Cultural History Through A National Socialist Lens

Studies in German Literature, Linguistics, and Culture

Edited by James Hardin
(*South Carolina*)

Cultural History through a National Socialist Lens

ESSAYS ON THE CINEMA OF THE THIRD REICH

EDITED BY
ROBERT C. REIMER

CAMDEN HOUSE

First published 2000 by Camden House.
Reprinted in paperback 2002.

Camden House is an imprint of Boydell & Brewer Inc.
PO Box 41026, Rochester, NY 14604–4126 USA
and of Boydell & Brewer Limited
PO Box 9, Woodbridge, Suffolk IP12 3DF, UK

ISBN: (cloth) 1–57113–164–7
(paper) 1–57113–134–5

Library of Congress Cataloging-in-Publication Data

Cultural History through a National Socialist lens: essays on the cinema of the
    Third Reich / edited by Robert C. Reimer
        p.   cm. – (Studies in German literature, linguistics, and culture)
        Some essays based on a seminar course entitled "Cinema in the Third
    Reich" offered by David Bathrick at Cornell University in the summer of 1996.
        Includes bibliographical references and index.
        ISBN: cloth 1–57113–164–7; paperback 1–57113–134–5 (both alk. paper)
        1. National socialism and motion pictures. 2. Motion pictures – Germany –
    History. I. Reimer, Robert C. (Robert Charles), 1943–   II. Studies in German literature, linguistics, and culture (Unnumbered)

    PN1995.9.N36 C85 2000
    791.43'658—dc21
                                                                99–089973

A catalogue record for this title is available from the British Library.

This publication is printed on acid-free paper.
Printed in the United States of America.

Contents

Preface

A FTER GERMANY'S DEFEAT in the Second World War, the Allies set up a commission to draft criteria for censoring films produced under National Socialism. In his introduction to *Catalogue of Forbidden German Feature and Short Film Productions* (1996), K. R. M. Short cites a number of themes that could have removed a film from public viewing in the immediate postwar period. These included glorifying Nazism, exhibiting racist sentiments, and distorting German history. Films that idealized Germany's military, dealt with German revenge, or presumably insulted Allied nations were also forbidden. Short points out that in spite of the number of forbidden topics, officials declared the vast majority of the almost 1,100 feature films produced during the Third Reich free of the propaganda that would have placed them on the list of banned films (xi-xii).

The distinction that the commission made between "bad" and "good" National Socialist films has prevailed for more than fifty years, at least in popular perception. On the one hand directors whose work was declared free of propaganda, such as Helmut Käutner or Kurt Hoffmann, continued their filmmaking without interruption. The same is true for actors like Hans Albers and Heinz Rühmann, whose popularity continued unabated after the war. On the other hand, Leni Riefenstahl, in spite of all her postwar efforts to recast her Nazi film career as the work of an outsider in the Third Reich, remains *persona non grata* among film historians and critics. This is ironic, since the film that made her a prominent figure in film courses, *Triumph des Willens* (*Triumph of the Will*, 1935) also sealed her fate as collaborator rather than fellow traveler.

The distinction between propaganda and entertainment continued years after the war. As an exchange student at the Technische Universität (Technical University) in Stuttgart in 1969, I attended a series of Nazi films that had been banned under the Allies because they dealt with topics that were forbidden. I recall that organizers of the event distributed informational handouts placing the works in context and explicating the propaganda intent of the films. In 1969, if I had had a television, I could also have watched — without explanatory notes — films by Luis Trenker, a successful Nazi director and actor, or works by Käutner, another Nazi director of films of light entertainment.

Today, more than fifty years after the defeat of the Third Reich, my students are shocked at the hateful messages of the more egregious Nazi propaganda films but accept as ahistorical diversions the comedies, musicals, and melodramas produced during the Third Reich. As a guest

professor at the Pädagogische Hochschule (teachers' college) in Lud-
wigsburg in 1997, I offered a course on the cinema of the Third Reich.
The sixty students, who came equally from the departments of history,
political science, and German, saw the sentiments found in *Der ewige
Jude* (The Eternal Jew, 1940), *Jud Süß*, (Jew Suess, 1940), and *Triumph des Willens* as transgressions against humanity. They had difficulty
placing films such as *Romanze in Moll* (Romance in a Minor Key,
1943) and *Quax, der Bruchpilot* (Quax, the Crash Pilot, 1940) within
the Nazi ideology but accepted them as Nazi films nonetheless. Many
balked at discussing *Glückskinder* (Lucky Kids, 1936) or *Münchhausen*
except outside of their historical framework, insisting these films were
somehow magically ahistorical. That my students saw these films as existing outside history is not surprising. During this later stay in Germany I had a television, and I could regularly view films of the Third
Reich era, which were often shown with no information that would
place them in an historical context beyond the television's notation of
the year in which they were made. The reaction of the students at my
home institution, the University of North Carolina Charlotte reveals
the same pattern of reception as exhibited by the students in Germany.

Until the appearance of Eric Rentschler's *Ministry of Illusion* and
Linda Schulte-Sasse's *Entertaining the Third Reich*, studies had followed the division suggested by Short's *Catalogue*, treating Nazi films
either as carriers of Nazi ideology or as harmless diversions. But the division is not as clear as critics or apologists would want. As artifacts of
popular culture, films borrow from other films and other arts, as well as
from contemporary institutions. That being the case, they reflect the
history and culture of their time, as well as influencing them.

The present volume grew out of a seminar entitled "Cinema in the
Third Reich" offered by David Bathrick at Cornell University in summer 1996. For six weeks participants in the seminar viewed and discussed scores of Nazi films under Professor Bathrick's guidance. Seven
of the essays here — those by Joan Clinefelter, John Davidson, Cary
Nathenson, Mary-Elizabeth O'Brien, Robert Reimer, Richard Rundell,
and Florentine Strzelczyk — are by scholars who participated in the
seminar and reflect ideas they initially presented in roundtable discussions at Cornell. Four of the essays — those by Franz Birgel, Heidi
Faletti, Thomas Nadar, and Roger Russi — were invited to address issues that were discussed at the seminar, but which are not represented
in the other essays. David Bathrick graciously consented to introduce
the volume.

*Cultural History through a National Socialist Lens: Essays on the Cin-
ema of the Third Reich* offers a view of Nazi Germany through an analy-

sis of over twenty films. These represent a sampling of the period's directors and the film medium's major genres. The overall premise of the essays is that, in spite of the control that Goebbels's film industry exercised over all aspects of filmmaking in the Third Reich, the films reveal an individuality that makes subsuming them under any one rubric or containing them within any one theory impossible. Films such as *Hitlerjunge Quex*, *Die große Liebe* (True Love, 1944), and *Unter den Brücken* (Under the Bridges, 1945) will be well known to readers. Others such as *Hans Westmar* and *Auf Wiedersehen, Franziska* (Goodbye, Franziska, 1941) will be less well known. Some films, such as *Glückskinder* (Lucky Kids, 1936) and *La Habanera* (1937) today seem void of Nazi ideology if viewed apart from the context of Nazism. Others such as *Der ewige Jude* (The Eternal Jew, 1940) shock us with virulent anti-Semitism and hate propaganda almost sixty years after their release. All of the films dealt with in the essays, however, regardless of their fame or notoriety, played an important role in a cinema that both reflected and influenced the dreams and lives of citizens during the Third Reich.

R. C. R.
December 1999

Acknowledgments

I WISH TO THANK the National Endowment for the Humanities and the Deutscher Akademischer Austausch Dienst for supporting my Cornell Summer and giving me the opportunity to work closely with the eleven other participants in the seminar and with our Director, David Bathrick. Thanks go also to my Chair, Michael Doyle, who recognized the value of the undertaking and granted me course reductions that enabled me to remain relatively honest about deadlines. Further thanks go to the many archivists who helped locate stills for the volume, Madeleine Matz at the Library of Congress, Mary Corliss at the Museum of Modern Art, and Hella Roth at Inter Nationes. For use of the many stills that appear in the book I wish to thank Inter Nationes, Transit GmbH, the Department of Motion Pictures of the Library of Congress, the Bundesarchiv-Filmarchiv Berlin, and the Museum of Modern Art Film Stills Archive. I wish to acknowledge the UNC Charlotte Foundation for a grant to cover publication costs of the stills. Finally I thank my daughter Kirstin Reimer for her editorial assistance and my wife Carol Reimer for her valuable input into my essay on Käutner and her assistance with the final assembly of the manuscript.

Chronology of Films

THE FOLLOWING LIST contains the titles of the films that are discussed or briefly referenced in the essays of this volume. Although some of the films that are discussed in the following pages are referred to in English-language publications and catalogs by English titles, the present volume uses German titles throughout, followed by a literal English translation the first time the film is mentioned in an essay. If films are followed by two English titles, the first represents the literal translation and the second an alternate English title by which the film may be known. Films that were made in Hollywood are marked with an asterisk.

1920

Das Cabinet des Dr. Caligari (The Cabinet of Dr. Caligari)
Der Golem: wie er in die Welt kam (The Golem: How He Came into the World)

1923

Die Straße (The Street)

1924

Die Nibelungen

1925

Potemkin (The Battleship Potemkin)

1927

Berlin, die Sinfonie der Großstadt (Berlin, the Symphony of the Big City)
Dirnentragödie (Tragedy of a Prostitute)
Der Fürst von Pappenheim (The Prince of Pappenheim)
Love
Metropolis
Ten Days that Shook the World

1928

Alraune
Spione (Spies)

1929

Asphalt

Der blaue Engel (The Blue Angel)

Mutter Krausens Fahrt ins Glück (Mother Krause's Journey to Happiness)

1930

Die Drei von der Tankstelle (Three from the Filling Station)

1931

Berge in Flammen (Mountains in Flames)

Berlin-Alexanderplatz

Die Dreigroschenoper (The Threepenny Opera)

Der Kongreß tanzt (The Congress Dances)

M

Der Mörder Dimitri Karamasoff (The Murderer Dimitri Karamasoff)

1932

Das blaue Licht (The Blue Light)

The Doomed Battalion

Kuhle Wampe oder Wem gehört die Welt (Kuhle Wampe or To Whom Does the World Belong; a k a Whither Germany?)

Der Rebell (The Rebel)

1933

Flüchtlinge (Refugees)

Hans Westmar

Hitlerjunge Quex (Hitler Youth Quex)

Liebelei

SA-Mann Brand

Terror oder Aufbau (Terror or Building Up)

Das Testament des Dr. Mabuse (The Testament of Dr. Mabuse)

Viktor und Viktoria

1934

The House of Rothschild *
It Happened One Night *
Ein Mann will nach Deutschland (A Man Must Go To Germany)
Monte Miracolo
Der Schimmelreiter (The Rider on the White Horse)
Der verlorene Sohn (The Prodigal Son)

1935

Ein falscher Fuffziger (A Counterfeit Fifty)
Hände am Werk (Hands at Work)
Tag der Freiheit: Unsere Wehrmacht (Day of Freedom: Our Armed Forces)
Triumph des Willens (Triumph of the Will)

1936

Glückskinder (Lucky Kids)
Der Kaiser von Kalifornien (The Emperor of California)
Schlußakkord (Final Accord)

1937

Der Berg ruft (The Mountain Calls); released as *The Challenge* (1937)
Condottieri (Giovanni di Medici, The Leader)
La Habanera
Juden ohne Maske (Jews Without Masks)
Der Mustergatte
Premiere
Der Purimshpiler (The Purim Player; a k a The Jester)
Der Schritt vom Wege (Step from the Path)
Versprich mir nichts (Don't Promise Me Anything)
Der zerbrochene Krug (The Broken Jug)
Zu neuen Ufern (To New Shores)

1938

Capriccio
Gestern und Heute (Yesterday and Today)
Heimat (Homeland)
Eine Nacht im Mai (One Night in May)
Olympia
Ziel in den Wolken (Goal in the Clouds)

1939

Der Florentiner Hut (The Italian Straw Hat)
Die Reise nach Tilsit (The Journey to Tilsit)
Robert und Bertram

1940

Bismarck
Der ewige Jude (The Eternal Jew)
Der Feuerteufel (The Fire Devil)
Das Fräulein von Barnhelm (Miss von Barnhelm)
Jud Süß (Jew Suess)
Kleider machen Leute (Clothes Make the Man)
Wunschkonzert (Request Concert)

1941

Das andere ich (The Other I)
Auf Wiedersehen, Franziska (Goodbye, Franziska)
Hauptsache glücklich (Happiness is the Main Thing)
Heimkehr (Homecoming)
Ich klage an (I Accuse)
Menschen im Sturm (Men in Struggle)
Ohm Krüger (Uncle Krüger)
Quax, der Bruchpilot (Quax, the Crash Pilot)

1942

Andreas Schlüter
Die Entlassung (The Dismissal)
Die Goldene Stadt (The Golden City)
Die große Liebe (True Love)
Großstadtmelodie (Big City Melody)
Pastor Angelicus
Rembrandt

1943

Damals (Back Then)
Germanin
Immensee
Münchhausen
Romanze in Moll (Romance in a Minor Key)

1944

Die Feuerzangenbowle (The Flaming Punch)
Der Führer schenkt den Juden eine Stadt (The Führer Gives a City to the
      Jews)
Große Freiheit # 7 (# 7 Freedom Street)
Opfergang (Sacrifice)

1945

Kolberg
Unter den Brücken (Under the Bridges, 1945; released in 1946)

1947

Liebe 47 (Love '47)

1953

Die Stärkere (The Stronger Woman)

1954

Tiefland (Lowlands)

1955

Urlaub auf Ehrenwort (Leave of Honor)

1956

Der Hauptmann von Köpenick (The Captain from Köpenick)
Die Trapp-Familie (The Trapp Family)

1958

Die Trapp-Familie in Amerika (The Trapp Family in America)
Urlaub auf Ehrenwort (Leave of Honor)

1984

Heimat

1993

Die Macht der Bilder: Leni Riefenstahl (The Power of Images: Leni
Riefenstahl; released in the United States as *The Wonderful,
Horrible Life of Leni Riefenstahl*)

INTRODUCTION

DAVID BATHRICK

Modernity Writ German:
State of the Art as Art of the Nazi State

MUCH OF WHAT HAS BEEN WRITTEN about German Cinema in the Third Reich has understandably concerned itself with questions revolving around the medium's relation to official Nazi policies between 1933–1945. Social historians dealing with its immediate impact as a tool of totalitarian persuasion have often narrowed in on what they perceived to be the overtly political propaganda value of certain films from that era. The Nazi youth films *Hitlerjunge Quex*, *SA-Mann Brand*, and *Hans Westmar*; Leni Riefenstahl's spectacular tribute to Hitler and the Nazi Party in *Triumph des Willens*; the anti-Semitic films *Jud Süß* and *Der ewige Jude*; or the *Durchhaltefilme* (films encouraging viewers to struggle through the increasingly hard times) *Kolberg* and *Der große König* often served to mark Nazi cinema for posterity as a "systematic abuse of film's formative powers in the name of mass manipulation, state terror, and worldwide destruction" (Rentschler 1996, 2).

While such an emphasis appropriately highlighted the extensive use of media by the Nazi regime to reshape the values and social imagination of the German people in the cause of war and ethnic genocide, its propaganda-driven methodological approach, together with its strong emphasis upon a particular canon, led to some misunderstanding concerning the nature of Third Reich cinema in its entirety. Of the approximately 1,100 feature films produced between 1933 and 1945, eighty-six percent of them were not officially coded as political by the regime. In addition to melodramas and detective stories, almost half of all films made in Germany at this time were comedies and musicals, many of them similar in genre if not in quality to movies coming out of Hollywood during the same period. After the war a vast number of these were gradually cleared for showing in East and West Germany.

Since 1970, there has been an evolution in the study of Nazi Cinema, consisting in a gradual "normalization" of the view of Third Reich cinema, fueled in part by its growing acceptance as a part of cinema programming inside and outside of Germany. My use of the word "normalization" should not be construed to mean exculpation; nor am I suggesting that there has been a shift toward neglect of the role that cinema played in the political and socio-economic life of Nazi Germany. On the contrary, the increased acknowledgment of Third Reich film as an ongoing source of entertainment has brought about intensified scholarly and critical efforts to understand the complex ways that the Nazi culture industry itself evolved in relation to cultural traditions and socio-economic contingencies within and beyond the temporal and geo-political parameters in which it was produced. Normalization in this regard would mean historicization and contextualization in its broadest aesthetic and thematic sense.

The present volume, which emerged from a seminar entitled "German Cinema in the Third Reich" at Cornell University in the summer of 1996 — jointly sponsored by the National Endowment for the Humanities and the Deutscher Akademischer Austausch Dienst — explores the cultural and aesthetic values of selected Nazi films within National Socialism's expanding entertainment industry. Such an emphasis comes in the wake of a growing interest among scholars in rethinking the question of Nazi cinema in light of the already extensive historical work that has been done on everyday life in the Third Reich.[1] One result of this focus on social life has been to demonstrate the similarity of cultural and industrial policies under Hitler to forms of modernization and mass culture in other advanced industrial societies of this period, in particular the United States. Among these are the building of the *Autobahnen*; the further development and application of the most modern industrial and technological design in the areas of machine technology, factory organization, and the communication industries; the continuation of the *Bauhaus* and art deco movements in home design and as a part of international expositions; and, particularly important for the film industry, the building in Germany of the same kind of consumer and leisure industries that were transforming the very self-understanding of class and national identities in Europe and the United States during that period.

The focus by historians on forms of modernization and the rhythms of everyday life is not intended to diminish the gravity of Nazi criminality or relativize the horror of Auschwitz. Rather, what such scholars argue is that precisely the programmatic effort to complete the project of modernity as the specific variant of a racist order enabled the Nazi elite to reconcile and thus facilitate the development of technological rationalization in the name of a spiritual and racial superiority. "By identifying technology with form, production, use value, creative (German or Aryan) labor, and German romanticism, rather than with formlessness, circulation, exchange value, and parasitic (Jewish) finance capital," writes Jeffrey Herf in *Reactionary Modernism*, "they incorporated technology into the 'anticapitalistic yearnings' that National Socialism exploited" (224). Moreover, their alignment of the war machine and *stählerne Romantik* (steel-like romanticism) (Goebbels, quoted in Herf, 195) with the fulfillment of a "good" German modernization also made it possible to link policies of exterminationist anti-Semitism and the militaristic realization of a pan-German Reich with the fulfillment of the *promesse de bonheur* (promise of happiness) lying at the heart of the advertising and entertainment industries. Nazi modernization, the argument went, can provide its citizens with everything: private, autonomous need-fulfillment within the larger security net of a contemporary, forward-looking and ultimately triumphant *Volksgemeinschaft*.

What is significant about the evolution of film from the end of the Weimar period to the collapse of the Nazi regime in 1945 is precisely the role it played in helping negotiate these seeming contradictions within the Nazi program. Here it is important to emphasize that the formal, structural, aesthetic, and entertainment value of individual films were often just as important as, if not more so than, their thematic and ideological content. Take for instance the question of propaganda. It is well known that both Goebbels and Hitler became increasingly opposed to the overly didactic propaganda methods that had been employed so successfully by the NSDAP in their rise to power in the 1920s. "Whatever you do, don't be boring," Goebbels told a group of directors from leading radio networks shortly after the Nazi takeover in 1933, "fantasy must employ all means in order to present the new message in a modern, contemporary, and interesting manner — interesting, instructive but not didactic."[2] The increasing number of "non-political" films, many of which had little or no direct discursive or even visual reference to the contemporary political scene, emerged out of a belief that the politics of entertainment had as much to do with state-of-the-art production values, creative cinematography, and sophisticated performance as with any explicit programmatic message. This did not mean that conservative values were abandoned or that ideology was ever unimportant. What was recognized, however, was the extent to which the style of a film, beyond suggesting something about one's mastery of the medium, also expressed the power and vision of those who produced it and controlled its distribution.

Goebbels's emphasis upon professional craft as a not-so-hidden larger political message of Nazi cinema anticipated in interesting ways Marshall McLuhan's later mantra "the medium is the message." As a statement about films being made in the Third Reich, such an insight has as much to say about the nature of their intended impact upon German audiences as it does about how we should be viewing them in the contemporary context. Whereas purely ideological or propagandistic treatments have tended to isolate Third Reich cinema within a framework inscribed primarily along the overdetermined lines of its anti-Semitism and its glorification of nation, *Volk*, and war, more culturally and historically grounded readings have sought to establish specific parallelisms and continuities between these films and other cinematic and political traditions inside and outside Germany.[3] This extraction of Nazi cinema out of the realm of pure demonology and its insertion into the coordinates of mass and high culture as they have developed both nationally and as a part of a global economic system allow us both to trace its moments of influence and to judge the often contradictory manner in which it appropriates and takes issue with these traditions within the Nazi context.

The present volume offers a number of textual analyses that consider the appropriation of earlier cinematic and literary traditions in the Third Reich. A particularly egregious example of cinematic cannibalism for purely propaganda purposes was the anti-Semitic documentary film *Der ewige Jude*, directed by Fritz Hippler in close cooperation with Joseph Goebbels. Joan Clinefelter, in an analysis focusing on the cinematic strategies underlying the film, demonstrates how appropriation in this case entailed a compiling of materials from every conceivable source — newsreel footage, film clips from Polish, German and American feature films, pro-Zionist film material from Palestine, studio footage, etc. — without attribution as to source and with the single-minded, unrelenting purpose of creating a coherent hate image. That this crude and brutal film premiered two months after the internationally acclaimed anti-Semitic feature film *Jud Süß*, with which it is conceptually linked, provided the unintended confirmation of a lesson that Goebbels himself had once offered concerning the importance of propaganda being "instructive but not didactic." Whereas *Jud Süß* had been an international box-office hit, the heavy-handed nature of *Der ewige Jude*, particularly the scenes devoted to the Kosher slaughtering of animals, literally drove sickened audiences out of the theaters, causing the film to close after a very short run.

Such was not the fate of the film *Hitlerjunge Quex*, which premiered in 1933. Heidi Faletti explores the ways in which three early SA youth films knowingly or unwittingly recycled topoi and stylistic devices from Weimar cinema. Such an analysis reminds us, for example, not only that a film like *Hitlerjunge Quex* is indeed a reply to Slatan

Dudow's 1932 film *Kuhle Wampe*, sponsored by the German Communist Party, but that the very similarity of these two party-initiated, prerevolutionary youth films, in political gest and at the level of cinematic style, mark the Nazi film itself as more a last breath of Weimar in transition than anything indigenous to the cinematic world of the Third Reich that began to emerge in 1936. Both are agit-prop films that direct their appeal to youth at a time of massive unemployment, proffering very similar utopian solutions to the problems at hand. This, of course, did not prevent *Hitlerjunge Quex* from having an important function in the Third Reich, above all as a martyr film replayed often within the ghetto of youth culture, but also because of its star signature. The appearance in the film of the renowned formerly left-wing actor Heinrich George — later a director of the Schiller Theater and major luminary through 1945 at Germany's premier studio, Universum Film Aktiengesellschaft (Ufa) — who in *Hitlerjunge Quex* literally performed his own conversion to Nazism, stands metonymically as a moment of transition and continuity. Like other Ufa stars such as Werner Krauss, Emil Jannings, Paul Wegener, Gustav Fröhlich, Sybille Schmitz, Fritz Rasp, Gustav Gründgens, Jenny Jugo, Hans Albers, Lilian Harvey, and Lil Dagover, George's embodiment of the Weimar cinematic heritage in the Nazi present lent a cultural familiarity that helped create its own kind of cultural legitimation.

Thus references to the cinematic German past in the Nazi present often came in the form of familiar faces as well as through thematic and stylistic citations from well-known films of the 1920s. But as Linda Schulte-Sasse has recently demonstrated, there is also a reservoir of familiar "underlying literary paradigms" from which these films drew and with which they were in dialogue (1996, 11). Richard Rundell gives us a reading of Veit Harlan's 1943 film *Immensee* that marks it as typical of a vast number of Nazi literary films that seemingly have no underlying political function other than to provide entertainment at a time of crisis, in this case the defeat at Stalingrad and the increased bombing of major cities. The dazzling Agfacolor, the high quality of the production values and the star allure of Kristina Söderbaum and Carl Raddatz, along with the sheltered world of Theodor Storm's novel, offered in their congruence little more than a nineteenth-century idyll (despite the film's twentieth-century setting) at a time of twentieth-century industrial devastation.

In Helmut Käutner's extraordinary *Romanze in Moll* the literary antecedents multiply in direct relation to the film's distancing itself from the Maupassant story on which it was supposedly based. Robert Reimer's tracing of its myriad other formal borrowings moves deftly from the eighteenth-century bourgeois tragedy, which, as has often been noted, came to serve as a kind of *Urschrift* for the Nazi imaginary in films like *Jud Süß*, to considerably more realist and therefore less tragic epigonal incarnations of nineteenth-century literary sources. *Romanze in Moll*'s refusal to be reduced, finally, to any one generic grid, be it a literary or a cinematic one, is as steadfast as the film's refusal to be pressed into a single ideological mold. Yes, its pessimism upset Goebbels, who, ever on the lookout for gloomy attitudes, initially banned it. Yes, its fascination with death (particularly that of a sacrificing woman) reproduces a metaphysics that lies at the heart of the Nazi death wish. Yet it is precisely its Chinese box of enigmas and its unresolved contradictions which explain the critical success of this complex film so resistant to easy interpretation. In refusing to submit to a single, all-encompassing reading, it denies the one thing which the Nazi public sphere will always ask of the desired unambiguous text.

Carl Froelich's *Heimat* is also marked by narrative and semiotic undecidability. Having revealed the disturbing manner in which this film refuses to resolve its antinomies, Florentine Strzelczyk wisely sees them as symptoms of the social forces the film seeks to negotiate and resolve. Zarah Leander's character remains locked at the crossroads of the old and the new, as do the characters she plays in most of her Nazi films. On the one hand, the film offers the extraordinary allure of a modern, independent woman, blessed with a surfeit of love and feeling, who brings reinvigoration and the forbidden flavor of America into a tired, late nineteenth-century German provincial town. At the same time, in part with the help of the forbidden, the film offers the ultimate restabilization of that very "Heimat" as the precursor of a modern Germany capable of respecting and harmonizing seemingly contradictory social values.

In the war film *Die große Liebe*, one of the genuine box-office blockbusters of the period, the antinomies generated by the "Leander effect" work themselves out, as Mary-Elizabeth O'Brien rightly emphasizes, "in the battle between love and duty, rather than between Germany and the allied nations, [which in turn] becomes the principle conflict of the film and, by extension, the times." Similar to Leander's earlier films such as *Heimat*, *Zu neuen Ufern*, and *La Habanera*, this conflict entails the taming of a shrew whose desire for both love and career, home and the exotic Other must be folded into the realities of what is presented as a viable compromise. Reimer is right in reminding us that love plays a commanding role in "most" of the Third Reich films, particularly, I would add, those that were made during war. What love means, of course, is anybody's guess, or might we better say anybody's projection. What love in fact quite often ends up doing is driving the narratives that it motivates into closures that in some way seem inadequate to the utopian longings they initially release.

Certainly music plays a key role in the staging of Leander's very powerful film presence as well as in narrating the terms of emotionality, longing and melodrama in many of her greatest films — in particular the ones she made with the director Detlev Sierck. Thomas Nadar shows how even at this early stage in his career Sierck had already worked out an elaborate strategy of distancing, drawing on Brecht and Weill for techniques of counterpoint between music and text, but then eviscerating the Brecht factor in his search for an emotionality that takes us to the center of feeling rather than circumvent it. The larger suggestions here are intriguing: a Sierckian notion of melodrama which distances the audience for reflection, while at the same time breaking the "aria effect" in order to further the pathos; a critical melodrama that would open up spaces for both indulgence and contradiction. Certainly these tensions were part of the reason for Rainer Werner Fassbinder's fascination with Sierck's later Hollywood films. We have seen how Fassbinder has drawn on the excesses of Ufa and Hollywood affect, particularly in his musical films about the Nazi period such as *Lili Marleen* and *Veronica Voss*, to create a kind of overdetermined emotionalized estrangement.

Assessing the official attitudes of the Nazi leadership toward the United States is one further means by which to explore the question of cultural modernity and modernization in the Third Reich. At one level, the discourse of "Americanism" as it emerged in the Weimar Republic was often employed by the far right as synonymous with metropolitan alienation and racial decadence against which a national culture must immunize itself. On the other hand, particularly subsequent to the *Machtergreifung* in January of 1933, we note an increasing tendency among the Nazi elite, more obvious in their practice than in explicit policy statements, to identify the Party and its rule with an Americanism represented generally by glamour and consumerism, and specifically by its often explicit acknowledgment of Hollywood production values and stylistic conventions as the norm. As has often been noted, actors from Babelsberg often modeled themselves on internationally renowned Hollywood stars, just as German directors of the time sought to copy the generic conventions of Hollywood, a cinematic system that continued to hold enormous attraction for German audiences of the period. Hans Dieter Schäfer has described the schizophrenic attitude of the Nazi powers in this regard as an example of *gespaltenes Bewußtsein* (split consciousness). Schäfer's term expresses the seeming two-sided nature of a policy apparatus that officially denigrated the materialist, "Jewish" values of American culture while it simultaneously promoted them for its own benefit.

What is interesting about Cary Nathenson's interpretation of *Glückskinder*, the extremely successful German remake of the American film *It Happened one Night*, is the extent to which the former successfully synthesizes its German values with its obvious strain for a Hollywood look. Here there is nothing split or schizophrenic in the way the lightness and comedic *joie de vivre* of these seemingly non-phallic representatives of American maleness are narratively and visually made to line up with the paradigms of a now "modernized," but also Germanized form of the reconstructed male. "American" here is slapstick, happy-go-lucky, pre-oedipal anarchy; the German realignment thereof is a man who has to be taught how to desire. Karsten Witte labeled this kind of national recoding of certain stylistic conventions from American cinema in German films of the Third Reich "*eingedeutschter Amerikanismus*" (Americanism writ German: *Lachende Erben*, 102). Its unconscious claim, of course, is to have it both ways, which is really the dream of reactionary modernism from the very beginning. The ultimate message of *Glückskinder* remains necessarily ambiguous. What narrative closure could possibly obliterate the still resonating comic-book mayhem represented by those three momentarily pre-pubescent adults screaming in a wild frenzy of song "I wish I were a chicken!"?

Luis Trenker's lifelong dialogue with American culture offers another, somewhat inverted and considerably more ponderous version of Americanism writ German. This time it is not the cinematography that bears the American side of the equation, but the *mise en scène* itself: in *Der verlorene Sohn*, the city of Manhattan reflects the values of an alienated, debilitating form of modernity that stands in contrast to the pristine beauty of the South Tyrolean mountains; in *Der Kaiser von Kalifornien* the American West represents the promise of the natural itself, whose meaning hovers as a floating signifier somewhere between the dreamed-of *Lebensraum* and an alternative space in which to carve out a better life. Franz Birgel argues persuasively against reducing Trenker's work to one-sided critiques of ideology, showing how the filmmaker's confusions about his relation to Hitler, Germany, fascism, and, finally, his own identity were translated into double messages, which resist the either/or of Nazi inscription. It is precisely this double figuration that has helped make Trenker a model figure for understanding the continuities from Weimar into the Third Reich (*Der Rebell*) and from the Third Reich into postwar Germany.

Wolfgang Liebeneiner is another paradigmatic transitional figure in this regard. Like Albert Speer, he was a successful bureaucrat, respected intellectual (Hitler anointed him a "professor" in 1943), and a renowned artist (as actor and director). Having established himself with such successful films as *Versprich mir nichts, Der Mustergatte, Ich klage an* and his two Bismarck films, he was made head of production at Ufa. Also like Speer, Liebeneiner seems to have survived his professional commitment to the Third Reich with his personal and artistic image unsullied, despite the fact that he worked closely with Goebbels on the euthanasia project and was deeply implicated in the day-to-day socio-economic and aesthetic operations of the Reich's major studio. In fact, as John Davidson argues in his article, it is precisely the continuity of Liebeneiner's aura as a sophisticated professional artist in its varying incarnations, in his work as well as in his person, that challenges us in seeking to untangle the complicated threads of complicity and continuity that link him to the afterlife of Nazi cinema in the Federal Republic.

Afterlife and continuity are also the concerns of Roger Russi's exploration of Leni Riefenstahl's undiminished efforts to stage her life and work as outside the parameters of the Third Reich. In her biography, Riefenstahl claims outsider status by asserting that her success as the creator of the acclaimed documentaries *Triumph des Willens* and *Olympia* allowed her to withdraw from public life in the Third Reich into an inner emigration and the making of her film *Tiefland*. But Riefenstahl also sees herself as outside political complicity on the basis of her role and vision as an artist. Ignoring the use to which this artistry was put or the impact that it had, Riefenstahl maintains her steadfast insistence on the transcendent powers of her own artistic professionalism as the redeeming final word.

And this final point returns us to our initial concern with state-of-the-art filmmaking. Like the Third Reich directors Veit Harlan, Wolfgang Liebeneiner, Helmut Käutner, and Arthur Maria Rabenalt, Leni Riefenstahl too has been recognized for her artistry, but unlike them, she has never been able to escape her past, although not for lack of effort. Her unremitting postwar efforts to exonerate herself of the ever recurring charges of Nazi collusion were rooted in a notion of art as well as *state of the art* which would seal the genius-artist off from the entanglements of a real-world society in which she or he will inevitably have to produce. Paradoxically, this is a notion that all these artists would share with none other than Joseph Goebbels himself — not that Goebbels was ultimately non-political or non-ideological, but rather because he realized from early on the political potential of the state of the art itself. Whether Käutner, Rabenalt or Liebeneiner ultimately ever used the spaces that this devil's pact permitted them in order to produce resistant or subversive film is another question altogether. What is important here is that there was a recasting within Nazi modernization of the political rules of the game — a recasting which was to link the films of Babelsberg much more closely to developments in Hollywood than was recognized at the time.

Notes

[1] Of particular importance has been the work of Ralf Dahrendorf, *Gesellschaft und Demokratie in Deutschland* (Munich: Piper, 1965); See Detlev J. K. Peukert, *Inside Nazi Germany: Conformity, Opposition, and Racism in Everyday Life*, trans. Richard Deveson (New Haven: Yale UP, 1987); Peter Reichel, *Der schöne Schein des Dritten Reiches: Faszination und Gewalt des Faschismus* (Munich: Hanser, 1991); Hans Dieter Schäfer, *Das gespaltene Bewußtsein: Über deutsche Kultur und Lebenswirklichkeit 1933–1945* (Munich: Carl Hanser Verlag, 1987); David Schoenbaum, *Hitler's Social Revolution: Class and Status in Nazi Germany, 1933–1939* (Garden City, NY: Doubleday, 1966); Rainer Zittelmann, "Die totalitäre Seite der Moderne," in *Nationalsozialismus und Modernisierung*, edited by Michael Prinz and Rainer Zittelmann, 1–20 (Darmstadt: Wissenschaftliche Buchgesellschaft, 1991).

[2] Helmut Heiber, ed., *Goebbels-Reden*, 2 vols. (Düsseldorf: Droste Verlag, 1971), I, 81–82. (My translation)

[3] The work of the following scholars has been particularly important within recent scholarly developments in the area of Third Reich cinema: Klaus Kreimeier, *Die Ufa Story: Geschichte eines Filmkonzerns* (Munich: Hanser, 1992); Stephen Lowry, *Pathos und Politik: Ideologie in Spielfilmen des Nationalsozialismus* (Tübingen: Niemeyer, 1991}; Eric Rentschler, *The Ministry of Illusion: Nazi Cinema and its Afterlife* (Cambridge MA: Harvard UP, 1996); Linda Schulte-Sasse, *Entertaining the Third Reich: Illusions of Wholeness in Nazi Cinema* (Durham, NC: Duke UP, 1996); Karsten Witte, *Lachende Erben, Toller Tag: Filmkomödien im Dritten Reich* (Berlin: Vorweg 8, 1995).

2

HEIDI E. FALETTI

Reflections of Weimar Cinema in the Nazi Propaganda Films SA-Mann Brand, Hitlerjunge Quex, and Hans Westmar

THE LAST YEARS OF THE WEIMAR REPUBLIC witnessed escalating violence between the right and left for political control of city streets. The combatants on both sides in the turf wars, known in German as the *Kampfzeit* (era of struggle), paraded through friendly and hostile neighborhoods, sang politically charged songs, proselytized — especially among German youth — fought, and even murdered. Three films produced in 1933, the first year of the Nazi regime, *SA-Mann Brand: Ein Lebensbild aus unseren Tagen* (SA Man Brand: A Contemporary Portrait), *Hitlerjunge Quex: Vom Opfergeist der deutschen Jugend* (Hitler Youth Quex: The Spirit of Sacrifice of German Youth), and *Hans Westmar: Einer von vielen. Ein deutsches Schicksal aus dem Jahre 1929* (Hans Westmar: One of many. A German Destiny from the Year 1929) recreate the era of struggle with Berlin as their backdrop. Released in the aforementioned sequence, the three films memorialize in their fictional heroes two men whom the Nazis had turned into martyrs, Horst Wessel, a member of the SA, and Herbert Norkus, a member of the Hitler Youth. With the streets as a battleground, the three films celebrate giving up one's life for the NSDAP as the highest calling an individual German might have. In recreating the era of struggle, the directors of the films, Franz Seitz (*SA-Mann Brand*), Hans Steinhoff (*Hitlerjunge Quex*), and Franz Wenzler (*Hans Westmar*) turn to Weimar cinema, appropriating for their cause images and style from the earlier films, many of which the Nazis had attacked because of their leftist content. In differing intensities, the directors incorporate motifs, style, and ambience of films familiar to an audience of 1933. Weimar elements are in this way recycled into a framework designed to politically benefit National Socialism and Joseph Goebbels's aims for propaganda. That is, Weimar cinema's film language carries over into the three martyr films, first appearing in *SA-Mann Brand*, the first feature film with explicitly Nazi themes, and becoming more evident in *Hitlerjunge Quex* and *Hans Westmar*. Before turning to the three films, it will be helpful to consider the legacy of Weimar-era film, as well as Goebbels's chief views on film as creative propaganda.

Weimar film's diverse approaches to the language and themes of cinema and its expressionist use of chiaroscuro lighting constitute the areas under study. This article makes no attempt to prove influences of the Weimar film epoch on Nazi films. Instead, it analyzes cinematic elements as analogies to conventions or particular films of the Weimar era. For the purposes of this article, the relevant trends are the films of the street, social realism in mainstream and leftist films, the New Objectivity, and national heroism in the mountain films. The two areas that concern us the most are the street and leftist films. The street film, following the lead of Karl Grune's *Die Straße* (The Street, 1923), features the perils of the kaleidoscopic city street, which seduces the bourgeois patriarch and spurs him to reject the family fold. Films of mainstream social realism, such as G. W. Pabst's production of *Die Dreigroschenoper* (The Threepenny Opera, 1931) focus on back-alleys, thugs, and crowds, highlighting at times the reality of their gritty nature, at other times giving them a picturesque look. Social-consciousness-raising films of the left, such as *Mutter Krausens Fahrt ins Glück* (Mother Krause's Journey to Happiness, 1929) and *Kuhle Wampe oder Wem gehört die Welt* (literally Kuhle Wampe or to Whom Does the World Belong; but also known as Whither Germany?, 1932), purport to document proletarian misery in their radically didactic narratives. Also of importance are the varied urban phenomena of the New Objectivity movement, which provide patterns of modernity, as for example those found in *Berlin, die Sinfonie der Großstadt* (Berlin, the Symphony of the Big City, 1927). Finally, not all films of the Weimar era came from the left. Elements of nationalistic films, for instance *Der Rebell* (The Rebel, 1932), which is proto-Nazi in its conception and imagery, also resurface in Third Reich features.

The film characteristics discussed above appear in sundry guises in the three films, but vary in exposure from faint to prominent. I have limited this study to examine the manner in which the films adopt and transform major traits of Weimar films. An overview of all possible analogies between the Weimar cinema and the Nazi trilogy of films is beyond the scope of this article. It should be noted that the NSDAP Ministry of Propaganda did not produce the three films, but, as commercial productions, the films were nonetheless intended to appeal to the new political climate. Their designation here as Nazi films rests not on their origin of production but rather on the ideologies they promote, especially that of self-sacrifice for the fatherland.

When the Ministry of Propaganda was established on 11 March 1933, it soon became evident that Joseph Goebbels considered the cinema the foremost medium for propaganda. His initial speech at the Kaiserhof on 28 March 1933 to members of the film community stressed artistry as the most effective means of conveying propaganda. The Propaganda Minister admonished filmmakers to eschew bald communication of the Third Reich's political agenda and instead to transform political themes and ideas into cinematic works of art with appeal to the *Volk*. Erwin Leiser highlights Goebbels's allusions in this speech to Sergei Eisenstein's *Battleship Potemkin* (1925), Luis Trenker's *Der Rebell*, and Fritz Lang's *Die Nibelungen* (1924) (1974, 10–11). Goebbels felt that Eisenstein's film could make anyone without ideological commitments into a Bolshevik because it expresses its themes in the form of an exemplary artwork. He saw similar qualities in Luis Trenker's *Der Rebell* and hailed its potential to convert people to National Socialism. He deemed *Die Nibelungen* topically modern, even with its mythically remote setting.

We should note that Goebbels's principle of artistry as vital to the communication of ideology influenced his judgment of the three martyr films. He dismissed *SA-Mann Brand* as too tendentious, but enthusiastically acclaimed the aesthetic achievements of *Hitlerjunge Quex*. He considered *Hans Westmar* in its first version, entitled *Horst Wessel*, to be inadequate as a portrayal of the consecrated legend of the SA hero and martyr. He ordered its premiere canceled, pending the deletion of direct references to Horst Wessel and the change of the namesake to Hans Westmar.

Of the three martyr films, *SA-Mann Brand* made the least use of Weimar cinema. *Hitlerjunge Quex* and *Hans Westmar* employ the Weimar tradition more actively, especially the leftist film and the street film. They use cinematic elements of Weimar film to denounce not only the Communists, but also the entire liberal Weimar civilization, even Berlin nightclubs, as decadent and effeminate. Indeed, compared to the other two films, Seitz's *SA-Mann Brand* appears to be a straightforward, low-keyed chronicle about an anonymous SA man. It is not necessarily a film that reminds viewers of Weimar cinema. Yet echoes of its predecessors appear in the film as the narrative unfolds in tableaux in a series of contrasts: dark streets, woodlands and fresh air, murky taverns, hearth and home. Despite Goebbels's criticism of the film, the *Filmprüfestelle* (Censorship Office) later gave it the ratings of "artistically especially valuable" and "valuable for national education" (Welch 59). Unlike the other two films, based on best-selling novels inspired by real-life heroes, this one was based on Goebbels's book, *Kampf um*

Berlin, which delineates his activities as *Gauleiter* (district leader) of the Berlin NSDAP (Schriefer, 1991, 78).[1]

Bavaria-Film-A.G. München released *SA-Mann Brand* on 14 June 1933. The premiere, held in Munich at the Gloria-Palast, was disrupted by an SA chief, Beckerle, who commanded that all SA and SS men exit the theater owing to the theater director's refusal to remove film posters by a Polish painter (Bettecken 5). The film drew controversial reviews. *Der Völkische Beobachter* praised it, while Goebbels's *Der Angriff* castigated the director's supposed dearth of talent and vision in portraying the Unknown SA Man (Welch 52). Goebbels later pilloried the film in *Kinematograph* (Berlin) for its rigid ideological stance: "We don't want to see our Storm Troopers marching across film or the stage. They're supposed to march in the streets" (quoted in Hoffmann 1996, 58).

Before beginning a discussion of Weimar elements in *SA Mann Brand*, I will present a brief synopsis of the film's action for those not familiar with it. The dominant sequence at the film's onset is a Communist attack on the SA meeting place, which the police quash. Afterwards, as Fritz Brand leaves and heads home at night, lurking Communist thugs try to shoot him, but fail because Anni Baumann, a Communist worker's daughter, and the sister of the attackers, accompanies Brand and warns him. Brand's close call is discovered by his neighbors: the kind-hearted and henpecked Nazi landlord, Huber, and an impecunious Nazi neighbor, Frau Lohner, with her Hitler Youth son, Erich. Brand and his father, an unemployed Social Democrat, clash on the subject of Brand's affiliations, but his mother is receptive to her son's vision of a liberated Germany.

At home, Anni Baumann argues heatedly with her two brothers concerning their attempt at murder. After her father beats her, she leaves for the Cafe Diana, the KPD (German Communist Party) hangout. There, Alexander Turrow, the Russian Communist leader, asks her to win Brand over to their side, saying that failure to do so would mean Brand's death. Turrow then arranges for the Jewish supervisor, Neuberg, to fire Brand from his job as tractor operator. After Anni warns Brand of Turrow's plot, he pretends to be a Communist.

For his sixteenth birthday, Erich Lohner receives a portrait of Hitler from Brand and a Hitler Youth uniform from his mother. Government officials, however, have forbidden public wearing of the uniform. In the interim, Brand, posing as a Communist, arranges for the transport of weapons from the KPD warehouse to the Nazis. Although shot during this venture, he recovers. After the government lifts the prohibition on wearing of the uniform, the SA men march through a Communist district. Erich seeks to march along with them, but is fatally shot. Like his father in the First World War, he dies willingly for Germany, here in anticipation of his own father in heaven. After Hitler becomes Chancellor, Huber asserts his male authority over his Catholic wife. The SA men celebrate wildly, and Brand's father too becomes a Nazi. At the conclusion, the Horst Wessel song enlivens a torchlight parade of Nazis. Fritz Brand appears as the standard-bearer for the Nazi spirit, as his profile appears in final close-up.

SA-Mann Brand presents self-sacrifice as the path to millennial salvation. Curiously enough, according to Martin Loiperdinger (1991a, 31–32 and 38), director Franz Seitz conceived it as a Heimat film with folksy traits. The collective setting, which has the main characters in one apartment house, sharing a *völkisch* (nationalistic) destiny, supports Loiperdinger's readings, for they all, with the exception of Frau Huber, end up as willing Nazis. Yet, the film also incorporates elements from leftist and street films, even if only minimally and in a mechanical fashion.[2] As a whole, the milieu and shabby attire recall the leftist cinema, but the actions and attitudes hark back to street motifs and turn the members of the proletariat (Anni Baumann's family) into criminal thugs. Elements of street films resurface here: as the streets themselves; taverns; the KPD; especially its villainous leader, Turrow, with his decadently luxurious abode; and Erich's patient mother.

The film recasts working-class districts with a moodily subjective slant. The lurkers at street corners and in doorways and cellars who shoot at Brand and kill Erich heighten the ominous atmosphere. Such an aura recalls the shadowy *mise en scène* of the street tradition. The proletariat Communist, there an unemployed victim, emerges here as a shiftless criminal, sinister and baleful. The contrasting use of dark (night streets and scruffy Communists) and light (woodlands and optimistic Nazis) reflect vestiges of expressionism also sometimes present in the street films. Even if the dark and light do not necessarily coexist in the same scene, they alternate from sequence to sequence, from the malevolent murk of Communism to the daylight wholesomeness of the Nazis. Moreover, the street still harbors perils; Brand's parents fear for his safety. Their son flees the cloying safety of his parents' home, only to return later, just as the protagonists do in the Weimar films *Die Straße* and Bruno Rahn's *Dirnentragödie* (Tragedy of a Prostitute, a k a Tragedy of the Whore, 1927). In the beginning, the SA man rejects domesticity and craves to live in the jungle outside. Yet, he maintains contact with his parents, despite the inherited duality of street and cozy household. A folksy harmony between Brand and his family, all ultimately united by their faith in the Nazi party and the Heimat, is the goal of the film's action.

The demonic street encompasses more than the street itself, extending its perils to the midway, bordello, and nightspots, all with the stereotypical denizens of the street films. Here, the murky innards of the KPD hangout, the Cafe Diana, accent the instinct-driven vices of the Communists. Turrow, the slimy local chief of Muscovite Communism, presides over the pub as a pimp, one of the street's prime tyrants in Weimar cinema. Indeed, he aims to use a worker's daughter, Anni Baumann, to lure Brand to the KPD. In the same mode, his sumptuous, bordello-like home and the alluring women present there portray him as a hedonistic, monied manipulator who belies the notion of a classless society. The Communist men who frequent the Cafe Diana are shown as loutish malefactors who not only shoot Brand and Erich but also menace Anni Baumann because she wants to protect Brand from murder. The film focuses on Anni, who recalls the striving young women in *Mutter Krausens* and *Kuhle Wampe*, but unlike them she acts against rather than for the proletarian cause. She is beaten ferociously by her father after she has flung insults at her two brothers, "work-shirking idlers," for the attempted murder of Brand: "You are cowards, who lie in wait for someone at night in order to shoot him down like a mad dog. Phooey" (Schriefer 1980, 23). The documentary bluntness of her diction and the brutishness of the men point to a kinship with the milieu of leftist cinema. The men, evil in the street sense, hark back in outward deportment to the rowdies of proletarian film, such as those harassing the released prisoner in Phil Jutzi's *Berlin-Alexanderplatz* (1931).

Frau Lohner, Erich's mother, whose husband had perished in the First World War, exemplifies the anxiety-ridden and patient mother. She descends from both the hardworking, humble matriarch in *Mutter Krausens* and the forlorn mother in Fritz Lang's *M* (1931), a throwback to the street film, who futilely calls her murdered daughter's name. Brand's own mother is also, but to a lesser degree, in this mode. Such screen mothers would appear to presage the submissive role reserved for women in the Third Reich in both celluloid and everyday life.

The sequences of marching SA men and Hitler Youths training in the open air offer a final dimension of the Weimar heritage found in such leftist films as *Mutter Krausens* and *Kuhle Wampe*. The resumption of these films' conventions of marching and athletic activities in *SA-Mann Brand* forcefully heightens the impact of Nazi enterprises. In this respect, it has been justly noted that in *Kuhle Wampe* the "scenes of mass enthusiasm (marches, competitive sports, streaming crowds), which for the filmmakers represented a political aesthetics, became in just a few years the dominant aesthetics of fascist politics" (Silberman 48).

Overall, although the Weimar elements in *SA-Mann Brand* formulate the red terror as a corruptly sinister, melodramatic opposition to the upright Nazi freedom movement, they have less of an artistic impact on this film than on the other two. The disjunction between villains and heroes is forced. Such stiffness and artificiality can be noted in other aspects of the film. The formulaic portrayal of the Jewish supervisor, Neuberg, who fires Brand for political reasons and who ultimately seeks a train to Switzerland, is a telling, even prophetic example of political intent overriding artistic effect. Moreover, Erich's death is almost random, as he rashly becomes a fortuitous target for a shot from a cellar window aimed at any Nazi in range. Brand, who is knowingly daring and destructive to the Communists, survives his wound and promises to make good Erich's death. Erich becomes a victim mainly because he wants to march, even if the march through a Communist neighborhood poses risks. From a Nazi standpoint, his death is heroic, and Erich himself believes just before he dies that he is following his father's example. Although Erich's death has less dramatic resonance than the pursuit and knifing of Heini Völker, the hero of *Hitlerjunge Quex*, it is distinguished by the pathos of his innocent suffering and his yearning for his own heroically fallen father in heaven, the subject of his final thoughts. As he goes "zum Vater [. . .] in Himmel" ("to my father [. . .] in heaven": Schriefer 1980, 107) he is inspired by the Nazi ideal of a heroic authority figure. Although Hilmar Hoffmann (53) and David Welch (58) maintain that the boy utters "Führer" and Francis Courtade (41) states that the name of the *Führer* is on his lips, Erich actually says "Vater" as he dies. The bond of patriotic martyrdom between Erich and his own father thereby takes on special religious significance.

The portrayal of allegiance to the NSDAP, the hazards of the opposition, and the virtue of sacrifice appear more nuanced, archetypal, and consequential in the second film of the Nazi martyr trilogy, Hans Steinhoff's *Hitlerjunge Quex*. Once again, an unemployed father and a recalcitrant son dominate the action, and a Hitler Youth must sacrifice his life. The merging of rebellion and sacrifice into a single figure, Heini Völker, generates a more focused scenario. Like Seitz's film, *Hitlerjunge Quex* has recourse to Weimar visions, but uses them more abundantly and creatively. As a cinematic achievement, it offers a distinct contrast to *SA-Mann Brand* with its greater flexibility in pacing, acting, humor, camera work, and music. As in the first film, the working-class milieu and its denizens are familiar constants. However, this milieu becomes demonized in two ways. Its pleasure-seeking and criminal Communists make it an underworld milieu of the kind met with in street films. Also the milieu becomes the site for violent events presented in the documentary manner of leftist films. Steinhoff's appropriation and restructuring of Weimar film elements presents National Socialism as the only viable political alternative and dramatizes the relentless forces that lead to Heini's brutal murder.

Numerous writers have noted that *Hitlerjunge Quex* is a reservoir of Weimar film elements. Lotte Eisner, for example, maintains that the film's style "is not a great way away from its political opposite *Berlin-Alexanderplatz*" (333). Erwin Leiser notes "conscious echoes of left-wing film classics," referring to *Mutter Krausens Fahrt ins Glück*, *M*, *Die Dreigroschenoper*, and *Kuhle Wampe* (1974, 36). Moreover, Elsaesser terms the film "itself the national-socialist 'reply' to *Kuhle Wampe* and its plea for an international proletarian consciousness" (42–43). Witte too acknowledges the film's adaptation of proletarian cinema (1986, 305). Eric Rentschler also alludes to the vestiges of these four Weimar films, as well as *Berlin-Alexanderplatz* in *Hitlerjunge Quex* (1996, 61).

The film was based on the best-selling novel *Der Hitlerjunge Quex* by Karl Aloys Schenzinger, who collaborated on the screenplay with B. E. Lüthge. In the novel, the fictional Heini Völker, a k a Quex, is a separate individual from Herbert Norkus, a real-life Hitler Youth who died at the hands of the Communists. The novel directly refers to Norkus's death and makes the Hitler Youth a conscious role model for Heini. According to Jay W. Baird, Baldur von Schirach, the creator of the Hitler Youth, and Goebbels, mythologized Norkus's martyrdom with the result that the "apotheosis of Norkus was the counterpart to the death, resurrection, and return of Wessel" ("To Die for Germany" 109). Steinhoff's film, as well as its reception by the NSDAP, conflated the real-life Norkus and the fictional Völker. The film eventually was widely celebrated as the hagiography of the fallen Norkus, butchered by a Communist gang.

Ufa decided to produce the film with little, if any, official nudging because the studio wanted to outdo Bavaria-Film's effort, to offer a product superior to *SA-Mann Brand* (Welch 59–60). The esteemed Hans Steinhoff, who later fashioned *Ohm Krüger* (Uncle Krüger 1941), a film of overt Nazi propaganda, was the director; the film had the support and influence of von Schirach. It was screened for Hitler at the Ufa-Palast in Munich on 11 September 1933, with great fanfare and eulogizing of Norkus.[3] If, in *SA-Mann Brand*, the actors were generally unknown, except for Otto Wernicke as Brand's unemployed father, *Quex* showcased mainly leading performers of the Weimar era, the most famous being Heinrich George. The casting of George, an actor who had played proletarian parts in *Metropolis* (1927) and *Berlin-Alexanderplatz* and was associated with left-wing politics, as Heini's unemployed father, has been aptly termed "Machiavellianism in perfection" (Courtade 43). The Hitler Youth roles, including that of Heini, were performed anonymously by real-life members of the organization. After having received the distinction "artistically especially valuable," *Hitlerjunge Quex* was well reviewed at home and internationally (Rentschler 1996, 55). Goebbels communicated his joy at the film's mix of art and character to the director of Ufa in a letter published in *Der Angriff* on 25 September 1933. As the exemplary film for Goebbels, it met his criteria for the integration of a political message into an aesthetic cinematic medium.

The strategy of *Hitlerjunge Quex* is mainly twofold: it perpetuates the tradition of viewing the street as ominous but places the cause squarely on the evil nature of the Communists. In addition, the film accents proletarian existence as hopeless in itself. Within these parameters, it is noteworthy that Heini, during his metamorphosis into a sacrificial hero, is beset by two worlds — of light and of darkness, of orderly Nazi wholesomeness and of Communist sloth, lechery, and squalor. His struggle is vindicated by his final apotheosis in the multiple dissolves of marching columns, which bring to mind the close of Trenker's proto-Nazi film, *Der Rebell*.

The basic elements of the action can be outlined as follows: Invited to an outing of the dissolute Communist youth group, Heini Völker, a printer's apprentice in Beusselkietz, feels drawn instead to the life-affirming discipline of the Hitler Youth after secretly watching the organization's outdoor activities. The Hitler Youth offers an inviting contrast to the beery milieu of Heini's unemployed father and the abusive treatment he and his mother receive from the father. In his newfound zeal, Heini warns the siblings and Hitler Youth members Fritz and Ulla Dörries of a Communist attack on their hostel. Stoppel, the local KPD leader, hears of Heini's tip and forces his way into the Völker's apartment. Finding the mother alone, he harasses her by threatening to kill her son. She resolves to kill both herself and her son by leaving the gas turned on overnight. She perishes, but Heini is rescued. At the hospital, Fritz and Ulla cheer up Heini with the gift of a Hitler Youth uniform. In the hospital garden, Cass, the *Bannführer* (youth leader), talks Heini's father into allowing his son to become a member of the Hitler Youth. When Grundler, a Hitler Youth seduced by the charms of the Communist flirt, Gerda, helps her to throw anti-Communist leaflets into the Spree, Heini and Ulla print fresh fliers during the night. Despite Stoppel's repeated efforts to lure Heini away from the Nazis, Heini is spotted distributing these fliers in Beusselkietz. He is then surrounded by the Communist gang and knifed to death by Wilde, its fierce Communist chieftain, in a deserted fairground tent. When his colleagues and Cass find him expiring, he stammers out the words of Baldur von Schirach's "March of the Hitler Youth." Upon his demise, multiple dissolves of marching columns carrying swastikas resound with the song's refrains.

Compared to the novel, the screenplay changed the order of crucial scenes and suppressed others for the sake of pacing and added suspenseful misunderstandings and increasingly confrontational dialogue. In the book, Heini's coming murder exists as a constant menace presaged by those of two others barely five months ago: "Norkus and Preiser had fallen in this service barely five months ago" (Schenzinger 216). After the mother's death, the father retreats from the action. Instead of the corruptible Hitler Youth Grundler in the movie, the only foil for Heini is the Hitler Youth Wisnewski, who is a merely irreverent wag and more in the background. Heini's death is brought on by a sudden, blunt blow to the head — unseen by the narrator, but probably from brass knuckles — as he is leaving a soirée he had enjoyed with Fritz and Ulla. In a final abrupt flickering of life, he sings an unidentified but familiar marching melody (to become the "March of the Hitler Youth" in the film). He dies in a hospital with his friends in attendance. After he is buried in a grave "between the dead comrades," the future is envisioned as a proliferation of banners and Hitler Youths marching to the same melody (255–56).

In both novel and film, the boy's striving for the ideal takes him through critical stages: his daily squalor, near death at the hand of his mother, a new life as a Nazi, and his death and apotheosis. The similarities to the cinema of Weimar promote a *déjà-vu* sense of continuity, satisfying Goebbels's dictum that films should provide viewers with familiar scenes. Street events echoing left-wing or street films unfold in the Communist-dominated areas of the streets including the fair. Such areas are full of traps, which are accented atmospherically by flitting shadows, drains, puddles, alleys, dens, knives, circular motion, midway booths, and raucous music. The upbeat, robust strains of the Hitler Youth song that launches the film contrasts with Heini's morbid surroundings.

A viewing of *Hitlerjunge Quex* brings to mind crucial Weimar film classics, whose leftist agenda the film parodies. Steinhoff's film suggests parallels to the portrayal of street life in *Kuhle Wampe, M, Berlin-Alexanderplatz, Mutter Krausens Fahrt ins Glück,* and *Die Dreigroschenoper.* The *Moritat* sequence that opens G. W. Pabst's *Dreigroschenoper,* for example, suggests the social relevance of Bertolt Brecht's play on which it was based, although the film was never approved by the playwright. Such a ballad of bloody deeds resurfaces in the *Moritat* singer's story in the fair sequences of *Hitlerjunge Quex.* The paranoia of pursuit found in Lang's *M* is reprised in the closing sequence of Steinhoff's film as the Communist thugs chase Heini and corner him in a carnival tent.

The primary link to Slatan Dudow's 1932 film *Kuhle Wampe,* banned by Goebbels, is its focus on the temptation of the proletariat. The human foible of giving into temptation in the celebration in *Kuhle Wampe* of the engagement of the two principles, Anni and Fritz, is a humanly understandable vice. Yielding to the enticement of excessive eating and drinking helps the poor briefly escape their drudgery. However, such a weakness among the Communists becomes negative behavior in *Hitlerjunge Quex.* At *Quex*'s onset, the close-up of an apple, which a boy tries to steal from a shopkeeper, prepares one for the treatment of this issue. The theft triggers in turn Wilde's speech about the downtrodden masses, a riot, and police intervention. The initial emphasis on extreme hunger here will be superseded by an accent on pure appetite as the more typical Communist peculiarity. The hilariously freewheeling drunkenness and gluttony of the party at the proletarian camp Kuhle Wampe in Dudow's film, reappears in *Hitlerjunge Quex* where it is reformulated in the lechery and eating excesses of the young Communists on the way to their forest encampment. In the spirit of boisterous fun, Gerda forces a surprise kiss on Heini, and Stoppel stuffs a phallic banana into her mouth. Despite the self-indulgent profligacy of the group, the Nazis as a whole, as Karsten Witte notes, cannot be tempted with any earthly fruit (1986, 306). Both the celebration in *Kuhle Wampe* and the wedding party in *Mutter Krausens,* released three years earlier, with its guzzling, overeating, and obscene dancing, offer antecedents for this event. As remarked, the athletic contests and political demonstrations in *Kuhle Wampe* may well have fostered a receptive climate for the marching feats in *SA-Mann Brand* and for the military formations, singing, and sports of the Hitler Youth in *Hitlerjunge Quex.*

The figure of Heini's father, Herr Völker, is probably the most palpable echo linking the film to its Weimar heritage. Heinrich George, the renowned leftist actor who plays Franz Biberkopf in Phil Jutzi's adaptation of Alfred Döblin's *Berlin-Alexanderplatz* and Herr Völker, the proletarian who switches allegiance from the Communists to the Nazis, provides continuity from Weimar to Nazi film. More importantly, the on-screen conversion of Völker parallels George's conversion from left to right, or at least his willingness to adopt a new screen persona. Consequently, any other parallels between the two films are subordinate to the political subtext supplied by George's presence. To be sure, the ruffians of the taverns and alleyways in Heini's world resemble the seedy habitués of local hangouts in Jutzi's film. Indeed, the squeaking, resonant, and measured speech of Reinhold, Biberkopf's nemesis, akin to Peachum's squeaky commands in *Die Dreigroschenoper*, resurges in Wilde's deliberate, strident exhortations. The overall shrillness of their voice patterns bespeaks their shallow, scruffy, and predatory natures. Also to be noted is a prime difference between the two films. For example, the panoramic montage sequences of criss-crossing traffic and street works, prominent at the onset of Jutzi's production, are not a distinct feature of *Hitlerjunge Quex*. The latter film inclines more toward moodily atmospheric street scenes rather than objective panoramas of urban phenomena. As a whole, the city sights are spatially more circumscribed, such as alley mazes and the midway. The interiors in both films, however, are markedly comparable with cramped living quarters and beery, rundown taverns.

Biberkopf and Völker are products of urban life. Economically distressed, gruff, and harried, they are prone to a violence fed by peer pressure and existential frustration. Biberkopf, having served prison time for the murder of a female lover, continues to manifest violence in his attack on his new lover, Mieze, during an altercation witnessed and halted by Reinhold, her future killer. In Steinhoff's film, Völker retraces a like pattern by beating his wife in retaliation for her reluctance to give him drinking money.

In spite of their violent nature that suggests Jutzi's and Steinhoff's main characters are cut from the same cloth, they are different. Heini's father evinces little of Biberkopf's vitality and charm; he appears a reductive version of Biberkopf. As a stereotypical patriarch, Völker suffers a sense of injured manhood because of his unemployed status. Certainly, he is as harried and frustrated as is Biberkopf, but, unlike the latter, who occasionally expresses a playful attitude toward life, Völker is mostly taciturn. His basic decency, manifested in his empathy for the apple thief, unfolds further, and following the film's intent, in his ultimate embracing of the Nazi cause after his talk with the youth leader Cass. The portliness of the Biberkopf character in Jutzi's movie produces a jovial effect, but the Völker character's rotundity is the symbol of vegetating joblessness. The contrast between Cass and Völker, disclosed in a comic moment in the hospital waiting room, appears meant to underscore the gulf between self-affirmation and self-denial, between National Socialism and Communism. When Cass, sunny and scrutinizing, asks Völker if he is Heini's father, the latter's first reaction is to shield his face in an embarrassed gesture. A lower sense of self-worth and more restricted possibilities, both indicative of Communism as a way of life, distinguish Völker from Biberkopf's indomitable vitality. Yet, there are significant enough parallels between them to suggest that this film is recycling and transforming a proletarian type in order to indict the Communism.

Just as Biberkopf, Völker can be brutal when opposed because of a need to express manly superiority and thus rise above his deprived, repressed existence. In this vein, he lashes out at his wife and son. When Völker beats his wife, a scene crucial to understanding the father's psychological motivations, Heini chances to arrive home from his printer's apprenticeship with a coin he covertly passes on to his mother, who fearfully proffers it to the father. Notably, Völker gloats over his ability as a dominant male to intimidate his wife into giving up the hidden money. When he forces Heini to sing the "Internationale" by beating him after hearing him intone the Hitler Youth song, it is clear that he is reacting to true peer pressure. He appears to dread the wrath of the leaders or any endangerment of his Communist status in the neighborhood clique. The fear of group pressure is not unfounded, for Stoppel later threatens the mother with Heini's death. Although Völker is rarely as jovial as Biberkopf, he does have occasion to display humorous whimsy. During the oft-cited talk between Cass and Völker, Völker is persuaded that his son belongs with the Hitler Youth and that Germany is that group's overriding object of allegiance. Then, in a reprise of the scene in a tavern, Völker hints jocularly to Stoppel that Deutschland, the site of Berlin and the Spree, is also the source of the beer they are drinking together. His new orientation renders him convivial. It is as if he can relax once he has been liberated from the stress of being a Communist. But his new persona has come at a price for the proletariat and the way it is portrayed in cinema. Instead of existing as an urban icon such as Biberkopf, Völker is reduced to a clichéd victim of international Communism who glimpses a new ideal in National Socialism. In order to serve the ends of propaganda, he has become diminished in complexity.

Minor characters likewise show metamorphosis from Weimar to their reincarnation in NS films. Jutzi's *Mutter Krausens Fahrt ins Glück*, dedicated to Heinrich Zille, the documentary artist of the Berlin slums, features a mother who, like Frau Völker, seeks a painless exit from life by releasing gas fumes from the kitchen stove. In the Berlin district of Wedding, Mutter Krause lives in dilapidated, crowded quarters with peeling plaster and a laconic proverb on the wall: "Nur nicht verzag, Glück kommt all Tag." ("Just don't lose heart, happiness comes every day.") Her dilemma is that she cannot turn in the entire earnings from her newspaper sales because her skittish son has squandered them in drink. Thus, she faces prosecution and homelessness. She chooses death as the happiness promised by the proverb, and decides that the little girl asleep in a box-like bed adjacent to the kitchen, the daughter of a subtenant, should join her. The child would otherwise have nothing in the world at all, as she views it.

The death of Mutter Krause is notably less melodramatic than the related situation of Frau Völker in *Hitlerjunge Quex*. Through concentrated and minimalist acting, the personality of the forlorn mother appears stoic, calculating, and worried, yet luminous with love for her wayward son. Her low-key suicide is truly deliberate: she puts a coin in the coffee machine, enjoys a finely brewed cup of coffee, and then pulls out the gas hose. Her final moments and those of her son come as close-up shots shifting from the wall clock's pendulum to the outlines of the mother's solemn, unconscious face which becomes nebulous and blurred as the fumes bring on death.

Not only is it more melodramatic, but Frau Völker's suicide is also fraught with symbolism. As the fumes from the gas stove penetrate the abode, visualized on the screen through special effects, their contours become indistinct and turn into curtain-like, waving strands. They are akin to banners (Bateson 304), and as such anticipate the final scene in which Heini ultimately dies stammering the lyrics of the Hitler Youth song about the billowing flag just before the Nazi flag fills up the screen (306–7). As the fumes spread, the musical score sounds the Hitler Youth song, but in a *minor* key. The combination of gauzy, almost festive filaments and anomalous music in the suicide scene suggests the disintegration of Heini's old way of life in favor of the new. Thus, a true twilight zone of transition is established.[4] The bright hospital room, where Heini awakens to behold Ulla and Fritz and be welcomed into the Hitler Youth, signals a fresh direction, which leaves the deceased mother behind. If the suicide scene lacks the austere gravity of Krause's demise, it is surrealistically designed to arouse empathy for the Nazi cause, adding to the Nazi film's hagiographic composition.

The *Bänkelsänger* (ballad singer) who seems to preside over the fair provides a striking accent to Heini's fate. He is presaged by the *Moritat* singer in Pabst's film, *Die Dreigroschenoper*, but Pabst's singer is invit-ingly folksy, in contrast to the sinister figure in Steinhoff's film. Heini's abortive desire for an eight-blade knife draws him to the midway, the prime stomping-ground of sleazy Communist idlers. This locus has been likened perceptively to the midway in *Das Cabinet des Dr. Cali-gari* (The Cabinet of Dr. Caligari, 1920) (Rentschler 1996, 62). Cinematically, it is another aspect of the pitfalls of the street. The ac-tivities of the midway, represented here by the free-floating, revolving, or spinning motion of such carnival attractions as the carousel and the shooting gallery, serve as archetypes of aimless excitation. In his song of murder, the ballad singer foretells Heini's doom. At first he is in the background, recounting bloody deeds in a singsong. The foreground shows Heini at a booth trying to win a knife. Stoppel, the leader of the Communists, wins the weapon and passes it on to Wilde, another Communist, who eventually will use the knife to kill Heini. The close juxtaposition of the glimpse of the knife and the distant singer intro-duces a note of tension. But one evening, when Heini runs into Gerda at the midway, the ballad singer is viewed in a medium shot and com-pels Heini's attention. His staring eyes and blank face, distorted by oblique top lighting, seem to gaze through the camera. Pointing at il-lustrations, he does not so much sing as speak in a measured and zom-bie-like fashion about grisly knifings: ". . . and whoever bleeds turns red"; ". . . and there he lies in the pool of blood"; ". . . helpless, like a poor child" (Arnold et al, 134–35). Then the Communist warehouse explodes and lights up the night sky. The fateful synchronization of the singer and explosion forecasts the fact and motive of Heini's coming murder as the result of his defection to the National Socialists. When Heini is finally killed by the Communists, their deed appears a cowardly act of murder. Yet the foretelling of a victim "lying in the pool of blood" also endows Heini's death with the force of predestination.

The structural elements recalling Lang's *M* showcase the fair and the street as iniquitous dead ends. Heini becomes a recycling of the protagonist of *M*. Ironically, he is used as the very moral opposite of a demented child murderer. In effect he becomes the victimized child it-self. At the fair, Heini eyes the eight-blade knife with the fixed stare of Lang's protagonist, who was drawn to an array of shop-window blades. Moreover, like the murderer in *M*, Heini is hunted down like a quarry and caught when his whereabouts are betrayed by an unwitting noise. In the second part of the film, after the warehouse bombing, streets and alleys become ever more tenebrous in the manner of Lang's film and earlier films demonizing the street, such as Karl Grune's *Die Straße*. While Stoppel tracks Heini in the streets, hoping to win him back, he is notably profiled by a lurking shadow redolent of the protagonist on the prowl in *M*.

The scene that is most evocative of key *M*, the one in which Heini gives himself away, is heralded by events that accentuate the knife as the tool of murder. When Stoppel flings it to a bevy of fellows in a Communist dive, who pounce on it, Wilde, the victor, pockets it. Upon hearing that Heini is in Beusselkietz distributing fliers, in defiance of all warnings, Wilde whistles his gang unit into action. Led by Wilde, the Communists slink down alleys in the predawn, blocking Heini's escape. Through a hole in a fence, he dashes into the fair and hides in a tent, dark and silent for the night. The midway, with its white carousel steeds frozen in mid-leap, is as spiritually inert as the warehouse that had hidden the murderer in Lang's film. Stunning montage lends immediacy to the attack: the mechanical drummer-boy activated by Heini bumping into it, Wilde's smirk as he signals his men to the source of the rattling, a quick extreme close-up of the boy's terrified face, an agonized cry, legs racing away, and the blurry ground, which then comes into focus as Heini collapses after having been stabbed by Wilde. In the light of dawn, Heini's friends rush over to him. Before dying, he feebly sounds out the refrain of the Hitler Youth song that tells of their banner flying before them. The members of the underworld in Lang's film, who are set to execute the murderer, are akin to the Communists that surround and kill Heini. Also, the mechanical drummer-boy represents a degraded image of Heini himself from a Communist perspective. As such, it stands in contrast to his apotheosis.

The finale harks back to the marching ranks of men marching through the clouds at the close of Luis Trenker's *Der Rebell*. In *Hitlerjunge Quex*, the shot of Fritz holding the lifeless boy in his arms dissolves into marching SA men and Hitler Youths. The columns march to the tempo of drums and the Hitler Youth song and become contained within the full-screen spread of the swastika banner.[5] Reflections of Weimar cinema enhance the propaganda effect of the film's closing vision, which shows Nazi marchers continuing Heini's struggle and succeeding. Hoffmann uses the legacy of the street purposefully to render the Communist milieu diabolical, to highlight a rift between the ordered Nazis and the rootless Communists. The broad range of transformed motifs contributes in varying degrees to Heini's exemplary path to martyrdom. As such, the film provides an overturning of the ideological assumptions of *Kuhle Wampe*. The proletarian milieu is reformulated as a malevolent underworld of the kind encountered in street films.

Although not as complex in style or content as *Hitlerjunge Quex*, *Hans Westmar*, directed by Franz Wenzler for *Die Volksdeutsche Filmgesellschaft*, is more challenging cinematically than *SA-Mann Brand*. Originally titled *Horst Wessel* and based on Hanns Heinz Ewers's novel of that name, the film adopts, according to Hull, the newsreel style of Russian models (32). In this respect, the demonstrations and battles of the streets in Sergei Eisenstein's *Ten Days that Shook the World* (1927) come to mind. The realism of *Hans Westmar* extends to the authentic look of its flags and posters (Hoffmann 1996, 55). Nevertheless, Goebbels, who never really solicited films about the SA, abruptly canceled its premiere, which was slated for 9 October 1933, finding that the film compromised the hero's stature and menaced the interests of the state and the German people (Hoffmann 1996, 55). He demanded revisions and a change in both the name of the protagonist and the title from Horst Wessel to Hans Westmar before allowing the premiere to take place on 13 December 1933.[6]

The film, scripted by Ewers, the novelist and screenwriter for the racy *Alraune* (1928), follows the chaste outline of his novel but omits its tedious subplots. He also augments the parts of the villains: Else Cohn, a KPD harpy bent on Westmar's demise, and the Muscovite, who decrees Westmar's death — played with chilling reserve by Paul Wegener. Furthermore, the film dramatizes Westmar's murder through a series of brief shot-countershot images. These reveal the agony in Westmar's twisting body, the horror on the faces of his friends, and the gleeful expressions of the assassins. The novel renders the scene more tersely: "Und Horst Wessel fiel, wälzte sich in seinem Blute" ("And Horst Wessel fell, writhed in his blood") (Ewers 217). As concerns specific Weimar references, the sports in *Kuhle Wampe* are replaced by a rigorous marching cult. This cult of marching materializes in another apotheosis, recalling again *Der Rebell*, when Westmar rises from the dead in step with his Nazis stalwarts in the victory of 30 January 1933.

Once more, the hero, here a songwriter and SA warrior, assumes a millennial dimension, as had Erich Lohner and Heini Völker. On the surface, *Hans Westmar* is the definitive feature film for the era of struggle. However, it diverges from objective fact. Loiperdinger comments correctly that since *Hans Westmar* attempts to play down the terrorist activities of the SA and limits them to stirring marches, it misrepresents the "struggle for the street" (1991b, 74–75). Vestiges of Weimar models are superimposed onto an ostensibly historical frame and are aimed towards an emotional appeal. This direction may have resulted from Goebbels's order to remake a film that came, for Courtade, too close to truth in its first version (47–48). The two pertinent aspects of Weimar film for our discussion of *Westmar* are the cinematic heritage of street films, in particular the way in which they present the KPD milieu, and the influences of New Objectivity and its treatment of the urban aspects of modernity. An analysis of these influences will follow a brief overview of the action of *Hans Westmar*.

A funeral chorus sounds over the opening credits (It will sound again once Westmar's death is impending). In Vienna, Westmar, a student, invites his German-American friends, Maud and her father, to see the sights of Berlin. In Berlin, the Russian envoy, also known as the Muscovite, tells the KPD leader, the German Camillo Roß, that abject misery is the best comrade for the party. Having already decried KPD brutality, Westmar is shocked at the decadence of Berlin nightlife and the indifference of its revelers to the slain soldiers of the First World War. At a KPD meeting, to which the SA have been invited, Westmar speaks against the rabble-rousing oration of the Jewish-Bolshevist KPD official, Kupferstein. A riot breaks out. Then, Kütemeyer, the SA man, is fatally beaten and tossed into a canal by four Communists. In protest, Westmar leads a march past the Karl Liebknecht House, the KPD headquarters.

Desiring to be one with his fellow men, Westmar turns to work in Berlin, first as a taxi driver and later as a subway construction worker. He also devotes himself to his SA unit, which swells to 100 men. After he has rescued a young woman, Agnes, from the blows of her drunken stepfather, the KPD clique pressures her to spy on Westmar. Both the Muscovite and Roß warn Westmar without avail to desist from his activities with the SA. He declines Maud's lovelorn plea that he emigrate to America. In his double life as SA man and subway builder, he converts some co-workers to National Socialism. Agnes secretly warns Westmar of her orders to spy on him. Owing to the effectiveness of SA demonstrations, marches, and posters, the KPD loses votes, and the Muscovite decides on Westmar's assassination. Cohn organizes a conspiracy with the landlady, Salm, which succeeds in its second attempt. Westmar is riddled with bullets in his room in the presence of Agnes and Klara, a Nazi colleague. While he is still alive at the hospital, another attack is crushed because Roß, disillusioned by the cynical ruthlessness of the KPD, alerts the SA. However, Westmar weakens and dies; his last word is "Deutschland," as his solemn face is bathed in shadows. KPD bands attack his funeral procession, but the police quash the street battle. Once at the cemetery, the focus is on the coffin, bedecked with swastika banners, then on Westmar's resurrection, as his spirit marches onward with the Nazis. The men stride through the

Brandenburg Gate, as Camillo Roß opens his clenched fist to form a Hitler salute.

As in the other two martyr films, in *Hans Westmar* decisive events unfold in the street and the locales associated with the street. Wenzler, like Seitz and Steinhoff, invokes leftist films as he reformulates the motifs of Weimar cinema. The spectacle of hunger goes back to the severe penury of Mutter Krause. The extreme abuse of Agnes recalls the all-too-human brutality of both Biberkopf and Reinhold in *Berlin-Alexanderplatz*. The scruffy taverns of those two films likewise reappear. However, these echoes are subsumed in the notion of the murkily evil streets, such as those in *Die Straße* and *Dirnentragödie*. As in the other two films, the cosmic dualism between light and dark, between Nazis and Communists, is of moment. It has been aptly demonstrated that the upbeat, natural, and disciplined SA men are linked to the open spaces of fields and sky, in contrast to the cramped spaces and smoky dives of the KPD (Loiperdinger 1991b, 56–59). Even the starving have come under the spell of materialism and lack spiritual sustenance. Hence, street hangouts form the baleful KPD locale, while the NSDAP becomes associated with the positive space of the open air. To be sure, the SA men are by necessity involved with the street by default in the era of struggle. However, their task in *Hans Westmar* is to master the street, to cleanse it of infestation and mayhem.

The stealthy ringleaders of the Communist gutter are indeed conceivable as distant variations on Caligari, the murdering doctor in Robert Wiene's *Das Cabinet des Dr. Caligari*, and Mabuse, the arch-criminal in Lang's *Das Testament des Dr. Mabuse* (The Testament of Dr. Mabuse, 1933). Caligari and Mabuse are both streetwise outcasts from the social order. By association, Paul Wegener's Weimar film role as the ferocious clay automaton, the namesake of *Der Golem: wie er in die Welt kam* (The Golem: How He Came into the World, 1920), infuses his role as the Muscovite with a sinister aura. Physically akin to Wilde in *Hitlerjunge Quex*, with dark hair and high cheekbones, the cool Muscovite displays the same immoral conduct as Steinhoff's villain. From a Nazi perspective he is the equal of Wilde, "a 'subhuman,' the product of miscegenation, venereal disease, and criminality" (Baird 1990, 123).

The slaying of Kütemeyer, who had distinguished himself in the brawl following Westmar's speech at the KPD gathering, takes place on a darkly hulking bridge. When four Communist workers beat him to death and drag him over the canal, the hands and head of his lifeless form are whitely illuminated. After he is thrown into the canal, white foam appears on the gloomy waters. The chiaroscuro lighting accents the prevailing murk of the setting, the diabolical thrust of the deed, and the radiant virtues of the deceased. Anticipating effects of film noir, it stresses the evil potential of the Communist streets. As a meaningful death, it presages the sacrificial fall of Westmar.

The strikingly violent murder of Westmar is the consequence of the criminal plots of the KPD. Cohn arranges with several workers and Salm, the vindictive landlady, to find Westmar alone. Fatigued by illness, Westmar is set to continue his studies at Greifswald, but must retrieve belongings from his room. There he meets Agnes and Klara and resolves passionately to stay with the SA and work to swell its ranks to ever-greater numbers. Responding to a knock at the door, Westmar opens it, and a worker from the KPD fells him with four pistol shots. A rapid montage of twenty-six shots in a matter of seconds follows — focusing mainly on the faces of the three workers from the KPD, Salm, and Cohn, whose face widens into a grin. Included are multiple shots of Westmar, almost freeze frames, as he falls. The contrasting juxtaposition of killers and martyr underscores the duality of evil and good, deceit and honor. Then, the scene shifts to the apartment of Westmar's mother, who futilely waits for her son's return. The focus on the table setting with empty plates recalls the mother in *M*, who hopes for the return of her already murdered child.

Hans Westmar is reminiscent of other Weimar films as well. For example, when Westmar shows Maud and her father, two German-American visitors, the nightlife of Berlin, his traditional beliefs in racial homogeneity and hatred of the cosmopolitan trends typifying the Weimar Republic are placed in relief. Maud is thrilled by international sights, but her father is disgruntled at the city's un-German aspect. When they seek his old neighborhood hangout, and he finds it has been turned into "Chez Ninette," he becomes indignant at his favorite pub's foreign name and new look. At the entranceway, posters announce exotic and risqué entertainment, such as "Berlin without a shirt." A black porter in a fez greets them in French. They are almost fearful of proceeding further. Once they are inside the ballroom, a mulatto woman sings in English amid glittering Hollywood decor. No Munich beer is available for Maud's father, who must settle for Moselle wine. The musicians, three blacks and one Caucasian, produce a lively rhythm for the dancing couples, but Westmar is visibly downcast because of his perceived absence of anything truly German. He exclaims that one can obtain caviar from Russia and tropical fruits, but nothing German. His mood turns gloomier at the sight of fat, drunken capitalist, extolling the virtues of free enterprise and requesting a performance of the "Wacht am Rhein" (Watch on the Rhine), a selection normally capable of arousing chauvinistically Germanophile responses. A black man dances to the beat of the song, which has been jazzed up. Westmar becomes even more disturbed than when the song was requested. Aghast at the song's profanation, he attacks the man, cries for the music to stop, and strides from the ballroom. He amazes Maud by lamenting that the nightclub does not represent Germany, which "is totally elsewhere" (Loiperdinger 1980, 23).

For Westmar, the decadence of the Weimar Republic is represented by this nightspot; it represents indifference to the lives lost in the last war and the hordes of unemployed workers and suicides. Its imagery harks back to Walter Ruttmann's 1927 *Berlin, die Sinfonie der Großstadt*, the renowned documentary of the city from dusk to midnight with its array of traffic, pedestrians, night life, and other urban aspects emphasized by the New Objectivity. The multiple dissolves of slanted neon signs, exhibiting the ethnic diversity of the city, which constitute the negative impressions of Maud's father in a taxi en route to his old hangout, recall the last movement of *Berlin*. Shots aimed at dancing feet provide another vestige of the film; there, dancing feet pulsated through the night as functional emblems of revelry. Westmar's final impression of Chez Ninette offers slanted, blurred, and distorted images of the whirling dancers and energetic performers. They convey a sense of chaos, also produced in *Berlin*, but by a different camera technique. Ruttmann used dissolves that could encompass anything of a hectic nature. Chaos and anarchy, viewed as mostly pure spectacle in Ruttmann's film, are hostile to Westmar's ideals. The nightspot, the site of cosmopolitanism, takes on for him an alarming street cast, and he sees it as a menace to German integrity.

Wenzler's *Hans Westmar* further references urban phenomena in the scene depicting its hero's employment as a subway construction worker, which evokes several key films. Like Freder in Fritz Lang's *Metropolis*, he feels compassion for his fellows and wants to work with them. The forerunners of this brief but key episode are, among others, Ruttmann's *Berlin*, Joe May's 1929 *Asphalt*, and *Berlin-Alexanderplatz*. In these films, the myriad city scenes typically include street workers with pile drivers and asphalt leveling equipment, as well as close-ups of machinery. In the sequence showing Westmar at work, the film is in line with the unemotional portrayal of street life favored by adherents to the style of the New Objectivity. As Westmar toils away, the machinery and scaffolding insist on his involvement in the real world. The scene is first introduced by the close-up of a machinery wheel, a transporter of iron, and intersecting pipes. Construction gear appears in the foreground before Westmar and his co-workers enter the scene. As the equipment surrounds them, a bond of fellowship between them is forged in the bowels of the city. When Westmar, during a pause, enlightens his co-workers that the Communist newspaper prints false reports about SA activities, they become suspicious of the KPD and more open to the NSDAP. Indeed, the gritty construction work makes possible the building of trust.

The trilogy of martyr films of 1933 celebrates the mythic ideal of sacrifice and presents the Nazi cause as a moral imperative. Plot elements overlap to a remarkable degree. Brand and Heini both have recalcitrant fathers who become Nazis. Even the patriarchal KPD man, Roß, salutes Hitler at the end. Anni and Agnes are both summoned to spy, but, as exceptions, betray their party out of love for a Nazi zealot. Turrow, the KPD puppet-master, Wilde, the Muscovite, and Cohn are obsessed with Bolshevik might and disdain the needy German people. The last words of the martyrs bespeak devotion to what are in a German context higher powers: the father in heaven, the banner, and Germany itself. The visionary endings, notably of *Hitlerjunge Quex* and *Hans Westmar*, suggestive of *Der Rebell*, exemplify the morality structure of these films.

The vestiges of Weimar cinema identified in this article as present in these films do not prove intent, nor have all such vestiges been identified here. Crucial films or complexes of films were selected for their representative import. Well-known motifs of Weimar films were reformulated in an attempt to nullify leftist or Communist ideas and promote and legitimize Nazi ideals. Leftist motifs, originally conceived as revelatory of human economic misery and hope, were revised to present the proletariat as self-indulgent, aimless, and conniving. Street elements were grafted onto the leftist heritage: darkened alleys, shadows, midways, dives, and predators, at times suggestive of expressionist overtones, are attributed to the feckless proletarian fold; they offer a dichotomy between the nocturnal forces of darkness and those of sunshiny, open-air affirmation. In contrast to the other two films, *SA-Mann Brand* offers more attenuated echoes of Weimar film, for their dramatic force is weakened by the film's mawkishly homey humor. Nevertheless, viewed as a whole, the trilogy offers the mythic sacrifice of the hero as a triumph over the street.

SA-Mann Brand (1933). *Erich Lohner* (*Rolf Wenkhaus*), *falling to demonic street forces in Berlin, becomes a Nazi martyr. Courtesy Museum of Modern Art Film Stills Archive.*

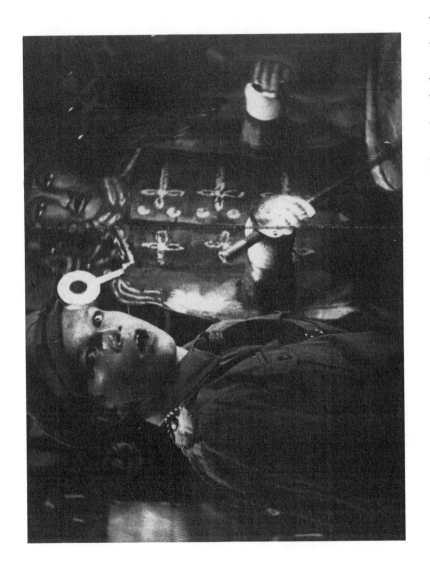

Hitlerjunge Quex (1933). Heini Völker (Jürgen Ohlsen) betrays his hiding place by bumping into a mechanical figure in a carnival tent. Courtesy Library of Congress and Transit Film GmbH.

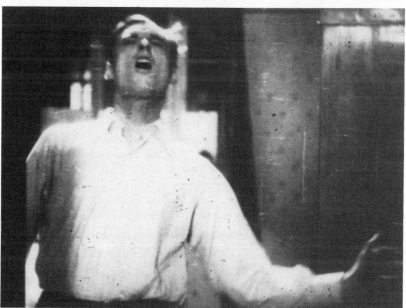

Hans Westmar *(1933). Director Franz Wenzler uses a rapid montage of 26 shots to create a startling juxtaposition of Communist killers and Nazi martyr. Courtesy Library of Congress and Transit Film GmbH.*

Notes

[1] See Viktor Reimann's views on these events in *Goebbels* (Garden City, NJ: Doubleday, 1976) 74–77. Goebbels probably planned coining "unknown SA man" during a riot-provoking talk in 1927 for a real SA man, who was wounded in the course of that talk in a struggle possibly staged by Goebbels's supporters.

[2] It should be noted that the proto-Nazi film *Der Rebell* is also echoed in *SA-Mann Brand* but only subliminally in the theme of rebellion and self-sacrifice; the other two films of the trilogy realize the imagery of *Der Rebell* more radically.

[3] For an overview of the premiere with its long lines of Hitler Youth and Baldur von Schirach's eulogy of the sacrifice of Norkus, see Jay W. Baird, *To Die for Germany: Heroes in the Nazi Pantheon* (Bloomington: U of Indiana P, 1990) 125–26, and David Welch, *Propaganda and the German Cinema* (Oxford: Oxford UP, 1983) 61.

[4] Also see Linda Schulte-Sasse who notes that rebirth is implied by the scene's unusual filmic style: ". . . the frame begins to 'swim,' transporting Heini beyond reality, erasing time and the existing symbolic order." *Entertaining the Third Reich: Illusions of Wholeness in Nazi Cinema* (Durham, NC: Duke UP) 266.

[5] The lyrics of the refrain are germane to the theme of sacrifice in the "March of the Hitler Youth" written especially for *Hitlerjunge Quex*: "Our banner flutters before us. /Into the future we proceed man for man. /We march for Hitler through night and through need. /With the banner of youth for freedom and bread. /Our banner flutters before us. /Our banner is the new time. /And the banner leads us into eternity. /Yes, the banner is beyond death!" (Arnold, et al. 253). Both the above march and the Horst Wessel song, the anthem of the Nazis, are the two major songs of the Nazi party.

[6] See Martin Loiperdinger, *Einstellungsprotokoll*, who maintains in the introduction that one cannot compare *Hans Westmar* at the present time with the original script of the film about Horst Wessel because it has been lost (ii).

3

FRANZ A. BIRGEL

Luis Trenker: A Rebel in the Third Reich? Der Rebell, Der verlorene Sohn, Der Kaiser von Kalifornien, Condottieri, and Der Feuerteufel

THE TENTH ANNUAL TELLURIDE FILM FESTIVAL of 1983 may be remembered for three significant events. The first was Andrei Tarkovsky's comment that cinema "was not and should not be an entertainment, only an art," whereupon he invited all those present who wanted to be entertained by his new film *Nostalghia* to leave. The second was Richard Widmark's rejoinder that films had room for both art and entertainment, and the third was a retrospective of Luis Trenker's films with the then almost ninety-one-year-old filmmaker present (Everson 1983b, 6). Trenker, who died in 1990, is known in Germany and Austria as skier, mountain climber, director, producer, actor, and writer of filmscripts, memoirs, novels, and books on mountaineering. He is further associated with environmental issues, guest spots on children's and talk shows, and promotions for Fiat automobiles and a line of organic health-care products. Like Leni Riefenstahl, Trenker began his film career in the mountain films of Arnold Fanck and went on to direct his own films during the Third Reich, but unlike Riefenstahl, Trenker was able to work again in the film industry after the Second World War. Trenker's appearance at Telluride and the screenings of his films at numerous Goethe Institutes in the United States for the 1983 tricentennial celebration of German immigration to America were part of an unsuccessful effort to rehabilitate the controversial filmmaker and to introduce him to a larger audience. In spite of these events and William K. Everson's work on his behalf, most American film historians have forgotten Luis Trenker or at best relegated him in a few short paragraphs to the category of Nazi filmmaker. His films deserve greater attention not only because some of them are well made, combining entertainment and art, but also because of their historical significance, which arises from their problematic interplay between politics, ideology, and cinema.

Today there are two conflicting narratives concerning the life and career of Luis Trenker, each asserting historiographic certainty. On the one side, Trenker argues that he was a loyal South Tyrolean, a Pan-German patriot who smuggled anti-Nazi statements into his films and who was first used and then oppressed by the National Socialists. As is the case with most filmmakers who worked in Germany during the Third Reich, Trenker's own accounts must be viewed with a degree of skepticism since they constitute more of a self-justification than a confession. Among Trenker's defenders are Everson and David Stewart Hull. Recent critics include Jan-Christopher Horak and Eric Rentschler, who focus on the anti-modernist tendencies and Nazi aesthetics of Trenker's films, viewing him as a blood-and-soil ideologue and chauvinistic anti-American agitator who benefited from Hitler's support. Placed within the context of Third Reich ideology and history, Trenker's films reflect Nazi ideology, lending themselves to interpretations as fascist works.

The question remains: What was Trenker? A rather naive *Naturbursche* (nature-boy) as he presented himself in public? A Catholic fascist? An opportunist? Amidst the opposing statements and views, the Trenker case will remain ambiguous and problematic. Florian Leimgruber's edition of Trenker's file in the Berlin Document Center exposes a person who, even in difficult situations, looked out for his own financial interests, maneuvering like an acrobat between the National Socialists and the Italian Fascists to his own benefit, and displaying all the traits of a "political chameleon" (4). The documents also reveal a non-conformist who, according to his denouncers in early 1934, wore a swastika pin and boasted of being Hitler's friend, but who also criticized the book burnings and treatment of Jews (13, 16–18, 173–74).

Scholars and critics today follow the approach formulated by Günter Netzeband, who states "film history of that period can only be described from a historical, anti-fascist position," whereby they tend to overlook the ambiguities, antinomies and paradoxes in Trenker's films (38).[1] Rather than functioning as Rorschach images, meeting the viewers' horizons of expectations, a closer examination shows Trenker's films to be more like gestalt pictures in which a viewer sees one image and after blinking sees an entirely different image. Whereas some critics find Nazi ideology imbedded in his films, others see veiled criticisms of National Socialism. The problem lies in the competing texts and subtexts of his films, which reflect the antinomy of Trenker himself.

Trenker's image in the U.S. has been shaped largely by Siegfried Kracauer, already one of the director's harshest critics in the early 1930s, and Erwin Leiser. Both authors, who had to flee Nazi Germany, focus on *Der Rebell* (The Rebel, 1932), co-directed by Kurt Bernhardt and financed by Deutsche Universal-Film AG. One of numerous films made between 1930 and 1932 about the German war of liberation against Napoleon,[2] *Der Rebell* was to become a prototype for *Hitlerjunge Quex* (Hitler Youth Quex, 1933), *Hans Westmar* (1933), and *SA-Mann Brand* (1933), three films about sacrificing one's life for National Socialism.

In his famous speech before representatives of the German film industry on 28 March 1933, Goebbels praised four films as artistic masterpieces: Sergei Eisenstein's *Potemkin* (The Battleship Potemkin, 1925), Edmund Goulding's *Love* (1927, based on Tolstoy's *Anna Karenina*), Fritz Lang's *Die Nibelungen* (1924) and Trenker's *Der Rebell*. Regarding Trenker's film, Goebbels stated that it "could even overwhelm a non-National Socialist." *Der Rebell* shows that "the proper attitude is not enough, great ability is also necessary" to create a cinematic work of art (Albrecht 1979, 27). Goebbels, who watched the film three times (at least twice with Hitler), realized that this was how the film of the future should be: "revolutionary, with very large mass scenes, created with an immensely vital energy" (1934, 244; 1987, 2: 342). Hitler even informed Trenker that he had seen *Der Rebell* four times and each time derived new pleasure from it (Wulf 371).

Since the National Socialists liked to represent the rise of the Nazi movement as an uprising by the people, this film about the Tyrolean revolt against Napoleon's troops became the prototype of the Third Reich's films about national uprisings. Like Fritz Lang's *Nibelungen*, the film was intended to evoke myths of the past and create a sense of pride among the Germans and Austrians after the Treaty of Versailles. According to Trenker, although he set this film in 1809, it was directed against the "chains of Versailles" and was intended to remind viewers of "the fate of Germany after the Versailles dictate of 1919" (Trenker 267, 270).[3] The historical and mythological significance of the Tyroleans' struggle against Napoleon's troops can be compared to the American colonists' War of Independence. In retrospect, the ending of *Der Rebell* with its apotheosis, in which the executed Tyrolean freedom fighter rises after being shot, raises his flag and leads a band of men who march toward heaven, "anticipates the Nazi's ritualized cult of death" as presented in the final scenes of subsequent films about Nazi martyrs such as *Hitlerjunge Quex* (Hoffmann 1997, 55).

This image of *Der Rebell* as a "thinly masked pro-Nazi film," as Kracauer claims is one interpretation (1947, 262), and to be sure, the Nazis appropriated the film for propagandistic purposes. In his analysis of Trenker's *Der Rebell*, Julian Petley reminds his readers that films must be seen "in interrelationship with a whole set of discourses at any particular point in time" (117). Yet Petley and other critics of Trenker ignore the discourse about the South Tyrol after the First World War, which appears as a recurring subtext in many of his films. As a condition for joining the Allies in 1915, Italy demanded, at the Treaty of London (26 April 1915), among other territories, the German-speaking South Tyrol. Woodrow Wilson's Fourteen Points regarding national self-determination did not apply to the German-speaking peoples, and a union between Germany and Austria after the First World War was prohibited.[4] Italy officially received the South Tyrol on 10 September 1919 at the Treaty of St. Germain. In spite of assurances that the natives' language, culture, and economic interests would be preserved, Mussolini's officials began a policy of enforced Italianization in 1923: the region was now officially called "Alto Adige," and the use of the names "South Tirol" or "German Tirol" became a punishable offense (Seton-Watson 689).[5]

In official speeches, Mussolini argued that "the boundary of the Brenner Pass is a frontier traced by the infallible hand of God" and stated that if necessary, Italy will push the border further north. Since Austria had been reduced to a small, economically weak republic dependent on Italy, the South Tyroleans hoped that Germany would come to their aid. In late 1925 and early 1926, the problem of the South Tyrol became a hotly debated issue in German and Austrian government circles, especially in Bavaria which borders Tyrol, until the matter was allowed to fade slowly out of the public arena (Suval 131–41; Steininger 1997, 119–36).[6] Hitler, in spite of his claims to bring all German nationals into his future Reich, stated as early as November 1922 that he was willing to renounce any claims to South Tyrol in order to gain Italy as an ally against France (Seton-Watson 695; Steininger 1997, 139). In volume two of *Mein Kampf* (1926), he explains in detail why he believes the alliance is necessary (626–29). Despite this, many South Tyroleans assumed that Hitler's acceptance of the Brenner border was merely a ploy to pacify Mussolini. The reunification of the Saarland with Germany in 1935 and the annexation of Austria in 1938 supported their belief that South Tyrol would become part of a greater Germany (Steininger 1989, 14–15; 1997, 146–47, 156–57).

Given that, as a South Tyrolean, Trenker saw the oppression under the Italian Fascist government first hand, his Pan-German nationalism was quite typical and comes as no surprise.[7] Trenker clearly states his views in *Der Rebell*, when its hero Severin Anderlan argues against fighting the Bavarian troops under Napoleon's command because they have the same language and customs as the Tyrolean peasants. Considering Trenker's personal background and the historical situation at the time of its production, *Der Rebell*, with its theme of liberation from foreign domination, appears in a more complex context and allows a different interpretation: a call for freedom from Italian rule. This may explain why Trenker initially looked to Germany for salvation, hoping that South Tyrol would become part of greater Germany. Because of its theme of a greater German South Tyrol, Mussolini banned *Der Rebell* in Italy (Drewniak 632).

Trenker's American diptych reveals a director more politically complex than his detractors grant. Both *Der verlorene Sohn* (The Prodigal Son a k a The Lost Son, 1934) and *Der Kaiser von Kalifornien* (The Emperor of California a k a The Kaiser of California, 1936) were very personal films for Trenker, but they can also, in varying degrees, be interpreted as both representations and criticisms of the dominant Nazi ideology. Although thematically in tune with the ideology of the National Socialists, the two films contain elements, which make a reading of the films as subtle Nazi propaganda problematic. Both films reveal the director's obvious fascination with the United States, its myths, its people, and its vast panoramas.

Trenker was inspired to make his third film, *Der verlorene Sohn*, while in New York after the completion of *The Doomed Battalion* (directed by Cyril Gardner, 1932), the Hollywood version of Trenker's and Karl Hartl's *Berge in Flammen* (Mountains in Flames, 1931). The film can be divided into three distinct parts. It begins as an overly sentimental Heimat film (homeland film) with idyllic scenes of the alpine countryside. The hero, Tonio (played by Trenker), suffers from wanderlust and longs for the big city. After an unexpected snowstorm kills Tonio's friend and almost takes the life of Lilian, the daughter of a stereotypical American millionaire, Tonio decides to leave the mountains he now hates. Trenker implies Tonio's journey to the United States through images of moving clouds cutting to a shot of the Dolomite peaks which, through a superimposition, dissolve into the New York skyline.

In part two, he meets with one disappointment after another: Lilian and her father are out of town; he runs out of money, is thrown out of his apartment and has to sleep on park benches. As Rentschler points out, the camera work and editing present Tonio as dislocated within the metropolis (1984, 608–9). Trenker presents several shots of derelicts and unemployed men during the depression which he claims not only foreshadowed but actually influenced Vittorio De Sica's neorealism in *The Bicycle Thief* of 1949 (Trenker 295, 454).[8] Tonio is filmed from a moving car as he walks aimlessly through the streets. Concealed hand-held cameras film the hungry Tonio staring into the windows of butcher shops, grocery stores and restaurants. Standing in the line of a

Salvation Army soup kitchen, Tonio remembers a religious procession back home, which painfully underscores the stark contrast between the New World and his Heimat. These innovative shots of New York during the Depression document in a *cinéma vérité* style a reality rarely seen in American films during the period.[9] Although eventually reunited with Lilian and her father at a fight filmed on location in Madison Square Garden, Tonio returns home rather than marrying the millionaire's daughter and staying in New York.

In part three, Tonio arrives home at Christmas time during the *Rauhnacht* celebration. (The twelve days between Christmas and the Epiphany are called the *Rauhnächte* in German. Among the festivities on the last of these nights, Twelfth Night in English, are various rituals to banish evil spirits). Tonio is re-integrated into the community and crowned king of the festival. The final shot shows Tonio and Barbl, his girlfriend, entering the local church where they pray to the Blessed Virgin.

The Polish film scholar Bogusław Drewniak includes *Der verlorene Sohn* among those films, which follow Goebbels's dictate to evoke feelings of animosity toward anything foreign and American (343). In his *Ministry of Illusion: Nazi Cinema and Its Aftermath*, Rentschler considers the film anti-American and groups it together with such overtly nationalistic *heim ins Reich* (back home into the Reich) Ufa films as 1933's *Flüchtlinge* (Refugees) and 1934's *Ein Mann will nach Deutschland* (A Man Must Go To Germany) (75–76). These propagandistic films, a popular genre during the Third Reich, usually dealt with oppressed German minorities abroad. Initially set during the First World War, later films such as 1941's *Menschen im Sturm* (Men in Struggle) and *Heimkehr* (Homecoming) depict the fate of German nationals after the outbreak of the Second World War and explain why these countries had to be invaded.[10] In Trenker's film, Tonio does not return to fight (as in *Ein Mann will nach Deutschland*), nor does he embody the Führer principle and return to help build the National Socialist empire (as in *Flüchtlinge*). If simply the theme of *Heimweh* (homesickness) and the desire to return home constituted a form of propaganda, the same argument would also apply to Detlev Sierck's *Schlußakkord* (Final Accord, 1936), which many critics consider free of Nazi propaganda.

In the mid-thirties there was little anti-American sentiment in Germany. As during the Weimar Republic, many during the Third Reich cherished the values of a preindustrial society and held conflicting views about America as the embodiment of modernism. Such views contributed to the ambivalence of the official National Socialist policy toward the United States (Trommler 338–39). Nazi criticism of American mass culture during the 1930s was racially motivated and directed mainly at jazz music because of its polyrhythms and African origins (Sanders 21–23). The government-controlled media only began an anti-American campaign after Hitler declared war on the United States, and then the propaganda was directed at popular culture (Trommler 339).

Like *Der Kaiser von Kalifornien, Der verlorene Sohn* is, in the words of Petley, "not so much anti-American as 'anti-capitalist'" (128). The portrayal of poverty and hopelessness in New York during the depression could be interpreted as anti-American, but in fact, it is unsparingly realistic, showing that not all immigrants realize the so-called American dream (Eisert-Rost et al. 29). Tonio's displacement in Manhattan functions as part of a Heimat film's implicit structure of polar opposites: the misery, chaos, and alienation of city life versus the sense of community and simplicity of rural life. New York serves as a contrast to the director's beloved mountains, where, as Trenker once stated, the poor peasants have a sense of belonging and are freer than New York's millionaires (Kalbus 2: 115). For this reason, he avoids a Hollywood-style ending. Tonio does not marry Lilian and live happily ever after in New York, but rather, returns home to Barbl. On a socio-political level, the film may be sending another message. Although Jews and leftists were forced to flee Germany after the National Socialists came to power, the film can also be interpreted as urging others not to leave the country — don't emigrate, the economy is picking up and unemployment is falling, stay at home where you belong.

Although the idealization of the simple rural life in *Der verlorene Sohn* was in accord with the Nazi's blood and soil movement in the arts, the film's emphasis on religion evoked displeasure from viewers at both extremes of the political spectrum. Trenker claims that Goebbels tried to prevent the distribution of *Der verlorene Sohn* in Germany (Everson 1984, 275), and there may be some truth to his story. *Der verlorene Sohn* was passed by the censors on 29 June 1934, but it was not premiered until 6 September 1934 (Albrecht 1969, 346). Because of government supervision through all phases of production, the time period between the official approval of a film and its first public screening normally took two days to three weeks.[11] Initial criticism of *Der verlorene Sohn* came from the leaders of the Hitler Youth, who viewed it as a work filled with concealed Catholic propaganda financed by the Catholic Church, and the Communist papers in Vienna also attacked the film (Trenker 305–6).

There are indications that already in 1934, the relationship between Trenker and the National Socialists was strained at times, but they con-

tinued to promote his film projects, even if the financial support for location shots in the United States was limited. The Trenker file at the
Berlin Document Center contains letters from February 6 and March 1,
1934, addressed to the Reichfachschaft Film, denouncing Trenker for
his anti-German comments (Leimgruber 13, 16–18). According to
other accounts, the filmmaker would get drunk at parties and give Nazi
officials a piece of his mind (Everson, 1983a). For the scenes filmed in
New York, Goebbels sent along a production director who not only
kept an account of expenses but also spied on him and sent reports
back to Berlin. As a result, Trenker's line of credit at the Berlin Film
Bank was stopped, but the American office of Universal Studios supported him (Trenker 299–301).

Trenker claims that he had declined Goebbels's offer to film the
1936 Olympic Games in Berlin because he desired to return to the
U.S. and make a sequel to *Der verlorene Sohn* (Trenker 310).[12] He
wanted to counterpoint the film with the story of a successful immi-
grant, the celebrated John Augustus Sutter. Because of his relationship
with Carl Laemmle, the German-born head of Universal Studios,
Trenker hoped to direct *Sutter's Gold* (1936), but the studio thought
he was not well known enough in the U.S. to direct and star in what
was originally conceived as a big-budget film (Everson, 1983a; *Variety*
12 May 1937, 13). Universal gave it to James Cruze to direct and cast
Edward Arnold in the role of Sutter. Trenker then decided to compete
with Hollywood and made *Der Kaiser von Kalifornien*, his version of
the Sutter story.

In *Der Kaiser von Kalifornien*, Trenker's relationship to Nazi ideology becomes more problematic and ambiguous. During the opening
credits, variations of Albert Methfessel's 1818 musical version of Ernst
Moritz Arndt's patriotic poem "Der Gott, der Eisen wachsen ließ"
(God Who Made Iron Grow) can be heard blended into the overture.
The opening sequence presents Sutter as an idealist and revolutionary,
publishing subversive political pamphlets written by Arndt, the German
author in opposition to Napoleon's conquest of Germany. When the
police come to arrest him, Sutter runs up the stairs of the church stee-
ple. Looking down upon the city, he contemplates suicide, whereupon
a spirit appears to him. This stranger, who according to Trenker represents Goethe, shows him a vision of the world he is to conquer.[13] Sutter
begins to travel west, following the sun. Rather than presenting the
journey, Trenker merely shows Sutter walking toward the ocean, creating the impression that he walked across the Atlantic.

After Sutter reaches California and receives a ten-year land grant
from the governor of Mexico, the film's propagandistic subtext be-

comes more obvious: Sutter will turn the region into a paradise on earth. Englishmen, Italians, Swiss, Austrians, and men of other nationalities come to work under his guidance in the thriving agricultural community. Having a German rule over the community not only stresses the contributions of Germans to the development of the United States, but also reflects Hitler's racist view of the country. In *Mein Kampf*, Hitler states, "The Germanic inhabitant of the American continent, who has remained racially pure and unmixed, rose to be the master of the continent" (287). The scene in which Sutter walks past the workers digging an irrigation ditch is reminiscent of the scene in Riefenstahl's *Triumph des Willens* (Triumph of the Will, 1935) where members of the Labor Service are presented from all parts of Germany (Horak 185; Koepnick 18). In both films, the men look up admiringly at their charismatic leader. When the governor's adviser fears that Sutter is attracting too many immigrants and will proclaim himself emperor of California, the governor responds with the words, "If you really want to see a man working, then take a look at this German."

Soon after Mexico cedes California in 1848, gold is discovered near Sutter's sawmill. Sutter fears that if news of its discovery were to spread, no one would want to work. His fears come to pass and by the time Sutter's wife and children arrive in California, only two men still share his ideals. All the others are digging for gold. Ten years later, Sutter is honored, named a senator of California and made a general in the U.S. Army. As he leads a horseback parade into San Francisco, people fill the streets, waving hats and arms in the air, reminiscent of countless films showing Hitler being greeted by his people. The California Supreme Court recognizes the legitimacy of Sutter's claim to San Francisco and Fairfield, but Sutter is not satisfied with a formal ruling. He demands that all his properties, including the cities, actually be given back to him and all the gold diggers be removed from his lands. After Sutter's speech, a general riot breaks out and all of San Francisco goes up in flames.

The final scenes of the film show an old and broken Sutter walking up the steps of the Capitol in Washington. As he stops to rest, the spirit appears again and presents Sutter with a vision of America's future, with twentieth-century skyscrapers, the pulsating power of machines and the modern city of San Francisco. He tells Sutter that he cannot keep the wheels of history from moving; he has been a great pioneer who put up a good fight and should be content because his heart will still beat in the forests and rivers of California. The film ends with an image reminiscent of the final scene in *Der Rebell* — shots of clouds with Sutter and two friends riding through them on horseback.

On one level, *Der Kaiser von Kalifornien* appears to follow Goebbels's new approach to propaganda as he explained at Berlin's Krolloper on 5 March 1937, "I do not wish, for example, an art which proves its National Socialist character merely through the display of National Socialist emblems and symbols." In accordance with Goebbels's vision of propaganda "as tendency, as character, as attitude" (Albrecht 1979, 48–49), Trenker's Sutter personifies the *Führerprinzip*, the principle of leadership, like Frederick the Great, Paracelsus, Ohm Krüger and others in films of the Third Reich. The film presents Sutter as a charismatic leader who acts out of a sense of inner conviction and a vision of a future utopian community. Like Sutter, many of the early leaders portrayed in films of the Third Reich fail, and the implication can be discerned that they were only forerunners of the true Führer, who shall not fail.

In addition, the theme of the settling and cultivation of the land in California has correctly been interpreted as a reference to the *Lebensraum* (living space) policy of the National Socialists (Horak 186). Trenker admitted as much in an interview upon his return from the United States in November 1935, when he advocated *Lebensraum* in reference to *Der Kaiser von Kalifornien*, stating that in contrast to *Der verlorene Sohn*, he wanted to

> capture the expansiveness of the world. We need the world. We are a people without space, and it is the most important project of our future that we can solve and carry out this problem. . . . Is it not providence that this first real colonizer of California was a German? (Leimgruber 35)

Trenker expressed these ideas almost four years before the beginning of the Second World War.

The paradox in *Der Kaiser von Kalifornien* lies in its subtexts: the almost parodistic references to Hitler and the final glorification of American capitalism. Apparently Goebbels and Hitler did not see the irony of a political fugitive fleeing to America. The text being printed by Sutter at the beginning of the film reads: "Whoever fights tyrants is a holy man, and whoever controls arrogance performs God's service. Because God dwells only in a proud heart, and heaven is too high for the base mind."[14] Although the National Socialists liked to use Arndt's writings for their own purposes, Trenker may have incorporated this tract as an anachronistic attack against the Nazi tyrants, which apparently went unnoticed at the time (Everson 1984, 275). In the scene in which Sutter walks past his workers building an irrigation ditch, he hands out cigars as he passes them. Since Hitler was an adamant nonsmoker who did not tolerate smoking in his presence, Trenker might have been having a joke at Hitler's expense. Watching Sutter give his angry speech in San Francisco, gesticulating and stamping his foot on the table, while the crowd turns against him, one wonders — in spite of identifying with Sutter throughout the film — whether or not Trenker might have been parodying Hitler, showing a man out of control, fighting a losing battle.

The fate of Sutter parallels that of the South Tyroleans in many ways. Whereas gold prospectors overran California, thousands of Italians moved to South Tyrol with government incentives and promises of improving their economic situation there. In early 1935, the Italian government began a systematic industrialization of the area in and around Bozen (Bolzano). Many farmers were deprived of their lands, receiving a small fraction of the market value, so that factories and homes for the Italian workers could be built. If one reads this film as an allegorical representation of events in South Tyrol, then Trenker's anti-modern devotion to farming becomes more poignant, and the final glorification of progress and industrialization becomes more problematic, since it would validate (albeit reluctantly) what was being done by the Italian government.

Although *Der Kaiser von Kalifornien* is a loose adaptation of Blaise Cendrars's novel *L'Or*, the Nazis accused Trenker of basing the film on a novella by the Jewish writer Stefan Zweig and of having had a good relationship with "the Jewish world of film rulers" (Drewniak 78). According to Trenker, Goebbels wanted him to add a monologue by Sutter condemning America's capitalist structure, similar to the condemnation of England at the end of *Ohm Krüger* (Uncle Krüger, 1941), which the director refused to do (Trenker 329–30; Panitz). Goebbels himself is less specific in his diary entries of 17 and 18 June 1936 regarding *Der Kaiser von Kalifornien*. He found the film wonderful and even more effective at the second screening on the following evening, but he writes that the conclusion contained an inconsistency [*Bruch*] and must be changed (2: 627–28). Hitler thought it was a shame that *Der Kaiser von Kalifornien* "concludes without any ethics and moral" (1982, 355). Trenker writes that after the film won the Mussolini Award for best foreign film at the 1936 Venice Film Festival, there was no need to make the additions Goebbels wanted (330).[15]

When it was released in the U.S., *Der Kaiser von Kalifornien* received a positive review in the New York Times on 8 May 1937 (Smith 23), but it was not a commercial success here.[16] During the period of occupation after the Second World War, when films banned in one zone often played in theaters of another zone (Hauser 282–83), the

Americans in Germany and the Allied Commission in Austria banned *Der Kaiser von Kalifornien* because they considered it anti-American; the Russians banned the film in Vienna because they considered it pro-American (Trenker 331).

In comparison with Universal's *Sutter's Gold*, which suffers from muddled characterization and an inconsistent plot, Trenker's film emerges as a more artistic and satisfying work. In his review for the *New York Times*, Frank S. Nugent describes Cruze's film as "tedious, illogical and fanciful . . . one of the major disappointments of the season" (27 March 1936: 25), and it became the biggest money loser in the history of Universal Studios (Frayling 10). Whereas in the Hollywood version, Sutter at one point becomes as greedy as the prospectors, Trenker presents his hero as a man of tremendous vision who wants to set up a utopian community, a man to whom responsibility to his fellow human beings and working the land is more important than gold. Granted, the view of the American West is a European one, influenced by the novels of Karl May. In addition, many German critics consider *Der Kaiser von Kalifornien* to be the best German-made Western despite the liberties Trenker took with historical facts and geography.[17] The beautifully filmed panoramas of the American West assume mystical dimensions, and the score by Giuseppe Becce gives the epic an operatic richness.

Some of the flaws in the film can be ascribed to the financial problems Trenker encountered while filming in the United States. Goebbels originally promised Trenker $100,000 for the location shooting, but then had the Reichsbank refuse him the foreign currency. Trenker then received $20,000 from the Dutch distributor, Tobis Maatschappij Amsterdam, for filming the sequences in Nevada, California, and Texas with a cast and crew of seventeen (Trenker 311–13). In the American Southwest, the director filmed only the location shots that were absolutely necessary. Carl Laemmle and Paul Kohner at Universal gave him some support for the American sequences, but most of the farming and mass scenes were later filmed in Livorno, Italy, where Tyrolean carpenters and painters re-created the western town of San Francisco. Trenker also filmed some exterior scenes in Berlin and the cathedral scene in Ulm. Because of the shoestring budget, interior scenes were mostly shot in real houses instead of studio sets.

After the completion of *Der Kaiser von Kalifornien*, Trenker went to Italy to film the German-Italian co-production *Condottieri* (1937, released in English as Giovanni de Medici, The Leader). For this large-budget film, the Italian government supplied 1,500 infantry and 500 cavalrymen, while the German government placed sixty of Hitler's SS bodyguards at the filmmaker's disposal. Trenker himself depicted Giovanni di Medici, applying the Führer principle to the Italian Renaissance prince who tried to unify his country. The parallels to Mussolini's Italy did not escape the American reviewer for *Variety*: "The men who rally around the hero look a good deal like Fascist blackshirts, salute a good deal like Fascist blackshirts, and talk a good deal like Fascist blackshirts" (*Variety* 14 July 1937: 21 and 31).[18] With this film, Trenker was obviously courting Mussolini. After first seeing this film on 17 March 1937, Goebbels considered it magnificently photographed but a bit overstated. He also wrote in his diary that Trenker "loses himself too much in mystical Catholic hocus pocus" (3: 82). After Hitler called him on the following day to express his disappointment in the film, Goebbels concluded that *Condottieri* is "not a heroic film, but a film of the Catholic campaign. I will have to edit it drastically" (3: 83). One scene in particular displeased both Goebbels and Hitler: the crucial confrontation between Giovanni and Pope Hadrian VI, when the SS men, dressed as Italian knights, kneel before the pope (Trenker 342–43; Hull 113–14).[19] Since Trenker's film premiered in Stuttgart only ten days after Pope Pius XI issued his encyclical "Mit brennender Sorge" (With Burning Care) on 14 March 1937, Goebbels ordered the film cut several times to remove the unacceptable scene of SS-men kneeling before the pope.[20] The available print does not actually show them kneeling, yet a high angle shot looking down on Giovanni from the perspective of the pope clearly indicates his submission to papal authority. One wonders whether Trenker was behaving as a naive and apolitical Catholic or being subversive when he filmed this scene. In order to pacify the Italians (who awarded it a prize at the Venice Biennial) and to recoup some of the investment in the film, Goebbels had it recut, released for a short time in Germany, and then quietly withdrawn from circulation (*Tagebücher* 1987, 3: 95–96, 103; Hull 113).

In order to escape the tense atmosphere in Berlin, Trenker started filming the German-British-Italian production *Der Berg ruft* (The Mountain Calls, 1937), a remake of *Der Kampf ums Matterhorn* (The Fight for the Matterhorn, 1928, directed by Mario Bonnard) in which he had acted. In the competition between the English and Italian teams to climb the Matterhorn, the British climber Edward Whymper reaches the top first, but four of his teammates fall to their death when the rope breaks. Whymper is accused of cutting the rope and put on trial. The Italian, Carrel (played by Trenker), climbs up the mountain to retrieve the broken rope and prove Whymper's innocence. The final scene shows Whymper and Carrel on top of the Matterhorn, which they have climbed together.[21] After its completion, *Der Berg ruft* was re-edited with interior shots filmed in England under the co-direction of Vincent Korda and released as *The Challenge* (1937). In addition to underscoring Trenker's personal theme of comradeship among mountain climbers from different nations, *Der Berg ruft* reflects Goebbels's attitude toward England at that time. He wanted German-English co-productions to counter the negative reporting about Germany in the British press, and he still hoped that Great Britain would become an ally of Germany (*Tagebücher* 1987, 3: 19). In this sense, the film presents a desired English-Axis alliance.

Trenker's attempt to straddle Berlin and Rome came to an abrupt end in 1940. On 23 June 1939, the German and Italian governments had reached an agreement whereby all German-speaking South Tyroleans could leave Italy if they opted for Germany by the end of December 1939. The option was later extended to 30 June 1940 for members of the clergy and South Tyroleans living outside the region.[22] The German and Italian governments pursued different goals in the resettlement of the South Tyroleans: Germany wanted to increase its labor force and military, populate conquered areas, and repay debts to Italy with property owned by the South Tyroleans; Italy, on the other hand, wanted to remove the unruly German-speaking inhabitants after the failure of its assimilation policy (Steininger 1997, 179). Since Hitler planned to resettle the South Tyroleans in conquered areas after the war, deciding to leave for Germany did not necessarily mean living permanently in Germany or Austria.[23] Many who chose to leave were motivated by rumors (spread apparently by Nazi propagandists) that those who stayed would be moved south of the Po River, to Sicily, or to Abyssinia (Eisterer 179–208; Steurer 213–16; Steininger 1997, 164).[24]

Like the other South Tyroleans, Trenker had to decide between remaining an Italian citizen and applying for German citizenship. His aging parents lived in the South Tyrol, and his four sisters had married Italians. In addition, he enjoyed Mussolini's favor, and his films were quite successful in Italy ("Feuer und Fett" 217). His production company, however, was in Berlin, where he had an apartment and spent much of his time. Trenker hesitated for months in making a decision and urged others not to opt for Germany (Trenker 432). Rumors soon spread to Berlin that he had decided in favor of Italy. Nazi political leaders, already displeased with Trenker's politics, began to distance themselves. In his diary, on 18 January 1940, Goebbels wrote:

> The option of the South Tyroleans has now been fortunately wrapped up. Luis Trenker, spineless creature, has decided in favor of Italy. We

shall fix him. The Führer never thought much of him, and I have warned people about him (4: 17).

In desperation, Trenker wrote to several people, requesting that they intercede on his behalf (Leimgruber 54–59). Finally, he wrote to Hitler on 27 February 1940, asking him whether he should break all ties to Italy and Mussolini, or whether he should continue to work in the spirit of German cultural understanding. He concluded: "You, my Führer, know all my works from *Rebell* to *Feuerteufel,* and you may rely on my knowing at the appointed hour where I must stand and belong" (63), but Hitler never responded, and Trenker never regained the favor of the party leaders. After a meeting with the filmmaker on 7 March 1940, Goebbels wrote:

> In the afternoon I receive Luis Trenker. He drivels on about his Germanness, which he betrays today with a cold smile. I remain unmoved and cool in my heart. A scoundrel and fellow without a Fatherland! Stall, and one day, eliminate (4: 65).

In order to save his career, Trenker finally opted for Germany on 28 March 1940 (Leimgruber 76–110). On 22 July 1940, he applied for membership in the Nazi party and was accepted on 1 October of the same year (4, 100–101). The files in the Berlin Document Center reveal that Trenker fabricated the claim in his memoirs that, given the choice between Germany and Italy, he decided to make no choice and thus to remain a German South Tyrolean citizen of Italy (Trenker 382–87). Nowhere in his memoirs does he mention having been a party member.[25]

Trenker's decision to opt for Germany came too late to help the reception of *Der Feuerteufel* (The Fire Devil), which had its premiere on 3 March 1940. For this film, he returned once again to the Napoleonic Wars. Like *Der Rebell,* this work presents the argument for a greater Germany by having the Prussian hussars of Ferdinand von Schill (an early form of the *Freikorps*) join the Alpine peasants, even though the king of Prussia and the emperor of Austria have ordered their troops to cease fighting. On the surface, the film appears to be another propagandistic, historical, anti-Napoleonic film, but Trenker managed to incorporate some dialogue regarding the 1939 situation of the South Tyrol into a scene, where the emperor and Metternich represent Hitler and Goebbels respectively:

> Emperor: Tyrol is ceded, and I will not hand over another shot of powder for a new uprising.
> Archduke Johann: What will happen to Tyrol? We have to help the poor mountain folk.

Metternich: The rebellion of the Alpine inhabitants is a social evil, which must be removed at all costs.

The discussion of Tyrol is really a reference to South Tyrol which had been a problem for Hitler and Goebbels, who made no attempts to regain the territory and found the situation there a nuisance that they wanted to end. After Austria was annexed to Germany in 1938, South Tyrol became a taboo subject for the National Socialists. On two occasions in 1938, Hitler's representative, Rudolf Hess, forbade all offices and party members from taking a position contrary to Hitler's declarations on the Brenner border (Alexander 342; Steininger 1997, 157). Because of this, Trenker had to remove most references to Tyrol during the filming of *Der Feuerteufel*, and the Tyrolean Josef Speckbacher, on whom the story is based, became a Carinthian woodcutter named Sturmegger. Because Trenker had urged his fellow South Tyroleans not to opt for Germany, he was shunned by them (Leimgruber 48–50), and a similar scene is presented in *Der Feuerteufel* when Sturmegger leaves the rebels' meeting. An old woman says in his defense that "he defended the soil of our homeland." In his confrontation with Napoleon, Sturmegger states: "I have the unshakable belief that in the end, not you, Mr. Bonaparte, will determine human history, but rather the Lord God." After the film's completion, Goebbels wrote in his diary on 16 February 1940: "New Trenker film *Feuerteufel*. Dreadful . . . rubbish. I have to cut out a lot. Trenker makes national films, but he's a real dirtbag" (4: 45). Trenker argues that the minister of propaganda realized that this film about Tyrolean freedom fighters hit too close to home: the comparisons between Napoleon and Hitler were too obvious (Trenker 379–80; Hull 196–97; Everson 1984, 279–80).[26]

In spite of Trenker's having become a party member, the Nazis blacklisted him and thus effectively banned him from directing and scripting any films in Germany. The director claims that Goebbels's ban also applied for a while in Italy (Trenker 386, 394).[27] *Germanin* (1943), directed by Max M. Kimmich, Goebbels's brother-in-law, was the only German film made between 1940 and 1945 in which Trenker was permitted to appear. In 1942, he worked in Rome as artistic supervisor on the Italian film *Pastor Angelicus*, a documentary about Pope Pius XII. Then, in 1943, he made a mountain film, *Monte Miracolo* in Italy. After Mussolini fell and German troops occupied South Tyrol in 1943, Trenker was forbidden to set foot in South Tyrol because he had urged his neighbors against opting for Germany and leaving their homeland (Trenker 431–32).[28]

After the Second World War, when the privatization of the giant Ufa group turned the German film business into a cottage industry run more by financial speculators than by specialists in the field, many of Trenker's proposed film projects fell through. He focused on writing, and after 1949, he made over thirty-two documentary films — mostly short films about South Tyrol, the mountains, and mountain climbing. After 1955 he directed three German feature films.[29] The city of Bozen honored Trenker with a retrospective of his films during its 1982 film festival. It was ironic that both Trenker and the signers of the 1962 Oberhausen Manifesto received awards at the June 1982 German Film Prize ceremony for their long and outstanding work in German cinema, since Trenker was a prime representative of the kind of films the manifesto's young authors had derided as "Opas Kino."

Trenker's own account of his activities during the Third Reich is, like Fritz Lang's story about how he fled Nazi Germany (Werner; Winkler; McGilligan 174–81), the product of selective and creative memory. After the National Socialists banned Jews and foreigners from working in the film industry on 28 June 1933, the remaining German directors were a privileged group. Trenker courted and was courted by the leaders of the Third Reich. Based on *Der Rebell*, they realized not only that his Pan-German nationalism agreed with their views, but also that he could make powerful feature films that would bring audiences to the theaters. In retrospect, one wonders whether the Jewish collaborators on this film, the co-director Kurt Bernhardt, the producer Paul Kohner, and Carl Laemmle, head of Hollywood's Universal Studios, were aware of how *Der Rebell* would be appropriated by the Nazis.

It cannot be denied that *Der verlorene Sohn* and *Der Kaiser von Kalifornien*, Trenker's third and fourth films, present themes prevalent in National Socialist ideology — such as the glorification of nature and simple rural life, along with the implied criticism of the capitalist system. Whereas the filmmaker believed in such conservative values, the Nazis cynically misused them. Although the theme of homesickness for Germany was abused in many propaganda films, in *Der verlorene Sohn* it appears as a well-motivated, personally felt human experience, revealing the director's true love for his native land. However, the mountain dwellers are not necessarily idealized. Trenker reveals their provincialism when they erroneously accuse the hero of *Der verlorene Sohn* of betraying his homeland, a theme the director returns to in *Der Feuerteufel*.

The two films Trenker made in the United States contain scenes that make it difficult to interpret them as Nazi propaganda in the guise of entertainment. Both Hitler and Goebbels objected to their final scenes. They wanted an ending other than the mystical glorification of American capitalism at the end of *Der Kaiser von Kalifornien*. The wild, pagan winter solstice celebration at the end of *Der verlorene Sohn* appears to be in accord with the Nazi revival, or rather creation, of so-called pre-Christian Germanic rituals, but it recedes into the background as Tonio and Barbl go into the church for the Christmas Mass and pray before the Madonna. As represented by these final scenes, Heimat for Trenker is a union of the South Tyrolean mountain regions, their local customs, and Roman Catholicism.

Throughout his life, Trenker remained a conservative Catholic and Pan-German nationalist.[30] The first indication of his Pan-German nationalism is clearly stated in *Der Rebell*, and the same idea of a greater Germany reappears eight years later in *Der Feuerteufel*, the last film he directed in Germany during the Third Reich. For most of his career, Trenker was too much of an individualist to be a mere blood and soil ideologue for the National Socialists, although they used him as such. The major lapses occurred in *Der Kaiser von Kalifornien* and *Der Feuerteufel*, where, to a large extent, he thematically and visually advocates Nazi ideas; but even there, the matter is ambiguous.

The recurring theme of personal reconciliation between men of different nationalities through comradeship, be they soldiers who fought on different fronts or competing mountain climbers, appears in such films as *Berge in Flammen*, *Der verlorene Sohn*, and *Der Berg ruft*.[31] Throughout his films Trenker shows his nationalism to be non-chauvinistic. Neither his continual use of the iconography of Catholicism nor the references of the characters to their faith fit easily into Nazi ideology. Hitler commented in one of his monologues in 1942 that Trenker had made two good films, *Berge in Flammen* and *Der Rebell*, but that "all of his other films are maggoty [*wurmstichig*], largely paid for by the Catholic campaign" (1982, 355).

As has been shown, Trenker enjoyed the favor of the National Socialist leaders until he made *Condottieri*, but even that error would have been forgiven if he had not waited so long to opt for Germany in 1940. Goebbels's diaries reveal how Trenker sank in his esteem: in 1933 Trenker was regarded as "a really great director" (*ein ganz großer Regisseur*, 2: 342–43), and still in 1936 "a genuine artist" (*ein echter Künstler*, 2: 616); by 1937 he was considered to be "not one of the great artists" (*keiner von den großen Gestaltern*, 3: 375), and in 1940 Goebbels vented his anger on several occasions by calling Trenker "a spineless creature . . . a real dirtbag . . . a traitor and patriotic hypocrite . . . a swine . . . a scoundrel without a fatherland" (*dieses Stück von Charakterlosigkeit*, 4: 17; *ein richtiges Miststück*, 4: 45; *dieser Vaterlandsver-*

räter und patriotische Heuchler, 4: 59; *dieses Schweinstück*, 4: 62; *ein Schuft und vaterlandsloser Geselle*, 4: 65).

In his old age, Trenker enjoyed the peak of his popularity as a storyteller on German television. In personal appearances, he cultivated the image of his own life as that of a prodigal son: like Tonio Feuersinger, he too left home for the big city, was humbled there, and returned home to his roots. According to Gerty Agoston's report in the *New Yorker Staats-Zeitung und Herold* (17/18 Sept. 1983), when Trenker visited New York on his way to the Telluride Film Festival, he brought along in his defense Goebbels's diary, but, one presumes, only the volume with entries from 1940.

The author would like to thank Muhlenberg College for a 1998 summer grant, which enabled him to research and write this article. He is also grateful to Ambassador Dr. Barthold C. Witte (ret.), former Undersecretary of State for Cultural, Scientific, and Educational Affairs of the Federal Republic of Germany, for many stimulating hours of conversation regarding the history of South Tyrol.

Der verlorene Sohn (1934). Tonio (Luis Trenker) standing in front of the Essex House, down and out in New York City. Courtesy Museum of Modern Art Film Stills Archive.

Der Kaiser von Kalifornien (1936). As Sutter (Luis Trenker) stops to rest on the Capitol steps in Washington D.C., the spirit reappears and presents him with a vision of America's bright future. Courtesy Museum of Modern Art Film Stills Archive.

From a 1932 Social Democratic brochure predicting disaster for
the South Tyrol at the hands of the Nazis and Fascists.
The caption reads "Death to South Tyrol!"

Notes

[1] Unless indicated otherwise, all translations are by the author.

[2] Some of the other films are *Die letzte Kompagnie* (The Last Company, 1930), *Luise, Königin von Preußen* (Louise, Queen of Prussia, 1931), *York* (1931), *Der schwarze Husar* (The Black Hussar, 1932), *Marschall Vorwärts* (Marshal Forwards, 1932), *Die elf Schillschen Offiziere* (Schill's Eleven Officers, 1932), and *Theodor Körner* (1932). Such patriotic films were still popular during the Third Reich, as is evident from productions such as *Schwarzer Jäger Johanna* (Black Hunter Johanna, 1934), *Der höhere Befehl* (Higher Command, 1935), *Der Katzensteg* (The Cat's Bridge, 1937), and *Kameraden* (Comrades, 1941). The genre culminated in the mammoth color epic *Kolberg* (1945). Produced at a cost of 8.5 million Reichsmarks, the film exhorts the German population to defend the country until the bitter end, just as the citizens of Kolberg had done in 1806. The ultimate example of a propagandistic *Durchhaltefilm* (a film encouraging viewers to struggle through the increasingly hard times), it was premiered in the Atlantic fortress La Rochelle and in Berlin on 30 January 1945.

[3] In his review of *Der Rebell*, which appeared immediately after its release, Siegfried Kracauer praises the film as magnificently made [*großartig gemacht*], but from his leftist position, he has strong reservations about its regressive attitude, the mythical image of the people and their antiquated ideals, the lack of historical distance, and the forced, unrelenting parallels to the contemporary situation, *Frankfurter Zeitung* 24 Jan. 1933.

[4] Initially, Italy's territorial claims on South Tyrol were in jeopardy. Because the United States had not participated in the Treaty of London (signed by Italy, Great Britain, France and Russia), Woodrow Wilson at first refused to recognize it along with the concessions it made to Italy. In addition, Point Nine of the Fourteen Points called for redrawing the borders of Italy "according to clearly recognizable lines of nationality." In January 1919, however, Wilson conceded to Italy's demand for the Brenner Pass as the northern border, which was a violation of the principle of nationality. René Albrecht-Carrié, "Foreign Policy Since the First World War," *Modern Italy: A Topical History since 1861*, edited by Edward R. Tannenbaum and Emiliana P. Noether, 338–39 (New York: New York UP, 1974).

Christopher Seton-Watson surmises that Wilson may have been "unhappy about the consequent transfer to Italy of 230,000 Germans, 'as if they were chattels and pawns.'" *Italy from Liberalism to Fascism 1870–1925* (London: Methuen, 1967) 527.

[5] The process of Italianization was based on the thirty-two points of Ettore Tolomei's "Provvedimenti per l'Alto Adige" (announced 15 July 1923)

which called for the eradication of all South Tyrolean Germanness. German towns were given Italian names. The use of the German language was suppressed in schools, courts, and administration (Steininger 1997, 77–93). German teachers were dismissed or sent to southern Italy and replaced by Italian ones who spoke no German. In order to teach their children the rudiments of reading and writing German, the South Tyroleans illegally organized secret "catacomb schools" (Villgrater 85–105). Incentives were given to the Italians to move into the region. Unable to penetrate the soul of the South Tyroleans, the Italian government devised means of taking away their soil and industrializing the area (Steininger 1989, 13–14; Gruber 230–32; Steininger 1997, 97–102). Italianization continued after the Second World War, causing small groups of South Tyrolean activists to engage in terrorist activities from 1956 until the late 1980s.

[6] Mussolini liked to present himself as the protector of Austrian independence. He opposed both a return of South Tyrol to Austria and a union of Germany with Austria. He feared that the latter would result in a strong German bloc at Italy's border and threaten a takeover of South Tyrol (Salvemini 102, 147–50).

[7] In his memoirs, Trenker reports how Italian fascists oppressed the South Tyrolean population. His diploma became invalid in Italy. The government forced the regional German-language newspaper to stop printing (187–90). Trenker also refers to "Blood Sunday," 24 April 1921, when 280 blackshirts from southern Italy joined 120 local blackshirts in Bozen (Bolzano) to attack a parade at the opening of the spring fair. A teacher was killed and approximately fifty other South Tyroleans were wounded during the armed assault (Steininger 1997, 52–54). After his election to the Chamber of Deputies, Mussolini proudly claimed in his maiden speech of 20 June 1921 his "share of moral responsibility" for the action (Salvemini 33).

[8] Even the reviewer for *Variety* states after a screening in Paris that the film contains "some of the most remarkable New York scenic photography ever made," 22 Jan. 1935: 15.

[9] Similar scenes appear in the gritty gangster films produced by Warner Brothers, but they were shot mostly in studios, not on location, and they often left the viewer with the final impression that the American system does work.

[10] The fate of the South Tyroleans under Italian rule would obviously have been a suitable topic for this film genre, but because of Hitler's desire for an alliance with Mussolini, such a film was never made.

[11] At the 1934 Venice International Film Festival, *Der verlorene Sohn* was awarded the Prize of the Italian Minister for Popular Culture, an award reserved for the foreign film with "the most important moral message." Ironically, this award did not prevent the anti-German Fascist prefect Mastromattei from banning the film in South Tyrol.

[12] In Hans Jürgen Panitz's three-part television documentary film *Luis Trenker* (1986), the narrator claims that the filmmaker competed with Leni Riefenstahl for the direction of *Olympia* (1938). Goebbels reportedly wanted Trenker to direct, but Hitler stated that Riefenstahl would make the film. The implication in Panitz's film is that Trenker went to the U.S. because *Olympia* had been given to Riefenstahl.

[13] This according to Everson in his lecture at Goethe House New York, 15 October 1983. On the other hand Jan-Christopher Horak interprets the apparition as depicting an angel, "Luis Trenker's *The Kaiser of California*: how the West was won, Nazi style," *Historical Journal of Film, Radio and Television* 6.2:185; according to Christopher Frayling, *Spaghetti Westerns: Cowboys and Europeans from Karl May to Sergio Leone* (London: Taurus) 19; and Lutz P. Koepnick, "Unsettling America: German Westerns and Modernity," *Modernism/Modernity* 2, 3: 14, the stranger represents the poet Ernst Moritz Arndt.

[14] In his discussion of the film, Klaus Kanzog (126–27) reveals that the text by Arndt which Sutter prints and the stranger later repeats comes from Arndt's *Kurzer Katechismus für teutsche Soldaten nebst einem Anhang von Liedern* (1812). *"Staatspolitisch besonders wertvoll": Ein Handbuch zu 30 deutschen Spielfilmen der Jahre 1934 bis 1945*, Diskurs Film 6 (Munich: Verlag Schaudig and Ledig, 1994).

[15] Everson surmises that the Nazi leaders wanted to suppress *Der Kaiser von Kalifornien* because its image of the United States may have been too negative: "World War Two was already in the planning stages, and Germany naively hoped that America might be an ally in that war, or at least could be persuaded to remain neutral. Thus German films of the 30's were careful to be flattering to America. . . . It is conceivable that the Nazis saw *Der Kaiser von Kalifornien* as being critical of the American government and wished to avoid rousing antagonism over here. In any event, the film's success as a Venice Film Festival prize-winner again forced the Nazis to allow its release" (1984, 278). Everson's hypothesis contradicts Trenker's story about Goebbels ordering him to have Sutter condemn American capitalism at the end of the film.

[16] After the film's U.S. release, the review in *Variety* stated that poor subtitling and continuity problems would "confine the picture's draw to German speaking houses — if any," 12 May 1937: 13.

[17] The *Variety* reviewer reported from Berlin: "Students of American history will not be a little interested to learn that in 1847 President Lincoln overstepped his constitutional powers by personally admitting California into the Union as a State. Geographers will have to move San Francisco up into the Sacramento Valley on their maps, and put Death Valley and the Grand Canyon just east of it, and the American flag will have to be radically altered. Then everybody will okay this picture — maybe," 19 Aug. 1936: 16.

[18] After its U.S. release, Frank S. Nugent expressed a similar view in the *New York Times* 5 Jan. 1940: 15.

[19] Even Leni Riefenstahl, whose relationship with Trenker was quite hostile after the war, corroborates his version of the event, *Leni Riefenstahl: A Memoir* (New York: Picador, 1995) 212.

[20] This encyclical condemned the National Socialist regime and ideology as illegal, inhuman, and anti-Christian. The encyclical was smuggled into Germany, sent secretly to hundreds of towns were it was printed locally and then distributed to the dioceses. On Palm Sunday it was read from every pulpit in Germany, and when it appeared abroad, the National Socialist government lost the support of many Catholics throughout the world. Within Germany, the encyclical provoked increased persecution of the clergy (Rhodes 195–210). Goebbels commented in his diary on 31 March 1937: "The Vatican impudence is still a major topic in the world press. Here they are working hand in hand: church, freemasonry, Marxism, democracy, and Jewry" (3: 95).

[21] Beate Bechtold-Comforty, Luis Bedeck, and Tanja Marquandt argue that *Der Berg ruft* reflects the National Socialist ideology through its themes of racism, sexism, the Führer cult, the male cult, and militarism. They do, however, admit that some elements of the film (ritualized and sensitive male friendships, and the implied homoeroticism) contradict Nazi ideology, "Zwanziger Jahre und Nationalsozialismus," in *Der deutsche Heimatfilm: Bildwelten und Weltbilden*, edited by Projektgruppe Deutscher Heimatfilm 47–51 (Tübingen: Ludwig-Uhland-Institut der Universität Tübingen, 1989).

[22] The Nazi term for the resettlement of the South Tyroleans was *volkliche Flurbereinigung* (redistribution of people); today, the euphemism would be "ethnic cleansing" (Steininger, 1997, 159).

[23] The South Tyroleans were to be transplanted to a *geschlossene Landschaft* (closed or complete settlement area) which meant driving out the indigenous population to make room for the new settlers. (See copies of letters by Heinrich Himmler reproduced in Eisterer and Steininger 1989, photo 30, and Steininger 1997, 294, 296). Some proposed regions were the Beskids (rejected because too many South Tyroleans knew the region from the First World War), Burgundy (rejected because it was under Vichy control), Alsace-Lorraine, the Ukraine, and the Crimean peninsula.

[24] Considering the oppression and forced assimilation of the South Tyroleans by the Italian Fascists, opting for Germany should not be equated with opting for National Socialism. Initially, the National Socialist government in Berlin reported that 90.7% of the population opted for Germany because that percentage of the Saarland's inhabitants had voted for annexation with Germany; later the number was lowered to 86%. The Italian government, however, claimed 72.5% voted for Germany so that its policy of Italianization did not appear as a total failure. Although 86% has become the commonly accepted figure, the actual number is unknown (Steininger 1997, 171). Reports of the

number of German-speaking South Tyroleans in 1939 vary. For example, it has been listed as 234,650 (Steininger, 1989, 13) and 266,985 (Jochmann, ed., *Hitler: Monologe* 443–44, fn. 98). By the end of May 1942, only 75,000 left South Tyrol for Germany and Austria because of obstacles set up by the Italian government and because the Nazi leaders still did not know where to settle them permanently. Difficulties in the reception camps caused many to return illegally to South Tyrol, and after 1945, many who had opted for Germany eventually returned to South Tyrol. Trenker views the planned forced transplantation of South Tyroleans to Poland, Burgundy, or the Crimea as worse than the Treaty of Saint Germain (382).

[25] Although Leimgruber reproduces a copy of Trenker's membership card (100–101), it seems that the filmmaker was neither active nor a member in good standing. The lines for monthly reports are blank, and less than one year later the filmmaker denies being affiliated with the party. A questionnaire filled out by Trenker on 23 June 1941 contains a slash (meaning no) after the question "Member of the NSDAP" (124). An employment card with the last entry from 1942 (apparently written in a hand other than Trenker's) reads: "NSDAP nein" (171). None of the documents reveal whether he later left or was expelled from the party.

[26] When *Der Feuerteufel* premiered in New York with the title *Der Heldenkampf um Heimaterde* (The Heroic Fight for the Home Soil), Wanda Hale commented in the *New York Daily News* that the film "is a strange picture to come from Germany . . . fans must have seen it with one eye closed, neither sensing anything prophetic about it. . . . To an outsider, it has a double edge and can be taken as a warning to Hitler and his supporters . . . whether to revolt or not must be the same arguments that are taking place in Nazi occupied nations today" (4 January 1941, rpt. Leimgruber 115). The party leadership was not unaware of the ambiguous messages films such as *Feuerteufel* (as well as films about the Irish revolt against England) were sending to viewers in occupied territories (Moeller 253).

[27] Some of the failed projects and contracts are reproduced in Leimgruber 112–66. According to a letter from the Office of the Reichsfilmintendant, Goebbels approved of Trenker making films in Italy, since Mussolini had given the director a contract. Apparently that film was never produced, and except for *Pastor Angelicus* and *Monte Miracolo*, he made no other films in Fascist Italy after 1940.

[28] In order to save himself and his career, he told Nazi officials that he had only advised his parents to stay (Leimgruber 71, 139).

[29] Of the six feature films Trenker made after the Second World War, the first three were Italian productions with a mostly Italian cast and crew: a reworking of 1943's *Monte Miracolo* with additional footage shot in Austria entitled *Im Banne des Monte Miracolo* (In the Spell of Monte Miracolo, 1949) but also released as *Der verrufene Berg* (The Infamous Mountain), *Barriera a Settentrione/Duell in den Bergen* (Duel in the Mountains, 1949), and *Il prig-*

ioniero della montagna/Flucht in die Dolomiten (Escape to the Dolomites, 1955) a k a *Im Schatten der Dolomiten* (In the Shadow of the Dolomites). The last three feature films were German productions: *Von der Liebe besiegt* (Overcome by Love, 1956), *Wetterleuchten um Maria* (Lightning around Maria, 1957), and *Sein bester Freund* (His Best Friend, 1962).

[30] On the occasion of Trenker's 1983 visit to Chicago, Hansjürgen W. Kienast wrote: "For Trenker, patriotism and true nationalism are living, altruistic, not egoistic systems of reference, for whose application no sacrifice is too high" (*Sonntagpost* 18 Sept. 1983).

[31] Kracauer's interpretation is quite different. Regarding *Berge in Flammen*, he writes: "Friendship between soldiers of different countries in the lulls of peace does not weaken the friends' determination to fight each other in wartime; rather, it ennobles this fight, transforming it into a tragic duty, a superior sacrifice. Trenker's mountain climber is the type of man on whom regimes in need of war can rely" (1947, 261).

4

THOMAS R. NADAR

The Director and the Diva: The Film Musicals of Detlef Sierck and Zarah Leander: Zu neuen Ufern *and* La Habanera

THE HIGHEST-PAID SCREEN ACTRESS, and arguably the most popular musical film star of Nazi cinema was Zarah Leander. Already a successful stage actress in her native Sweden, with three films as well as a dozen phonograph recordings to her credit, Leander thrilled Viennese audiences on stage in Ralph Benatzky's 1936 musical comedy *Axel an der Himmelstür* (Axel at Heaven's Gate). Her first German-language feature film, *Premiere*, quickly followed in 1937, directed by Geza von Bolvary for Gloria Film in Vienna. Her success on the screen resulted in the Ufa film studio in Babelsberg signing Leander to a long-term contract and painstakingly turning her into a film diva.

Leander first performed for Ufa in an expensive epic titled *Zu neuen Ufern* (To New Shores, 1937), based on a novel by Lovis H. Lorenz. The studio assigned major talents to the project, including Detlef Sierck, who adapted the screenplay with studio writer Kurt Heuser, and directed the film. Most importantly, the studio wanted the best musical numbers for Leander, so it took no chances and, at considerable expense, hired well-known composer Ralph Benatzky to write the extensive score for the film.

The choice of Sierck as director may seem odd in retrospect, for he has never had a reputation as a director of musical films, despite the fact that he made a number of them during his career.[1] However, all directors faced a challenge during this time, for in Germany, as in Hollywood, motion pictures learned to sing as soon as they had learned to talk, studio contracts forced important directors to make musical films whether or not they had interest in the genre. In point of fact, the film Sierck made just prior to *Zu neuen Ufern*, *Schlußakkord* (Final Accord, 1936), an extremely popular melodrama, was filled with classical music. It also happened to star the actor assigned to the Leander-Sierck project, Willy Birgel, playing a symphony conductor accused of murdering his wife.[2] Critics had praised Sierck's skillful handling of the musical numbers. His unique ability to integrate music into drama allowed him to create melodrama, in its classical sense, which the director sought to achieve in *Schlußakkord*, in *Zu neuen Ufern* and finally in *La Habanera* (1937).[3] Although melodrama was not a new genre, Sierck felt that his distinctive mixture of music and drama was highly innovative. He wanted no part of the traditional musical theater or operetta style, in which the characters can break into song at any moment as if it were the most natural thing in the world — a theatrical tradition that dominated the film musicals of the 1930s. Film audiences may have thought it was perfectly acceptable for Lilian Harvey in *Der Kongreß tanzt* (The Congress Dances, 1931) to sing "Das gibt's nur einmal, das kommt nicht wieder" (That Only Happens Once, That Won't Come Again) along the entire distance from her glove shop in the city out into the Vienna Woods, but Sierck found the convention artificial. Even more problematic was that in most musical films, studio songwriters added the songs almost as afterthoughts. Although no one would dispute the entertainment value of these musical numbers for an audience, the songs could, if necessary, be cut completely, or interchanged with others if desired, as long as the tunes were catchy and the lyrics amusing. The tunes from *Die Drei von der Tankstelle* (The Three from the Filling Station, a k a Three Good Friends, 1930) with Lilian Harvey, Willy Fritsch and Heinz Rühmann — "Ein Freund, ein guter Freund" (A Friend, a Good Friend) and "Liebling, mein Herz läßt dich grüßen" (Sweetheart, My Heart Says Hello) — could have been reused in any of a half-dozen of the later Harvey-Fritsch vehicles, such as *Glückskinder* (Lucky Kids, 1936), with its equally non-film-specific hit "Ich wollt' ich wär ein Huhn" (I Wish I Were a Chicken). Certainly the same criticism could be leveled at most of Leander's film musicals, including her German-language debut film, *Premiere*. In it she plays the star of a musical revue involved in a murder mystery and sings "Merci, mon ami, es war wunderschön" (Merci, mon ami, It Was Wonderful), her first German hit, which became one of her signature tunes. A marvelous song, undeniably, but one the actress could have sung in any of her subsequent Ufa films. All, that is, but the two she made with Detlef Sierck. The director argued that if the films were to be effective, the musical numbers would have to derive naturally from the action and be staged as an integral part of the dramatic action.

In *Zu neuen Ufern*, Sierck wastes no time introducing his new singing star. Following an expository scene in which an outraged man protests the indecency and immorality prevalent in London as witnessed by the shocking songs and scandalous behavior of singer Gloria Vane (Zarah Leander), the star performs her first musical number, the show-stopping "Yes, Sir," before a sellout crowd at the Adelphi Theatre. Sierck shoots the song as a music-hall entertainment and even reminds the viewer that it is meant to represent a live performance by interrupting Gloria after she completes the first verse. A fistfight breaks out in the audience over the propriety of Vane's song, her revealing costume, and her questionable moral character. Only when Sir Albert Finsbury (Willy Birgel) comes to her rescue in the manner of a dashing cavalier is she able to perform the concluding verses of the song, this time without interruption. Not simply an entertaining opening number for the star, the director uses "Yes, Sir" as a means of character exposition, creating at the beginning of the film a deceptive, but alluring stage persona for this apparently scandalous woman. The lyrics, specifically tailored to the character in the film, present Gloria as a coquette who breaks the heart of every man she meets. However, as Marc Silberman points out, "Gloria's stage personality, her shameless and aggressive sexuality turns out to be just that, a role she plays which hides her true, backstage personality. What she sings is a lie" (Silberman 56).

The most important song in *Zu neuen Ufern* is the mournful "Ich steh' im Regen" (I'm Standing in the Rain), which Sierck uses as a *leitmotif* throughout the film. In the scene immediately following her performance in the Adelphi Theatre, Gloria Vane joins Albert Finsbury and other acquaintances in the fashionable apartment of one of Finsbury's friends, where she sings the song. The lyrics reveal a hitherto hidden side of Vane's character: she has the capacity to love deeply and give herself completely to the man she loves. The instrumental accompaniment suggests raindrops hitting against the windowpane described by the lyrics. However, Sierck avoids this popular but obvious film cliché, and stages the song in a highly dramatic fashion: the party guests enjoy a flaming punch in front of the fireplace in the darkened room. As she watches the melting sugarloaf dripping incessantly into the crystal bowl, Gloria appears lost in thought about her unhappy love affair with the dashing-but-penniless Sir Albert Finsbury, and seems to sing primarily to herself.

As the scene progresses, Gloria continues her song, while the audience sees the object of her affections altering the amount of a check given to him by a friend. As she sings "der Zeiger der Kirchturmuhr geht von Strich zu Strich" (the hand of the tower clock moves from number to number)," Albert alters the amount on the check by adding an additional *Strich* (stroke) of the pen. Sierck ensures that the song lyrics have a more significant context in the narrative: Gloria's hopeless love for Albert will result in her noble but foolhardy sacrifice, which will send her to prison in Australia. Once again, Sierck reminds the viewer that this song is being performed live, and breaks off the song without a resolution. When it is heard again in the next scene, it is heard only in the nondiegetic musical score, that is, in the dramatic background music or musical underscoring. Albert and Gloria say goodbye before he sails away to Australia to seek career advancement as an officer in Her Majesty's army. As the two talk about their relationship and their future, the background music reminds the viewer of the lyrics of the song heard earlier. Indeed, Gloria will wait for Albert, not only in the rain, but also in England and in Australia, and perhaps for her whole lifetime if necessary. Only now does Sierck show the raindrops splashing against the window of the carriage, their sound imitated by the pizzicato musical accompaniment of the strings.

The third of Benatzky's songs in *Zu neuen Ufern* is also the most unexpected and non-traditional musical number in the film, the "*Moritat* von Paramatta." Sung by Lina Carstens while Sierck's *mise en scène* presents the forgery trial of Gloria Vane, the song acts as a dramatic commentary on the action. Once again the director separates the song's verses with a montage comprised of several short dramatic scenes, some of them in pantomime. The ballad singer's description of the notorious women's prison, Paramatta, near Sydney, leaves no doubt in the viewer's mind that the woman in the dock has no chance for justice. The song tells the viewer that all men and women have to pay for their sins. Only nondiegetic music accompanies the moment in which Gloria is sentenced to seven years of hard labor in the penal institution. In the concluding portion of the montage, through the magic of a lap dissolve, the crude drawing of the prison is superimposed onto the image of the real barred and chained gate of Paramatta. Lina Carstens intones the final refrain of the *Moritat* with a prayer that the rest of us might be spared a similar fate.

In his analysis of this sequence, Marc Silberman has pointed out what he regards as an homage both to Brecht and Weill's "Mackie-Messer" and to G. W. Pabst's 1931 film version of *Die Dreigroschenoper* (The Threepenny Opera), (Silberman 58). This observation is based on the musical presentation of the ballad singer with her crude illustrations of the events described in the song, as well as the director's *mise en scène* for the song, which is such an integral part of the narrative. Certainly one might argue that Sierck could not have easily avoided the temptation to imitate the revolutionary and innovative style of his contemporary fellow artists. As Fritz Lang comments in an interview with Gero Gandert, "Did Brecht influence me? Of course he did. Nobody who tried to come to grips with the time could escape his influence."[4] Sierck had, in fact, directed a stage production of *Die Dreigroschenoper* in Bremen during the 1928–1929 season, as well as the

premiere of *Der Silbersee* (The Silver Lake), written by Kurt Weill and
Georg Kaiser, in Leipzig on 18 February 1933. While Sierck has referred to G. W. Pabst as a "great movie director," he nevertheless insisted that he never saw the director's classic film adaptation of *Die
Dreigroschenoper* (Halliday 22).

The question of the influence of Brecht and Weill on Sierck has only
recently moved out of the realm of critical conjecture. With the publication of the expanded new edition of *Sirk on Sirk* in 1997 on the occasion of the 100th anniversary of the director's birth, evidence has come
to light regarding this important theatrical and aesthetic connection. In
a lengthy but heretofore unpublished portion of his interview with Jon
Halliday, Sierck comments that the success of the revolutionary *Dreigroschenoper* encouraged him to attempt something new in his two
pictures with Zarah Leander. The director saw a unique combination of
music and drama in the innovative approach of Brecht and especially
Weill to musical theater. The songs and musical numbers were integrated into the dramatic text in order to develop and comment upon
it.[5] The insistence of Brecht and Weill on using actors who could sing a
little, rather than singers who could act, shifted the emphasis onto the
dramatic component of the song rather than its musical structure. In
the early works of Brecht and Weill, Sierck found the solution to his
problem of how to create effective film melodrama. He never stops the
action entirely in order to indulge the viewer with a song — the music
and the lyrics always carry the story forward (Halliday 50–51). Sierck
stresses that the Weillian style, not the Brechtian style, fascinated him
most. For those who have long regarded the playwright and composer
as having had a similar aesthetic agenda, the director's distinction may
come as a surprise. Sierck suggests that he was not attracted by the often heavy-handed political message and self-conscious theatricality advanced by Brecht, but rather by the composer Weill's attempt to render
the music more accessible to the audience. Sierck, like Weill, used a
simpler, more popular musical idiom, and carefully integrated the songs
into the dramatic work.

In *Zu neuen Ufern*, Sierck attempts to create a new form of film
melodrama closely following the principles of Brecht and Weill. However, the composer Ralph Benatzky's approach to his film score does
not always share this aesthetic goal. This is apparent in the song he
composed for Zarah Leander to sing in Paramatta. Not surprisingly,
Sierck stages it rather traditionally: as an operetta-like scene in which
Gloria and the other women prisoners sing as they weave baskets and
brooms that are sold on the streets of Sydney. The character is consumed by her unrequited love for Albert, and she sings "Ich habe eine

tiefe Sehnsucht in mir" (I Have a Deep Longing Within Me) while the other women inmates join in on the refrain, providing the angelic harmony for her song.[6] While highly entertaining, this song (and, to a certain degree, "Ich steh' im Regen") could have been used in any of a half-dozen of Leander's films. The fact that both of these works repeat the familiar motifs and well-worn clichés of scores of popular torch songs makes them immediately recognizable to the listener. Nothing in the text refers to the specific dramatic situation in the film. The song simply reveals the fact that Gloria Vane is filled with a "deep longing" for Sir Albert Finsbury, just as the earlier number expressed her resolution to wait for him, forever if need be. It is director Sierck's staging of both songs that seamlessly integrates them into the dramatic narrative.

Sierck fills the first thirty-five minutes of the film with songs that serve as character exposition or as dramatic commentary on the action. Once the scene changes to Australia, however, the dramatic plot and its development take on greater significance, while the musical score retreats into the background. Only near the end of the film does Gloria Vane sing her final number, a complete reprise of "Ich steh' im Regen" that she performs in the tawdry Sydney Casino, where she attempts to earn her living after being released from Paramatta. It is an excruciating moment for the viewer, who recalls Gloria's triumphant "Yes, Sir" sung to her jubilant fans at the Adelphi Theatre in London. In the casino, the patrons are much more interested in the scantily clad cancan dancers and the bleached blonde chorus girl who assaults their ears with her military drum and her highly suggestive "Ich bin eine Jungfrau, Schatz, du mußt mir glauben" (I'm a Virgin, Honey, You've Got to Believe Me). Gloria's dirge-like torchsong could not be more out of place, and the audience pelts her with rotten fruit and vegetables, and only a reprise of the "Jungfrau" number allows the singer to escape with her life. Coincidentally, Albert, who is out on the town celebrating his forthcoming marriage to the governor's daughter, sees Gloria's humiliation. In the short scene after the performance, Albert tells Gloria that he has finally realized how much she has loved him over the years. Her admission to her former sweetheart that she no longer loves him comes as a devastating revelation to him. In the following scene Albert is seen contemplating, then carrying out his suicide. The nondiegetic musical underscoring becomes linked to the diegesis, that is, the narrative, as the character hears in his guilty conscience the imagined voice of Gloria whispering the words of "Ich steh' im Regen." Sierck stages the scene in his best melodramatic manner, once again imitating the pizzicato figures in the song's accompaniment with the raindrops hitting against the windowpane, and ending with a sudden gunshot and then silence.

The tragic end of Sir Albert Finsbury and its musical underscoring is an element highly characteristic of Sierck's films. Thirty-six years after making *Zu neuen Ufern,* the director commented:

> The type of character I always have been interested in, in the theatre as well as in the movies, and which I also tried to retain in melodrama, is the doubtful, the ambiguous, the uncertain. Uncertainty, and the vagueness of men's aims, are central to many of my films, however hidden these characteristics may be. I am interested in circularity, in the circle — people arriving back at the place they started out from. This is why you will find what I call tragic rondos in many of my films, people going in circles. This is what most of my characters are doing (Halliday 46).

Sierck's choice of the specifically musical term rondo to describe the dramatic turns of the plot is particularly revealing. It also helps to explain his use of the songs in the film. In particular, he employs "Ich steh' im Regen" as a "tragic rondo" in the four most significant scenes in the film: Albert's altering of the check, the lovers' farewell scene in London, Gloria's performance in the Sydney Casino and her final reunion with Albert, and his subsequent suicide.

The final musical number in the film accompanies the reconciliation of Gloria and Henry Hoyer (Viktor Staal), the farmer who has bought her freedom from Paramatta by agreeing to marry her. This melodramatic scene is set in a church near the prison where a boys' choir intones a triumphant "Gloria in excelsis deo" as the camera fades out on what seems to be an optimistic, if uncertain, future for the couple.

Marc Silberman interprets this closure from the perspective of the 1990s: "the religiously intoned celebration of [Gloria's] union with a man she hardly knows underscores the contradictions that this resolution must accommodate" (51). If this happy ending strikes contemporary viewers as both artificial and ambiguous, not to mention reminiscent of Sierck's later glossy Hollywood melodramas, we must recall that for audiences in 1937 this type of marriage was both a reality and rather desirable. The women who entered into such a union — and society as a whole — saw this as receiving a second chance in life, as being saved from a fate worse than death. Gloria Vane might have chosen to return to prison, and Henry Hoyer could have refused to marry her, knowing of her previous liaison with Finsbury. The couple brings about their own happy ending in the film. It is not some higher authority as suggested by both the religious setting and diegetic liturgical music performed by the boys' choir.

If Sierck was not entirely successful in *Zu neuen Ufern* in creating a cinematic melodrama along the lines of the Brechtian and even more particularly Weillian model, he came much closer to this ideal in his next collaboration with the Swedish actress. Only a few weeks after production ended on *Zu neuen Ufern*, Leander and Sierck began work on their second and final film together, *La Habanera*. The director not only wrote the screenplay with Gerhard Menzel, a leading scriptwriter at Ufa, he also insured that the musical sequences would be a more integral part of the narrative by insisting on writing the lyrics for two of the three songs featured in the film.

Leander plays Astrée de Avila, née Sternhjelm, but Sierck makes the audience wait forty minutes for her first song — nearly half the film's running time — as the film moves forward from 1927 to the present, here 1937. Sierck wrote "Du kannst es nicht wissen" (You Can't Know or There's No Way That You Could Know) as a musical set piece that serves primarily for character exposition and the advancement of the narrative in the film. The song delineates the relationship between Leander's character and her son, Juan, a relationship that has grown extremely close over the course of his ten years. Not for a moment does the viewer doubt that the fair-haired Nordic Juan is her son and has little or nothing in common with his father, swarthy Don Pedro de Avila, played by Ferdinand Marian, an important Ufa star of the thirties and the forties who specialized in villain roles. The nostalgic "Du kannst es nicht wissen" recreates the delights of a Northern winter, so completely unimaginable in exotic Puerto Rico, where the action is set. It also catalogues the sights and smells of that most German of all holidays, Christmas. The song even ends with a direct quote from that quintessential German carol "Vom Himmel hoch" (From Heaven on High), composed by Martin Luther, which, the lyrics reveal, Astrée has had to teach her son in secret for fear of arousing the wrath of his tyrannical father.[7] Sierck regarded this musical sequence as one of the most important in the entire film. It appeared on the movie's original poster art The director did not intend the song to be a hit tune for Leander, but rather attempted in integrating the song into the film to create his distinctive form of melodrama and advance the film's narrative.

Sierck also wrote the lyrics for "Kinderlied" (Child's Song), a light-hearted combination of spelling song, nursery rhyme, and bedtime duet for Juan and Astrée. As in the previous musical number, the lyrics allow the mother to describe the beauties of the winter in Sweden to her young son, who has never seen snow in sultry Puerto Rico. Eric

Rentschler notes, "When Astrée sings to her son about the Swedish snow, one becomes privy to her memories of home and her yearning for her lost Heimat."[8] The cuckoo mentioned in the song is a bird as foreign to these surroundings as the Black Forest cuckoo clock seems out of place on the wall of the boy's room. All of these references point towards Northern Europe, as does the revelation of Astrée's Christmas present for little Juan, a sled. The viewer wonders what possible use the boy will make of such an impractical gift, but in the brief dialogue that concludes the musical scene, his mother reveals her plan to leave Puerto Rico and return to Europe, taking her son with her. In his attempt to integrate songs into the film, Sierck has compressed a great deal of information into two very short songs. Just as Sierck uses the whimsical "Kinderlied" to contrast with the earlier dramatic number, "Du kannst es nicht wissen," he also uses the duet to lighten the mood of the film by positioning it between two dramatic expository scenes dealing with the outbreak of tropical fever on the island. Ufa marketed both "Kinderlied" and "Du kannst es nicht wissen" as potential hit tunes in order to promote the film, having Leander record them, and publishing the sheet music. While neither song became a megahit for the studio or the singer, Sierck was justifiably proud of his creations, as he modestly noted in later life, "I think they were maybe something a little out of the ordinary" (Halliday 51).

The most important song in *La Habanera*, and Leander's most popular recording ever, is "Der Wind hat mir ein Lied erzählt" (The Wind Has Told Me a Tale or The Wind Has Sung Me a Song). Even though the studio had allowed Sierck to write the lyrics for the other songs, it wanted to be sure that the film contained one major hit for its biggest singing star. Ufa gave the task to two of the studio's best staff music writers, composer Lothar Brühne and lyricist Bruno Balz, both of whom were associated with many of Leander's hit songs. Although Sierck was not directly responsible for the song's text, he treated "Der Wind . . . " as he did "Ich steh' im Regen" in *Zu neuen Ufern*, as a kind of musical *leitmotif* sung repeatedly throughout the film. The song varies as the dramatic context changes. It is this song that is first heard in the film, sung in German by the Puerto Rican entertainers who perform for the passengers of the cruise liner that has just arrived in port. A short time later, a chauffeur reprises the song, much to the exasperation of his two captive passengers, Astrée and her aunt Ana. It would seem that everyone on the island knows this tune! Sierck uses this siren song to motivate Astrée's decision to leave the ship and remain behind in Puerto Rico. Its seductive melody suggests the irresistible nature of this tropical paradise which later turns into a prison for the heroine.

Near the end of the film, the heroine finally performs the song herself. Dressed in an elaborate native costume, with her hair beautifully coifed, she entertains the guests at her dinner party. Is Astrée singing to show her husband she is still his faithful, loving wife (although he reminds her that she hasn't sung "Der Wind . . . " for him in the past nine years)? Or is she singing to tell her former sweetheart, Dr. Sven Nagel, that she still loves him after all these years of separation? The text does not specify which man is the object of Astrée's longing: "The wind . . . knows for whom [my heart] is beating and burning! It knows for whom! It knows what my heart needs . . . [a heart] that also needs me." Sierck stages the number in an ambiguous manner so that each character can imagine that Astrée sings just for him. By the end of the song, however, the viewer has no doubt which of them is her true love.

Following Don Pedro's death from tropical fever, Astrée sails back to her European homeland with her beloved son, Juan, and her soon-to-be-husband, Sven. As their ship leaves the harbor, the last music that they hear is the siren song of the island, "Der Wind . . . " The *mise en scène* is virtually identical to the opening sequence: passengers on a cruise ship sung to by native entertainers. This final reprise of the song serves as a reminder for Astrée not only of the sorrows of her life there but also of the undeniable pleasures she experienced in these exotic surroundings. The film's conclusion is, in many ways, not the anticipated happy ending that the viewer has hoped for, and the director seems to have his own doubts regarding the uncertain future of the heroine. He comments many years later:

> Well, Zarah Leander's feelings on that boat are not entirely linear. She has been in the place ten years, the ten best years of her life. As she looks back she is aware that she is getting out of rotten — but definitely interesting — circumstances. Her feelings are most ambiguous (Halliday 52).

No discussion of these two films, made shortly after the Nazis took over Ufa in mid-March 1937, would be complete without some indication of their value as propaganda works. Both *Zu neuen Ufern* and *La Habanera* were primarily intended as entertainment of a purely escapist nature, containing virtually no political references or undertones.

If a subtext exists in either of these films, it is that a woman can find true happiness only with a husband who is neither a soldier of fortune nor a playboy, while a man will find complete fulfillment only in his work (that is, work useful to society, such as being a farmer, a doctor, or a soldier) with a loving wife at his side. While this attitude clearly reflects the Nazi philosophy, it fits the code of many other ideologies as well.

The negative depiction of foreign cultures in the films may also reflect the new order in Germany, as Marc Silberman has written:

> [*Zu neuen Ufern*] conforms closely to the hundreds of escapist films produced during the Third Reich in which a happy end, prompted by social authority, can redeem even the most complicated and morally questionable situations. Moreover, the negative portrayal of English society and its brutal colonial politics coincides with the official National-Socialist view of British perfidy. (62)

We need to recall, however, that all the characters in *Zu neuen Ufern*, both good and bad, are British, and the audience will in all likelihood reject the decadent Sir Albert Finsbury while it identifies with the two protagonists, Gloria Vane and Henry Hoyer. *La Habanera* seems to demonstrate more pronounced xenophobic tendencies. It presents foreigners, that is the native population of Puerto Rico, as less noble and less scrupulous than their Aryan counterparts. Astrée does, after all, leave Puerto Rico in the company of her blond-haired son and her Swedish sweetheart. The ending of the film seems in accordance with the Third Reich's injunction to all Germans living in foreign countries to return to their homeland. Once again, the ambiguous situation Sierck has created for the film works against this interpretation. Eric Rentschler suggests that the film's conclusion both "anticipates the double-edged endings of the director's later [Hollywood] melodramas," and "subversively undermines the script's 'Heim ins Reich' rhetoric" (1996, 142).

To be completely fair, the same charges can be leveled at nearly all of the eight films Zarah Leander made over the following seven years for Ufa. Her third film for the studio, which sealed her position as the prima donna of German film musicals, was *Heimat* (Homeland, 1938) directed by Carl Froelich. Although adapted from a stage play written in 1885 by Hermann Sudermann, the situation of a world-famous opera singer who finally reconciles with her father when she returns to the land of her birth certainly resonates with Nazi ideology.

The diva's most politically controversial film, Rolf Hansen's *Die große Liebe* (True Love), became the highest-grossing movie of 1942. Leander plays Hanna Holberg, a popular Danish singer in Berlin (not unlike a combination of Astrée Sternhjelm and the music-hall entertainer Gloria Vane,) who falls in love with and later marries a handsome Luftwaffe Lieutenant, Paul Wendlandt (Viktor Staal).

Die große Liebe not only provided audiences with needed diversion from the realities and the hardships of war, it instructed them in the necessity of doing their duty, and of making sacrifices for the Third Reich. During a military concert for the troops stationed in occupied Paris, Hanna raises the morale and spirits of the Wehrmacht with her rousing "Davon geht die Welt nicht unter" (It's Not the End of the World). The lyrics describe how one should react to a failed love affair: "Chin up, things aren't all that bad." In 1942, however, audiences under stood the song much differently. According to Cinzia Romani:

> The air raids and all the tragic goodbyes between Paris and Rome seemed only half as bad, thanks to this song. It gave comfort and hope to all the women who, left alone on the home front by their husbands, brothers and fathers, sang it to themselves (86).

For her final musical number, Hanna Holberg sings the hymn-like "Ich weiß, es wird einmal ein Wunder geschehen" (I Know That One Day a Miracle Will Happen). The text suggests the woman's powerful faith that she and Paul will be reunited despite the war and their own personal differences. Once again, audiences interpreted the text as a comment on their own situation:

> In 1942 people only thought about one miracle: the victory over the enemies of the Reich. The women who remained on the home front while their men fought in the war were able to identify with the heroine of the film, a woman who disregards her own desires and wishes in order to be the kind of wife her Luftwaffe captain expects her to be. (Romani 86).

Toward the end of the film, Hanna rushes to Paul's side after his plane is shot down. At the final fadeout, the couple looks resolutely at the German warplanes passing overhead, and they know their future together will be a positive one despite all the dangers. While the ending of this film resonates for the contemporary viewer with Nazi ideology, it is not unlike the conclusion of *Zu neuen Ufern* — minus, of course, the triumphant boys' choir singing "Gloria in excelsis deo." Since Leander teamed once again in *Die große Liebe* with her earlier costar, Viktor Staal, audiences may well have seen the happy union of Hanna Holberg and Paul Wendlandt as not dissimilar to the marriage of Gloria Vane and Henry Hoyer.

Recognizing the political significance of Leander's role as Hanna Holberg in *Die große Liebe*, Dr. Joseph Goebbels's Ministry of Propaganda recommended that she be named a *Staatsschauspielerin* (Actress of the State), the highest award given to actors by the German State. Hitler denied the actress the prize in anger over her refusal to become a

German citizen. Leander knew that the end was in sight. She went on to make one final film, *Damals* (Back Then, 1942). When a bombing raid damaged her home in Berlin in early 1943, Leander returned to her native Sweden to wait out the end of the war there. Zarah Leander remained closely identified with her 1937 success, *Zu neuen Ufern*, as her first postwar radio interview in the Federal Republic of Germany in 1948 shows, in which she and the interviewer playfully refer to the film's hit songs:

> Interviewer: Is it really you?
> Zarah Leander: "Yes, Sir!"
> Int.: And this is no deception?
> Z. L.: No, Sir!
> Int.: You know, I was standing in the rain ("Ich stand im Regen") so to speak, I was waiting with the microphone and I was quite sad. I had, how should I say it, I had a deep longing for this interview within me ("Ich hatte eine tiefe Sehnsucht in mir").
> Z. L.: Never cry on account of love ("Nur nicht aus Liebe weinen").[9]

The director who had helped turn Zarah Leander into a film diva, Detlef Sierck, left both the Ufa studio and Germany shortly after the premiere of *La Habanera* in December 1937, traveling first to Italy, then to France via Switzerland, and finally journeying from Holland to the USA in 1940. But the two musical films Sierck and Leander made together are among their most treasured works. Michael Wilmington, film critic for the *Chicago Tribune*, writes: "It is in the films directed by Douglas Sirk that we see the Nazi era cinema and the movies themselves at their best and most devious."[10] *Zu neuen Ufern* and *La Habanera* are as impressive today as they were sixty years ago when German audiences saw them for the first time. These films remain a tribute to the two remarkable talents that made them. More significantly, the two films reflect the successful attempt by a master filmmaker to expand the boundaries of the film musical.

Zu neuen Ufern (1937). Sir Albert Finsbury (Willy Birgel) greets Gloria Vane (Zarah Leander)
on the stage of the Adelphi Theatre after her show-stopping number, "Yes, Sir."
Courtesy Library of Congress and Transit Film GmbH.

La Habanera (1937). Astrée Sternhjelm (Zarah Leander) sings the "Kinderlied" with her son Juan. Courtesy Library of Congress and Transit Film GmbH.

Du kannst es nicht wissen

Lied aus dem Ufafilm: „La Habanera"

Text von Detlef Sierck

Musik von Lothar Brühne

Music (Lothar Brühne) and lyrics (Detlef Sierck) to "Du kannst es nicht wissen" from La Habanera. Copyright 1938 by Ufaton Verlagsgesellschaft mbH (BMG UFA Musikverlage, Munich).

Music (Lothar Brühne) and lyrics (Detlef Sierck) to "Kinderlied" from La Habanera. Copyright 1938 by Ufaton Verlagsgesellschaft mbH, used by permission of BMG UFA-Musikverlage Munich.

Notes

[1] For the Ufa studio, Sierck made, in addition to the films discussed in this article: *Das Hofkonzert* (The Court Concert, 1936); for France-Suisse Film he completed *Accord Final* (1939) which borrowed only the title but not the plot of his earlier film *Schlußakkord* (Final Accord). For Universal International, as Douglas Sirk, he made several low-budget musicals: *Has Anybody Seen My Gal?* (1951), *Meet Me at the Fair* (1952), *Take Me to Town* (1952), and *Interlude* (1956).

[2] Sierck would return to this theme and modify it somewhat in his film *Interlude* (1956).

[3] As the director noted in later life, "Well, the word 'melodrama' has rather lost its meaning nowadays: people tend to lose the 'melos' in it, the music. . . . *Schlußakkord* was one kind of melodrama; and *Zu neuen Ufern* and *La Habanera* were another kind of melodrama. But all three were melodramas in the sense of music + drama." See Jon Halliday, *Sirk on Sirk*, 2nd ed. (London: Faber and Faber Ltd., 1997) 107.

[4] Interview with Gero Gandert, quoted in Lotte Eisner, *Fritz Lang* (London: Secker & Warburg, 1976) 116.

[5] For an overview of Brecht and Weill's approach to create a new form of musical theater, see Thomas R. Nadar, "Brecht and His Musical Collaborators," A Bertolt Brecht Reference Companion, edited by Siegfried Mews, 261–67 (Westport, CT: Greenwood Press, 1997).

[6] Incidentally, if Leander's two songs in the film seem curiously (or irritatingly) passive, it is typical for most of the thirty songs the star recorded between 1937 and 1943. Ulrike Sanders notes that the actress really suffers when she is in love; she requites herself, she hopes for miracles, she waits patiently, she suffers silently and conceals her pain, she represses memories or is consumed by yearning. She remains passive and makes no demands on her lover, for his well-being is more important to her than her own and she does not want to bother him with her problems. Sanders concludes, "In not a single one of these songs does one find any evidence of a woman ready to take her life in her own hands instead of waiting for destiny or her lover to intervene." In *Zarah Leander: Kann denn Schlager Sünde sein?* (Cologne: Pahl-Rugenstein, 1988) 168.

[7] Studio composer Lothar Brühne wrote the music for the film's three songs. He created some of Leander's most popular hits, including "Kann denn Liebe Sünde Sein?" (Can Love Be A Sin?), "Von der Puszta will ich träumen" (I Want to Dream About the Puszta), and the three hit songs for *Die große Liebe*.

[8] Eric Rentschler erroneously conflates the two songs Leander sings to and with her son into one that he describes as "a simple Swedish lullaby, a Christmas standard" (1996, 132). *Kinderlied* is in part a lullaby, but the direct quotation of "Vom Himmel hoch" in *Du kannst es nicht wissen* hardly qualifies it as a "Christmas standard."

[9] Rebroadcast on 15 March 1992 by Westdeutscher Rundfunk as part of its tribute on the eighty-fifth birthday of Zarah Leander, "Zeitzeichen: Stichwort: 15. März 1907." In addition to the direct quotations from the three major hit songs from *Zu neuen Ufern*, Leander's parting comment to the interviewer recalls yet another of her most popular film tunes, "Nur nicht aus Liebe weinen" (Never Cry on Account of Love) from *Es war eine rauschende Ballnacht* (An Intoxicating Night at the Ball, 1939) written by Hans Beckmann and Theo Mackeben. Fans of Fassbinder's *Die Ehe der Maria Braun* (The Marriage of Maria Braun, 1979) will recall that Maria and her friend, Betti, sing this tune in order to cheer themselves up.

[10] Michael Wilmington, "Series of Nazi-era Films Reveals How Illusion Can Mask Evil," *Chicago Tribune* 27 May 1995, C1+. Wilmington refers to *La Habanera* and *Schlußakkord*, which were shown as part of the Goethe-Institute-sponsored Nazi Film Retrospective, "Ministry of Illusion," organized by Eric Rentschler.

5

CARY NATHENSON

Fear of Flying:
Education to Manhood in Nazi Film Comedies:
Glückskinder *and* Quax, der Bruchpilot

> In a time when the entire nation is being weighed down
> with such heavy loads and worries, even entertainment is of
> particular political value.
>
> —Joseph Goebbels

AS THE ABOVE QUOTE from Joseph Goebbels illustrates, the Propaganda Minister understood the significance of entertainment.[1] Entertainment, especially in film, meant more than mere distraction from the hardships of everyday and wartime life. Entertainment was embedded in the Nazis' vision of a central authority omnipresent in the lives of its subjects. Goebbels continues: "a national leadership . . . must make it its duty to lovingly and helpfully accompany the people, not only in their concerns, but also in their joys, not only in their burdens, but also in their leisure" (Albrecht 1969, 480). To "accompany" is a euphemism; while no work of art can be devoid of ideology, the unprecedented control the State held over film production in the Third Reich attests to a conscious effort to employ the medium to guide and instruct. Goebbels's audience on this occasion, the Hitler Youth, and the title of his talk, "Film as Educator," leave no doubt as to the pedagogical intentions of National Socialist cinema. To this extent, then, all films under the Nazis were propaganda films.

Unlike the more transparently programmatic agitation of the anti-Semitic propaganda films such as *Der ewige Jude* (The Eternal Jew, 1940) and *Der Führer schenkt den Juden eine Stadt* (The Führer Gives a City to the Jews, 1944), the instructional design in an entertainment film is more difficult to prove. The pedagogical moments contained in entertainment films more likely stemmed from filmmakers' unconscious reflections of Nazi society and its desired self-image rather than from a directive of the Propaganda Ministry. Films made primarily in order to entertain the mass audience offer a glimpse into the everyday fears and joys Goebbels's film industry deemed desirable — or necessary — to portray. Discussion of such films illuminates recesses of society left underexposed by examinations of what is traditionally viewed as propaganda. By reading backwards from the completed entertainment film the lessons it held for its contemporary audience can be reconstructed.

Such a reading of film comedies produced between 1933 and 1945 reveals a profound concern with the state of masculinity under the National Socialists. This demonstrates a level of continuity with the perceived gender imbalance of the Weimar Era. The political and economic destabilization that followed Germany's defeat in the First World War was perceived by many as a threat to the patriarchal foundation of society. The increasing presence of women in the public sphere as suffragists, sex reformers, and, more typically, white-collar workers,[2] exacerbated such masculine insecurity. The cultural artifacts of Weimar are replete with symbolically (and literally) emasculated men.[3] Although this crisis was more one of masculine subjectivity rather than a loss of genuine political power, masculinity seemed — and not only from a fascist perspective — dangerously unstable.[4] Men would have to be shown how to be men again.

Film comedies produced under the Nazis portrayed and thus taught the re-establishment of a patriarchal universe with fixed and immutable gender roles. The comedies accomplished this through humor based on men's transformation from figures of fragility to figures of authority. The cross-dressing farce *Viktor und Viktoria*, released at the end of 1933, comes during the transition period between Weimar and the fascist reconstitution of masculinity. The gender instability does not arise from the woman who portrays a man portraying a woman (the humor is in just how solidly feminine she remains, despite her best efforts). This film distinguishes itself from those that follow in that it still tolerates a foppish man who, after tossing away a gun to avoid a duel, joyously sings, "praise God, I'm rid of that thing!" Two later comedies, *Glückskinder* (Lucky Kids, 1936) and *Quax, der Bruchpilot* (Crash Pilot Quax, 1941), demonstrate that such an unreconstructed Weimar male did not survive this transition. On the contrary, these two different types of film comedy (the screwball and the war comedy) attest to Nazi society's continuous struggle with its fear of the incomplete man.

In order to re-establish patriarchal gender roles in these films, a depiction of gender in an unfixed condition had to be demonstrated. Films that modeled the National Socialist New Man had to evoke his opposite first. The danger inherent in this strategy was that the negative example might more strongly impress itself upon its viewers.[5] While melodramatic entertainment films also portrayed gender insufficiency and restoration, comedy more easily resisted the hazards of the necessary negative example.[6] Instability and confusion form the basis of humor in most comedic modes. In the realm of the comic situation the rules and roles of everyday society are repealed, at least for the comedians.[7] Yet because comedy, unlike drama, often reveals its artifice to the audience and involves them in what Kenneth McLeish calls "a state of conspiratorial irony" (Horton 9), audiences are less likely to identify, emulate, or feel threatened by the aberrant comedian. When humorously presented, the problems of gender identity become laughable, and so less threatening.

The use of comedy to address gender identity is nonetheless not without pitfalls for a totalitarian ideology. While comedy may present a specific behavior as ludicrous and therefore harmless, the very moments of chaos and uncertainty required to make comedy funny are also potential moments of subversion, for they are gaps in the chain of normalcy.[8] These films run a further risk since they do not merely portray humorous errant behavior: they also demonstrate *transformations* from that behavior to another one more conforming to the society's dominant ideology. In totalitarian societies, this mutability must be portrayed as a singular event that guides away from deviance and toward conformity to the exclusion of all other options. Should the comic methods stray from their narrow, one-time application — assisting the male lead character to a more acceptable masculinity — the film's lesson threatens to decay into one of free will and individual choice. This may account for the almost complete absence in Nazi comedies of physical or acrobatic comedy (which requires the appearance of bodies out of control) or the extensive use of sight gags (which show audiences how to combine elements and to construct alternate perceptions of reality).[9] Comedy in the service of fascism presents tightly controlled releases of humor that must be recaptured at the film's conclusion. However, the traces of anxiety exposed by the mechanisms of the repression and reformation of gender in these films linger after the conclusion. The fears behind the laughter can guide the contemporary viewer to a political understanding of these seemingly apolitical Nazi comedies.

The classic forum for the humorous collision of gender roles is the screwball comedy. Perfected on the Hollywood soundstages of the 1930s, the screwball comedies presented eccentric heroes that stood outside of conventional society, its means to success and its norms. The foundation of the screwball comedy's humor rested on a battle of the sexes waged between the lead characters. Their struggle expressed the possibility of resistance against calcified masculine and feminine roles, albeit a resistance embedded in the relative safety of laughter and mainstream culture. American screwball comedies often conclude in marriage, but the union rarely indicates an unequivocal acceptance of social conformity. This often also holds true for gender conformity. Andrew Britton, writing about the screwball comedies of Cary Grant, argues that these films are "comedies of male chastisement," which so thoroughly abuse traditional masculinity that the heterosexual couple that emerges is one "whose sexuality is no longer organized by the phallus" (Jenkins 247). Even when the results are not as radical, the harmonious endings of American screwball comedies usually reflect more a compromise with societal convention than a complete surrender or retraction of alternatives.

Glückskinder illustrates how severely the liberating elements of the American screwball comedy suffer when the genre is transplanted into the more restrictive cultural environment of Nazi Germany. But economic considerations likely weighed heavier than ideology upon the decision to produce this film. By the time the Nazis seized power, the German film industry was in decline. Audiences for domestic films dwindled as production costs soared, leading to "an overall sense of crisis, which by 1937 reached alarming proportions" (Rentschler 1996, 104). Imports from Hollywood, on the other hand, arrived at the rate of about one per week during the 1930s and enjoyed great popularity until the war (Schäfer 128–29). The enormous success of subtitled and dubbed versions of *It Happened One Night* (1934) shocked the Ufa, Germany's premier film company, into a new strategy against its U.S. rivals: imitation as competition. *Glückskinder* is a result. In plot and setting, Paul Martin's film is little more than a remake of Frank Capra's screwball comedy, but a German remake. For most critics and viewers, that was enough: "Bravo! Bravo! What the Americans can do we can do too!" boasted the *Film-Kurier* after the premiere (Kurowski 167).

Glückskinder serves as more than an impressive example of German film's epigonic talents, however. Martin employs the ebullient chaos of the American screwball comedy and society — *Glückskinder* is set entirely in New York and its characters are Americans — and corrals that freedom into an order that restricts both sexuality and gender roles. This early Nazi comedy demonstrates how comic formulae reflect and ultimately serve the National Socialist's ideology of gender, and especially of masculinity.

The story line of *Glückskinder* differs from *It Happened One Night* only slightly, but enough to warrant summation. Gil Taylor (Willy Fritsch), poet and intern at the New York *Morning Post*, is determined to make a name for himself in journalism. He is therefore gullible enough to believe his friends Frank (Oskar Sima) and Stoddard (Paul Kemp) when they inform him that the editor has assigned him to cover night court. But the cub reporter loses all objective interest in the proceedings when Ann Garden (Lilian Harvey) is brought before the judge on charges of vagrancy. As the judge begins to pass sentence, Taylor announces himself to be the startled woman's fiancé. The judge puts an end to this blatant ruse by marrying the pair on the spot. The newlyweds exit the courtroom to the cheers and laughter of the crowd.

Taylor's editor, however, finds it less than humorous that every other paper in town has turned his antics into front-page news. Taylor, Frank, and Stoddard are promptly dismissed. They adjourn to the apartment of the married (albeit unconsummated) couple to sing one of the film's two hits, "Ich wollt', ich wär' ein Huhn!" (I Wish I Were A Chicken!) in celebration of their new-found sloth. But Garden soon sets in motion a plan to get the trio employed again. A millionaire's niece (conveniently played by Harvey in a double role) has disappeared. Garden pretends to be that niece in order to draw out the real woman and get a scoop for the *Morning Post*. The confusion and mistaken identities that are the hallmark of the screwball comedy lead first to a rift between Taylor and Garden and then to joyous reunion when Garden helps the men find the true heiress. The reporters are rehired, Taylor's poetry is published, and the sham marriage becomes true love.

Glückskinder is motivated by the actions of an unorthodox woman who begins on society's fringe and ends up safely "domesticated." But while the story line resembles *Taming of the Shrew*, the shrew in *Glückskinder* is not the unruly woman, but a man who cannot rule. The poet is the problem child in *Glückskinder*. The film imbues the designation *Lyriker* (poet) with a meaning tantamount to "effeminate," even "unnatural." As a poet with no other successes to qualify him as masculine, Gil Taylor is an incomplete man. His position at the *Morning Post* is tenuous and his poetry goes unread by the editor. Taylor's impetuous behavior at the night court exposes him as immature and naive in both his profession and the world outside the newsroom. Part of the problem, but also the humor, is that Gil Taylor does not even know he has a problem. His immodest confidence in his talent as a poet deafens him to the cruel laughter at his expense. And the poet is the butt of all jokes, three in the first twenty minutes of the film alone. The unkindest cuts of all are not even jokes, per se, but simply affirmations that Taylor is, indeed, a poet. "Ah, a poet," is all the explanation his editor needs to confirm his worst suspicions about Taylor's inadequacies.

The knowledge behind the humor is that the word poet in this context marks Taylor as impotent. The thread of poet jokes throughout the film link his professional failings to his implied sexual shortcomings. This is made explicit from the start of the formulaic battle of the sexes waged between the newlyweds. Although Taylor has chivalrously rescued Garden from prison, she can easily see his lack of any further conventional manly qualities. Taylor's repeated attempts to prove the contrary exhaust themselves with the assertion "I am a poet!" Garden's single word retort counters those attempts just as assuredly: "*eben*" (exactly).[10] Taylor thus cowed, Garden has little reason to fear the impending wedding night in his "remarkably tidy" bachelor apartment. When Taylor nonetheless makes a veiled claim to his marital right to sex with the threat, "I'll show you what a poet is!," Garden knows herself to be safe. He does show her what a poet is: he does nothing and retreats behind the ruse that Garden did not say "please."

What little genuine sexual tension there is in this sequence (as opposed to the corollary scene in *It Happened One Night*) is actually initiated by Garden, not directly toward Taylor, but rather toward his canary. Once more, Taylor demonstrates the poet's aversion to seduction. He represses Garden's flirtatious whistling by covering the already caged bird and reproaching her: "That's a little man [*Männchen*]!" Taylor makes a suggestive joke that implies his own gender inadequacy in order to dampen the sexual energy of the moment. This pattern repeats itself throughout the film. Sexual overtures and allusions are either empty threats or end in awkward excuses or prudish jokes that expose the poet's crippled heterosexual masculinity. As if to emphasize the difference between Willy Fritsch's character and his predecessor in *It Happened One Night*, Taylor later sings, "I wish I were Clark Gable." The gulf between the two romantic heroes is as obvious as it is structurally necessary in order for *Glückskinder* to impart its lesson in masculinity.[11] *Glückskinder* is aided here by the general anxiety Nazi films, particularly comedies, have about sexuality. "The imitation of the American comedy is ruled by the exclusion of sexuality that is only permissible in repressive forms" (Witte 1976, 350). Sex, like humor, has a subversive potential feared by all totalitarian regimes.

As a classic of German cinema, *Glückskinder* was recently reissued on video. The advertising blurb on the cover promises performances by "the unforgettable romantic duo Lilian Harvey and Willy Fritsch and the comedian duo Paul Kemp-Oskar Sima." This advertisement also displays a subtle understanding of the film's organization. The juxtaposition of the lead characters as two couples where the words "romantic" and "comedian" are interchangeable describes not only the constellation of the actors but also the film's structure as two parallel love stories. The male duo is, of course, a standard comic feature that predates film. These duos typically display no overt sexuality of their own, and when they appear in romantic comedies, their primary function is to shepherd the lead couple toward happiness. In this role as helpers to the primary heterosexual couple, the male duo may act as if they were the primary lovers' parents. In the comedy *Ein falscher Fuffziger* (A Counterfeit Fifty, 1935), Hans Moser and Richard Romanowsky have just this role; the pair act as guardians and marriage brokers for an orphaned young woman in their care. The parental role, a "substitution function," as Karsten Witte calls it, serves "to legitimate the attraction to each other as well as to conceal it" (1995, 86). The dilemma in romantic comedies for the male-male relationship, which critics have described as at least latently homosexual or even love,[12] is to remain a humorous, guiding counterweight but not to develop into a romantic couple akin to the main heterosexual couple. The more restrictive (or fearful) a society is of homosexuality, the more its films will embed the male couple in a protective, legitimizing context. In Nazi society, that context is an environment that is platonic, male, and homosocial, such as the newsroom of the *Morning Post* in *Glückskinder*.

The film initially presents the *Morning Post* as a chain of male relationships. The first scene in the newspaper office begins with a tracking shot that follows a messenger boy down a long row of men at their desks. A phone call from a drunken and incapacitated reporter activates a network of male friendship and, ultimately, deception that results in Taylor getting sent to cover night court. Frank dispatches Taylor with the solemnity of a military officer speaking to a novice recruit, or as a father to a son. Failure on Taylor's part would be understood as a slight against all the men of the *Morning Post*. "I will return a success or not at all," vows Taylor as he marches out of the office. Frank and Stoddard are relieved. The drunken colleague has been covered for; the homosocial unity has been preserved.

But, of course, it has not. The disruption caused by Ann Garden, or more accurately, by Gil Taylor's insufficient handling of the problem Garden presents, is therefore also a threat to the integrity of the homosocial environment that contains the relationship of Frank and Stoddard. Taylor's bogus marriage immediately results in the banishment of the male figures from the newspaper. Now unemployed, Frank and Stoddard take on the traditional comic role of guardian angels and matchmakers to the heterosexual pair. This task requires the men to become a corollary couple, even role models for the errant twosome, but as such their own relationship threatens to exceed the boundaries of the homosocial context of the *Morning Post* and become homosexual. This danger is evident in the film's use of cross editing. Taylor and Garden are shown in a tender, sleepy moment on the subway. The next shot cuts to Frank and Stoddard, looking just as tender across the aisle opposite the pair. Another sequence presents a series of cross-cuts linking the hetero (but not yet sexual) couple in bed and the homo (but no longer just social) couple sharing a darkened bedroom. At first, it is not even discernable that Frank and Stoddard are in separate beds. The stabilization of the first couple will be necessary to prevent the further destabilization of the latter.

The humor of the male couple plays dangerously on an anxiety prevalent among the Nazi leadership: that the homosocial order they were creating could decay into homoerotic desire. The repression of this anxiety did not even stop at murder. The deportation of homosexuals to concentration and death camps is the most horrendous expression of this phobia. Nor did this fear shy away from murder within the ranks of the Nazi elite themselves. Homophobia was one of the motivations behind the Night of the Long Knives, the murders in 1934 of the leadership of the more radical and often openly homosexual SA. The "second revolution" so feared by Hitler appears to have been sexual as well as economic in nature.[13]

The film's happy ending constrains the subversive potential of the couple of Frank and Stoddard. Taylor learns to be a man; Garden is safely integrated into the passive background reserved for wives in National Socialist society; the men are allowed to rejoin the homosocial world of the *Morning Post*. One of the film's final shots symbolizes the stabilizing effect of Taylor's education to masculinity. The shot resembles a wedding photo: the two happy couples in the middle (Garden and Taylor, the rich niece and her boyfriend), next to them the millionaire uncle, and framing the entire shot from opposite ends, Frank and Stoddard.[14]

Writing in *Der völkische Beobachter* (1934), Adolf Hitler expressed the National Socialist View on gender:

> When one says, the world of the man is the state, the world of the man is his struggling, his commitment to the community, one could perhaps say that the woman's world is small. For her world is her husband, her family, her children and her house. But what would the larger world be if no one wanted to tend to the smaller one?[15]

In *Glückskinder* Ann Garden becomes one of Hitler's dutiful attendants. First, she must act in the larger world of men in order to make it safe for her to inhabit her smaller sphere. She materializes out of nowhere and is a "problem for everyone," as the night court judge claims. And indeed, her initial impact is to throw the male world into chaos. Yet immediately after her disruption, Garden begins her work to create an improved male order. We never learn what led up to her court appearance; she is the *Fräulein Niemand* (Miss Nobody) of the film's other song title. Like the Gods of ancient tragedies, Garden has arrived shrouded in mystery in order to bring a healing disturbance. Ann Garden is not the problem, but the solution in *Glückskinder*.

The Nazi's obsession with the fragility of masculinity resulted in comedies that have as their primary objective the reformation of the outsider or deviant male lead. Female characters, when they have any more than marginal narrative importance, usually serve as catalysts for the development of the male. The behavior of the female character becomes regimented as well, but this occurs as a consequence of the stabilization of the male's position rather than as a result of any direct sanction or reward for her own actions. As an expression of the humorous danger of the abnormal situation, she is granted a surprising level of freedom — a fool's freedom — to move outside the norms until the man gains, or regains, the ability to fulfill his masculine destiny. "Romantic comedy tolerates, and even encourages, its heroine's short-lived rebellion because that rebellion ultimately serves the interests of the hero" (Rowe 112). To this limited extent, women in comedies exercise a degree of authority denied most female characters of other Nazi era films.[16]

The film portrays Garden as a helpless waif in the big city for precisely the length of the court scene. From the moment she leaves the building as Mrs. Gil Taylor, she takes complete control of her own destiny and Taylor's as well. She moves effortlessly into a domestic role, shopping, preparing a meal for her husband, eagerly awaiting his return. When the new husband arrives with unexpected guests (Frank and Stoddard), Garden complains like a cliché wife of twenty-four years, not twenty-four hours. The satire of the tensions of marital bliss hides a deeper meaning. Behind the humor of playing house also begins the socialization process that turns Taylor into a more conventional man. To instigate this process seems to be Garden's sole purpose for being.

But Garden's mission of stability cannot tolerate such indolence for long. After the new quartet of friends culminate their brief period of carefree living in the "Chicken Song" routine, the men are all too willing to remain in their musical domestic paradise where they are "the master of all creation" yet also "stupid but happy." The camera work attests to the film's fear that its most decadent fantasy might become permanent reality. The four dance and sing from one tightly framed room to the next "and constantly threaten to crash into walls" (Rentschler 1996, 122). Garden alone resists the temptation of permanent sloth. Just as she once created a necessary disturbance in the men's lives with her arrival, she now forces their development further with her departure. "It's all my fault," she admits as she prepares to leave. By leaving, Garden focuses the attention of the men once more on the connection between success in the sense of "getting the girl" and in the sense of getting the story, and thereby becoming productive members of society. True happiness, she will teach them, is won by masculine heroes in the real world, not by feminized "chickens" of silver screen fantasies.

Garden's manipulation of the trio ultimately leads them to discover the millionaire's niece, thus lifting the shroud of confusion to signal that the time has come for the happy ending. Taylor is a hero, yet his education to manhood has not concluded. Not until Garden submits to the questions of the reporters, to whose ranks Taylor now belongs, is Taylor complete. The shot of Garden framed by the interrogating men recalls the structure of the end of the "Chicken Song" scene, reminding the viewer that what was wrong has now been corrected. As Taylor has learned that Garden is not just a serendipitous wife, but a story to be told — by him — he has been properly ordered in the masculine world. A man is not a man until he can objectify and control those around him. The woman's role is to submit to this objectification, and if necessary, to bring it about by her own will. The differences between *It Happened One Night* and *Glückskinder* are most conspicuous here. Gable resists precisely this objectification of Colbert and learns that the desirable heterosexual relationship is a partnership that can span social disparity. The exchange of power is one-sided in *Glückskinder*. With Taylor's masculinity now restructured in accordance with society's expectations, Garden's ability to motivate him (and the narrative) is exhausted.[17] Were she truly a goddess she would now dissolve into the ether from whence she came. Instead, she completes the joke from earlier in the film by saying "please" and consummating the marriage. Taylor's newfound control becomes absolute when it is extended to include Garden's body. Although Taylor gets Garden to "beg for it," in the end it was Garden who taught him how to want it.

Glückskinder illustrates how humor is based on mistakes: mistaken identity, mistaken assumptions. First, Taylor is mistaken in thinking that the editor has sent him to night court and is interested in his poetry. Then, Taylor confuses his function as reporter with that of rescuer, and marries Garden instead of turning her into a story. He is further mistaken when he believes that everything will go his way. All of these errors are necessary for Taylor's development and the attainment of his never-questioned goals. But there was more at stake than the aspirations of one individual: Taylor has been re-integrated into his society and thus that society itself has been legitimized. The microcosm of Taylor's immediate surroundings demonstrates this broader stabilizing effect. The *Morning Post* runs smoothly and successfully once more and Frank and Stoddard retire discreetly into the shadow of the harmonious and conventional heterosexual marriage of Taylor and Garden. There is neither likelihood nor reason for Taylor ever to be mistaken again. The transformation of Gil Taylor, and thus the comic opening in *Glückskinder* and its potential for subversion, is more surgical incision than gaping wound. The conclusion of *Glückskinder* rescinds its comic means for the sake of ideological conformity.[18] The *felix culpa* is a singular event, lest the viewer remember the sin more than the sinner.

In 1941, two German film comedies appeared that trace the progress of the *Glückskinder* model: *Hauptsache glücklich* (Happiness is the Main Thing) and *Quax, der Bruchpilot*. Both employ techniques similar to those developed in the earlier film in order to advance their male protagonist toward a masculinity compatible with Nazi ideology. In *Hauptsache glücklich*, an otherwise conventional housewife resorts to deception to stir her complacent husband to the greater ambition she knows him to be capable of. In the story of *Quax, der Bruchpilot*, slumbering manhood also awakens, but here female intervention is secondary to pressure exerted from within the community of men itself. While *Glückskinder* concludes with the reformed husband and wife in bed and *Hauptsache glücklich* acknowledges the debt masculine subjectivity owes to women, women are completely absent by the end of *Quax, der Bruchpilot*. The film demonstrates that the homosocial world now can take care of itself.

It seems surprising at first that both later films share the same male lead: Heinz Rühmann. Diminutive in stature, doughy, with a boyish face, and a pleading voice, he is almost asexual compared to the dashing Willy Fritsch. Yet the highly popular Rühmann turned out to be the ideal actor for the gender-education comedies. His understated masculinity made his characters ripe for correction. As a clown-like figure, however, he enjoyed freedom from narrow categorization, and so his feckless persona was always more entertaining than alienating for his audiences, and for the political elite. Rühmann's characters therefore model a more dramatic transition to manliness while generating greater laughter and familiarity than those of Fritsch.[19] These features allow

Rühmann's films to concentrate both the gender education and the humor onto one exaggerated figure. This reduces the audience's exposure to credible or seductive negative examples while the films still model a transformation to ideological masculinity.

Rühmann's gender comedies consequently employ different strategies than the screwball comedy *Glückskinder*. While the two do share many structural and even plot elements, *Quax, der Bruchpilot* is a war film. The plot follows the standard formula of dozens of war films, German or American: a misfit becomes a hero when he learns to overcome his individuality for the sake of a greater whole. Although the film takes place in 1928 with no overt references to war, a military atmosphere pervades the flight academy where the majority of the scenes take place. The instructor declares that pilots form a "stormy front" that "fights for the idea." They fly, he promises, not into the sky but into "world history." In the context of 1941 Germany, audiences would unlikely distinguish whether a private air school or the *Luftwaffe* "makes a man" of Quax. Hans Hellmut Kirst contends that Rühmann never grasped the propaganda value of his film and that he "not even for a moment" felt he was aiding the war effort (140). The war effort aided Rühmann, however. Soldiers were apparently assigned to assist the film crew in Bavaria. Included in the film's publicity material, an allegedly fictitious letter demonstrates a desire to associate Quax with the military. In this letter, a soldier identified only as Max writes to his girlfriend from the "field," expressing his enthusiasm for the project.

As in *Glückskinder*, a poet is once again cause for concern. In order only to win the third prize, a vacation for himself and his girlfriend, a civil servant in a small-town tourist office has submitted a mediocre poem to a contest. Unfortunately, his talent so impresses the jury that he collects the grand prize: flying lessons. The amateur poet and reluctant pilot is immediately branded a suspicious interloper at the flight school. Quax's alien status is accentuated by director Kurt Hoffmann's shot composition. He is at least a foot shorter than the other students who line up for an initial inspection. His uniform is ill fitting and his headgear resembles a dunce cap. Quax's insistence on the title "Mister" before his name accentuates his dubious qualifications for such masculine heroism. "Are you part of the group?" flight instructor Hansen (Lothar Firmans) barks at him. The inappropriate giggle Quax gives when Hansen orders him to board *Emma*, the training plane, further underlines the obvious negative response to that question. In the prudish and all-male environment of the flight school, Quax's insinuating a heterosexual connection to *Emma* is marked as an immature display of an inappropriate sexuality. The masculine ideology of *Quax*, *der Bruchpilot* is less dependent on the male-female bond than *Glücks-kinder.* The flyer is a different, higher level of masculine identity. A plane, Quax will learn, is an object of desire, but not in the mundane sexual manner reserved for women.

But what sets Quax apart most from the others is his fear of flying, which he attempts to mask with arrogance. The pilot who is afraid of flying is obviously a source of the film's comedy, but it is also the measure of Quax's development to proper manhood. Fear of flying represents fear of controlling, of dominating. Just as Taylor could not become complete as a man before turning Garden into a story for the *Morning Post,* Quax remains inadequate until he has learned to use his plane to territorialize and master his world. Quax's fear is depicted primarily through camera work. When he flies for the first time, the hysterical student is captured from the point of view of the audience. We look headlong into his screaming, crying face; the wind further exaggerates his terrified expression. The shot thus subordinates Quax to the force of the plane and nature, and to his unmanly fear.

This experience is recalled later when the other students attempt to scare the errant — and thus disquieting — Quax into leaving the school. While he sleeps, they hoist his bed into the air and blast him with a powerful fan. The shot of his face is identical to that of the previous scene. His bed has become as frightening a place as the plane and thus represents both a privatization and a sexualization of his fear. The students then douse Quax with water and turn his own prize-winning poem into a threatening chant, advising Quax to leave, "better today than tomorrow!" Drenched in water and crying, Quax resembles a child who has awoken from a nightmare to find he has wet his bed. This primary experience of shame and loss of control is thereby equated with his inability to fulfill his adult obligation to control — here, to fly.

Whereas Taylor is forced to leave the homosocial environment in order to regain entry as a full-fledged member, Quax must undergo his transformation from within the confines of a masculine universe. The flight school is an entirely male operation. Even the handyman fills the post of *Mädchen für alles* ("girl for everything," or girl Friday). The students and instructors form a big family, albeit one without female relatives. The sole woman who temporarily enters this masculine realm is the pilot Hilda. Her extremely brief screen appearance early in the film functions to highlight Quax's underdeveloped state. The neophyte flyer/man peels potatoes in the kitchen when Hilda's plane lands. "See," the handyman goads the already humiliated Quax, "even women fly." Although the school functions as a self-contained male universe, the implication here is that someone else, someone less male if not necessarily female, is supposed to do the housework.[20]

Hilda notwithstanding, flying is a male calling. "We need men," Hansen tells his students. So, it seems, does everyone, for flying is not merely a hobby in *Quax, der Bruchpilot*, but a mission of vital interest to the entire community. Quax must learn that with his prize comes an immense degree of social responsibility. The fawning attention he receives from the town elders thwarts his early attempt to quit the school and return home. The community needs a hero, and the unlikely Quax becomes one as soon as he puts on his flight suit.

But why flying? Certainly, air travel harbingers modernization and economic development for the otherwise sleepy village. Quax's skillful landing of his plane in the main square will later convince the mayor that the town needs an airport, not a streetcar line. This ridiculous logic is nonetheless the only practical argument offered in a film that otherwise portrays flying as a crucial yet mystical passion. The townspeople celebrate Quax's mission with a folk song, "Heimat, deine Sterne" (Homeland, Your Stars). Flying extends the cramped homeland into the skies and gives it the tools to take the heavens that before could only be claimed in song.[21] Fearless men are needed to master the technology and harvest those stars. Flying, as Hansen cryptically proclaims, is "more important than you think."

Women, on the other hand, have a considerably less prominent role in *Quax, der Bruchpilot* than in *Glückskinder*. This is, in part, a structural difference between the genres of the screwball and the war comedy. Still, women are important motivators in Quax's development to masculinity. The first woman in his life, Adelheid (Hilde Sessak), is an opportunist. When Quax fails to win the vacation, she abandons him for a local merchant wealthy enough to take her wherever she wishes. Yet even in her negative role, Adelheid assists Quax. She brands him a coward when he returns home prematurely from the flight school and thus shames him into returning.

Marianna (Karin Himboldt) fills a more significant and positive role. Innocent and pure, Marianna is a healthy alternative to the materialistic Adelheid and therefore the proper woman for a heroic man. Himboldt would perform an almost identical role for Rühmann three years later in his most famous comedy, *Die Feuerzangenbowle* (The Flaming Punch, 1944). She stands in crass contrast to a more sophisticated and sexy woman, whom Rühmann, of course, will abandon.[22] Here, too, however, the *felix culpa* model applies. Quax's attempts to impress Marianna, signs of his personality flaws of egotism and arrogance, become vehicles for his discovery as a natural flyer. Quax's reckless commandeering of a hot-air balloon turns from tragedy to triumph when he demonstrates skillful use of a compass. Marianna inspires Quax's heroic character and suppresses his effeminate qualities. But Marianna is most valuable to Quax in that she is disposable. Ann Garden may be powerless, but she is still present at the conclusion of *Glückskinder* because her presence is the implied guarantor of Taylor's stability. Once Marianna has helped release Quax's talents as a pilot and placed him in the heterosexual world, she disappears. We last see her well before the film's conclusion when the returning demi-hero flies into the village. After a kiss from his betrothed, Quax is dragged off by the jubilant mass, notably made up almost entirely by men. Marianna releases Quax to the more important company of men and planes.

If *Quax, der Bruchpilot* were a romantic comedy, it would revolve around the stormy love affair between student and teacher. The most important person in Quax's education is not a woman but a man: the flight instructor, Hansen. Their relationship is a passionate and narcissistic struggle for control. Hansen's mechanisms of control are his stern words, his unquestioning sense of purpose with which he acts, and, most of all, his sharp gaze. That gaze catches the misfit Quax, literally across a crowded room, on the evening of his first, disastrous day. Eyeline-match shots connect Hansen's disapproving scowl to Quax's simpering expression of shame, highlighted by the fact that he is also clearing dinner plates. Yet, as the misfit, Quax resists Hansen's complete control by offering an inconsistent mixture of respect, fear, and buffoonery. Quax thus also controls Hansen because he is the latter's object of fascination.

This results in a series of encounters so similar to lovers' quarrels and reconciliations as to throw the entire homosocial-homosexual divide into doubt. The risks *Quax* takes with the heterosexual veneer of Nazi society reflect the increased urgency of the mission of the wartime gender comedy. The aftermath of Quax's misadventure with the hot-air balloon exemplifies this risk. Hansen castigates the student's reckless endangerment of Marianna, but then adds: "I do not even want to talk about what you have done to me!" Quax's disobedience injures Hansen more than it does any woman. Hansen's concern for the student has led to humiliating fissures in his otherwise iron composure. During their final reconciliation scene, Quax declares that what he wants most is to "stay here — with you — forever." There is no mention of Marianna. Unlike the one-sided lesson imparted by Garden to Taylor, Hansen and Quax train each other. Hansen learns to recognize signs of masculinity beyond the superficial. Quax masters the art of self-control and control in general. As if trying to convince himself, Hansen insists that "Discipline, discipline, discipline, discipline!" will be required if Quax is to remain permanently at the school. The unruly Quax needs discipline, but so does Hansen, to ensure that their mutual attraction does not distract from the higher devotion to flying.

The exchanges between Hansen and Quax do not go unnoticed by the other students. They jealously remark that Hansen treats Quax like a son. Actually, Hansen considers all of his students to be his sons. He refers to them as "children," and takes them all under his (airplane) wing for instruction. Like the parental role played by Frank and Stoddard that legitimizes their partnership, the substitute father-son relationship functions to contain the erotic tension in the flight school. The students then are, for Hansen, offspring training to replicate their father. This is especially true for Quax, the most difficult and therefore favorite object of Hansen's narcissistic desire. Hansen's efforts ultimately bear fruit; Quax becomes a flight instructor who quotes Hansen verbatim to his new students. Hansen has born of himself a son. Hansen's gaze now focuses on Quax with the eyes of a proud father instead of a lover.[23]

The key to Quax's transformation from poet to pilot is the discovery of his hidden strength. Whereas *Glückskinder* employs the social and sexual tactics of the screwball comedy to effect change, this later comedy reflects more strongly Nazi racial theory and its conception of the true nature of Germans. Quax, it turns out, is a born flyer. The school physician detects this quality when the hapless Quax scores off the charts in every category. Such a racial-biological twist had already been used in *Robert und Bertram* (1939). There, the bumpkin (and poet!) Michael — a symbol for all German manhood — is revealed during his mandatory military service to be a natural leader of great physical strength.[24] Here, as in Quax, training and discipline exposed and then harnessed inner ability: "What the Prussians can make out of a guy!" remarks Michael, in awe of his new self.[25] Quax's instinctive talents clearly would make a return to his former life at the tourism office an abomination against nature. But nature alone is not enough; Quax must be refined. "Train him!" the doctor implores the bewildered Hansen. "He's a tough nut — you'll have to crack him."

For Quax this means to break through his shell of effeminate socialization in order to release his core masculinity. To do so, Hansen launches a frontal assault on reason. When Quax says, "I just thought. . . ." Hansen snaps back "Better you shouldn't think!" Flying is a matter of feeling, not thought. The weakling, of course, is the most intellectual and therefore most resistant student. He alone has read a book on the theory of flight. Hansen, however, has no patience for "gray theory," but only praxis. In his first lesson, Hansen dresses the students as pilots, as if merely changing their textile shells would also alter their internal qualities. And, eventually, it works. Quax simply goes into the air so often that he finally internalizes Hansen's mantra that "reason alone is not enough."[26] The release of Quax's true self creates a man of action in every regard. Whereas the "unnatural" Quax sought to accomplish everything through smooth words, he finds himself speechless when he wants to propose to Marianna. The conflict between nature and reason thus forced to a head, nature emerges victorious: Quax just kisses her. Fear of flying and fear of manhood turn out to be the same thing. Both are overcome when the heart is free to speak louder than the head.

A dramatic shift in camera work seals Quax's triumph. When the hero Quax now flies, the point of view is his own. The audience sees the skies and the landscape as if through Quax's controlling eyes. Town and nature bend to his will with each confident maneuver of his plane.[27] The continuity established from *Glückskinder* to *Quax* is a masculinity that is defined by its will to dominate and to tell its own story.

But like *Glückskinder*, *Quax, der Bruchpilot* also does not trust its comic devices alone to secure the irreversibility of its education. The final shot in *Quax* abruptly abandons comedy and film realism for a direct appeal to the audience. While the camera gradually zooms in to a screen-filling close-up, Quax gives a speech on the need for order and a world "more real than imagined."[28] Heinz Rühmann's tightly framed face betrays no more of its softness; the shot crops out his clownish femininity. The containment of the frame excludes the possibility of further humor, but also of further deviance. The memory of the insufficient man and his transformation is eradicated. Only the desired outcome remains.

Glückskinder (1936). Ann Garden (Lilian Harvey) models for Gil Taylor (Willy Fritsch) —
in his own pajamas — how a real man acts. Courtesy Stiftung Deutsche Kinemathek, Berlin.

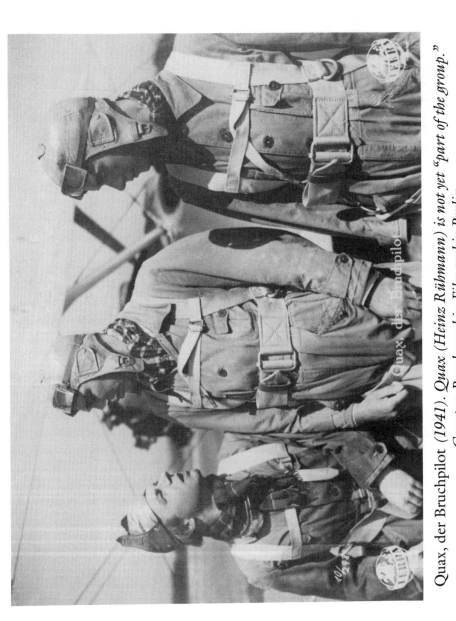

Quax, der Bruchpilot (1941). Quax (Heinz Rühmann) is not yet "part of the group."
Courtesy Bundesarchiv-Filmarchiv Berlin.

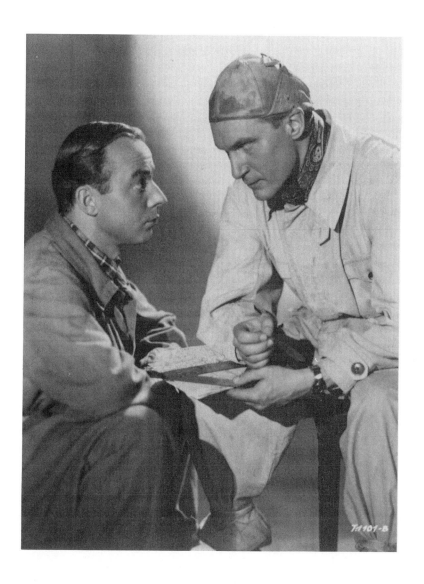

Quax, der Bruchpilot *(1941). Discipline, discipline, discipline, discipline! The master's (Lothar Firmans) piercing gaze focuses Quax on flying. Courtesy Bundesarchiv-Filmarchiv Berlin.*

Notes

[1] Joseph Goebbels, "Der Film als Erzieher: Rede zur Eröffnung der Filmarbeit der HJ," (Berlin 12 October 1941), cited in Gerd Albrecht, *Der Film im dritten Reich* (Stuttgart: Ferdinand Enke Verlag, 1969) 480. Unless otherwise stated, all translations are my own.

[2] The seminal text on this new generation of office workers is Siegfried Kracauer's *Die Angestellten* (1930). Kracauer's analysis is helpful, though ultimately limited by its narrow understanding of what constitutes a political consciousness. A more differentiated, albeit fictional, account from a woman's point of view is Irmgard Keun's 1931 novel, *Gilgi — eine von uns* (Gilgi — One of Us). Atina Grossman has written extensively on the sex reform movement, for example in her essay, "The New Woman and the Rationalization of Sexuality in Weimar Germany," *Powers of Desire: The Politics of Sexuality* Eds. Ann Snitow, et al. (New York: Monthly Review Press, 1983) 153–71.

[3] Ernst Toller's play *Hinkemann* (1924) features a war veteran that truly gave his all for the *Vaterland*.

[4] "Even after the post-war chaos — revolution, counter-revolution, hyperinflation — had been 'stabilized,' the authoritarian Right still felt humiliated and had by no means given up hope of re-establishing the traditional order; and socialists and communists still felt the disillusionment of having had their revolutionary hopes of 1918 dashed. This led to feelings of 'emasculation' on the left as well." Richard W. McCormick, "Private Anxieties/Public Projections: 'New Objectivity,' Male Subjectivity, and Weimar Cinema," *Women in German Yearbook* 10, eds. Jeanette Clausen and Sara Friedrichsmeyer (Lincoln: U of Nebraska P: 1995) 6.

[5] Although he was primarily successful in inciting anti-Semitic fervor, Ferdinand Marian's exaggeratedly nasty depiction of the title character in *Jud Süß* (Jew Suess, 1940) backfired in this manner for part of its audience. The evil with which he saturated his role translated for many female viewers into a powerful erotic allure. The "villain" was soon awash in fan mail. See Linda Schulte-Sasse, *Entertaining the Third Reich: Illusions of Wholeness in Nazi Cinema* (Durham: Duke UP, 1996) 81.

[6] Schulte-Sasse analyzes gender and the function of the "feminized male" in several films.

[7] Mikhail Bakhtin's discussion of the carnival in his essay *Rabelais and His World* is the foundation for this understanding of comedy and the temporary suspension of norms of acceptable behavior (trans. Helene Iswolsky; Cambridge, MA: M.I.T. Press, 1968) esp. his introduction (1–58) and chapter on the "popular-festive" (196–277).

[8] The dual possibilities of laughter as diversion or subversion is an inherent risk of the comedy under fascism. The comedy in the service of the State can tolerate only so much laughter at its own expense, preferably none at all. A greater threat still is inappropriate or "false" laughter of an audience member. Laughter, where unexpected, is an unnerving challenge to the primacy of a film's narrative and ideological vehicles: "An out-of-synch laugher is a potential terrorist in the dark, someone who refuses to let the screen cast its spell. No matter how isolated a presence, the figure lurked in the wings as a specter, an élan vital and dissenting voice with an incendiary potential." Eric Rentschler, *The Ministry of Illusion: Nazi Cinema and Its Afterlife* (Cambridge, MA: Harvard UP, 1996) 113. Such laughing "terrorists" reduced more than one Ufa production to harmless comedy this way.

[9] *Viktor und Viktoria* is again pivotal. This was the last significant use of physical humor and sight gags until Wolfgang Staudte's *Akrobat schö-ö-ön* (1943), itself a singular event in Nazi film comedy history.

[10] "What that one little 'exactly' doesn't say" pondered the critic for the *Film-Kurier*. Garden's ability to exasperate her new husband with her one-word agreement found resonance and sympathy in the review from 19 September 1936. Ulrich Kurowski, ed., *Deutsche Spielfilme 1933–1945: Materialien II*, 2nd ed. (Munich: Stadtsmuseum München, 1978) 167. The claim that one is a poet should instill the listener with respect, the author claims: "But when instead of awe only another still more emphatic 'exactly' is the response, must not even the strongest man admit he is in checkmate?" Even the strongest man would be stopped in his tracks, let alone the apparent weakling Taylor.

[11] It is not just that Clark Gable was more macho than Willy Fritsch, rather Gable's masculinity is not marked by *It Happened One Night* as insufficient in the context of the film's subtext of social justice. In fact, Gable's character "marks the long-delayed birth of a hero suitable for the Depression. . . . He's broke; he's out of a job; he can't even run fast enough to catch the guy who stole Ellie's suitcase. He's a surprisingly frank embodiment of the ineffectuality of the American male in the face of the Depression. He can do only one thing well: take care of someone who's lost." Elizabeth Kendall, *The Runaway Bride: Hollywood Romantic Comedy of the 1930's* (New York: Knopf, 1990) 45.

[12] Critics such as Frank Krutnik, who (paraphrasing *New York Times* film critic Molly Haskell) "suggests that the male comedy duo . . . excludes heterosexuality to form a latently homosexual 'union of opposites (tall/short, thin/fat, straight/comic) who, like husband and wife, combine to make a whole.'" Frank Krutnik, "A Spanner in the Works? Genre, Narrative and the Hollywood Comedian," *Classical Hollywood Comedy*, eds. Kristine Brunovska Karnick and Henry Jenkins (New York/London: Routledge, 1995) 37–38. Arthur Dudden makes the bolder claim that "Stan Laurel and Oliver Hardy were really a love story." "Dimensions of American Humor," *East-West Film Journal* (2.1.1987): 13.

[13] Mosse argues that the murder of SA chief of staff Röhm and many other real or accused homosexuals in the Nazi ranks illustrates the "danger to accepted sexual norms inherent" in such homosocial environments (1985, 158). Nazi theorist Alfred Rosenberg wrote in his diary after the killings: "The Berlin gigolos in brown shirts will disappear — the old, our old SA will return." Burkhard Jellonnek, *Homosexuelle unter dem Hakenkreuz* (Paderborn: Ferdinand Schöningh, 1990) 97. With a perverse lack of irony, Rosenberg labeled the executions a "men's enterprise."

[14] At least Frank and Stoddard are allowed to remain in the picture. In the 1939 anti-Semitic comedy *Robert und Bertram*, the similarly ambiguous male pair in the title is enlisted to bring together an (also newly educated) German man and his true love. Once their task is completed, they are prevented from leaving any lingering discord in the homosocial/heterosexual world by ascending to heaven in a hot-air balloon! The undesirable men of the real world are killed; their film comedy counterparts are disposed of with fairy tale methods.

[15] Hitler writing in *Der völkische Beobachter* (10 September 1934), cited in Rita Thalmann, *Frausein im Dritten Reich* (Frankfurt a. M.: Ullstein, 1987) 77.

[16] Anke Gleber's findings about film dramas produced under the Nazis do not apply to the comedies: "The dynamics of meaning and image in Nazi cinema is the exclusive domain of male propaganda, a propaganda operating at the expense of the female image, which is defined only in terms of absence and lack." "'Only Man Must Be and Remain a Judge, Soldier and Ruler of State' — Female as Void in Nazi Film," *Gender and German Cinema: Feminist Interventions*, eds. Sandra Frieden, et al. (Providence/Oxford: Berg, 1993) 116.

[17] One must wonder what is in all this for Garden. Claudia Koonz proposes the following thesis to explain the "active" woman's passive cooperation with men, at times even with inferior men: "Men would never relinquish their power, women could never wrest it from them; hence many concluded that the only effective women's strategy lay in cooperating with men and reaping protection as a reward. Experience had taught them that competition with men did not pay but compromise might." *Mothers in the Fatherland: Women, the Family, and Nazi Politics* (New York: St. Martin's Press, 1987) 12. Ann Garden is looking for a man she can train to protect her so that she can "compromise" with him.

[18] This sublimation of personal fantasy in favor of the greater good is a characteristic of modern comedies (since Shakespeare), according to Horton: "The characters, no matter how much they have turned the everyday world upside down during the narrative, must act like 'adults' to the degree of committing themselves to each other and thus to life within society. They change: society remains the same." Andrew Horton, "Introduction," *Com-*

edy/Cinema/Theory, ed. Andrew Horton (Berkeley: U of California P, 1991). American screwball comedies show that this re-integration need not always be total, but there is no such room for alternatives in the Nazi screwball film.

[19] As the loveable "little man," Rühmann invited identification with the average male of the audience: "There was not a family in our country that did not feel it had a Rühmann among its ranks. Numerous contemporaries felt themselves to be like him." Hans Hellmut Kirst, *Heinz Rühmann: Ein biographischer Report* (Munich: Kindler Verlag, 1969) 48.

[20] That implied "someone" is the woman, the wife in the background that is never shown. The closest we come to seeing such a person on screen is the figure of the "Mädchen für alles." Next to Quax, he is the most feminized member of the school. He is the only one not to fly and is relegated solely to domestic duties. The "girl Friday " in this case is a male, and he is thus included as a member of the school, but he also serves as a warning to the pilots that such a fate awaits them should they fail.

[21] Konrad Vogelsang contends that "Heimat, deine Sterne" is an important propaganda tool in *Quax:* "Due to its very simple structure, this catchy song was widely popular. . . . Embedded in harmless entertainment films, such songs could do more damage than other songs of the Hitler Youth or the army. Emotions were awakened and were supposed to sharpen one's awareness of love and loyalty for the homeland." *Filmmusik im Dritten Reich: die Dokumentation* (Hamburg: Facta Oblita, 1990) 19.

[22] The choice of the more marriageable woman by the man who must learn to make such a choice illustrates, according to Stephen Lowry, the suppression of the erotic threat to gender norms so typical in Nazi films, *Pathos und Politik: Ideologie in Spielfilmen des Nationalsozialismus* (Tübingen: Niemeyer Verlag, 1991) 237.

[23] A possible model for the character of Hansen was Ernst Udet, an accomplished flyer revered by Rühmann. "Rühmann admired Udet without reserve — but he never forgot himself in the process" (Kirst 129). Kirst's limiting appendix to his description of the relationship between Rühmann and Udet reveals what it intended to conceal: that an observer may have detected an erotic level, or at least its potential, in their friendship. But as Rühmann later recalls in his autobiography, his relationship with Udet did not end as well as that of Quax and Hansen. In the war, Udet was the actor's commander, a role the friend would not take seriously at least once too often: "That was my mistake. I was a soldier and should have followed his order. Ernst Udet never forgave me that." *Das war's: Erinnerungen* (Frankfurt a. M.: Ullstein, 1983) 173.

[24] The "German Michel," the caricature form of Michael, patron saint of the Germans, was often portrayed in Nazi propaganda as a slumbering giant awaiting the Nazi call to awake: "Deutschland erwache!"

[25] The Kurt Hoffmann apologist Ingo Tornow dismisses this link between *Quax* and Nazi biology with the facile claim that such theories were not "genuinely National Socialist," but simply appropriated from other sources, *Piroschka und Wunderkinder oder von der Vereinbarkeit von Idylle und Satire: Der Regisseur Kurt Hoffmann* (Munich: Filmlandpresse, 1990) 37.

[26] Viktor Klemperer notes in his journal of Nazi rhetoric and beliefs that Hitler himself often emphasized the supremacy of the instinctive and physical over the rational: "The development of character clearly occupies only second place; in his opinion it arises more or less on its own if the physical dominates education and suppresses the intellectual." *LTI: Notizbuch eines Philologen* (Leipzig: Reclam, 1990) 8–9.

[27] At yet another level of control and reality, the intersection of ideological and narrative fiction is embodied in the actor Rühmann. An expert pilot himself, Rühmann flew for all his own scenes in Quax: "Two cameras were mounted on his plane — one in front of him and one on the wings. And Heinz Rühmann flew, acted, ran the cameras, monitored the lighting, background, settings. 'It was difficult, but magnificent!'" (Kirst 141). Thus Rühmann controlled everything, even where Quax could not yet.

[28] "Mehr Sein als Schein," the reverse form of the idiom. *Die Feuerzangenbowle* also concludes with a speech by Rühmann.

6

FLORENTINE STRZELCZYK

Far Away, So Close: Carl Froelich's Heimat

THE WORD HEIMAT IN GERMAN culture has always signified an
opaque concept. Connoting birthplace, childhood, mother, family,
country, and nation simultaneously, it is drenched in the longing for a
wholeness and unity no longer accessible to those who left it. The foreign and the distant, therefore, form an integral part of the concept of
Heimat. Heimat indicates a place but often means the nation; it signifies personal identity but possesses politically explosive forces. The concept has formed a key word in German culture that is crucial for the
understanding of German national identity and history.

In the following, I will focus on Carl Froelich's film *Heimat* (1938)
and analyze some of the politically explosive forces inherent in Heimat
by concentrating on the particular representations of femininity that the
film offers to its audiences.[1] Froelich's film is based on the popular
drama *Heimat* (1893) by Hermann Sudermann. Enthusiastically received in its time, the play was performed all over Europe and the
United States. Sarah Bernhardt, in the role of the fallen daughter
Magda, toured with the play and contributed considerably to its success
(Mannens 183). *Heimat* addresses turn-of-the-century conflicts between the individual and the family/community, the temptations of the
foreign and the confines of home, and the roles ascribed to women in
Heimat. Froelich's film adaptation of Sudermann's drama was also an
extraordinary success. Not only was his family melodrama awarded the
National Film Prize of 1939, but Froelich himself was recognized as
best director at the Biennale in Venice that same year.

The key role of Heimat in German culture has shaped diverse cultural expressions to the present day. During the eighties, for example,
Edgar Reitz's film *Heimat* (1984) became a crucial cultural event that
refueled discussions about German identity and the legacies of the
German past. Both Reitz's and Froelich's film display the strong tensions and pressures of German culture and society through the positions of its female characters in the Heimat. Reitz uses a number of
sequences of Froelich's *Heimat* in his film, thereby not only pointing to

the textual continuities and discontinuities of Heimat in Nazi and pres-
ent-day Germany, but also to Heimat as a site framed around women.
While Reitz focuses his narrative on women, thus constructing German
Heimat as a motherland, Froelich features a woman in conflict with a
patriarchally defined Heimat.

Rather than concerning itself with the veracity of its historical setting, like many historical films, Froelich's *Heimat* employs historical
circumstances to legitimize the present through the past (Happel 11,
39–40). In 1938, the ruling National Socialists reshaped and tightened
the boundaries of the German Heimat, on the one hand by annexing
Austria and the incorporation of the Sudetenland and on the other by
separating those who belonged from those who did not by means of
the Nuremberg racial laws. Surprisingly, however, *Heimat* is saturated
with the attraction of the exotic and with the desire to go beyond the
narrow boundaries of Heimat. The star of the film, Zarah Leander,
plays the role of an opera singer returning *heim ins Reich* from America,
and blends the appeal of eroticism and self-assertiveness with ethnic
otherness, wanderlust, and homesickness. This contradictory attraction
to both the exotic and distant and the familiar and close was crucial for
the success of the film, which is dependent on the female star as its
emotional center, and on her ambiguity toward Heimat. In order for
the film to function as entertainment, it invites the audience to participate in the ideological widening of the narrowly defined Heimat while
at the same time insisting on its restrictions.

The concept of Heimat played a crucial role both in the literature
and the public sphere of the Third Reich. Concerns for the protection
of Heimat that had emerged during the Weimar Republic formed the
basis of a unified German *Volksgemeinschaft* (national community) that
would transcend local, class, and political divisions. Quests for a purified Heimat legitimized plans for racial cleansing through elimination
of foreign and degenerate people as well as for territorial expansion as a
form of Heimat protection, thereby even masking Nazi militarism
(Williams 376–79). The "Heimatization" of Germany, as Alon Cofino
calls the dissemination of the concept into all levels of society from the
Second Empire on, can also be observed in the feature films of the
Third Reich (66).

Numerous films produced during the Nazi era hold the theme of
home and belonging at their cores. Their themes include leaving home
for far away places, returning home to one's community, longing for
the security of Heimat amidst the chaos of foreign cultures, or the experience of being driven from one's home. "I'd like to sit here like this

forever," exclaims Barbl in *Der verlorene Sohn* (The Prodigal Son, 1934) while enjoying a panoramic view of her Heimat from a mountaintop. While Dorothea, in *Jud Süß* (Jew Suess, 1940), admits to her own wanderlust by saying, "I would love to travel," she questions her travel companion Süß somewhat disquietingly, "Don't you have a homeland?" In these films as well as in *Heimat*, women not only express the tensions between the borders of the familiar and the strange, but they also negotiate the ideological limitations and expansions of Heimat.

But an approach that concentrates on the divergent forces at work in Nazi film runs counter to the majority of scholarly opinions on the films produced during the Third Reich. Specifically, modern scholarship has often either concentrated on the criticism of Nazi ideology which attempted to control, fix, and petrify all meaning, or, quite to the contrary, insisted on the purely melodramatic function and entertainment value of the films, or even emphasized their subversive strategies.[2] In his book *The Ministry of Illusion: Nazi Cinema and Its Afterlife* Eric Rentschler calls for a more precise awareness of "form, address, and appeal of Nazi films," rather than reducing them to either "ideological containers" or harmless and escapist entertainment packages (15). He then suggests reading these films in the context of both a culture industry in the service of mass deception and an emerging entertainment industry (15). In the film *Heimat*, however, the charismatic persona of the newly emerged star of Nazi cinema, Zarah Leander, represents both the desire to rebel against and the obligation to submit to the pressures of German Heimat. By transforming not just women, but beautiful stars, into the protagonists of Heimat, the concept could be popularized and finally packaged for mass entertainment.

The change in focus in scholarship on Nazi-era Cinema, as exemplified by Rentschler, has found its counterpart in the area of cultural history. The anti-modern iconography of Heimat, according to which an archaic German community celebrated its unity, presents only one aspect of the Third Reich. Another element is fascist Germany's simultaneous embracing of modernity, inviting Germans to widen the narrow boundaries of Heimat and to awaken the desire for the strange and foreign. According to the German cultural critic Hans Dieter Schäfer, this double bind is responsible for the split consciousness in which many Germans between 1933 and 1945 perceived their reality. Schäfer shows, for example, how travel abroad, especially to the Americas, enjoyed great popularity with many Germans. In 1933 traveling was declared a "national duty," a duty which 180,000 Germans are supposed to have performed in 1938 (Schäfer 155). Regular contributions to entertainment magazines featured articles and photos on great American cities.[3] Until 1939 international student exchanges between Germany, other European countries, and especially the United States took place both on the high school and university level. Through this contact and a more widespread fascination, America became a yardstick for German achievements.

The underlying excitement about American culture and lifestyles was expressed through widespread broadcasting of American radio programs, through books and publications about the U.S., and especially through American films. Until mid-1940, audiences could see a new American film every week, and they attracted far more viewers than domestic films. American stars were part of the star cult, and magazines published look-alike contests and rankings of American stars (Schäfer 164–67).[4] American swing and jazz music were also extremely popular, even though they were discouraged by the Nazis. Their attempts to replace American artists with homegrown jazz and swing bands failed (Kater 13).

The increased production of consumer goods that the government strongly supported during the pre-war years was also intended to compete with American-style products and life-styles. Rather than folk women weaving folk goods and preparing folk food, German women experienced the advantages of electric stoves, washing machines, and coffee makers (Schäfer 157). Advertising displayed modernization, efficiency, and technology that would allow women to spend quality leisure time (157). Clothing, make-up, and beauty products even became the subjects of courses preparing young girls in the art of womanhood (159–60). Moreover, carefully displayed eroticism in magazines and journals imitated the eroticism of American models.[5] While internationalization presented a threat to German Heimat and its values, a different kind of internationalization that featured America as the land of infinite possibilities also widened it. It is this ambiguity that, in part, determines the Janus-faced form of the film *Heimat.*

The contradictory realities that Schäfer describes deeply affected women and their experiences during the Third Reich. While women and mothers were transformed into the imagined protagonists of an idealized home and Heimat according to Nazi ideology, economic realities required women in the work place. To encourage women to take up their roles as wives and mothers, the government passed the 1933 *Ehestandsdarlehen Gesetz* (law regulating loans for newly married couples) which granted young middle-class couples loans at substantially reduced rates if the wife gave up her job (Eichborn 48–64). In contradiction to this promotion of women as mothers, wives, and focal points of the family, the Nazis actively encouraged the return of women to the work force with the beginning of rearmament in 1936 (Koonz 1991, 235–38). A 1938 issue of *Frauenwarte* illustrates this contradiction: "At a time when men will be needed more and more in technical professions, women will have to fill the vacancies," requiring them to "balance their femininity with their work" (488). The article promotes care-giving, teaching, and agricultural professions, each of them alluding to nurturing attributes associated with women. The title picture shows an intimate scene, a young woman dressed as a nurse and surrounded by and caring for children, with a caption that reads "comrade in the service of the people." Text and image suggest that the recommended balance can be found by transcending motherhood and joining in the care of the larger national community. This double-bind structure works to expand the notion of self-sufficiency of women in Heimat by incorporating images of female autonomy that also underlie the film *Heimat*.

The examples of filmic and historical scholarship discussed here show a less monolithic and more contradictory — a modern yet also anti-modern — face of Nazi politics and society, in which the careful promotion of lifestyles was constantly balanced against the ideological fixation of gendered social and political positions.

Heimat is set in 1885 in the small town of Ilmingen, to which Magda von Schwartze, now known as the famous American singer Maddalena d'all Orto, returns home after eight years away. Driven by homesickness, she accepts a small role in the local music festival, hoping to reconcile with her father, Oberst von Schwartze, and be accepted back into the family. She had left in order to avoid the shame of an illegitimate child from her misalliance with the local banker, von Keller. With the help of her friend and admirer, Heffterdingk, and through her art, she eventually regains her father's sympathy despite his otherwise rigid code of ethics and gains re-entrance into family and Heimat for herself and her daughter.

Sudermann's drama utilizes major elements of the *Rührstück*, the German version of the melodrama and a sub-genre of the middle-class tragedy, but adds naturalistic and sometimes art nouveau elements. The subject of *Heimat*, like many melodramas of the eighteenth and nineteenth centuries, is the nuclear family, which serves as both a refuge and a private sphere in opposition to the public sphere. The narrative action stems from a conflict that threatens to unravel the emotional dependencies in the family which, according to the conventions of the melodrama, are to be reconstituted in the course of the dramatic action (Viering 124). Acts of altruism and sacrifice, mostly on the part of the female characters, resolve the conflict. At the same time, the intensity of their renunciation intensifies the melodramatic effect (127). Whereas the conflicts in the melodrama are generally not acted out but rather internalized by the characters, in Sudermann's *Heimat* there is also a naturalistic element that questions the social pressures behind such dynamics.

The film takes up these turn-of-the-century pressures in accordance with the ideological perspective of 1938. While narrative structures in film melodramas usually assume the moral correctness of the nuclear family and achieve narrative closure through the restoration of these family relationships, in Froelich's film, the reconstitution of the family merges in the final scene with the reconciliation of the larger community of Heimat (Carroll 198). Rather than settling the clash between father and daughter through action, however, the film solves the melodramatic conflict by appealing emotionally (through music and framing) to the national community, thereby superseding the family as the primary social order.

The emphasis on the emotional is evident from the film's first sequence, which depicts Magda as psychologically incomplete. In this sequence, before the credits begin, Magda sings the theme song, "Drei Sterne sah ich scheinen" (I Saw Three Stars Shining). The song portrays the oppositions at work in the concept of Heimat, the axis between home and the foreign. Heimat appears here in the form of Magda's dream of a garden with a tree in it, introducing the idea of closure and of bound and rooted space. The close-up of Leander's face shows traces of tears, and her eyes are directed toward a faraway Heimat visible only to her inner eye. This initial sequence depicts her wandering mind longing to return to her Heimat; her body is not shown. The effect of this mind and body split is to cloak the idea of Heimat in a secret, the nature of which we are to discover during the film. From this opening sequence, however, it becomes clear that Magda is psychologically divided because she is separated from her Heimat.

This initial sequence sets up tensions that become further substantiated in the following scenes. Both the discussion at court involving the prince and local dignitaries of Ilmingen about the music festival and the casting of the star singer, and the subsequent scene between Aunt Fränze and Magda's father, Oberst von Schwartze, revolve around the absent Magda. In the community and its core, the family, there is an absence, a need for Magda the artist and Magda the daughter to return. The court discussions about the nationality of the artist who is to sing Bach's *St. Matthew's Passion* show the German homeland in need of German artists. Magda's eight-year absence has also shattered the von Schwartze family. A disagreement between Aunt Fränze and the Oberst develops due to his plea for money, which is needed so that Max, his younger daughter Marie's fiancé, may be released from his military obligations and marry. Fränze rejects the Oberst's request and blames him fully for Magda's desertion and the subsequent collapse of the family. Not only is von Schwartze scarred and damaged by the loss of Magda, but so is Magda's sister, Marie, called Mieze, whose future is measured against Magda's past. The conflict between Magda's career and her family duties increasingly clash, until they are resolved within the uniting forces of Heimat in the final scene.

The core conflict in the film between father and daughter expands in a concentric movement into larger conflicts concerning the very essence of Heimat. Initially, Magda is driven away by Heimat, because its social structures condemn her for being an unwed mother. If she wants to return into the family she must submit to the family's patriarchal code of ethics by admitting her sexually active past and marrying the father of her child. If she becomes part of the family structure, as wife, daughter, and mother — if in other words she chooses life — she will have to give up art and her international career. "I believe gypsies like us are at home right here, Magda," suggests Rohrmoser, Magda's friend and mentor, "Your voice is too good for this dump." "This dump is my Heimat," she replies. The conditions of membership in Heimat and the position of women within it reveal the tensions between family and career, art and life, independent woman and dutiful daughter, or between homeless traveler and Heimat dweller, as powerful, ever intensifying oppositions that press for answers. Rather than provide solutions, however, the film seeks to transcend these conflicts visually, spatially, and emotionally within the communal space of Heimat.

A number of melodramatic effects, particularly the use of Christmas imagery and classical music, support the merging of all conflicts into the space of community. Although the Ilmingen Music Festival takes place in February, the town's decorations for the festival, the setting, and the activities give the illusion of Christmas. This is supported by the biblical references in the names of von Schwartze's two daughters: Marie, the dutiful and pure one, and Magdalena, the whore, but also the repentant sinner. Moreover, Christmas is the day on which many

Western cultures celebrate the unity of the holy family, which in return unites the larger community of Christians. The popular imagination not only connects Christmas with specific winter activities and landscapes, but also with childhood memories, especially the security of belonging to a family. Christmas images that grow out of the idealization of the nuclear family evoke social stability and the permanence of community. When Magda rides up and down in front of her father's house in her carriage, the falling snow in front of the cozily lit windows intensifies the power of the family idyll in its Heimat. Furthermore, on a sleigh ride Oberst von Schwartze first encounters his granddaughter who bears a feminine form of his name, Leopoldine. Finally, the closing scene features Magda performing Bach's *St. Matthew's Passion* in the local cathedral. The music, often played at Christmas concerts, unites not only the family, but also the nation as family within Heimat, further illustrating how the concept of Heimat and the language of melodrama are closely linked.

Heide Schlüpmann has pointed out the importance of music and space in the heroine films of the Third Reich. The spatial dimensions of the scene often mediate the insertion of the female protagonist into patriarchal order, while music imbues the images with mythical and irrational qualities (55, 58). In the last scene of *Heimat,* Magda is framed by the powerful architecture of a gothic cathedral, filled with the music of Bach. This frame positions her symbolically within the national community. The camera zooms in on Leander performing Bach's aria "Buß und Reu" (Penance and Remorse). She becomes one with Heimat as her image dissolves into the tower of the cathedral. The camera moves upward to the top of the tower, reinstating the patriarchal order, and the power of the music sweeps away all conflicts.

As Michael Meyer has written, the National Socialists not only considered music the most German art form, but also thought it to be fundamental for "creat[ing] a German people's community" (59, 61). The Nazis regarded the folk song as the basis of all German music, and promoted singing within the family. Classical composers like Bach and Beethoven symbolized German national identity and unity, and their music was used during official and public events (123). In *Heimat,* classical music structures the beginning and the end of the film and offers an emotionally powerful solution to the family conflict by channeling it into a larger whole. In her 1939 Vienna dissertation "Vergleich zwischen Drama und Film *Heimat,*" Dorothea von Littrow explains this solution as the difference between 1893 and 1938. While Sudermann's drama featured the fight of the individual against society, "today the community restrains the individual" (86). The community assembled in the gothic church witnesses Magda's remorse and can forgive. She symbolically becomes part of another order that transcends both her father's Wilhelminian order and her own individualistic one. The appeal to the audience's emotions and the protagonist's posture of suffering work together to purge the prodigal daughter and to purify and rejuvenate the community by promoting unity, ostensibly beyond social, economic, and especially generational and gender struggles, in order to strengthen the family of Germans. The combination of music, the Christmas-like setting of the melodrama, and the dynamics of Heimat serve to endorse such an ideology.

Froelich's *Heimat* owed its popularity in large part to the way it adapted its source for a contemporary audience. The success of Sudermann's drama, on the other hand, was largely due to the attraction of the ambiguous character of the female protagonist Magda and her urge to realize herself as an individual without compromise, outside the narrow social customs and boundaries of her time. Sudermann's Magda borrows her convictions from popularized formulas of Nietzsche's philosophy, but as an interpreter of Wagner arias she simultaneously embodies the characteristics of both Madonna and the Bacchae (Viering 117, 129–30). With Magda, Sudermann employs the two images that most dominated the literary and artistic imagination in the second half of the nineteenth century: the *femme fatale* and the *femme fragile*. This concept of the *femme fatale* carries over into the film and disrupts and casts doubt on Magda's subordination to family and community. The film widens the boundaries of Heimat by allowing viewers to experience at a distance the foreign places, exotic desire, and sexuality that had all become so closely associated with the persona of Zarah Leander.

At the center of *Heimat* are both its protagonist Magda and the star playing her, Zarah Leander. The Swedish actress replaced Marlene Dietrich as the leading female film star in Germany and stepped into the diva role of Greta Garbo.[6] Leander's appearance combined a foreign, almost exotic, eroticism with a mysterious androgyny that characterized so many *femmes fatales* in literature (Schickedanz 22–49). Her alto voice, robust body, and the strong characters she portrayed suggested masculine traits, while her foreign accent, red hair, and facial features gave her an exotic feminine aura. This exotic femininity could incite longing for an otherness in contrast to the streamlined Aryan physique that dominated the official propaganda, although as a Swede, Leander fit into the Nazis' racial definition of what an Aryan was. In a 1938 feature, the popular magazine *Koralle* compares red-haired women to dangerous seductresses, bacchanalian courtesans, and, interestingly, innocent saints (566). The article ascribes to Zarah Leander a "beguiling spell" that flows from her dark voice and her "Titian red" beauty that could even be perceived in a black and white movie (567). While these contradictions between masculine and feminine traits, Bacchae and saint, elicited a wide range of audience reactions, the emphasis on exotic foreignness extended an invitation to cross the borders of a narrowly defined Heimat, at least in fantasy. Through public appearances and press releases Leander's carefully styled and marketed otherness resulted in her becoming the *femme fatale* par excellence to many Germans at the time (Seiler 32–33; Winkler-Mayerhöfer 100).

In nearly all of her films, Leander plays sexually assertive foreign women whose masculine drive, however, is always tempered by a feminine fragility of suffering. *Heimat* casts these traits into the popular imagery of *femme fatale* and *femme fragile*. While the *femme fragile* is characterized by her aesthetic suffering and spiritual fragility, the *femme fatale* possesses, because of her sexual appetite, demonic powers over men (Wittmann 82–85). While the play casts Magda as a *femme fatale* — her urge for personal freedom and sexual emancipation causes the men who love her shame, or pain (in the case of the pastor), or even death (in the case of her father) — the film balances her vamp-like man-devouring sexuality with aspects of the suffering and nurturing female. The success of *Heimat* is, to a large extent, based on the play between these two constructs of femininity, the *femme fatale* linked to exotic, dangerous sexuality and the *femme fragile* who expresses the qualities of Heimat. Both represent opposing positions in an ideological battle concerning the affirmation and revocation of female autonomy and the extension and delimitation of the concept of Heimat.

The *femme fatale* elements generate an image of woman as dominant, successful, and emancipated. When Magda first arrives in Ilmingen by train, crowds have gathered at the main station to catch a glimpse of her, now known as one of the stars the New York Metropolitan Opera. In the course of the film, her expensive and revealing clothing, her furs, her jewelry, her servants, and her other extravagant habits represent her Americanness and cosmopolitanism. The view of the cosmopolitan metropolis as a force for disintegration and as a site of seduction and irresistible temptation, which had already been the subject of polemics during the Weimar Republic, was absorbed into the blood and soil ideology of National Socialism (Wehrling 721). Third Reich films like Veit Harlan's *Die Goldene Stadt* (The Golden City, 1942) or Luis Trenker's *Der verlorene Sohn* not only portray the racial impurity and moral abyss of the city in contrast to the pure and rural landscapes of Heimat, but also associate the city with unrestrained female sexuality. Trenker's famous Manhattan sequences viewed America — and especially New York City — equally as a site of a disintegrative internationalism and as feminized spaces with the power to lure the male protagonist away from Heimat (Rentschler 1996, 85–89). Unlike Trenker's strategy of mystifying German Heimat by exorcising the foreign and the female, *Heimat* seems to be at ease with the foreign. Moreover, the film appears to celebrate it. The entertainment value of America in the popular imagination at the time and its function as a yardstick for German achievements shape the protagonist's appearance and behavior. Americanness becomes the object of desire as an extension of the aura of the female star.

The camera favors Magda's physical appearance and fashionable clothing over the schoolmarmish uptightness of the female upper class of Ilmingen. During the reception scene where she is introduced to the notabilities of the town, her quick wit and worldly manners contrast with the narrow-mindedness of the other women. Maddalena d'all Orto is a success story. She has lived the American dream, climbing up from the bottom of the social hierarchy to the top through hard work and individual strength. Her career as an artist started in the morally questionable night club scene of European and American metropolises. When one of the Prussian officers questions her about the racially and socially objectionable population of New York's melting pot, she deliberately shocks her audience by situating the beginning of her own career amidst blacks, prostitutes, and servants. Far from showing her as a social outcast, the reception scene casts her in complete control of the conversation and the interaction with male and female guests. Her admission of her morally suspect past has the effect of heightening the eroticism of the forbidden and irresistible exotic attraction the American diva presents to men and women alike. This fascination with America as the place where such success stories are possible echoes in popular journals and magazines of the time. Journals like *Koralle* reported obsessively on America during the pre-war years. A series of reports dealt with how to find work in New York, other features included working women in the U.S., newest dance styles in New York, or the marriages of American stars.[7] America, in the film and popular culture of the time, often portrayed female self-confidence as irresistible femininity combined with material success.

Focusing on Magda's captivating energy, the film turns against the idleness of the upper classes. During a reception where the ladies of the town's high society confront her, Magda emphasizes that her art is not a pastime as art is for the daughters of the higher social classes, but a way to earn a living through hard work. Magda's experience with the lower levels of society on her way to success and independence contributes to her ability to appear as the intelligent, confident, and emancipated "New Woman" of the Weimar Republic, which Nazi ideology attempted to battle with the slogan: "emancipation from emancipation" (Mosse 1966, 42). In the film, Magda's criticism of both upper class lifestyles and patriarchal concepts of professional women, however, is directed toward other women and re-channeled into a competition about beauty and youth. While the prince and all the other men are captured by Magda's provocative aura and charm, the camera scans the morally appalled and self-righteous faces of the female audience while she performs the song "Eine Frau wird erst schön durch die Liebe" (Only Love Makes a Woman Beautiful). Her body language and flirting with her male audience challenges the standards of the good, petit bourgeois morals maintained by the women in the scene. However, Magda's contagious sex appeal begins to conquer even the initially hostile women, and even pious Aunt Fränze, returning home after the reception, involuntarily hums the song. While the patriarchal system and its restrictive concepts of female sexuality are the root of Magda's conflict with her father and Heimat and have driven her away in the first place, the film redirects the critique of the patriarchal system toward its accomplices and beneficiaries, the upper-class women. Because Magda convinces men not through arguments but through her charm, and women act as her adversaries, patriarchal authority is not generally questioned. The film appropriates the Weimar concept of the New Woman by draining it of its socially and politically charged potential and adding it to the charm and sex appeal of the *femme fatale*.

Magda appears self-confident with men, for example, when she ridicules her former lover von Keller, but she needs male negotiators to organize her life and career. Rohrmoser — colleague, trainer, father substitute, and nanny — provides emotional and professional support. While Rohrmoser tries to convince her to continue with her profession as artist, the cathedral organist, Heffterdingk, mediates between Magda and her family and tries to convince her to stay in her homeland. The emancipating narratives in the film showing a successful career woman are undermined by the fact that men — chiefly Magda's father — propel the action. While she seems autonomous on one level, she also depends on the patriarchal system.

The images of female autonomy and emancipation presented so openly on the surface are therefore in many ways elusive underneath. For example, the song "Eine Frau wird erst schön durch die Liebe," superficially a music-hall chanson interpreted with the gestures and body language of a *femme fatale*, is about true love, which men need to discover below the erotic surface of women. Being loved, not being desired, makes women beautiful. While camera movements evoke the *femme fatale*, the text points instead to a *femme fragile*, a vulnerable femininity. Hiding beneath the *femme fatale* posture of the diva Maddalena d'all Orto is therefore "nothing but a woman's heart." In other words, even when she appears most in control of both her sexuality and her destiny, as during the performance of the song at the reception, she renounces both in favor of a consuming love that is celebrated as true femininity.

Magda's loving heart is in the right place. Her father admits to her: "You've kept your good heart, but I can see something in your eyes that worries me." Magda is a caring sister: she finances the payment required by the army for the soldier Max, enabling him to marry Mieze. She is a caring daughter who longs, despite her professional success, to return to her father's home and reconcile with him. Yet most of all she is a dedicated mother who loves her illegitimate child. Although she is willing to sacrifice herself to an unhappy marriage with von Keller, the father of her daughter, in order to save her family's honor, she rejects his marriage proposal when she learns that he plans to send her child abroad. Even her professional success is motivated by motherhood. "Then the fight began, the fight for my child," she says to von Keller, explaining how she found the strength to bear financial hardship and pursue a career. The film further reveals Magda's masculine professional ambition as merely a role she had to play out of necessity.

Immediately after Magda confesses to her father that she has a child and his rejection of her, she must perform as Orpheus in Gluck's opera *Orpheus und Eurydike*. Heartbroken, she feels unable to sing when Rohrmoser teases her that her lips are too red for the role of the man she has to play that night. When she appears on stage, the camera displays an androgynous image, the dress-like Greek costume, the deep voice, the painted lips and tears. Interpreting Orpheus's pain about the loss of Eurydice, her performance turns into mourning for her lost Heimat. In Magda's male role, Heimat takes on the qualities of a love object. On the one hand, androgyny here functions to express the conflict between an imposed male role and her true female identity. On the other, however, it signifies the longing for home, as Heimat itself is always marked by feminine qualities and is therefore desired from a male position. Magda adopted her public persona as a career woman with masculine drive in order to survive outside a protecting Heimat. Even her stage name, Orto, meaning kitchen garden, reveals a longing for domesticity that belies her professional success and places her within the boundaries of a garden whose tamed nature and clear structure signify the essence of Heimat expressed in the first song, "Drei Sterne sah ich scheinen."[8] While in many films of the Third Reich, different women characters embody the opposition between *femme fatale* as seductress and career woman on the one hand and *femme fragile* as self-sacrificing mother and wife on the other,[9] in *Heimat* the heroine's character alone supports notions of ambitious self-realization, assertive sexuality, female vulnerability, and Madonna-like motherhood simultaneously.

Zarah Leander portrays Magda as a strong woman, stronger than her father and the patriarchal system. As a New Woman, Magda contradicts all proclaimed ideals of women's roles as housewives and mothers during the Nazi era. She is ambitious, successful, courageous, even egocentric, but on another level her strength is revoked through her suffering as a mother and her remorse for her sexual past. As Gudrun Brockhaus shows in her essay "Male Images and Female Desire," the most frequent type of woman in the German women's novel of the Nazi era was not at all "the blond and braided Gretchen," obedient and subservient, but rather the "autonomous heroine," whose masculine traits, rebellion and independence, are encompassed in a motherly femininity that casts woman as an embodiment of nature and eternity (78–79). Leander, as Magda, personifies this "autonomous heroine" whose masculine potency is refracted through the cliché of suffering motherhood or, as Heide Schlüpmann puts it, the image of the penitent (54). Whereas Marlene Dietrich, despite her popularity, was sometimes negatively reviewed because of her "undisguised eroticism" that would "completely negate the idea of a woman," Leander's *femme fatale* aspects were subdued through elements of a suffering *femme fragile* (Schäfer 168). The embodiment of female autonomy in the female protagonist is mitigated by her simultaneous portrayal as vulnerable and motherly, and by her commitment to her homeland.

The heroic melodrama of the thirties and forties is, according to Schlüpmann, such a feminized genre that it often attributes feminine characteristics to male heroes in artist roles (58). In National Socialist melodramas, however, women artists exhibit the feminine and emotional qualities of art, for instance vocal music, men perform artistic roles that are typically considered as masculine, such as sculptors or architects, or they play composers like Beethoven or Bach. This gender split, according to Schlüpmann, counters the femininity of the melodramatic genre (58). In *Heimat*, the organist Heffterdingk appears at first sight as a feminized artist. His mediating qualities and his unconditional devotion to Magda, however, softly but firmly propel her return to her Heimat. Employing his female attributes he functions as an agent of patriarchy. In all one-on-one encounters between the two, the camera establishes a visual hierarchy by positioning his face above hers, with her either being seated or kneeling and looking up to him in trust. As the conductor of the closing Bach concert, he not only orchestrates the emotional reconciliation of the family von Schwartze, but he also dominates the final scene as the conductor of the orchestra and choir that perform Bach's *St. Matthew's Passion*. In this scene, Magda repents of her sinful past, which purifies and prepares her for readmission into Heimat. Heffterdingk performs the role of a catalyst who continuously smoothly directs Magda toward denouncing her outgoing femininity and sexual assertiveness in exchange for a desexualized inwardness.

As in the beginning sequence, the last shot focuses in a close-up on her face, while we hear her sing. Her hair lit from behind, her dress emphasizing the vertical, the camera again denies her sinful body to the viewer by angelically transcending and desexualizing it. This suppression of female sexuality corresponds to the emotional and mythic elevation of archetypal woman as part of the male symbolic order. The unwed mother is transformed into a purified Madonna. "What is negated in reality is being glorified as a metaphor," concludes Schlüpmann (58). Women, in other words, figure as icons of Heimat, as long as they can be inserted into the patriarchal order as mothers, daughters, and wives. The film *Heimat* packages these gendered dynamics for mass consumption, playing out the exotic and sexual aura of Zarah Leander that incites the audience to taste the strange and far away and transgress the narrow borders of Heimat, only to lead it *heim ins Reich*.

The Third Reich was obsessed with order and coordination; reordering, subordinating, uniting, classifying, categorizing. "Our socialism goes far deeper," asserted Hitler in 1936, "It not only changes the external order of things, but it also reorders the relations between people and state and national community" (Rauschning 180). Goebbels explains the manner, however, in which people should be redirected toward community and state. He based his idea of coordinating competing areas of the public sphere on an orchestra:

We do not want everybody playing the same instrument. We only require that everybody plays according to a plan and that the emerging concert . . . is based on a symphony. No one should have the right to play however he wants (Rühle 82).

These concepts of order also determine the conflicts in *Heimat* about Heimat.

In the film, the traditional German Heimat is on the verge of breaking down and in urgent need of reordering. All levels of society are shown as split, antagonistic, and enclosed in their own world, separated from the others. Even worse, the social function of the different classes seems exhausted. The main function of the aristocracy, represented by the prince, has become the organization of festivals rather than the assumption of leadership in the political affairs of the country. The prince appears as a character without authority, but possesses a superficial charm and a preference for the London night club scene where he heard Magda sing for the first time. The film presents highly valued members of the upper class like Aunt Fränze, the pious, narrow-minded would-be-artist, and von Keller, the unscrupulous, corrupt womanizer, ironically. The wives of high society members, as discussed earlier, live a life of luxury and bigotry, supporting and supported by a gender- and class-based hierarchical social order.

The military also is shown a problematic position in the film, as a class and an institution. It has preserved a strong code of honor, yet its social and political status is devalued. Oberst von Schwartze's pension, for example, is not sufficient to provide the financial means required by the army as payment for the wedding permit that would allow his daughter's fiancé to marry. As the scenes at the ball and reception illustrate, the military lives an encapsulated life, reveling in better times and celebrating a set of traditions and values out of touch with other members of society. Entangled in its traditions and without political vision, the Prussian military, with its superiority complex, is treated with ironic sympathy. As exemplified in Oberst von Schwartze, the military's attitude lacks flexibility and human generosity. Von Schwartze is introduced as a strict patriarch who values obedience, discipline, and honor above all. His daughter has violated this system: "You have betrayed us. You have sullied your father's uniform. You have scorned the principles of order [Ordnung] that are the immutable laws in this house." Against his laws she sets the individualistic life maxim of a younger generation: "There is only one principle important to me: the honesty of my feelings, faithfulness to myself." The film treats the attitudes of the different social classes, the military, and different generations critically, while also showing sympathy toward the closed world that each represents.

At the same time, however, the film expresses the longing for a new and different order that unites all conflicted parties and convictions and encompasses each individual within a larger whole. This notion is expressed for the first time in the folk song "Drei Sterne sah ich scheinen," when Magda sings it at the beginning of the film. By imagining a linden tree within a garden rather than nature per se, Magda expresses her longing for a familiar identifiable order. What separates the garden from nature is the controlled order of the latter within the former. Later in the movie, Mieze tries to oppose Magda's naturalistic philosophy of the right of the individual by stating that there is a higher order to which everyone should adhere: "You are not that important. We all are not that important. Do it for father, do it for us. . . . Somehow, things need to be in order," she closes helplessly. But Mieze cannot imagine what kind of order could not only reunite her family, but also reconcile diametrically opposed concepts of life as represented by Magda and her father. Nor can anybody else. Von Schwartze, after hearing about his daughter's arrival, attempts to distract himself by concentrating on the newspaper: "What a man this Bismarck is. Authority must prevail. All the time. Always." Von Schwartze admires Bismarck as a man of authority and discipline, who had the strength and the leadership to found the German Reich in 1871. The tensions between social classes, genders, and life philosophies prevalent in the film, however, point to a solution in the future when the German people would be not only politically, but also socially and culturally, united under one idea. From the perspective of the audience in 1938, it would seem that within the past lay the seeds of the present and that the turn of the century represented in the film prefigured political constellations that the Third Reich appeared to have solved.

Heimat exemplifies how the demands of a new age can no longer be fulfilled with the values and traditions of an older time. "I grew up in this world. I don't know another one," von Schwartze admits helplessly to Heffterdingk, who replies:

> But you do know of this other world, Mister von Schwartze. It is ascending with new visions and a new honor. It touches our hearts and cannot be stopped even by you. This life that also stirs within you is too big, too powerful not to burst open these old forms. You feel it too, you just refuse to admit it.

It is Heffterdingk who speaks these prophetic words that point to a future that can only be known to the audience. The context of 1885 provides the screen on which the situation of Germany in 1938 is projected. The failings perceived in the past propel the social and political changes experienced by Germans of the present.

By 1938, Hitler himself had achieved the unity of the German people within Germany by suppressing, threatening, and eliminating the opposition to National Socialism. He had also succeeded in reuniting the different "family members" of the German nation. The reintegration of the Saarland into the Reich, the annexation of Austria, and the incorporation of the Sudetenland completed this German family romance. In other words, by 1938 Hitler had brought about a new order by managing to unite the various, heterogeneous members of the German nation and mold them into a unified whole. The new order, the new honor, and the new world that the soft-spoken musician Heffterdingk so prophetically announces near the end of the movie is definitely Hitler's world. The past legitimizes the present, and German history appears as teleological progress toward a glorious future.

What Heffterdingk envisions and Hitler accomplished for a short time, however, was not all that new. It is rather a familiar world in which Prussian values of order, discipline, and obedience could be reconciled in a modern nation-state and fueled by Hitler's aim to unite Germans of different regions, classes, political convictions, and gender. In this context, the language in the film becomes crucial. The language of the military has invaded the private sphere: von Schwartze speaks of "treason" [Verrat] and "interrogation" [Verhören] when discussing his daughter Magda's past; Mieze's fiancé Max uses the phrase "to stand at attention" [strammstehen] to address the family conflict; Magda's thinking revolves around the "battle" [Kampf] for Heimat and for her child; and Heffterdingk casts Magda's position vis-à-vis her father in terms of "battle" [Kampf] and "victory" [Sieg]. This militaristic rhetoric forms a disturbing subtext that, in the case of Heffterdingk, seems to contradict the feminized traits that many male artists in Nazi films carry. In the fascist rhetoric of suffering, however, man is often ascribed feminine characteristics. Nazi ideology ascribed to the fascist man, as a servant of his party, the traits of devotion, dedication, relinquishing of the self — all traditionally feminine qualities (Brockhaus 74). Indeed, Heffterdingk's vision seems to be part of this higher, ideally orchestrated system that proclaims itself at the end of the nineteenth century and that Hitler strove to fulfill.

The language of war and the prophetic promise of a higher ideal world in which unity, not war, will prevail, relate to the split consciousness of the time. On the one hand, Germany's increased economic production and the transformation into an American-style consumer society invited Germans to enjoy life's pleasures. On the other hand, the party employed numerous campaigns to encourage people to prepare themselves for war. Together with the Volkswagen, Hermann Göring introduced a "folk gas mask" in 1937 and increased air raid and blackout exercises. In addition, military exercises frequently included folk fairs (Schäfer 182). In this way, the state succeeded in keeping the hope for peace and the fear of war alive simultaneously. Numerous contributions to the magazine *Koralle* in 1938 praised the possibilities of widening one's horizons through travel, and celebrated the American lifestyle. In contrast, it also published reports about the newest weapon systems, the armaments of the major powers, and geopolitical considerations about shifting power balances. It is this disturbing contradiction of war and peace that characterizes Heffterdingk's vision.

Neither the solution to the conflict nor Heffterdingk's prophecy are acted out in the film. The solution shown is an emotional one following Goebbels's orchestra principle that promises to dissolve national conflict and opposition within a unifying harmonious whole. In the last cathedral scene, Heffterdingk appears symbolically as the conductor of this newly composed and orchestrated national community in which gender struggle, family conflict, and generational and individual differences can be solved. The solution remains vague: Magda is likely to keep singing, probably under Heffterdingk's judicious supervision, but instead of ambitious career goals, she will perform her art in the service of the homeland. Her blond child will grow up in Germany within a traditional family, von Schwartze will have the honor of his daughter restored, most likely by marriage to Heffterdingk, and Max and Mieze will be able to get married. The prodigal daughter has returned home, and has matured through pain and remorse. She is still a strong individual; her strength, however, will no longer benefit just herself, but serve the German community.

The notion of Heimat itself can be understood as a system of ordering. On the one hand, the concept of Heimat separates what is familiar and close from what is foreign and strange, or decides who is to be considered an insider or outsider. On the other hand, Heimat also functions to order people around a principle of unity. Both aspects of Heimat are related, as the unified experience of Heimat requires that different voices and identities be assimilated, suppressed, or excluded.

The cultural critics David Morley and Kevin Robbins therefore conclude in their analysis of Heimat that "xenophobia and fundamentalism are opposite sides of the same coin." That is, belonging to Heimat is a way to conserve one's own culture and identity while excluding the alien and foreign (Morley and Robbins 4). In *Heimat*, the conflict is about the fundamentals of patriarchal order, which pressure genders and generations to unite. While the narrative closes in a uniting wave of emotions and music, the subtext of war indicates that such unity can only be reached through pressure and force.

Carl Froelich's 1938 melodrama *Heimat* is marked by the powerful contradictions that characterized the Nazi pre-war years. While the film invites the widening of a narrowly defined Heimat by allowing viewers to safely experience the foreign and exotic, in the end, the film reconfirms the restrictions imposed by Heimat. This contradiction between the far away and the close depends on the persona of the newly discovered *femme fatale* of German film, Zarah Leander. In most of her films, her androgynous qualities negotiate female autonomy, sexual self-assertiveness, and career-oriented emancipation with fragility, altruistic suffering, and motherhood. As Magda, she plays the rootless vagabond who travels the Americas, but desires nothing more than to return home. She reenters Heimat in a glorious spectacle that stylizes her into an icon at the price of her sexuality. Her strengths are not revoked, but re-channeled toward service for the homeland.

These tensions about Heimat, nation, and the position of women still exist today, as evidenced by the reactions to Edgar Reitz's 1984 film *Heimat*. Rejecting the fatherland and its Nazi crimes, Reitz focuses on an alternative motherland centered around the labor of women in order to rehabilitate German identity. However, this new perspective does not provide a fundamentally different treatment of the gender thematics addressed in Froelich's *Heimat*. Like in Froelich's film, women figures, in the end, only sanction patriarchal arrangements. The discourse of Heimat elevates woman as an icon for the price of controlling and manipulating her in its center. Froelich's film, in its ideological assumptions seemingly so far removed from today's culture, has, nevertheless, passed on some of its ideological baggage to contemporary films like Reitz's *Heimat*. Far away, but so close.

In which way did Froelich's *Heimat* function as entertainment for the male and female viewers of the thirties? From today's perspective, it is difficult to assess the audiences watching films such as *Heimat*. However, we can discuss the appeal of these films in terms of textual analysis. In *Heimat*, the ambiguity, anchored both in the aura of the female star and in the melodramatic narrative, gives the film its human face. Feminist approaches to film have recognized a powerful binary model of sexual difference at work in the cinematic text that grants only the male spectator the privilege of visual pleasure, whereas the female spectator assumes a position of narcissism (Mulvey 6–18; Doane 1982, 78). More recent feminist approaches to cinema, however, maintain that the cinema offers a variety of fantasies "in which the spectator takes up several subject positionings" (Stacey 31). By fostering the illusion of crossing the boundaries of Heimat, then, Froelich's film encourages fantasies of rebellion and resistance, radical individualism, unrestrained sexuality, exotic far-away places, and consequently offers multiple ways of interpretation of both the characters and the narrative. Moreover, these border crossings can be enjoyed from a position of safety and security in German Heimat, as the film evokes so powerfully in its closing scenes. Reveling in exotic Otherness and crossing the borders of a narrowly defined Heimat, function as a means to reaffirm and revalidate such boundaries of Heimat. This kind of "safe fantasy," finally, popularized and proliferated the "Heimatization" of Germany, that is, the concept of a newly orchestrated and restructured National Socialist community.

Heimat (1938). Zarah Leander as Magda seeks reconciliation with her father, played by Heinrich George. Courtesy Library of Congress and Transit Film GmbH.

Family members look up as Magda (not shown) sings the "Buß und Reu" aria from Bach's St. Matthew's Passion. Courtesy Library of Congress and Transit Film GmbH.

Notes

[1] The English translation of Heimat as homeland must necessarily be inadequate. Throughout the essay, therefore, the unitalicized form Heimat will be used to refer to the concept and the italicized form *Heimat* to refer to the film.

[2] See for example, Erwin Leiser, *Nazi Cinema*, trans. Gertrud Mander and David Wilson (New York: Collier, 1975) 16–17; David Stewart Hull, *Film in the Third Reich* (New York: Simon and Schuster, 1973) 6; and Klaus Kreimeier, *Die Ufa-Story: Geschichte eines Filmkonzerns* (Munich: Hanser, 1992) 268–70.

[3] See for example, "Symphonie der Nacht," *Koralle* 6.19 (1938): 670–71; "New Yorks neuer Mittelpunkt — Radio City," *Koralle* 6.44 (1938): 1556–57; "Weihnachts-Shopping in Hollywood," *Das Magazin* 6.160 (1937): 29–31; "Gigant New York," *Das Magazin* 6.161 (1938): 38–41.

[4] For example "Verheiratet mit einem Filmstar," *Koralle* 6.32 (1938): 1125–27.

[5] "Sophistication: Ein wichtiger Begriff des amerikanischen Lebens, der in keinem Wörterbuch steht," *Koralle* 6.40 (1938): 1400–1401.

[6] A review about Leander's first Ufa film, *Zu neuen Ufern* (To New Shores, 1937), measures her performance against the appearance and acting of Greta Garbo. "Zu neuen Ufern," *Deutsche Filmzeitung* 16.32 (1937): 5.

[7] Lotte Zielesch, "Ich suchte Stellung in New York," *Koralle* 6.20 (1938): 711, 714, *Koralle* 6.21 (1938): 749–50, *Koralle* 6.22 (1938): 804–5; "Krankenschwestern in USA," *Koralle* 6.16 (1938): 560–62; "Big Apple: Ein närrischer Tanz macht in Amerika Mode," *Koralle* 6.22 (1938): 806–7; "Verheiratet mit einem Filmstar," *Koralle* 6.32 (1938): 1125–27.

[8] I would like to thank Sandra Hoenle, University of Calgary, who drew my attention to this detail.

[9] For example in *Kora Terry* (1940) or *Opfergang* (Sacrifice, 1944).

7

JOAN CLINEFELTER

A Cinematic Construction of Nazi Anti-Semitism: The Documentary Der ewige Jude

WHEN THE FILM *Der ewige Jude* (The Eternal Jew) premiered on 28 November 1940, the National Socialist press recognized it as a "symphony of disgust and horror."[1] Since 1945, film critics and historians have agreed with this assessment, although for reasons quite different than the Nazis. Conceived as documentary proof of the Jewish threat, *Der ewige Jude* stands as the purest visual representation of National Socialist anti-Semitism. As such, the film has been treated extensively in scholarly literature. Typically, scholars describe the film's origins in October 1939, its seven revisions, its content, and the public's reaction.[2] In another approach, critics attack the veracity of the film's claims and point to the outright falsification of statistics, history, and quotations.[3] However, scholars have paid little attention to the film's structure and how its component parts are used to compose an anti-Semitic document. That is, they fail to analyze the film as a cinematic construct.

The filmmakers produced *Der ewige Jude* as a documentary intended to cinematically sell anti-Semitism to the German public, but the film did not function as a typical documentary. The filmmakers did not invite the viewers to reflect on the factual material assembled; nor were they interested in having the viewers interpret the film's message for themselves. Instead, *Der ewige Jude* imitates the affective structures of fictional film, thereby evoking in the audience a visceral rejection of Jews and a wholesale acceptance of Nazi anti-Semitism. The self-referential structure of the film creates a seamless visual argument for the necessity of the Nazis' anti-Jewish policies. By combining documentary footage from the ghettos with clips cut from newsreels, other National Socialist documentaries, and even Weimar-era and Yiddish films, the director and editors of *Der ewige Jude* assembled an indictment against the Jews and their influence on German culture. The filmmakers consciously used the techniques of the cinematic medium to create a film that is more pseudo-documentary than documentary.

In the following, I will consider four major segments of *Der ewige Jude*: the documentary segment of the ghettos and the subsequent unmasking of the Jews; the film's use of the American feature film *The House of Rothschild* (1934); the sequence on degenerate art; and finally the segment on Weimar film culture. In so doing I will illustrate the interplay between these segments and how they interact with the narration and music to create the archetypal anti-Semitic film. Operating as key scenes, these segments unfold before the audience, pulling the narrative toward its dramatic conclusion. Indeed, far from devising a documentary designed to sway the audience with facts, the film's director, Fritz Hippler, sought to craft a cinematic spectacle that would seize the viewers' emotions. The images, narration, and music combine to tell a compelling story of a pervasive evil and the battle to combat it; a story that would hold audiences spellbound — ideally long after they left the theater. By analyzing *Der ewige Jude* as a cinematic construct, I will demonstrate how the National Socialists represented their ideology to the movie-going public, and how they packaged and sold anti-Semitism in the theaters of the Third Reich.

Throughout, my analysis borrows from Hilmar Hoffmann's interpretation of *Der ewige Jude* as an example of a compilation film. Hoffmann defines compilation film as a "parasitic genre" of cinema; it takes footage from other films and uses it in ways that are most often contradictory to the original film's themes and style (Hoffmann 1988, 154). Segments from other films are thus transformed into "realistic visual particles" that are manipulated, resequenced, and reinterpreted to construct an alternative reality (154). Hoffmann's concept of a compilation film offers an excellent interpretive model for a fuller analysis of *Der ewige Jude*. Expanding upon Hoffmann's general notion, the film can be thought of as a potent potion of images derived from a variety of sources, mixed together with the essence of National Socialist ideology — anti-Semitism. In the final product, each cinematic ingredient is transformed into visual proof of the "Jewish problem" and the necessity of the Nazis' solution.

Der ewige Jude utilizes the entire range of the photographic medium by splicing together clips from documentary footage shot specifically for the film, feature films produced in Hollywood and during the Weimar Republic, newsreels and documentaries made by the Ministry of Propaganda, as well as still photographs and photomontages. For example, the film employs clips from the following Nazi documentaries: *Hände am Werk* (Hands at Work, 1935), *Terror oder Aufbau* (Terror or Building Up, 1933), *Gestern und Heute* (Yesterday and Today, 1938), *Juden ohne Maske* (Jews Without Masks, 1937), and *Triumph des Willens* (Triumph of the Will, 1935).[4] There are clips taken from at least five German newsreels and seven feature films.[5] The film also brings together material from five other media: music, print media, painting, sculpture, and two 1937 exhibitions organized by the Nazis: *Entartete Kunst* (Degenerate Art) and *Der ewige Jude* (The Eternal Jew).

By recycling newsreel and documentary footage and incorporating it with footage shot in the Polish ghettos and excerpts taken from fictional feature films, director Fritz Hippler and his staff heightened the perceived documentary character of the film and hence strengthened the illusion of the images' accuracy. This heightened sense of truthfulness bolstered the audience's predisposition to believe that the film tells the truth. More importantly, by intersplicing newsreel, documentary, and fictional film footage within a framework that purports to be a documentary itself, the boundaries between fact and fiction, between ideology and reality, collapse. At the points where such collapse occurs, the film reinforces its claims to historical veracity. Anton Kaes refers to this as the "reality effect" (1990, 115). The fiction of feature films is transformed into documentary reality, visual documents and facts are conjured into illusion, and all the while the unseen narrator assures the viewers that this cinematic fabrication is real. From the film's opening sequences until its concluding scenes, *Der ewige Jude* constructs an illusory world designed to legitimate the Nazis' anti-Semitic ideology and policies.

Der ewige Jude opens with a lengthy sequence of images of the newly created Jewish ghettos in Nazi-occupied Poland. After the opening credits, animated text informs the audience that the film uses documentary footage in order to show Jews in their original state, or as the narrator explains, before "they put on the mask of civilized Europeans." Thus the film begins with an ideologically driven construct of reality that will be sustained throughout: Jews have always lived in the ghettos and in fact they *choose* to live like this.

Although created under extraordinary circumstances, the film represents the ghettos as ordinary, as normal. Never mind that Nazi occupational authorities created the ghettos by forcing Jews out of their homes and into the ghettos as racial refugees. Never mind that the film depicts the effect of the Nazi administration and disruption of the lives of millions of Polish Jews rather than their normal lives. The normative interpretation that Hippler placed on this documentary footage and the film as a whole lends the film a kind of truth-value. That is, the film constructs a National Socialist reality, a world in which dangerous Jews lurk in every street; a world that depicts and therefore justifies Nazi anti-Semitism, and ultimately, the Nazi extermination of the Jews.

Joseph Goebbels, Minister of Propaganda and head of the Reich Chamber of Culture, may have had in mind a film on Eastern European Jews before the German invasion of Poland on 1 September 1939. However, the photographic documentation of Polish Jews had to be delayed until the German invasion was concluded.[6] From early October through November 1939 — immediately after the German victory over the Poles — Fritz Hippler, head of the German newsreel service *Deutsche Wochenschau* and director of several important newsreels, took camera crews to film Jews in the ghettos of Łodz, Warsaw, Lublin, and Cracow.[7] Hippler's footage, which was the only film shot specifically for *Der ewige Jude*, lent credence to the film's claim to documentary truth.

In radio interviews and in print, Fritz Hippler touted *Der ewige Jude* as a documentary counterpart to the highly successful feature film, *Jud Süß* (Jew Suess, 1940). However, while non-Jewish actors had played Jews in that box office smash, Hippler stressed that *Der ewige Jude* faithfully depicted reality. Indeed, the documentary quality of this film was one of its selling points. As Hippler explained in the Nazi press:

> No Jew was forced into any kind of action or position during the shooting. Moreover, we let the filmed Jews be on their own and tried to shoot in moments when they were unaware of the camera's presence. Consequently we have rendered the Ghetto Jews in an unprejudiced manner, real to life as they live and as they react in their own surroundings. All who see this film will be convinced there is never a forced or scared expression in the faces of the Jews who are filmed passing by, trading or attending ritual services.[8]

Although Hippler's assessment of the filming seems disingenuous, he touches upon the value of *Der ewige Jude* as a National Socialist documentary, and, more importantly, its usefulness as a construction of an anti-Semitic reality. By asserting that none of the scenes were staged, that no Jew was forced or terrorized into performing in front of the Nazi cameramen, Hippler offers the film as a slice of daily life. He claims that the camera does not lie but rather records the actuality of the ghettos.

Even if the ghetto images left the viewers unconvinced of the filmmakers' anti-Semitic message, the impression that the ghetto scenes depict ordinary, normal Jewish life remained. As the camera — mounted on a vehicle — moves through the ghetto streets, it offers the audience mini-narratives of supposed normalcy. Against the dubbed background noises of the streets, the narrator explains the meaning of the images. The ghetto segment is comprised largely of vignettes that cut between various groups of Jews walking the ghetto streets and working. However, the filmmakers intersperse these general views of life with extended narratives, all created cinematically.

For example, after a series of shots of Jews in the streets, the camera records one man's movements. He walks toward the camera, pauses, turns around, and ducks inside a doorway. The camera then cuts to the next scene, in which a male figure passes in front of the camera, now placed inside a ghetto residence. The use of match-on-action creates continuity between the action in this home and the man on the street. Because of the way the film is sequenced, the viewer can assume that the male figure in the home is the same man just seen ducking into a doorway outside. Now transported into a Jewish home represented as both authentic and normal, the narrator explains that Jews do not live as Germans do. Jews at the table grab food with no manners; a woman eating looks to one side, and the shot, which seemingly reveals what she is looking at, dissolves to a wall covered with flies. To emphasize the filthy living conditions, the camera then cuts back to another woman at the table who also looks away, her glance followed by another view of a pest-covered wall. The camera next returns to the room, recording the household activities of the women. Then the scene shifts again — this time a woman passes into another room, seemingly of the same home, and serves men at a table. The camera then observes the men praying. Thus, through the magic of editing, the filmmakers have constructed a fictional space, the "normal ghetto home," and cast it as documentary fact.

The crowd shots of the ghetto, medium close-ups of Jews, young and old, working and living in their miserable quarters, schools, and synagogues are later dispersed throughout the film after their use in the film's initial sequence. Each time ghetto footage is used, the film repeats its claims that it depicts the daily lives of Jews. The narrator describes the Jews as lazy, given to trading and bartering rather than honest work. He says that they prefer their filthy conditions; they are not like the Germans. Moreover, they represent a danger to any German who dares to pity them.

This sequence also demonstrates the film's use of cinematic techniques to construct an image of "world Jewry." By using close-up and medium close-up shots, dissolves, and fades, the filmmakers create a sequence that represents Jews as criminals unmasked. This segment begins with a series of quick mug shots of Polish Jews in traditional Orthodox dress. The screen fades to black and then reveals a close-up of a bearded Jewish man wearing a hat and glasses. This image then dissolves into another shot in which the same man is shown, now shorn of his beard and dressed as a west European businessman. The screen fades to another man, shot so that about three-fourths of his body can be seen. He too is an Orthodox Polish Jew, dressed in a caftan and yarmulke. This medium shot dissolves into a close-up of the same man. Again through the dissolve, he is transformed into an assimilated Jew, shaved and in western dress.[9] The sequence of medium shot, close up, dissolve to shaven, westernized Jew is repeated once more. The sequence ends with a cut to a line-up of six Polish Jews in Orthodox dress, including those just transformed. As the camera pans down this line, with careful editing, the same Jews reappear at the end of the line, this time all shaven and westernized. The film thus creates an illusion that claims to reveal the Jews' methods of infiltrating society.

This unmasking sequence visually and aurally reinforces the allegedly criminal nature of the Jews. The segment opens with close-ups of individual Jews that imitate mug shots, and it ends with what can only be described as a police lineup. Such representations of the Jews as criminals reassert the message in the narration immediately preceding the sequence, in which the commentator compares the Jews to rats as the screen fills with the film's infamous images of rats scurrying about. The narration then claims, "This Jewish race of parasites is responsible for most international crime" (Hornshøj 60). The narrator supports his claim by giving statistics on Jewish involvement in various kinds of crimes. For example, the film's unseen expert asserts that Jews conducted ninety-eight percent of all prostitution in 1932. Such statistics, attributed even to a specific year, are typical of the film's invention of facts to prove its anti-Semitic message. In this way, fabricated facts and cinematic sleight of hand combine to concoct the film's leading villain: the assimilated Jew.

By fabricating the criminal nature of the Jews, the film sets up the viewer for a variation on the theme of "Jew-as-criminal" and the "Jew-as-undetectable-interloper" illustrated in the unmasking sequence. Not only are the Jews "other" in terms of daily life and morality, but (and even more dangerous) they attempt to conceal their inherent difference by masquerading as Aryans. As the film exposes the Jewish attempt to assimilate into western society, the narration drives the message home:

> These physiognomies refute conclusively the liberal theories of the equality of all men. Jews change their outward appearance when they leave their Polish haunts for the wider world. Hair, beard, skullcap, and caftan make the Eastern Jew recognizable to all. If he appears without his trademarks, only the sharp-eyed can recognize his racial

origins. It is an intrinsic trait of the Jew that he always tries to hide his origin when he is among non-Jews.

A bunch of Polish Jews — now wearing caftans — now ready to steal into Western civilization (Hornshøj 60–61).

The film's images and narration, then, substantiate the idea that Jews are criminals and that only experts can see through the Jews' assimilation disguise. As if to acknowledge the viewer's observation that the film's metamorphosed Jews appear incapable of fooling anyone, the narrator explains that "Of course, these ghetto Jews do not yet know how to look at ease in fine European suits" (Hornshøj 61). The film then cuts to a clip of men and women in evening dress at a party. Nothing indicates that these are Jews, other than the narrator's claim. And that is precisely the point. Once Jews begin adopting western dress and manners they become undetectable and therefore dangerous. This innocuous film clip ends the unmasking sequence by underscoring earlier themes while offering more visual fabricated evidence. To make the seamless nature of these sequences and the narration clear, consider the text and bear in mind the images that accompany them:

A bunch of Polish Jews — now wearing caftans — now ready to steal into Western civilization [unmasking sequence]. Of course, these ghetto Jews do not yet know how to look at ease in fine European suits [clip of the party]. These Berlin Jews are more adept. Their fathers and forefathers lived in ghettos, but that's not apparent now. Here in the second and third generation, Aryanization has reached its zenith. Outwardly they try to imitate their hosts. People lacking in intuition let themselves be deceived by this mimicry and think of Jews as just the same as they are. Therein lies the dreadful danger. These assimilated Jews remain forever foreign bodies in the organism of their hosts, no matter how they seem to appear outwardly (Hornshøj 61).

Again, the film's commentary reinforces and even calls to mind images that the viewer has already seen: the opening shots of the Jews "as they really are" in the Polish ghettos; the criminality of the Jews, "proven" with images and statistics; the scene of the scurrying rats and the equation of Jews to vermin; and finally the unmasking sequence. In this way, *Der ewige Jude* reiterates its message through images, narration, and music, even as the film simultaneously rolls forward with its message. This segment of the film also carries with it a subtle subtext that rises to the surface at the end of the film. Most Germans cannot see through the Jews' many disguises, but the National Socialist regime can; the Third Reich will end the subterfuge once and for all.

Throughout, *Der ewige Jude* hammers its anti-Semitic message into its audience. The incessant narration and pacing of the film were designed to avoid any possibility for the viewer to reflect on the message or images. Indeed, the film is both tedious and oppressive as it drives forward with what can be best described as a cinematic *Blitzkrieg* of anti-Semitism. The film's oppression of the audience underscores the differences between this film and most other documentaries. *Der ewige Jude*, unlike other documentary films, does not appeal to the intellect and does not invite audience reflection. Instead, the film operates on a visceral level, arousing fears, feeding prejudices, and confirming, if not fomenting, audience hatred of the film's object of interest, the Jews. In part, such an assault on the audience — and on the Jews — serves the filmmakers well, for it assists the audience's willingness to accept the ideological gloss placed upon the supposedly objective documentary images of the Polish ghettos. Moreover, the film's pacing facilitates the collapse of the always-thin line between the real and the fictional by placing an equal value on documentary film and fictional film and by using them interchangeably.

In so doing, the film orchestrates an emotional response from the audience much in the same way that feature films do. The film operates on two levels, both of which confuse fiction and fact in order to legitimate and represent the National Socialist worldview. It uses narrative films to lend the documentary the emotional impact of a feature movie while simultaneously using documentary footage to provide the fictional film with the semblance of objective truth.

In all, at least seven feature films are spliced in throughout *Der ewige Jude*. These clips perform two vital, often interrelated functions. Feature film clips that have been removed from their context are either transformed into mini-documentaries of past Jewish crimes, or they are used to condemn the Jews and their influence on German culture. I will return to the latter function later in the article. Here I would like to focus on the filmmakers' use of an American feature film, *The House of Rothschild*.

Released in the United States in 1934, *The House of Rothschild* was directed by Alfred Werker and starred George Arliss, Boris Karloff, Loretta Young and Robert Young. In *Der ewige Jude*, Hippler splices together clips from this Hollywood film to construct supposedly objective, non-German testimony to provide further evidence against the Jews. These clips immediately follow the unmasking sequence discussed previously. With its scenes removed from their context and mistranslated, the clips of *The House of Rothschild* seem to advance the narrator's claim that assimilated Jews can only change their outward appearance, not their inner essence. The narration also reinforces earlier themes as the clips are introduced:

Here we show an excerpt from a film, about the House of Rothschild. American Jews produced it as a tribute to one of the greatest names in Jewish history. They honor them here in typical Jewish manner, delighting in the way old Meier Amschel Rothschild cheats the state which made him welcome by feigning poverty to avoid paying taxes (Hornshøj 61).

In the first clip, Meier Amschel Rothschild urges his children to act hungry as he hides his money (and the roast beef!) from the approaching tax collector. As the tax collector and his men search the house for the hoarded gold, *Der ewige Jude* provides no context to explain the clip's original argument that the family must hide its wealth because Jews were taxed much more heavily than the non-Jewish businessmen. Instead, the film substantiates everything the viewer has seen about the Jews in the ghettos and heard from the narrator: the Jews do hoard their money; they do pretend to be poor; they are bilking their "host countries" out of money and trade. Thus this excerpt from a fictional film is recast as documentary evidence and fiction is recast as truth. As a result, the Rothschild family represents the National Socialist image of all Jewry.

This collapse of fiction into fact develops further in the next clip from *The House of Rothschild*. Amschel Rothschild, now old, lies in bed surrounded by his five sons. He tells them that they should each open banks in different European capitals and aid one another in building their businesses. This last excerpt, which seems to be two clips carefully spliced, becomes the foundation for the film's next theme: the Jews have created a network of financial markets that enable World Jewry to control the flow of international capital.[10] The Rothschild film clip thus transports viewers back into time and allows them to peer over the shoulders of the Jews as they hatch their international financial conspiracy! After the clip is shown, the narrator conducts viewers back into the present, and helps them interpret the consequences of the plot they have "witnessed":

By the beginning of the twentieth century, the Jews sit at the junctions of the world's financial markets. They are an international power. Though but 1% of the world's population, with their capital they terrorize the world stock exchanges, world opinion, and world politics (Hornshøj 62).

The narrator then continues, re-documenting this theme of financial collusion with still photographs and newsreel segments of New York City, its stock exchange, and leading Americans, Englishmen, Frenchmen, and Germans whom he derides as Jews. This list includes the "half-Jewish mayor of New York, La Guardia," the secretary of the treasury under Franklin D. Roosevelt, Henry Morgenthau, and the first Socialist premier of France, Leon Blum. The film thus doubles back to the earlier theme: that outwardly a Jew may appear to be fully assimilated, but underneath he remains "a rootless parasite, even when in power. His power does not come from his own strength, it lasts only as long as his misguided hosts are prepared to carry him on their backs" (Hornshøj 62).

Thus documentary film, newsreels, and photographs of real people frame *The House of Rothschild*, a fictional feature film. Such juxtaposition of the fictional with what can be purported as truth blurs the distinction between fiction and reality. Careful editing and narration here support the claim made in the opening credits that *Der ewige Jude* is a documentary film. By blending some facts with ideologically-driven fictions, all within the larger framework of a documentary film, these clips from *The House of Rothschild* are invested with a new and wholly National Socialist meaning. Deprived of its original context — and even its original narrative — this American film lends yet another layer of fabricated truth to *Der ewige Jude*.

Thus far in the film, Hippler has used narration, editing, and intercut documentary with fictional films to construct the National Socialist image of "the eternal Jew" in a natural environment. In roughly the middle of the movie, the filmmakers change tactics. Rather than documenting Jewish ghetto life and criminality, the film alters its focus by orchestrating a sequence that contrasts "pure German" art and values with the "racially degenerate" culture of the Weimar Republic. Even as this segment refers to earlier themes and images, it raises the emotional ante. Here, claims the film, is what happened when those disguised, criminal Jews infected German political and cultural life. Just before this section, the film uses documentary footage to demonstrate just how the German Jews seized control of the Weimar Republic and its professions: "Not by honest work," the narrator informs the viewer, "but by usury, swindling and fraud," all of which were portrayed earlier in the documentary segments shot in the Polish ghettos (Hornshøj 63). But not only have the Jews taken control over and thus perverted German finances, government, and professional life; according to this section of *Der ewige Jude*, they have also taken possession of German culture.

Moreover, the narrator claims that the German idea of art is foreign to the Jew, who represents a danger of its corruption:

Jews are most dangerous when they meddle in a people's culture, religion and art, and pass judgement on it. The Nordic concept of beauty is completely incomprehensible to the Jew and always will be. The rootless Jew has no feeling for the purity and neatness of the German idea of art (Hornshøj 63).

With these comments, Bach's *Toccata and Fugue in D Minor* begins to play, and icons of supposedly Nordic sculpture appear on the screen. The black background sets off the white marble of the sculptures and provides an absence of context. According to the Nazi conception of art, these "Aryan" works were eternal; the stark black-and-white contrast underscores their timeless nature. The images scroll down the screen, fading in and out, at times superimposed upon each other.

The procession begins with the Parthenon, followed by Ancient Greek and Roman sculpture. A black break in the sequence signals a new age, capped, as in the first segment, by an architectural piece. Just as the Ancient Greek and Roman works appeared beneath the Parthenon, the medieval works are housed beneath Gothic vaults. These vaults frame the Bamberger Reiter, a perennial *völkisch* (nationalist) and Nazi example of Nordic art.[11] The figure's female equivalent, the statue of Ute von Ballenstedt from the Naumburg cathedral appears beneath him and on the left side of the screen. Then the head of what may be an Adam figure dissolves in on the lower right of the Ballenstedt image; finally the head of a woman, perhaps Eve, dissolves in slightly below and to the left of the Adam.

As in the ancient art section, the placement of the medieval figures in the frame alternates from left to right and then to the center. Similarly, the gazes of the images also vary as they look left, right, or directly at the viewers. Such alteration of placement and gaze combines with the downward scrolling to add an element of movement to the otherwise static figures. The variation of placement and gaze continues as Botticelli's *Venus*, Michelangelo's *Birth of Adam*, and a representation of a Madonna and Child float solemnly down the screen.

The "Nordic art" having been displayed, the film suddenly shifts from scrolling to a series of very fast cuts, fades, dissolves, and layering of black-and-white shots of modernist paintings and sculpture. The music changes, too. Most of the modern art section has either the narrator speaking or a continuation of Bach's fugue, faintly heard. The minor chords of the organ lend a sinister tone to the fleeting Expressionist images. About halfway through this sequence, the music changes from Bach to indistinct jazz.[12] The pace of the modern art segment is chaotic throughout as the photographs of modernist art flicker across the screen. The narrator explains the confusion:

> What he [the Jew] calls art must titillate his degenerate nerves. A smell of fungus and disease must pervade it; art must be unnatural, grotesque, perverted, or pathological. These pictures, fevered fantasies of incurably sick minds, were once extolled by Jewish art critics as outstanding. These days we find it hard to believe such pieces were once purchased by almost every state and city gallery. Jewish art dealers and Jewish artists extolled them as the only true modern works of arts [sic]. German cultural life was niggerized and bastardized — painting, architecture, literature and music — all suffered in the same way. For more than a decade Jews wielded their pernicious power: as art dealers, music publishers, editors and critics. They decided what should be art and culture in Germany (Hornshøj 63).

At least some of viewers would find the arguments and even the images familiar. The works shown in this segment had been defamed on many previous occasions, most infamously as part of the *Entartete Kunst* (Degenerate Art) exhibition that traveled throughout the Reich from 1937 through 1939. Indeed, this segment of the film is kind of a mini-exhibition of degenerate art on film. It also appears that the November 1937 exhibition *Der ewige Jude* contained a section on degenerate art. Although information is sketchy, most scholars agree that for the film *Der ewige Jude*, Hippler adapted the art segment as well as the later segment on "Jewish film" from this exhibition.[13]

Throughout this art segment, the film once again constructs a Nazi reality. Sculpture by the Ancient Greeks and Romans and by medieval and Renaissance artists are transformed into expressions of the eternal, culture-producing Germans.[14] The film then reinterprets paintings and sculpture created by Germans as visual proof of the Jewish invasion of and control over German culture during the Weimar Republic. Using film techniques that serve to distance the viewer from the artworks shown strengthens the claim that modernist art was alien to Germans. For instance, modern paintings, for which color was a crucial ingredient, are shown in black-and-white photographs. The stills also flash across the screen in a series of more than forty rapid-fire cuts, visually representing the uneven rhythms of jazz, also considered degenerate. In this way the audience is manipulated into reacting on an emotional level and submitting to the narrator's conclusion that what they see is abnormal. At the end of the sequence, a film clip of black male and female singers overlaps the paintings as the strains of a jazz song reinforce the narration. This juxtaposition visually and aurally represents the Nazi contention that degenerate art and music were somehow simultaneously Jewish and black.[15]

A long litany of prominent Germans accused of being Jewish follows this segment to further emphasize the scope of Jewish penetration into German culture: newsreel clips and photographs name Kurt Tucholsky, Alfred Hirschfeld, "the 'relativity' Jew Einstein," and Max Reinhardt, among others (Hornshøj 63). This list of Jews prominent during the Weimar Republic then dissolves into a commentary on the corrupt, infected, and degenerate nature of Weimar film culture.

The segment on Weimar film continues the film's thematic leitmotifs while again sharpening the emotional impact of the film's message. Just as the previous section on degenerate art turned the republic's culture against itself, here the Nazis appropriate Weimar cinema as proof of the Jewish corruption of all things German. This section of *Der ewige Jude* uses clips from six feature films. With the exception of *Der Purimshpiler* (The Purim Player, a k a The Jester, 1937) — a Yiddish film made in Poland by Joseph Green — all were made in Germany. These clips, however, are not simply used to demonstrate the supposed Jewish influence in the German film industry before 1933. Rather they are transformed into visual proof of Jewish conspiracies and degeneracy. Just as "Jewish, Weimar" art infiltrated and poisoned "German culture," claims the film, so "Jewish, Weimar" film demonstrates the extent of the Jews' invasion into Germany. Again, fictional films become documentary evidence to prove the National Socialist belief system.

The narrator claims that Jews controlled the Prussian Ministry of Culture, and numerous theaters and cabarets. Film clips of the director Max Reinhardt and film director Richard Oswald follow to substantiate this assertion. Then the film turns once again to feature films — and specifically to comedies, which to the Nazi eye are not at all amusing — to claim that: "The presentation of all that is disreputable and repellent for Jews becomes a subject for comedy" (Hornshøj 63).

Once *Der ewige Jude* returns to feature films, the filmmakers edit in a brief clip from *Spione* (Spies, 1928) in which only the lower part of Rosa Valetti's face can be seen. The shot focuses its attention on her torso, her legs splayed as she sits facing the audience. The unspoken text is that she is a prostitute, and not only in films. A clip of Jewish comedian Curt Bois from *Der Fürst von Pappenheim* (The Prince of Pappenheim, 1927) follows the clip of Valetti. Dressed as a woman, Bois plays out a comedy of mistaken identity. The voice-over informs us that Bois is enjoying a "particularly perverted role," but the implication of homosexuality would be clear to anyone who lived in the Third

Reich (Hornshøj 63). According to the film, this cinematic role proves that Bois enjoys dressing in drag, and perhaps worse.

After an excerpt from the film *Der Mörder Dimitri Karamasoff* (The Murderer Dimitri Karamasoff, 1931), the filmmakers splice in yet another clip from a feature film, this time Fritz Lang's *M*. Here, Peter Lorre, portraying a murderer of children, confesses his maniacal compulsion to the city's criminals who have tracked him down. Yet again, *Der ewige Jude* transforms an excerpt of a feature film into a visual statement of "fact" while distorting the film's original intent. Before the clip, the narrator claims that the film exonerates the murderer while blaming the children for their own deaths. Reinterpreted in such a way, *M* becomes a film made by Jews, portraying the Nazi version of Jewish values, and starring a Jew. And, Lorre's part in *M* becomes documentary proof of Jewish criminality and immorality, themes already introduced in *Der ewige Jude*. That is, the film implies that "Lorre the Jew" is not just an actor playing a part; he *is* a child murderer.

This reinterpretation of Lorre as an actual Jewish murderer of children plays upon the viewers' emotions, evoking a visceral rejection of Lorre's character, of the film itself, and of Weimar film and Jews in general. In this instance, *Der ewige Jude* also tacitly but powerfully evokes an age-old prejudice that existed well beyond the confines of both Weimar- and Nazi-era films. That is the filmmakers intended the *M* clip to remind viewers of the familiar charge of blood libel, the fictional Jewish sacrifice of Christian children.[16] By using Weimar-era feature films to legitimate ancient anti-Jewish myths, *Der ewige Jude* transforms both fictions into fact. At the same time, the theme of blood libel foreshadows a later scene in the movie and will be remembered then, during the scene of the kosher slaughter.

The Nazis themselves recognized the effect of this blurring of reality by using feature film footage. In his article for the journal *Der Deutsche Film*, the critic Erwin Goetz, writing under the pseudonym of Frank Maraun, explained the function of the fictional film clips in *Der ewige Jude* by using what can only be described as Nazi logic:

> The quotes from the feature films do not, however, call into question the documentary character of the film. These quotations will be clearly announced, so that even the most unknowledgeable viewer will be able to distinguish clearly between what is reality and what is fiction. Moreover, the feature film episodes that are edited into the film maintain . . . the sense and significance of documentary proof. When there are scenes with Jewish actors from German films of the Weimar Republic [*Systemzeit*], scenes with Fritz Kortner, Rosa Valetti, Curt Bois, Siegfried Arno, Fritz Grünebaum, Curt Gerron and Peter Lorre,

then here too, fiction becomes reality. It is the reality of the cultural activity of the Jews in the cultural life of their host people. Such activity by the Jews means destruction, immorality, perversion, enslavement through media in every form . . . and also the glorification of impudence, of insolence, of hatred for the law, of sympathy for the criminal. Fiction reflects reality in the excerpts from films which were shot in pre-war Poland by Jews for Jews.[17]

For the Nazis, fiction and reality are interchangeable. Goetz places equal value upon the documentary footage shot in Poland, the section on Jewish art, and the film excerpts in the Weimar film sequence. Additionally, he points to the film's self-referential character. As I have shown, *Der ewige Jude* constantly refers back to earlier themes, images, and arguments as the film moves toward its conclusion. However, understanding the film's repetition of themes as well as materials is a complicated enterprise. Perhaps by focusing on one final segment of the film, its self-referential nature can be laid bare.

According to the above quote from Goetz, "Fiction reflects reality in the excerpts from films which were shot in pre-war Poland by Jews for Jews." This statement refers to the use of *Der Purimshpiler* in *Der ewige Jude*. Now a Yiddish classic, the comedy *Der Purimshpiler* plays on the notion of Purim, a Jewish festival primarily for children. The clip used in *Der ewige Jude* shows a lively crowd seated around a long dining table, eating with table manners that are less than perfect. Viewers cannot tell what all the raucous discussion is about because the dialogue is in Yiddish, the subtitles are difficult to read, and the narrator's voice frequently drowns out the dialogue. However, viewers do not have to try to comprehend this excerpt because the narrator interprets for them:

> The following scenes show the Jewish festival of Purim, photographed by Warsaw Jews themselves for use in a cultural film. This harmless-looking family celebration commemorates the slaughter of 75,000 anti-Semitic Persians by Biblical ancestors of our present-day Jews. The Bible says that on the next day, the Jews rested, feasting and exchanging presents. They agreed to name the two days Purim, insisting it be remembered by their children's children, from one generation unto another.

> Educated Germans, objective and tolerant, regarded such tales as folklore or an example of some strange custom. But that is the tribe of Israel rubbing its hands and celebrating this feast of vengeance, even if the bowdlerized West European clothing conceals the Eastern origins of present-day Israelites (Hornshøj 64).

The narrator constructs several reinterpretations here. First, *Der ewige Jude* recasts the comedy *Der Purimshpiler* as a documentary. The film's comic elements are now intended to produce a kind of disgusted laughter among the Nazis' audience. Or to put it another way, the audience no longer laughs with the film's characters but at them. Appearing within the framework of *Der ewige Jude*, this clip turns *Der Purimshpiler* against itself, thereby retaining the cinematic strengths of the clip — especially its comedy — but reinterpreting the humor in a way not originally intended. Thus, the comedy is distorted into a film that the Jews made themselves as a cultural or educational film. It contains documentary value because it shows the Jews not only as they really are, but as they see themselves.

Second, the narration completely reinvents the events and meaning of Purim. No longer a celebration of the defeat of Haman and his plan to exterminate the people of Mordecai, a plan that even the Persian king recognized as indefensible, *Der ewige Jude* transforms Purim into a feast marking the extermination of anti-Semites. It also ignores the Purim tradition of refusing to gloat over the defeat of the Persians.

Finally, the narrator ridicules Germans tolerant of Jewish ritual. He berates such Germans for failing to understand that beneath surface appearances, the Jews are celebrating murder — just as they do not understand that while Jews might look like Germans, underneath they are really the enemy. In this way, the film circles back to the unmasking sequence and to the film segment that showed clips of two "Jewish murderers" — Dimitri Karamasoff and Peter Lorre's character in *M*. The narrative explanation of Purim also prepares the viewer for yet another scene in which the film claims Jews relish the slaughter of innocents — the sequence depicting the ritual slaughter of animals at the close of the film.

The clip of *Der Purimshpiler* in which celebrants sit around a dining table also refers back to the documentary footage shot in the Polish ghettos for the opening segment of *Der ewige Jude*. Specifically, the Purim meal — Jews around a table at home, eating with few manners — evokes the memory of the earlier scene of Jews eating a meal in the Polish ghetto. And the connection of the two segments reinforces the illusion of truth in these scenes. The first was shot in the ghettos by a camera that recorded what was really there. The Purim segment comes from a film the Jews themselves made. Each reinforces the truth of the other. Together, they validate the truth of the entire film and its indictment of the Jews.

Through the medium of film, Hippler crafted a cinematic representation of an ideological construct: anti-Semitism. Further, by relying on the medium of film — particularly film footage represented as un-staged — and billing *Der ewige Jude* as a documentary, the National Socialists invested their creation with the claim to truthfully represent "the Jews as they really are." Indeed, the silver screen provided the Na-zis with the ideal medium for constructing an alternative reality that le-gitimated and proved their ideology. With the ability to edit, to dissolve from one image to another, to mix documentary footage with fictional film, to splice together footage from a wide variety of cine-matic genres, to add music and narration, the film *Der ewige Jude* be-comes a *Gesamtkunstwerk* that portrays on multiple levels the National Socialist image of the Jew.

Der ewige Jude also marshals its visual and narrative evidence from a variety of sources and weaves them together into a seamless whole. The filmmakers edited narration, images, and even music together so that they refer to each other, tying the various themes and film segments to one another. The film's major segments also operate as mini-narratives, stories that collapse fiction and truth into the National Socialist vision. In the process, the film completely reinterprets its evidence to fulfill its role as documentary proof of that vision. As a result, *Der ewige Jude* confronts historians and others with a film that purports to be a docu-mentary and yet completely twists and misrepresents its component parts.

Ironically, in the end, this film can indeed be considered a docu-mentary, but not the documentary that the Nazis intended. It is not "a film contribution to the problem of world Jewry" as the opening titles proclaim. Instead, the film visually documents the National Socialist ideology of anti-Semitism — more than any other film produced by the Nazis. With moving and still images, documentary footage and films, music and narration, *Der ewige Jude* portrays a cinematic argument that legitimated the approaching Holocaust, the first transports of German Jews to the East beginning shortly after the film was released. This film offers us a glimpse of the world from a wholly Nazi point of view; it documents the Nazis' "reality." In the end, this might be the real value — and horror — of *Der ewige Jude.*

Es wird bald viele Kriege geben,

The makers of Der ewige Jude (1940) misuse footage from the American film The House of Rothschild (1934). Amschel Rothschild advises his sons that war is coming. Courtesy Library of Congress and Transit Film GmbH.

Der ewige Jude (1940). Through dissolves, filmmakers superimpose the Star of David on world capitols, implying international Jewish domination. Courtesy Library of Congress and Transit Film GmbH.

Notes

[1] Fritz Hippler, "Wie 'Der ewige Jude' entstand," *Der Film*, no. 48, 30 November 1940, cited in Peter Bucher, "Die Bedeutung des Films als historische Quelle: 'Der ewige Jude' (1940)" in *Festschrift für Eberhard Kessel zum 75. Geburtstag* (Munich: Fink, 1982) 300.

[2] Stig Hornshøj-Møller and David Culbert have written one of the best articles on *The Eternal Jew*, "'Der ewige Jude' (1940): Joseph Goebbels' Unequaled Monument to Anti-Semitism," *Historical Journal of Film, Radio, and Television* 12 (1992): 41–67. Hornshøj-Møller and Culbert include a chronology of the film (Appendix A, 55–56) as well as an English translation of the narrative (Appendix B, 56–67). Because it is difficult to get a copy of this film, I will cite this article's translation of the German narration, using "Hornshøj" as the abbreviated citation in the text.

Other useful texts include: Michael Siegert's "Der ewige Jude" in *Propaganda und Gegenpropaganda im Film 1933–1945* (Vienna: Österreichisches Filmmuseum, 1972) 63–79; Peter Bucher's article "Die Bedeutung des Films als historische Quelle: 'Der ewige Jude' (1940)" in *Festschrift für Eberhard Kessel zum 75. Geburtstag* (Munich: Fink, 1982) 300–329; Régine Mihal Friedman, "Juden-Ratten — Von der rassistischen Metonymie zur tierischen Metapher in Fritz Hipplers Film *Der ewige Jude*," *Frauen und Film* 47 (1989): 24–35; and Friedman's *L'image et son Juif: Le Juif dans le cinéma Nazi* (Paris: Payot, 1983), especially chapter 5.

[3] The most extensive study of the film's factual base (or rather, its lack of one) is Yizhak Ahren, Stig Hornshøj-Møller, and Christoph B. Melchers, *Der ewige Jude: Wie Goebbels hetzte: Untersuchungen zum nationalsozialistischen Propagandafilm* (Aachen: Alano, 1990).

[4] For identification of and *Bundesarchiv* catalog information on the clips used in *Der ewige Jude*, see the endnotes in Peter Bucher, "Die Bedeutung des Films als historische Quelle: 'Der ewige Jude' (1940)." For example, see 325 n. 100 (*Hände am Werk*), 326 n. 127 (*Terror oder Aufbau* and *Gestern und Heute*), and 323 n. 48 (*Juden ohne Maske*).

[5] For the newsreel clips, see Bucher, "Die Bedeutung des Films als historische Quelle: 'Der ewige Jude' (1940)," especially the endnotes on pages 325–28. The seven feature films are (roughly in the order in which they appear): *The House of Rothschild*, 1934, directed by Alfred Werker; *Spione*, 1928, directed by Fritz Lang; *Der Fürst von Pappenheim*, 1927, directed by Richard Eichberg; *Der Mörder Dimitri Karamasoff*, 1931, directed by Fyodor Otsep (a k a Fedor Ozep); *M*, 1931; and *Der Purimshpiler*, 1937, directed by Joseph Green. The scene in which the camera "flips" from a view down a Polish ghetto street to a street in what is purported to be Jerusalem may be taken

from *Land of Promise*, made by Leo Hermann in 1935. Some sources also claim there are clips from H. Berendt's film *Zucht in der Liebe* and the Yiddish classic *Yidl mitn Fidl*, however I have not been able to identify these clips in the film.

[6] According to Stig Hornshøj-Møller and David Culbert, Goebbels "tried to send a film crew to shoot in the Polish Ghetto" after the November 1938 *Kristallnacht*, or Night of Broken Glass convinced him that the Germans needed to be further educated on the dangers of the Jews. However, he could not obtain permission from the Polish government. Thus, the idea for a documentary film to instruct the German public on the finer points of anti-Semitism may have begun in November 1938, a full year before any footage was shot. See Hornshøj-Møller and Culbert, "'Der ewige Jude' (1940)," 41.

[7] The filming in Łodz, which included the scenes of the ritual slaughter and the synagogue scenes, was done 11–13 October 1939. See Hornshøj-Møller and Culbert, "'Der ewige Jude' (1940)," 53, n. 6.

[8] Fritz Hippler, *Die Judenfrage*, 28 November 1940, 188, as quoted in Hornshøj-Møller and Culbert, "'Der ewige Jude' (1940)," 48.

[9] In a similar manner, Süß Oppenheimer transforms from an Orthodox Jew into a "German" through the use of the dissolve in the film *Jud Süß*, released just a few months before *Der ewige Jude* in 1940.

[10] The makers of *Der ewige Jude* left nothing to chance in this segment and went so far as to misrepresent the translated subtitles. The original film has Amschel saying to his sons: "Our five banking houses may cover Europe, but you will be one firm, one family, the Rothschilds, who will always work together." The subtitles here, however, read: "Unsere fünf Bankhäuser werden Europa beherrschen." (Our five banking houses will control Europe.)

[11] For another example of the Bamberger Reiter as a favorite symbol for the National Socialists as well as for *völkisch* groups, see issues of *Das Bild*, a monthly magazine published by the German Art Society from 1934–1944. The profile of the Bamberger Reiter typically graced the magazine's masthead, and was used by the German Art Society throughout the 1920s.

[12] For more on degenerate music see Michael Kater, *Different Drummers: Jazz in the Culture of Nazi Germany* (New York: Oxford UP, 1992) and idem, *The Twisted Muse: Musicians and their Music in the Third Reich* (New York: Oxford UP, 1997).

[13] The clips from the movies *Der Fürst von Pappenheim, Der Mörder Dimitri Karamasoff*, and *M* were taken from the earlier film *Juden ohne Maske* which played as part of the 1937 exhibition also called *Der ewige Jude*. According to Peter Bucher, at least part of this film — available only on nitrate stock — is located in the Bundesarchiv-Filmarchiv, Zg. Nr. 53 789.

[14] Nazis borrowed the argument that the Germans descended from "culture-producing" Aryans of Greece, Rome, and Italy from nineteenth-century racial theorists. See for example, Houston Stewart Chamberlain, *Foundations of the*

Nineteenth Century, 2 vols., trans. John Lees, with an introduction by George Mosse (New York: Howard Fertig, 1968); Arthur de Gobineau, *Essay on the Inequality of the Human Races*, trans. Adrian Collins (New York: Putnam's Sons, 1915). Two of the better secondary treatments of Nazi art and racial theories are Franz Roh, "*Entartete*" *Kunst: Kunstbarbarei im Dritten Reich* (Hannover: Fäckeltraeger Verlag, 1962), and the collection of documents in Joseph Wulf, *Die bildenden Künste im Dritten Reich: Eine Dokumentation* (Gütersloh: Siegbert Mohn Verlag, 1963).

[15] The claim that degenerate art was Jewish and "Negro," as well as Marxist, was a constant theme of both the Nazis and the *völkisch* cultural critics of the 1920s. The Nazis also launched a "Degenerate Music" exhibition in 1938, a kind of musical equivalent to the "Degenerate Art" exhibit. The main advertising poster for the degenerate music show had a caricature of a Black man — complete with swollen lips — who sported a Star of David badge on his lapel.

[16] For an excellent treatment of the blood libel and its impact before the Third Reich, see for example, Sander L. Gilman, "Kafka Wept," *Modernism\Modernity* 1 (January 1994): 17–37. See also the very brief treatment of this segment of the film in Hans-Jürgen Brandt, *NS-Filmtheorie und dokumentarische Praxis: Hippler, Noldan, Junghans* (Tübingen: Max Niemeyer Verlag, 1987) 64.

[17] This quote has been edited in the translation because most of the original text is one extremely long sentence. Frank Maraun, "Symphonie des Ekels: *Der ewige Jude* — ein abendfüllender Dokumentfilm," *Der deutsche Film* 4 (1940): 157, cited in Brandt, *NS-Filmtheorie und Dokumentarische Praxis*, 73–74.

8

ROGER RUSSI

Escaping Home: Leni Riefenstahl's
Visual Poetry in Tiefland

LENI RIEFENSTAHL'S FACE glows with mystery and beauty in *Das blaue Licht* (The Blue Light, 1932), a film that she both directs and casts herself in the leading role. The face belongs to Junta, a witch, a wild woman, and a nature child whom Riefenstahl ultimately immortalizes in a portrait contained within a medallion that appears at the film's end. Many years later, at the end of *Tiefland* (Lowlands, 1954) Riefenstahl takes this idolization a step further. The camera presents Riefenstahl again, this time as a Spanish beggar-dancer, Martha, a Gypsy-like figure, walking at the film's end up a mountain, past the camera, and into a blazing sunset. The figures of Junta and Martha are both representations (of Riefenstahl as the character) and self-representations (of Riefenstahl as Riefenstahl), each attaining a form of apotheosis. Junta becomes a sacrificial lamb or saint. Martha rises to the mountain heights with the sunset blazing halo-like around her. Finally, Riefenstahl godlike comes to life every time her films are played.

The figure whom Riefenstahl plays in both films is what Siegfried Kracauer once loosely defined as "a sort of gypsy girl" (1947, 258). Both Martha and Junta are extreme outsiders. The two films clearly show that they can never earn the trust of the villagers. Their attempts at dialogue or interaction remain unreciprocated, and even elicit violent reactions from the villagers. Riefenstahl creates these mysterious, romantic Gypsy figures and places them in the otherworldly sphere of fable and legend. Geographically remote mountains offer a place of freedom and bliss, while both films portray the lowlands as evil and destructive places. The avoidance of realism and the remove from reality in person, location, and genre suggest an attempt at escaping historical circumstances into pure imagery and allegory. By casting herself as Martha and Junta, Riefenstahl, by inference and very likely by design, assumes the position of the outsider, the abused other. The naive, basically good outcast who is resented by the villagers — whether they are the greedy ones from Santa Maria or the desperate ones from Roccabruna — enacts a fantastic image. In *Tiefland* especially, Riefenstahl produces this remote otherness, while exacerbating the discrepancy between the historical and the filmic present. By using Roma[1] who are inmates in a nearby Nazi concentration camp as extras for the crowd scenes in the film, she sees herself as temporarily rescuing them from the camp. The result is a pure fantasy painstakingly created while barely out of earshot the world went to pieces.

This essay examines Leni Riefenstahl's last feature film, *Tiefland*, as *the* filmic construct representing the director's escape into the aesthetic. Shot between 1940 and 1945, *Tiefland* is her return to the genres of *Heimatfilm* and *Bergfilm* and represents the most readily perceivable aspects of this escape. While Riefenstahl casts herself as the mysterious yet kind Gypsy dancer who must choose between the evil Don Sebastian of the lowlands and Pedro, the good shepherd of the mountains, the film's primary focus rests almost as much on the camera work and photography as on the narrative itself. As Ray Müller's film *Die Macht der Bilder: Leni Riefenstahl* (The Power of Images: Leni Riefenstahl; released in the United States as *The Wonderful, Horrible Life of Leni Riefenstahl*, 1993) documents, even at age ninety, Riefenstahl does not see nor care to see beyond questions of visual representation and the poetry of motion. A discussion of her films is complicated by the director's postwar revisions. For example, she completed *Tiefland* in 1954, one year after recutting *Das blaue Licht*, which suggests a conscious attempt at saving her reputation.

When Ray Müller asked Leni Riefenstahl about the production of *Tiefland*, she answered:

> It was actually an emergency solution, because I . . . let us say . . . I wanted to avoid having to make war films. I did not want to make a war film, and *Tiefland* was a neutral theme. And because the film *Olympia* made so much money, I was completely free and had sufficient money to make a film from purely artistic perspectives.[2]

While Glenn B. Infield's discussion of Riefenstahl's activities during the war years contradicts Riefenstahl's statement about her financial situation and reveals it as half-truth, I would like to draw attention to Müller's representation of her during this part of the interview (186–99). His composition seemingly recreates the kind of portrait shots that she composed of herself as Junta, Martha, and as Riefenstahl. As she speaks, Alpine peaks tower behind her against the blue sky. Whenever Müller works critically, the camera meets her gaze at eye level. With this change of perspective Müller's film goes counter to Riefenstahl's own technique to shoot upward giving her subject a larger than life appearance. On most occasions the camera focuses on Riefenstahl, eye-to-eye, showing a wide-eyed, often defiant woman in her nineties. While she repeatedly attempts to step back into the Junta and Martha personae, Müller stops her retreat with interview shots cast in a barren room with Riefenstahl sitting at a table and facing the camera. At these moments, Müller's interview turns into an interrogation.

By giving Riefenstahl a prominent voice in *Die Macht der Bilder*, Müller appears to present an objective view of one of the most notorious film directors at work during the Third Reich.[3] He allows Riefenstahl to comment on and explain her situation then and now. Thus, he permits her to participate in the decisions of her representation. For example, early in the interview during the discussion of *Das blaue Licht*, Riefenstahl fiercely argues about an appropriate perspective for the Alps as backdrop. Both Müller and his cameraman have chosen an angle that would diminish the grandeur of the mountains. In spite of Müller's nudges to address her life's work within the historical context, she remains consistent in her preoccupation with aesthetic representation.[4] Even when she is engaged in an activity as inevitably political as an interview, visual dramatization remains her foremost concern. Ever obsessed with appropriate representation, she raises the strongest objection not when Müller points out such things as samples of her correspondence that contradicts her professed relationship to Goebbels, but rather when the light, distance, and camera-angle are not set up to her liking. The extent to which Riefenstahl seeks to control her portrait occasionally approaches the ludicrous, for example, when she thinks it ridiculous to have to walk during an interview at the old Babelsberg studio. When the interview seems to have less to do with the life of Riefenstahl and more with giving the viewers an impression of the work done during the early thirties at Babelsberg, it appears Riefenstahl is ready to break off the project. While I agree with Müller that Riefenstahl considers herself a pure aesthete, as his filmic representation of her frequently confirms, his attempts at breaking that image — one which Riefenstahl herself has created — through photos and document inserts, are far too gentle. Since Riefenstahl likely would have refused to cooperate had he been more forceful or confrontational, the film ends up in a double bind between reifying Riefenstahl's image of herself and a documentary image whose historical context lends the image a semblance of truth.

To facilitate an examination of Riefenstahl's representations in *Tiefland*, a look at her first feature film *Das blaue Licht* proves helpful. The films mark the beginning and end of her career as a film director. Moreover their production spans the rise and fall of the Nazi regime. Yet since neither has any explicit reference to the politics of the Third

Reich, Riefenstahl has continued to maintain in her own defense that the films represent purely aesthetic works of art.[5]

Das blaue Licht tells the story of Junta, a young, spirited, wild woman who lives on her own. Shunned by the villagers, she suffers their hostilities daily. Her skill at climbing mountains, as well as her beauty, drives the young men wild. Junta has discovered a cave full of crystals that shine blue in the full moon. Obsessed with her or with the blue light to which only she has access, one by one the young men fall to their death trying to reach the blue light, Junta, or both. When a painter from Vienna, Vigo, comes to the village, he begins to follow Junta. Ultimately he discovers her secret and reveals it to the villagers by guiding them to the cave in the hope that Junta's and the villagers' lives will improve. Harvesting the crystals brings the villagers great wealth and at the same time ends the bane of the blue light. Young men no longer will fall to their death trying to discover its source. Junta, however, finds the cave despoiled and falls to her death in what is most likely a suicide.[6] Vigo finds her at the bottom of the mountain. The camera lingers on this final moment, zeroing in on the two faces, his above hers. The artificiality of the moment becomes apparent. True to Riefenstahl's desire to remain within the realm of the fantastic, this is a beautifully stylized death scene. Reinforcing and recalling the initial portrait shots, Riefenstahl shows the heroine enveloped in soft direct light with not a hair out of place. When the camera pulls back, it blends the valley with the mountain shadowing Santa Maria. A narrator informs us that Junta's legend lives on, telling of the great injustice done to her and of the great wealth it brought the village.

As Eric Rentschler points out, Riefenstahl actually recut this version of *Das blaue Licht* in 1953 (1996, 42).[7] The original 1932 version contains a contemporary frame to Junta's story. A car with a newly married couple arrives at the hotel in Santa Maria while a voice-over gives an account of the town. The young woman spots a medallion worn by one of the playing children. When she inquires about the face on it, someone fetches a book. Focusing on the open pages, the shot fades into the interior story. At the end of the film, the camera returns to the young woman. The last shot of the waterfall mirrors earlier scenes with Junta.[8] By removing this outer frame, Riefenstahl not only eliminates the original distance to the romantic portrait at the center but also intensifies the focus on Junta, whose face in the medallion now frames the film. The introductory credits reflect the framing medallions, as Riefenstahl's name stands at its beginning and end. The ubiquity of Junta's name reflects the repetition of Riefenstahl's name. The voice-over introduces (and concludes) Junta's legend by repeatedly naming her. For example, there is a slate tablet that displays *Historia dell Junta* (History of Junta) at the film's beginning and end. And the medallion with Junta's face blends in over the engraved tablet. As Junta's face is thus framed, immortalized, so is Riefenstahl's. The re-editing in 1953 of *Das blaue Licht* seems intended to recast Riefenstahl's image as does the allegorical *Tiefland* completed in 1954. A glowing portrait of the innocent outsider materializes from the two films, which relentlessly insists that the performer and the performed are identical, inseparable.

In *Das blaue Licht*, Riefenstahl creates not only Junta but also nature itself as the central figures of the film. Magnificent shots of peaks, waterfalls, roiling cloud formations, steep slopes, panoramic shots taking in the Sarn valley as far as the eye can see; all these images vie with the characters for dominance. Frequently, the scenery dwarfs the characters or even lets them disappear in nature. Ultimately, Riefenstahl conflates Junta and nature. As the mountain loses its mysterious light, so the disturbing outcast surrenders her life. Yet both survive, the mountain as conquered monument, Junta as a memento.

From the beginning of the film, Riefenstahl constantly presents images in which nature and Junta are fused. The first frame shows the valley with the waterfall and mountains. While a narrator begins to tell the legend of Junta, the wide view blends into a shot of a single crystal sitting in clear water. Junta's white hand appears and reaches for the crystal. As it rests in her palm, the two seem to merge. The frame blends into a full body profile shot of Junta with the mountain framing her on three sides. The camera looks up to her, holding her there like a painting. This initial portrait shot and numerous others make it easy to regard the film as a tour through a gallery of romantic paintings (Schulte-Sasse 1996). Riefenstahl creates a considerable number of shots during which the camera lingers for several seconds, just as one fully takes in a painting before moving on to the next one. Most frequently, Junta's face serves as the subject of these prolonged gazes.

Riefenstahl shows Junta's downturned eyes gazing demurely or totally focused upon the crystal. The same slightly upward angle allows the figure to fill or at times transcend the screen, giving it a towering presence. The same technique will return in *Triumph des Willens* (Triumph of the Will, 1935), *Olympia* (Olympia, 1938), and *Tiefland*. In these later films, for example, Riefenstahl presents the figures of Hitler (*Triumph des Willens* and *Olympia*) and Pedro (*Tiefland*) in the same monumentalizing way. They stand larger than life, heads raised, looking down upon their respective empires — the mass parade and the herd of sheep grazing at the mountainside. Likewise, the first shot of

Don Sebastian in *Tiefland* presents him on his horse looking down upon his fighting bulls. While Don Sebastian appears both majestic and exotic — he resembles a matador with his wide-brimmed, ornate hat — a reverse shot captures the approaching farmers as if they were a flock of gloomy, black crows. They humble themselves by dropping to their knees and removing their hats. Their gaze remains downcast. The ensuing dialogue reinforces the visually introduced power dynamics through Don Sebastian's contemptuous demeanor. Later on he will call the farmers rabble and vermin. Thus, already at the beginning of *Tiefland*, similar to the scenes that introduce Hitler in *Triumph des Willens* by having him descend out of the clouds, or Vigo by having him tower above Santa Maria, Riefenstahl invests her respective heroes with an almost overwhelming sense of power.

In *Das blaue Licht*, Riefenstahl spends considerable footage on the scene building up toward the introduction of the hero (or is he the villain?). Junta turns her head to look over the valley where Vigo is arriving in a carriage. A series of progress shots follows. As the carriage approaches the village and Vigo eventually gets out, continuing on foot, Junta descends from the mountain. Several shots show her either disappearing into the rocks next to the waterfall or reemerging from them. These shots show her mostly in silhouette and as a minute part of the landscape, which fills the screen. At the same time, Riefenstahl's use of shadow and light fuses Junta's dark figure into the dark mountainscape, while the slow moving, brightly lit pans of the camera show Vigo's approach, keeping the carriage at all times separate from the forest it traverses.

Seen at first from a bird's-eye perspective, the carriage becomes larger than the screen as the view gradually levels out. When Vigo climbs out, he is too large for the screen. Several frames show him either with his legs or his head cut off. Meanwhile Junta has reached the bottom of the waterfall and begins to dash through the dark village streets. A cut reveals Vigo with his back to the camera, looking down at the village. He appears gigantic as he sweeps his broad-brimmed hat from his head. He too, like Riefenstahl's other heroes, Hitler and Pedro, towers over the rest of the world.

Out of a dark alley, Junta darts into the light. Her open face and her dress contrast strongly with the churchgoers whom she observes. While the priest crosses himself after exchanging glances with her, three older women dressed in black eye her suspiciously. The entire scene consists of a series of full-length body portraits alternating with careful close-ups revealing the churchgoers' faces. Riefenstahl keeps these portraits separate from one another by intercutting shots showing Junta's face.

The play of dark and light, strange and familiar, open and closed facial features, invokes the absolutely clear-cut, either-or world of fairy tales, a point to which I will return in more detail below. Interestingly, while Junta is seen in bright light, in a complete reversal from the nature scenes, all the villagers seem dark, almost sinister. After this intense identification of camera-eye with Junta's gaze, the camera follows the churchgoers inside and introduces Lucia and Tonio. In Tonio the obsessions for the blue light and for Junta are completely fused. Lucia's appearance lets her disappear into her surroundings as much as Junta's lets her stand out.

Junta and Vigo do not meet until the next day, after another young man has killed himself on Mount Cristallo and an angry mob chases after her. The villagers perceive Junta and the mountain as one. Their mysterious powers, the remoteness, invincibility, her gaze and the blue light, all are seen as forces robbing the young men of their senses. Not being able to conquer either the mountain or Junta, the young men despair. Escaping the mob, twice Junta flits away out of the village, always from the dark into the light, from the village path into nature. In nature again, Riefenstahl reverses the play of shadow and light when shown from a distance. The climbing scenes frequently show Junta's silhouette, allowing her to disappear into the dark of the mountain, only always to reemerge. This is the case when Vigo and Tonio follow her to the cave. While Tonio becomes the last young man to fall to his death, perhaps as penance for having been one of the villagers who attacked Junta, Vigo continues to follow her through the cave to her lookout. There she bathes in the moonlight. The next day, when Vigo tries to communicate his intentions about the cave of crystals to her, it becomes apparent that they do not speak the same language. Riefenstahl uses Junta's near-muteness to set her apart. Fritz Göttler, quoting Enno Patalas, makes the point that the films of Riefenstahl may have come closest to the Nazi ideal of a purely musical and visual film in which speech has become virtually superfluous.[9] Thus, in *Das blaue Licht*, Junta has only a few lines. She talks mostly to Guzzi, the shepherd boy.[10] The minimal dialogue highlights her otherness, her otherworldliness. The near static presentation of the interaction between Vigo and Junta results in a series of portrait-shots, drawing attention to the singularity of each portrait moment, which evoke Riefenstahl rather than Junta.

Upon Vigo's revelation concerning the crystal cave, the villagers triumphantly pillage the mountain. When Junta climbs back to her cave, the camera follows her to the precipice. She lets herself fall. There is a cut to Vigo, who follows Junta's path until he comes upon her in a meadow. As he takes her in his arms, her face glows brightly. Even in death she is beautiful and glowing, "a beautiful soul, purity of desire, generous, purpose-less being. Her body is yearning and image" (Wysocki 75). This dramatic moment mirrors the scene from the film's opening sequence, wherein Junta's hand gently picks up a glowing crystal. Similarly, the camera again blends to the stone tablet with the title "Junta's story" before the next frame shows her face in the medallion. The last shot shows the same view of the village as in the film's opening sequence. The narrator concludes his story by iterating its moral: Junta's sacrifice for the village's wealth. A simple voice-over transforms the villagers' animosity that accompanied all of their encounters with her into a tale of adoration. Now sanctified, Junta has become larger than life, similar to the mountain. At the same time, mirroring the camera's first move from the mountain, which it can capture only imperfectly, to the view of a single crystal, Junta ends up trapped in the medallion, a sentimental commodity.

The production of *Tiefland*, with its many interruptions and setbacks, spanned nearly the entire Nazi era and extended into the first years of the Federal Republic. All told, it lasted twenty years from 1934 to 1954. Riefenstahl insists that the film focuses on a neutral subject. With it, she intended to celebrate the black and white medium at the time when color began to take over film. Nevertheless, it is important to review the political context within which she produced *Tiefland*. Robert von Dassanowsky suggests that the film should be considered as "a work of inner emigration" (125). Perhaps if Riefenstahl had completed the film during the war we could have read her retreat from documentary into allegory as a conscious attempt to reject Nazism by turning away from public events and toward private concerns. But the late date of the film's final cut, 1954, weakens this interpretation. I do not claim that there is a direct correspondence between the historical events and the production of the film, but they constitute the backdrop.

While the SS killed the leadership of the SA during the "Night of the Long Knives" on the weekend of 30 June 1934, Riefenstahl was in Spain preparing to film *Tiefland*. She fell ill and had to stop her work on the film. Riefenstahl shelved the project when she was commissioned to shoot *Triumph des Willens* and *Tag der Freiheit: Unsere Wehrmacht* (Day of Freedom: Our Armed Forces, 1935). She then went to Hitler in order to gain the rights to shoot and produce *Olympia* between 1936 and 1938.[11] After accompanying the troops on the 1939 invasion of Poland as a war correspondent and having observed the execution of civilians, possibly Jews, she returned to Berlin and soon resumed her work on *Tiefland*. Surprisingly, Riefenstahl had the freedom and status to return to Berlin, despite having been commandeered to accompany the soldiers. Able to continue her old project, she sent her production manager, cameraman, and art director to Spain to begin preparations to continue the shooting of *Tiefland*.

The invasion of France forced her team to relocate to the Karwendel Mountains. As Riefenstahl recalled in 1992, "on the hilly meadows in Krün near Mittenwald, the mill, the citadel, and our film village Roccabruna were reconstructed in the style of their Spanish counterparts" (1992, 265). But to her dismay, the village was not built according to her specifications and had to be rebuilt. She discovered Franz Eichberger, who would play Pedro, and sent him to Berlin for elocution training while she went to scout for locations in the Dolomites. Her friend and one time mentor Arnold Fanck eventually shot the introductory scenes of *Tiefland* where Pedro kills the wolf, but Riefenstahl considered the bulk of the footage unusable because he had shot from too great a distance from the half-tame wolf.

During this time, two of Riefenstahl's filmcrew members, Harald Reinl and Hugo Lehner, selected Roma as extras from a concentration camp near Salzburg (Zigeunerlager Leopoldskron). Riefenstahl to this day denies that Roma extras were borrowed from a concentration camp.[12] She also insists that she met them again after the collapse of the Third Reich, implying that they had survived the war (267). Yet Müller, in his documentary *Die Macht der Bilder*, inserts a series of photos and documents that contradict Riefenstahl's personal account of the events. He supplies, for example, two photographs of Romani families, a photo of a truck filled with Roma and another truck with a German officer in front of the truck directing traffic. Müller also includes a list of the Roma men and children documenting their employment for her production company, Riefenstahl Film Limited.

Between 1941 and 1944 Riefenstahl completed most of the on-site and studio filming of *Tiefland*, although with great difficulties. Her art directors, Erich Grave and Isabella Ploberger, created the interior of the citadel at the studio in Babelsberg. Around the time Riefenstahl began filming in the studio, the first allied air raids on Berlin took place. There was another hiatus when Riefenstahl fell seriously ill. By 1943 Riefenstahl's production company was apparently near bankruptcy.[13] Letters from that time document her struggle for further financial support (Infield 187). About the time Kurt Gerron received a direct order from Goebbels to make a documentary about Theresienstadt, Riefenstahl secured studio space in Prague, where she began editing *Tiefland*. Helma Sanders-Brahms notes that Riefenstahl finished shooting the film in May 1945 (176). When the Allies declared victory, the film was in the process of being synchronized. American forces chanced upon her in her mountain retreat near Innsbruck, where members of the French forces eventually confiscated all her film materials. Between 1949 and 1952 Riefenstahl faced the Baden State Commission for Political Cleansing, which ultimately attested her status as fellow traveler [*Mitläufer*], someone who followed the dictates of the Nazi regime without either opposing nor supporting it. She fought to retrieve her confiscated film materials. She then proceeded to put together *Tiefland* in spite of several lost parts, including materials from Spain that were intended to highlight Don Sebastian's background (Berg-Pan 166).

Tiefland relates the story of Martha, a Gypsy dancer, and the shepherd Pedro. Pedro lives a simple life high in the mountains. After defeating a wolf that preyed on his herd in the opening sequence, he decides to descend to the lowlands in order to give his master, Don Sebastian, the wolf's fur as a present. The simple action sequence uses the inevitable directness found in folk tales. Swiftly, Riefenstahl sends her hero into the conflict situation. Passing through the village square, Pedro encounters Martha for the first time. Riefenstahl de-emphasizes this first meeting by having neither acknowledge the other's presence. The camera first follows Pedro arriving through the arched gate, then follows him to the village fountain, where his path intersects hers. She walks ahead of a traveler's wagon into Roccabruna. The camera leaves him and follows her path to where she makes camp. There she prepares for her dance. A cut back to Pedro sees him arrive at the kitchen of Don Sebastian's estate.

Don Sebastian rules there in a despotic manner, yet his power is not absolute. Bankrupt, his mismanagement has made him a debtor of the mayor, who eventually forces him to marry his ambitious daughter Amalie. The film suggests that Amalie is the power behind her father, the mayor. In her opposition to Martha, she seems as tyrannical as Don Sebastian. After a formal gathering during which he insults Amalie, Don Sebastian sees Martha for the first time and observes her dance. He requests her to dance for him. When she acquiesces to his wish and visits him, he quickly reveals his real intentions. He makes Martha his mistress. When he must marry, Don Sebastian coerces her to enter a sham marriage with Pedro. Pedro agrees because he is totally smitten by her, but on the wedding night, he discovers Don Sebastian's plan. When he appears at the mill, Pedro confronts him. After a fierce knife fight that mirrors Pedro's struggle with the wolf, he leaves Don Sebastian dead at the feet of the angry townsmen. While they celebrate the death of the tyrant, Pedro together with Martha returns to the mountains.

Similar to the way Riefenstahl trains the camera on Junta in *Das blaue Licht*, here she keeps the camera on Martha in *Tiefland*, noticing her first from a distance as she walks into town. Then the camera, together with the village children, observes her inside the wagon as she gets ready for a performance. The scene is punctuated by Martha's dramatic closure, in which she literally lets a curtain fall after she steps out of the wagon. Riefenstahl employs the same upward profile shots that she used in her first film. A series of shot-reverse-shots highlights the exchange of glances between her and the village children. While the children watch the mysterious Gypsy woman preparing for a dance, her glances take in their Romani features. The happy raggle-taggle bunch evokes the romantic, streetwise image of the Gypsy. Similarly to the way in which Junta's hand seems to merge with the crystal, Martha's hand becomes one with the castanets. Riefenstahl's shots of Martha elicit a spiritual image of a natural, endowed with the gift of dance. These shots cast Martha as an idol. Soft, direct light on her face sets it aglow. The scene, apart from the faint musical score and the giggles of the children, is virtually silent. The entire exchange is organized visually.

Just as the children seem drawn in, dazzled by Martha's appearance, so the villagers stand spellbound as she dances in their midst. They are totally absorbed in her dance. Riefenstahl edits the tavern sequence to enhance Martha's sensual qualities: the camera focuses first on the dancer, allowing film viewers an exclusive view of her dancing, and then it focuses on the men ogling the dancer. The camera then abruptly cuts outside to a chance meeting between Pedro and Don Sebastian, but just as abruptly it returns to again focus on the dancer. The scene, in an ironic way, mirrors Riefenstahl's dance of filmmaking in that both the dancer and the director seemingly do not understand or realize that their audience becomes aroused. Just as Riefenstahl seems startled whenever her work elicits virulent criticism, Martha shows surprise when one peasant can finally no longer contain himself and lurches forward to embrace her. Repelled, she pushes him away. The tavern sequence can also be read as a staging of Martha's or by inference Riefenstahl's own innocence. It suggests that the dancer is so focused on her dancing that she becomes unaware of her surroundings. Similarly, it would seem Riefenstahl could create *Triumph des Willens* solely with aesthetic concern in mind.

Once the spell of the dance has been broken, the camera swings away from Martha to Don Sebastian, who commands everyone's attention. Martha and the camera gaze at him as he demands a private dance at his castle. The next scene shows him in his domain, and it is clear that here the master rules absolutely: Don Sebastian seems power incarnate until his death at the hands of Pedro. He has no peers, insults the family and friends of the wealthy mayor, and treats the peasants as slaves.[14] He is the one character who addresses everyone else informally, even the mayor. When Martha appears at the castle, Don Sebastian dismisses her traveling partner — whose behavior suggests that he too considered Martha his property — and usurps his place. Don Sebastian can play the guitar well, although it is only a tool to him: with it, he can get Martha to dance for him. Everything that takes place at his castle prepares us for his rape of Martha. Twice, however, Riefenstahl shows Martha consent to his forced embraces. Both scenes end in portrait shots lingering momentarily. It is difficult not to see this scene as another of Riefenstahl's stagings of her own naiveté, as someone who succumbed to the advances of the National Socialists while remaining apart and innocent.

Martha's escape from Don Sebastian's estate accelerates the film's action, despite the lack of chase scenes. The camera captures important moments, such as Don Sebastian threatening the unsuccessful searchers, their discovery of Martha's scarf, and Pedro's temporary rescue of her. While characters are mostly shown at the culmination point of an action, the music and the cloud shots create the rising tension. Riefenstahl uses a gathering thunderstorm to indicate the imminent climax. A series of quiet interior shots alternates with the increasingly stormy exterior.

In a scene that mirrors the beginning of the film, Pedro kills Don Sebastian with his bare hands, telling him "You are the wolf." The farmers then recognize Pedro's status as hero by removing their hats in a salute. At the same time, it begins to rain. Riefenstahl shows the open hand of the fallen tyrant capturing raindrops. Then the camera observes the couple walking uphill toward it and past in a procession-like step. It follows the couple as they step into the blazing light of the sunset. The last scene is an apotheosis, frozen as the last portrait in the film.

Both *Das blaue Licht* and *Tiefland* employ elements of the folk tale. The folk tale uses a clearly defined reality removed from, for example, the hard realism of a documentary. Riefenstahl consciously chose the legend and fairy tale as narrative modes. As she relates to Müller, her film, in contrast to Arnold Fanck's mountain films, seeks the otherworldly or mystical qualities of the fairy tale or legend in an attempt to create greater harmony between form and content. For example, *Das blaue Licht* captures the mystical power of the mountains when Tonio falls to his death or when Junta discovers the despoiled crystal cave and intentionally falls to her death. *Tiefland*, also provides examples of fairy tale imagery: when Pedro descends into the valley, the music trills happily and the camera pans uphill and downhill focusing on the translucent water as it burbles down a meadow; a grandiose shot of a waterfall ends the scene. In another scene, as Pedro returns to the lowlands to assume his position as miller in Roccabruna and become Martha's husband, the gathering clouds, rising winds, and finally thunderclaps clearly determine the mood of the scene. Riefenstahl brings together strong visuals and a musical score of an ominous crescendo to create one of the best-edited sequences in the film.

Perhaps Riefenstahl chose to create a fairy tale as a way to keep the film "neutral" — that is, removed from the historical moment — or to keep the political dimension in a safe story-telling context. She uses "fairy tale" [*Märchen*], "mountain legend" [*Berglegende*], and "fable" [*Fabel*] to indicate a world removed from that of the raw realism of mountain films (*Macht der Bilder*). She does not seem concerned with the distinct differences of the three types of tale, yet each suggests a particular horizon of expectation. The fable has a moral intended to edify the audience. A legend — from the Latin, *legenda*, that which must be read — traditionally records an important event or person's deed.[15] Unlike other folk tale genres, fables and legends carry with them an imperative that something can be learned and ought to be remembered. Their content, then, is inherently educational, which suggests it is also political to a degree.

Riefenstahl's use of these types of folk tales allows her to create a world separate from her own. The worlds of *Das blaue Licht* and *Tiefland* remain one-dimensional, inhabited by archetypes rather than fully developed, three-dimensional characters. Thus, simple plots string together powerful images of landscapes and people in both fable-like films. The characters have no psychological depth. They are ultimately only images motivated mostly by action. Although their geographic locale may be realistic, their purport lies in the symbolic or spiritual. Riefenstahl uses types of narrative that embrace distilled, crystallized action and imagery, wherein pure art becomes possible, art removed from any and every messy, murky social context.

In Junta and Martha, Riefenstahl presents two similar yet different Gypsy types. Junta is a Gypsy in the romantic tradition, wild, independent, untamable, a child of nature. Riefenstahl depicts her as self-sufficient. Like the nymphs of mythology, she is linked to her environment. Thus, when the villagers destroy the crystal cave, they destroy her. At the same time, these villagers in *Das blaue Licht* reflect a centuries-old suspicion of the Gypsies, and of Junta in particular, which suggests a break in style. Since fairy tales usually rely on absolute values, such as good/bad or beautiful/ugly, suspicion or any other kind of emotion belongs in a more realistic setting. In *Tiefland*, Martha would seem to be an entirely different Gypsy construct. Considering the operatic setting, her character may be a nod toward Carmen, the flamenco dancing, fiery Gypsy. Yet, she is a rather weak character, mostly depicted in poses, even when she dances. Clothes, castanets, and hair may be reminiscent of the romantic Gypsy figure, but the acquiescing sadness in her is uncharacteristic of the fairy tale world. Again there seems to be a break between the intention and the realization of the character. If we then remember as well that Riefenstahl's characters are Romani extras playing Spanish villagers, the whole enterprise takes on a very cynical air.

One may read the film as the fable of the overthrow of a tyrant, as Sanders-Brahms has done. The performance of Martha is, however, in no way subversive. She yields to the power of the moment, be it embodied in Don Sebastian or Pedro. Riefenstahl's scissors cut an image of herself as spellbound victim. While the scene that introduced Martha showed her leading a horse with wagon, the final shot shows Pedro leading her in a stiff, procession-like step. They parade past the camera, which follows them as they slowly step into the blazing sunset. The scene visualizes a glorious moment. As such it is stunning, but it seems unmotivated as far as the previous scenes are concerned. It suggests that Riefenstahl did not want viewers to overlook the sanctification of the two characters.

In conclusion, by directing *Das blaue Licht* and *Tiefland* as well as casting herself in the female protagonist's role, Riefenstahl fails to separate her reality from the fantastic worlds of Junta or Martha. Her personal intrusions into their separate, fantastic worlds link with the myth of herself. As she keeps spinning and respinning her own myth with the help of her critics and her supporters, the fairy tale worlds of Junta and Martha end up an integral part in the Riefenstahl myth. She may be preoccupied with the films' imagery to the exclusion of everything else, yet the visual and verbal shape a narrative that invites more than quiet gazing. An extended piece of communication, the dialogue must always be completed by the audience, prompting some kind of social interaction. As Riefenstahl shows in *Tiefland*, when the dancer presents her dance, she affects her spectators. While she, as a performer, may be completely absorbed in her art, the product takes on a life of its own, which may have dangerous consequences. Thus, in the film, a brutish villager attacks the dancer and is repelled. This part only gives the spectacle a new direction, as the laughter of the other villagers suggests. At this point the dancer's position seems infinitely more dangerous. Only Don Sebastian's invitation saves her from the aroused group of males. While the scene asks to be read as "look at what unwittingly happened to this innocent," the fact that Riefenstahl cut these images together in 1953 clearly suggests that this represents a most cynical kind of self-propaganda. It reifies her self-image whose truth-value she maintains to this day.

Ultimately, the formal constraints of the fairy tale reassert themselves in the happy ending. Riefenstahl returns to the Gypsy princess-type by turning Martha, after her moment of three-dimensionality and psychological depth, into the reward of the tyrant-slayer Pedro. The simple tale, however, betrays its storyteller. While a more complex tale elaborating the psychological depth of its characters would have created room for an *apologia*, the simple tale clings to one-dimensionality. The victim remains true to its one-dimensional type. Given the time during which Riefenstahl cut the film materials, one is struck by the director's cynical opportunism. Martha ends up with the new master, the innocent pure mountain-hero (and killer when the situation demands it) to whom the villagers bow respectfully. As Riefenstahl plays Martha, the end of *Tiefland* suggests an enactment of the director's own retreat to the Bavarian Alps, this remote place of innocence and purity. One is left wondering how much of the final product is the result of Riefenstahl's scissors, recutting the images to suit the political sensitivities of 1953.

Tiefland (1954). Children, perhaps played by Romani extras, look on as Martha (Leni Riefenstahl), a Gypsy dancer, prepares for a performance. Courtesy Library of Congress and Transit Film GmbH.

Tiefland (1954). Performing in a tavern, Martha does not realize the effect of her seductive dance on the men. Courtesy Library of Congress and Transit Film GmbH.

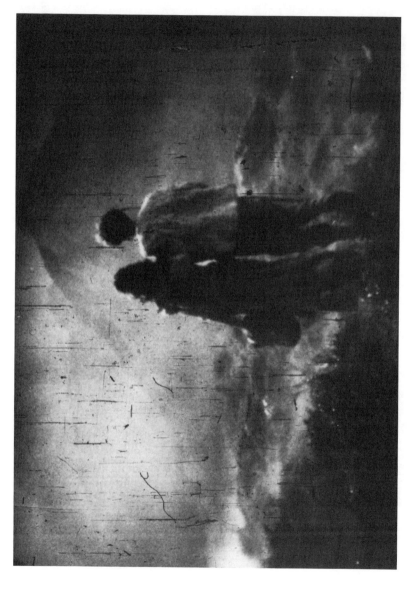

Tiefland (1954). In the final scene, Martha and Pedro (Franz Eichberger) walk off into a mythical landscape. Courtesy Library of Congress and Transit Film GmbH.

Notes

[1] "Roma" is the proper name of the peoples Non-Roma have called "Gypsies." It is used as noun and adjective. "Romani" is also an adjective. Whenever "Gypsy" appears in the text, I refer exclusively to the historical and cultural stereotype.

[2] *Die Macht der Bilder — Leni Riefenstahl* (The Power of Images — Leni Riefenstahl; *The Wonderful, Horrible Life of Leni Riefenstahl*), Directed by Ray Müller (Channel Four Films et al., 1993). Unless noted, all translations are my own.

[3] Infield calls her "Hitler's favorite filmmaker," Glenn B. Infield, *Leni Riefenstahl: The Fallen Goddess* (New York: Thomas Y. Crowell Company, 1976) i; Susan Sontag refers to her as "a close friend and companion of Hitler," *Under the Sign of Saturn* (New York: Farrar, Straus and Giroux, 1980) 81; and Linda Seger considers Riefenstahl "the most controversial and one of the most important filmmakers, male or female, in the history of film," *The Developing Power and Influence of Women in Television and Film* (New York, NY: Henry Holt and Company, 1996) 20. Riefenstahl seems to attract superlatives regardless of who speaks about her or her work. I think directors such as Luis Trenker or Veit Harlan deserve this "most notorious" status equally. Strangely enough, unlike Riefenstahl, her male colleagues were allowed to continue their careers after the war.

[4] For a succinct summary of the problematic aspects of her work see Klaus Kreimeier, *The Ufa Story: A History of Germany's Greatest Film Company*. Translated by Robert and Rita Kimber (New York: Hill and Wang, 1996) 252.

[5] For example, she insisted in a filmed interview with John Musilli and Stephan Chodorov in December 1972 in Munich that to her mind even *Triumph des Willens* is not a propaganda film, but rather a documentary that catches the spirit of that historical moment. At no point does Riefenstahl permit herself to perceive that, while she may have captured that spirit of the time with the film, at the same time she helped create that spirit by producing a monument that fitted into the National Socialists' programs of self-representation. Others also did not recognize this correspondence between her aesthetic project and the historical environment within which it was created. Ironically, Riefenstahl received the "Diplôme de Grand Prix" for *Triumph des Willens* on 4 July 1937 at the *Exposition Internationale des Art et des Techniques* in Paris.

See also Julia Knight, *Women and the New German Cinema*, (London: Verso, 1992) 1–21. In her introductory chapter entitled "The Absent Directors," she presents a brief historical overview of the early German women directors and points out that several of the earliest women directors also established their own production companies, collaborated in script writing, etc. Thus, during that time, it seems to have been quite common for a director to exert considerable influence over a project. Seen in this light, Riefenstahl's personally controlled filmmaking reflects the practices of the time.

[6] While Kracauer considers the absence of the blue light the reason for Junta's death (1947, 259), Linda Schulte-Sasse considers her death a suicide (127).

[7] Also see Rentschler, *The Ministry of Illusion* (Cambridge, MA: Harvard UP, 1996) 27–51; and David B. Hinton, *The Films of Leni Riefenstahl* (Metuchen, NJ: Scarecrow Press, 1978), 1–26. Hinton contends that Riefenstahl added the contemporary frame to the film, recut it, and re-released it as *Die Hexe von Santa Maria* (The Witch of Santa Maria) (24–25).

[8] See Renata Berg-Pan, *Leni Riefenstahl* (Boston: Twayne Publishers, 1980) 79 and Rentschler (1996, 42–43) for a fuller discussion of the frame. Riefenstahl does not discuss the frame in her memoirs.

[9] Enno Patalas wrote in 1965 that the perfect movie "would have been one in which there would have been no speech at all, but rather only music and sound (the films of Riefenstahl came closest to this ideal). Nazi films are entirely musical throughout . . . it is as if the films sounded by themselves, as if they set free superfluous feelings that otherwise would not could not have expressed itself." Attributed to Patalas by Fritz Göttler in "Kolberg: Nichts geht mehr," in *Das Jahr 1945: Filme aus Fünfzehn Ländern*, edited by Hans Helmut Prinzler, 188–89 (Berlin: Stiftung Deutsche Kinemathek, 1990)

[10] Berg-Pan, in my opinion, makes too much of what she perceives to be an erotic tension between Guzzi and Junta (87–88). Junta appears to be unaware of the power of her sexuality. While the male characters respond to her in a sexually aggressive manner, Riefenstahl keeps Junta innocent except for the very last image. The death pose is far too sensual and goes counter to the image of innocence that the entire film creates.

[11] Berg-Pan cites among others Infield for corroboration (140–43).

[12] Bogusław Drewniak suggests that Riefenstahl filmed at Maxglan, in Krün, in the Dolomites, and in Barrandov. He concludes with "When the film was shown a year later in the German theaters with moderate success, one looked in vain for the extras of Maxglan," *Der Deutsche Film 1938–1945: Ein Gesamtüberblick* (Düsseldorf: Droste, 1987) 456. Hinton also makes reference to the use of Roma as extras. Rentschler gives a brief account of Nina Gladitz's documentary *Zeit des Schweigens und der Dunkelheit* (Time of Silence and Darkness, 1985) and the ensuing legal action. He states after Riefenstahl contested the first verdict, the second trial confirmed Gladitz's findings: "that the director had selected sixty gypsies from a group of 250 concentration camp inmates and forced them to act in *Lowlands* without pay" (1996, 310).

[13] See Berg-Pan (Leni Riefenstahl 165) also Hinton (The Films of Leni Riefenstahl 84–86).

[14] The credits list them as "Leibeigene," a term signifying a clearly defined social status especially from ca. 1000–1500. The word choice suggests yet another distancing as it evokes a time and social conditions far in the past.

[15] For a discussion of the legend as genre, see, for example, Max Lühti, *Once upon a time: On the Nature of Fairy Tales* (Bloomington: Indiana UP, 1976) 35–46 and 83–94. Also see Lühti's *The European Folktale: Form and Nature* (Bloomington: Indiana UP, 1982) 2–12 and 14–17. For a discussion of the fable as genre, see Peter Hasubek, ed., *Die Fabel: Theorie und Rezeption einer Gattung* (Berlin: Erich Schmidt Verlag, 1982).

9

RICHARD J. RUNDELL

Literary Nazis?
Adapting Nineteenth-Century German
Novellas for the Screen: Der Schimmelreiter,
Kleider machen Leute, *and* Immensee

CO-OPTING THE NINETEENTH-CENTURY German literary heritage
for the cultural and ideological aims of National Socialism was a
significant priority in the policy of the Nazi film industry, both before
and during the war. Of the 465 feature films produced in Germany
during the war years 1939–1945, no fewer than 243, or more than
half, were based on previously published literary originals such as novels, plays, and short stories (Drewniak 485).

Three particular film adaptations of novellas from mid and late
nineteenth-century German Realism, a genre which has considerable
status in the German literary canon, were successful and diverting entertainment and at the same time lent cultural legitimacy to the National Socialist appropriation of literary classics. Theodor Storm's *Der
Schimmelreiter* (The Rider on the White Horse), published in 1888,
was filmed by Curt Oertel and Hans Deppe in 1934; Gottfried Keller's
Kleider machen Leute (Clothes Make the Man), published in 1874, was
filmed by Helmut Käutner in 1940, and Storm's *Immensee*, published
in 1851, was filmed by Veit Harlan in 1943.

All three of these novellas lent themselves unusually well to cinematic realization, owing to the distinct narrative structure and techniques of the novella, as well as their style of characterization and
character development. Storm's perceptive insight, that the novella is
the sister of the drama, has implications also for adaptations of the form
as motion pictures (Neis 10). Many common features of the novella
form were ideally suited to the screen: the circular structure, frame stories, flashbacks, sudden narrative shifts, and use of symbols. Moreover,
these films were welcome star vehicles featuring pairs of the most
popular luminaries of Third Reich cinema in the romantic leading roles.
Mathias Wieman and Marianne Hoppe starred in *Der Schimmelreiter*,

Heinz Rühmann and Hertha Feiler in *Kleider machen Leute*, and Carl Raddatz and Kristina Söderbaum in *Immensee*.

What little critical attention has been paid to *Der Schimmelreiter*, *Kleider machen Leute*, and *Immensee* has tended to dismiss these movies as trivial diversions of purely entertainment value and almost no political import. But the screenplays of these three films include a number of significant changes from the literary originals that bear closer examination. Of particular interest are those changes that have a potentially ideological message, whether overt or implicit, despite the films having been regarded as almost totally apolitical.

Adapting literary texts for the screen has been going on, of course, since the very hour in which motion pictures were born, and the debate on how to do it, even whether to adapt literary texts at all, has been more or less uninterrupted for a century. Since the mid 1960s, scholars and critics have settled on the term "filmed literature," although the term has also had a pejorative connotation at times, implying dilution of an original. The two media, literature and film, are sufficiently distinct that Ingmar Bergman once noted "film has nothing to do with literature; the character and substance of the two art forms are usually in conflict." American novelist Norman Mailer put the dichotomy even more graphically by arguing that "film and literature are as far apart as, say, cave painting and a song" (Beja 51). But neither of these assertions denies the fact that many motion pictures are based on literary works rather than original screenplays. This being so, one cannot avoid comparing the adaptation with the original. In the foreword to his book *German Film and Literature: Adaptations and Transformations* Eric Rentschler notes with dismay that this kind of comparison usually amounts to "fidelity analysis," that is, determining the extent to which the motion picture has faithfully rendered the book (2).

The comparative approach blurs the reality that the two media, film and literature, possess features of production and reception so distinctly different as to make comparison not only awkward but almost meaningless in many cases, however appealing the book-movie association may be. This is the point that Bergman and Mailer seek to make. The criteria for judging visual and verbal art are not identical, nor need they be, and what has been termed the "adaptation-as-betrayal" approach to comparison is invariably disappointing (Horton and Magretta 1).

However, when filmmakers choose to take an established literary classic as their point of departure, comparison is not only unavoidable but perhaps even an aim of the filmmaker. It is, after all, the fame of the literary original that will make people wish to see it made into a movie. Even when one realizes from past experience that one is likely to be disappointed, sheer curiosity makes us want to see films made from books we have read and found interesting.

More to the point than the issue of whether scholars trained in literary analysis can effectively apply their analytical skills to the modalities of film is the simple reality that feature films almost without exception are, and have to be, about something. That something is inevitably a story of some kind, and stories have an inescapably literary association, even when told orally. In the United States, this reality motivated the Academy of Motion Picture Arts and Sciences to distinguish between "original" and "adapted" from its beginnings in 1927, formalized since 1957 into two screenplay awards, one "based on material from another medium," the other "written directly for the screen." Both categories flourish in the USA and in most European film cultures.

The criteria by which we form our judgments of how successful a film adaptation of a literary work may be are necessarily subjective and difficult to codify. Essentially, one finds oneself determining what the film adaptation has changed from the literary original, usually in terms of what has been left out or added. Changes to the period, locale, or narrated time of the book are considered. This approach entails the risk of quickly turning into an uninspired inventory that too easily depends on the viewer's skill at catching small and often trivial differences.

In his essay on Hans Schweikart's 1940 adaptation of Gotthold Ephraim Lessing's 1767 play *Minna von Barnhelm*, the film being entitled *Das Fräulein von Barnhelm* (Miss von Barnhelm), film scholar Karsten Witte makes the point that film versions are aimed at readers and promise familiar images from well-known books. But Witte also maintains that, like any other translation, a film adaptation invariably betrays its original. Readers are turned into spectators; they forget the reader in themselves and lose sight of the literary tradition (in Rentschler 1986,103). Marc Silberman, in his chapter in the same book on Gustav Ucicky's 1937 film adaptation of Heinrich von Kleist's 1808 comedy, *Der zerbrochene Krug* (The Broken Jug) expresses a similar position by using the term "transposition" as well as "adaptation" (87). However, one might differ with Silberman and maintain that an adaptation almost always goes beyond transposition in the musical sense of merely shifting to a different key while not omitting or adding anything.

Of the filmed literary adaptations made in National Socialist Germany, many are labeled in the screen credits with the qualifiers "nach" (based on), "frei nach" (based loosely on), or even "frei nach Motiven von" (loosely based on themes from), indicating that the filmmaker took liberties with the original and wanted to avoid being condemned for infidelity. This crediting practice may also have had legal and copyright ramifications, as it does today.

The following analyses of three films adapted from nineteenth-century literary originals have different emphases stemming in part from the nature of the films being examined and the records of their respective production and reception. I examine *Der Schimmelreiter* with particular stress on the contemporary reception of the film. I compare *Kleider machen Leute* with its literary source. Finally, in my analysis of *Immensee*, I pay special attention to the circumstances of its film production. Together, these varying focal points may facilitate the appreciation of a group of films that have been hitherto underexamined. A film adaptation is, in an important sense, also an interpretation of a literary work in and for a particular time. While much recent scholarship has tended to concentrate on the wave of "filmed literature" since 1960, the National Socialists were no less intent on adapting and interpreting well-known literary works for their own purposes. Just why the three filmed novellas under consideration here are of particular interest will become clearer in the following analyses. All three works were exemplary in terms of employing cultural and social values that Goebbels and the Nazi film industry were especially eager to foster.

Theodor Storm's last work, his masterful novella, *Der Schimmelreiter*, was written when Wilhelminian Germany was in full flower as a growing world power. Indeed, 1888 — the year of the novella's composition and of Storm's death — is familiar to historians as the "Three Kaiser Year" of Wilhelm I, Friedrich III, and Wilhelm II. The suspenseful tale of Hauke Haien, the outsider who rises to a position of leadership as "Deichgraf" (responsible for all matters pertaining to the dike system of a region), set in the late 1830s, is generally considered to be Storm's most mature work. One scholar termed it "Faust without transcendence" (Loeb 121).

As one of the classic short prose works of German literary realism, *Der Schimmelreiter* continues to enjoy a secure place in the German school canon, and a surprising amount has been written about this novella, particularly around 1988 on the hundredth anniversary of its publication and its author's death. Despite the sophisticated and complex levels of its narrative framework, few literary texts lend themselves with more visual promise to an effective transformation into cinema. The images of the North Frisian landscape and coastal seascape, which play such an evocative, atmospheric role in the novella, seem predestined to film.

Der Schimmelreiter was first adapted by screenwriter-directors Curt Oertel and Hans Deppe as a low-budget, black-and-white sound film in

1933 and had its premiere on 12 January 1934, less than a year after the Nazis assumed power. This film adaptation lent itself splendidly to illustrating the National Socialist image of the German character, which was just being made the official view, as well as facets of a Nordic "blood and soil" ideology. Mathias Wieman, the actor portraying protagonist Hauke Haien, bore a distinct facial resemblance to the idealized Teutonic physiognomy featured in propaganda posters of the period.

Felix Schmeißer noted in the *Husumer Nachrichten* of 17 January 1934 that the film was not a very faithful rendition of the novella and ought rightly to have been labeled "freely adapted from themes by Storm." But he conceded that the film was a beautiful and powerful work. "Magnificent above all are the landscape images of our coast, the endless marshes with their tree-lined farms and bays surrounded by reeds, the picturesque beaches with their fishermen's cottages and small Frisian churches, the grey shore in storm and silence. . ." (quoted in Spurgat 24).

This quotation focuses one's attention on the fact that, although *Der Schimmelreiter* was a sound film, there are long segments without dialogue, in which the mood of the North Sea dikes is established visually. Moreover, the especially effective music score based on folk melodies was a fine example of the employment in film of what was widely regarded as the most German of all the art forms. Also, one sees clear allusions to the Heimat movement of the nineteenth and early twentieth centuries in *Der Schimmelreiter*, in decor, landscape, music, and costume, all of which have been rendered with painstaking historical accuracy to evoke the specific region in which the film was set and shot. Indeed, the sense of Heimat is powerfully evocative in all three films under discussion. The film reminds the viewer of the work of silent-film directors like Sergei Eisenstein, but also the films of Leni Riefenstahl, and there is an oddly documentary quality to this film adaptation of *Der Schimmelreiter*.

A review from the family magazine *Daheim* of 15 February 1934 called the film a "picturesque new creation" and noted that "the speeches are limited to an absolute minimum; indeed, the silent scenes are the most powerful" (Holander 110). An advertisement for the premiere of *Der Schimmelreiter* in the *Lübecker General-Anzeiger* of 2 March 1934 also stressed "the unique landscape of North Frisia in its indescribable charm, with its tough, laconic people who must defend their homeland and soil in daily struggle with the sea" (Spurgat 72).

But the 1934 *Der Schimmelreiter* was far more than a simple, yet powerful paean to the raw Frisian coast. Also in *Daheim*, one could read the following political approbation:

> This film is very timely. "Blood and Soil" is its content, the idea of a leader [*Führergedanke*] lives in it, the question of reclaiming land is posed, the great hymn of the death-defying sacrifices of the individual for the common good signal the heroic ending (Holander 110).

An ideological and propagandistic reading of the film is clearly delineated here. The parallel between Hauke Haien and Adolf Hitler was unmistakably emphasized in the repeated low-angle close-ups of Hauke Haien, which looked as if they would fit seamlessly into Riefenstahl's *Triumph des Willens* (Triumph of the Will, 1935). Indeed, Hauke Haien's will is triumphant in *Der Schimmelreiter*. Although he is ultimately swept away with his wife and daughter in the flood, his new dike withstands the great storm, and the agricultural polder he leaves behind is his gift of new *Lebensraum*.

Storm was regarded as a great German during the Nazi era and considered a literary forerunner and passionate advocate of a Greater German Empire [*Großdeutsches Reich*]. *Der Schimmelreiter* was not only assigned reading in schools, but also for soldiers of the Wehrmacht. A school edition of the novella approved by the Reich Ministry of Education included this introductory note:

> It is the German people's eternal current of power that Storm symbolizes in his Hauke Haien. Thus shall there always be a Hauke Haien in the German people . . . who risks great things and is capable of achieving them, whose life is a clear decision. . . . [Hauke Haien] is a leader figure [*Führergestalt*], able to lead (Holander 109).

The film itself received from Propaganda Ministry censors the ratings "künstlerisch" (artistic) and "besonders wertvoll" (especially valuable), not only the highest possible labels at the time, but given to only six out of 240 films produced in 1933 and 1934 (Holander 109). The National Socialist or *völkisch* tone was thereby set for public viewing of *Der Schimmelreiter*. It was so dominant that one is somewhat surprised that Storm's novella managed to shake off its brown mantle in the years following the Second World War.

The story of *Der Schimmelreiter* is sufficiently protean that it lends itself quite smoothly to ideological re-reading. This was the case in a 1978 West German version, which attempted with an international cast to present a love story heavy with conflicts and plot strands between individuals, depoliticized in Hollywood fashion. Closer to a socialist-realist model is a 1984 East German-Polish version shot on the Baltic coast near the site of the legend which was the source of Storm's novella. This adaptation de-emphasizes the personal (there are far fewer close-ups of Hauke Haien, for example) and stresses class-conscious aspects in its depiction of a hard life for the working peasantry. Every political color and every generation seems comfortable with the values of *Der Schimmelreiter*. It seems worth noting that Hauke Haien has quite a bit in common with some of the classical heroes of the American Western film.

Whereas *Der Schimmelreiter* had been filmed early on in the Nazi era, Gottfried Keller's masterpiece comedic novella, *Kleider machen Leute* had its film premiere in a version written and directed by Helmut Käutner on 16 September 1940, slightly more than a year after the war between Germany and Poland had begun, but prior to the German invasion of the Soviet Union and the entry of the USA into the war. Keller's novella is one of ten in the cycle entitled *Die Leute von Seldwyla* (The People of Seldwyla), published in two volumes in 1856 and 1874. The fact that Keller spent the great majority of his life (1819–1890) in Switzerland has never seemed to be a particular hindrance to the inclusion of his writing in the German literary canon, and Keller was certainly valued as a sympathetic writer in the literary politics of Nazi Germany.

Keller's novella is narrated by a not-quite-omniscient third person who is clearly on the side of the protagonist Wenzel Strapinski, trying to understand — if not wholly condone — the various reasons why Wenzel does not speak up and admit that he, a poor tailor, has been masquerading as a nobleman. Käutner's film, on the other hand, is content to let the camera tell the story rather than resorting to the literary device of a voice-over narrator. Keller's novella begins with a narrative description of Wenzel in a dejected humor. Käutner's film, if it wished to begin similarly, would have had to provide some sort of visual or dialogue cues that would serve this expository function. However, Käutner chooses a wholly different point of departure in order to avoid the use of an immediate flashback. The screenplay begins a week or two prior to the novella, while Wenzel is still working as a tailor in Seldwyla. A long establishing pan shows us a street scene in mid-winter with children in a Twelfth-Night procession, singing. A medium exterior shot of the tailor shop is followed by a reverse interior shot of Wenzel sitting cross-legged, sewing.

The novella summarizes initial exposition with a single clause, explaining that Wenzel is on the road, "because, with the bankruptcy of the master tailor in Seldwyla, he [Wenzel] had lost both his wages and his employment and was obliged to leave town."[1] The film, on the other hand, gives us this background in more character-establishing detail, added by Käutner — Keller's single clause is fleshed out to showcase Heinz Rühmann as Wenzel in yet another lovable-loser role. Wenzel is shown to be an easily distracted daydreamer who is fired because he ruins an elegant frock coat ordered by the mayor by cutting it too small.

Wenzel leaves the tailor shop with the elegant coat in lieu of severance pay, and the significance of the film's title that "clothes make the man" is stressed from the outset. Before his departure, Wenzel's absentminded daydreaming is given substance in a playful dream sequence, also purely Käutner's invention, and a popular film convention of the time. Underscored solely by music, without dialogue, the tailor's mannequins come to life as the camera now takes on Wenzel's point of view; fashionably dressed gentlemen bow to Wenzel as he enters a grand ballroom for a gala. The camera cuts to the arrival of a stylized coach and, in a long shot, the entrance of a lovely woman in a ball gown. As we pan in, we see that she is wearing only the skeletal hoops of her petticoat and is otherwise naked. We then cut to Wenzel's face, embarrassed by his own racy daydream, and back to a revised version of the dream with the woman now fully clothed. The nudity is only momentary, surely not more than a few frames in length, but it must have been titillating at the time without breaching Nazi prudishness.

The woman is, in fact, the character of Nettchen, played by Rühmann's wife, Hertha Feiler, but we do not yet know her screen identity. Only when the master tailor shakes Wenzel out of his reverie do we return to the narrative and cut to find Wenzel walking toward the neighboring and hostile village of Goldach. This is the point at which Keller's novella commences: "On an unfriendly November day, a poor little tailor was walking on a country road toward Goldach" (7).

Novella and film merge here, but only briefly. The above comparison illustrates several fundamental differences in narrative exposition between written text and film sequence. Käutner chooses to present background in such a way as to give us a far deeper understanding of Wenzel's film character. We know him, for example, by his first name, while the novella's protagonist continues to be called "the tailor" until the coachman, playing a trick, tells the personnel at the inn that he is "Count Strapinski."

As the film proceeds, Wenzel meets a sage old vagabond who introduces himself as the puppeteer Christoffel; this is a newly invented character not present at all in the novella. As a fine coach unexpectedly stops to offer the modishly garbed Wenzel a ride into Goldach, Christoffel says, "Resign yourself, tailor, and seek your fortune." This scene provides both an impetus and an alibi for all that is to come. Käutner suggests, unlike Keller, that Wenzel has been set upon the path to his adventure by someone who has some power over him (a puppet master); the motif will recur. But interestingly, the fact that Wenzel actually undergoes the kind of development which results in real insight by the end of the story is clearer in Käutner's film than in the novella.

As the comedy of mistaken identity gathers momentum, Käutner stays close to the narrative flow of the novella and its dialogue in the scene of the Lucullan feast at the inn. The inn's celebrated partridge pie is topped with a small coronet as the appropriate decoration; as Wenzel devours the dish, a special-effects dissolve leaves only the coronet lying on the platter.

As in the novella, Wenzel's attempt to escape after the meal is foiled by the unctuous innkeeper, who supposes that the mysterious nobleman is seeking "a certain convenience" to which he is then courteously conducted. From the hallway, we see the closing of a door with a small, heart-shaped window, followed by a reverse shot from within, through the little window, again through Wenzel's eyes. This shot, as he is hiding in confusion in the toilet, gives the visual impression of a kind of benign imprisonment and illustrates the shift in point of view that endears us to Wenzel. Keller's Wenzel resolves at this point to make the best of the peculiar situation while it lasts. He will enjoy the privileges that arise from his new identity, although this now makes him a knowing impostor. But Käutner nicely preserves some of Wenzel's innocence by having him mutter sotto voce, "I'm not a count," every time he is thus addressed. This is an important difference between novella and film, because the film's Wenzel is depicted as more reluctantly opportunistic; at no point are we encouraged to lose sympathy for him.

The card-playing scene at the estate of the wealthy government official, where Wenzel is to meet Nettchen, is another of Käutner's variations on Keller's original. The wealthy men have placed their bets with silver coins (Belgian *Brabantertaler*), and Wenzel is forced to admit that he has no such coin with him. Keller lets the suspicious Melcher Böhni donate Wenzel's ante for him, even though Böhni has seen Wenzel's peculiarly pricked fingers, which hint that he may not be a nobleman. Böhni wants to see what will happen and therefore does not tip his hand. Käutner, on the other hand, lets Wenzel solve the coin problem by himself, enhancing our impression of the hero's ingenuity. Wenzel impulsively removes a silver button from his stylish frock coat, placing it on the table shyly in lieu of a coin. The other players find this eccentric but amusingly acceptable behavior for a nobleman. Wenzel mumbles "Valuta-Schwierigkeiten" (currency problems), and play commences.

This throwaway line is notable in the context of the year in which *Kleider machen Leute* was made — 1940. The words "currency problems" can certainly be read as a wry comment by Käutner on the difficulties that Germans were having with foreign exchange, which was severely limited or proscribed altogether for many people. Käutner was no anti-fascist resistance fighter, but he managed to maintain a kind of near-neutrality, which bore its own perils. He was able to "resist political and artistic indoctrination," but also "succeeded in making political problems visible in private conflicts."[2]

The button scene in *Kleider machen Leute* is trivial as a political utterance, and one cannot infer that it "slipped past" the censors. Still, the censors were attentive to just such tidbits as "currency problems"; the scene's very presence is noteworthy in a political climate in which double meanings were scrutinized carefully. The issue of veiled criticism of the National Socialist regime in motion pictures has been addressed and explored in fascinating detail by a number of recent books (particularly Rentschler's *Ministry of Illusion: Nazi Cinema and Its Aftermath* and Linda Schulte-Sasse's *Entertaining the Third Reich*). There is peril in reading too much into every marginally questionable sentence of dialogue or cinematic image, however. One must attempt to watch the entertainment films of the Third Reich with some awareness of the consciousness of the filmmakers, moviegoers, and censors of the period. Moreover, Goebbels was shrewd enough to allow modest dissent that did not transgress party ideology or threaten its policies.

More political, although not oppositional, is another of Käutner's changes. In the novella, Wenzel Strapinski is confused with a Polish count; in Käutner's film, the count is not Polish, but rather Russian. Poland in 1940 was an enemy belligerent, recently defeated and occupied, whereas the USSR was still allied with Hitler's Germany by the Molotov-Ribbentrop mutual non-aggression pact of 1939. Käutner's shift of Wenzel's mistaken nationality is meaningful only to a moviegoer who recalls the small details of the novella.

Käutner takes the Russification a step further by inventing another new character who is not present in Keller's novella, namely the genuine Russian count who had been expected in Goldach and with whom Wenzel is being confused. Named Alexei Stroganoff, he is not outraged at the imposture, but rather curious (as are we viewers) as to what will happen. Several occasions arise where Stroganoff could easily expose Wenzel, but the real count hastily asserts that he is actually Count Strapinski's servant. When Wenzel finally confesses the truth to him in private, Stroganoff decides to go along with the deception for a lark, henceforth answering to the name "Ivan" and maintaining that he was once a tailor. This script change compounds the comedy of errors and further sweetens the suspense.

The tailor motif that runs through Keller's novella figures in a scene of the film where it is not used in the novella, in the song that Wenzel sings to entertain the guests at the estate. Keller has Wenzel sing in Polish, which none of the guests speak. The reader however sees the German text, a humorous pseudo-folk song about the swineherd Kathinka wading about in the muck of a hundred thousand pigs (Keller 20). The guests think it is a genuine folk song, and Nettchen remarks how lovely national identity (das Nationale) always is. But Keller's conceit will not work in a film. If Wenzel sings in Polish (or Russian), neither the guests in the film nor the movie-going audience will understand him. So the device of not understanding a foreign language must be dropped in the film. The song is now not only sung in German, but is another song entirely, a satirical song about tailors. Moreover, it is sung not by Wenzel, but by Nettchen, and the element of irony is pointed in the opposite direction, at Wenzel, not at the guests.

Käutner invents still another character pair to clarify a plot element that is vague in Keller's novella: a noblewoman and her aunt, who have installed themselves in the hotel in Goldach to await an assignation with Count Stroganoff. We see the noblewoman for the first time in an abrupt cut from the feast scene in the inn; it is initially unclear who she is and why she is in the film. Only later does it emerge that her horoscope had recommended a romance with a foreign nobleman. For the remainder of the film, she serves to provoke jealousy in Nettchen, and as someone to whom the real Count can reveal his identity. After he has told her the truth, he talks about how the whole deception has the element of a game and says, quite as much for our benefit as for the noblewoman's, that he is in effect controlling Wenzel's life. Much like a puppeteer controls a puppet; Stroganoff can stop the game at his pleasure. The puppet master Christoffel in the beginning of the film is reflected here. Käutner further uses the Stroganoff character as a source of funds for Wenzel's extravagances, so that the unnecessarily improbable novella sequence where Wenzel wins his own money in a lottery can be omitted.

The changes noted above enhance the script in useful ways and may thus be regarded as positive. But Käutner also omits some of the novella's more charming features, ostensibly for reasons of economy. The delightful digression in Keller in which he catalogues the house-names in Goldach has been cut. Käutner also trims the parade of allegorically decorated sleighs to a minimum, so that almost all that remains is Keller's clever inversion of the novella's title. In novella and film a banner pronounces "Leute machen Kleider" (People Make Clothes) on the head sleigh of the Seldwyla contingent, and "Kleider machen Leute" (Clothes Make People) on the last sleigh. In the film, however, the sleigh procession is shown in a spirit of jolly revelry without any allegorical allusion.

The ritual dance at the celebration finds its cinematic realization as a Shrovetide festival scene, with dancers wearing grotesquely gigantic heads and performing elaborate steps just prior to Wenzel's exposure as a fraud by his erstwhile employer. This scene has and needs no dialogue in the film; the building tension is underscored by music, and the accelerated tempo that is achieved by the editing contributes similarly to the suspense. As Wenzel is unmasked, the camera cuts quickly to his point of view, and we see an Eisenstein-esque montage of shocked faces reacting to the startling news.

While fully a third of the novella's plot follows the climactic exposure of Wenzel, Käutner has cut this down to Wenzel's flight, his last-minute rescue by Nettchen, and a conciliation that seems hurried and impatient. For Käutner to have included the sizeable segment concerning Wenzel's childhood, he would have had to use a flashback at a point in the film where things have drawn to a natural denouement.

The film *Kleider machen Leute* is from start to finish a Heinz Rühmann vehicle. It capitalizes brilliantly on the comic actor's considerable gifts, which he displayed in a career that included *Die Drei von der Tankstelle* (Three from the Filling Station, a k a Three Good Friends, 1930), the most commercially successful film of 1930–1931 (Jacobsen, Kaes, and Prinzler 98), *Quax, der Bruchpilot* (Quax, the Crash Pilot, 1941), a highpoint in Nazi film comedy, and *Der Hauptmann von Köpenick* (1956), his most successful postwar film. Keller's novella lent itself ideally to such a star vehicle, but the film has received only marginal critical attention and has generally been seen as light entertainment. In *Cahiers du Cinema*, Louis Marcorelles calls *Kleider machen Leute* "a lightweight film like a sketch tossed off quickly, but one which shows a sure feeling for the atmosphere of a period like the best films of [Vincente] Minnelli," a director of frothy Hollywood musicals (27). Käutner's origins as a cabaret artist may inform his aesthetic touch in this film. Neither Rentschler, Schulte-Sasse, nor Jacobsen, Kaes, and Prinzler include it in their indexes. And yet, the sovereign command with which Käutner appropriates a well-known nineteenth-century literary property and converts it into a film comedy with wide appeal illustrates one premise which this brief discourse seeks to explore, namely, that such stories make fine movies, no matter what the ideological underpinnings.

Immensee has long been Storm's most popular novella. Written in 1849, it was his first published prose work. An enormous amount has been written about this *Erinnerungsnovelle* (novella of remembering) in a more or less steady stream up to the present day. Just as one imagines that there is nothing more to be said about the novella, another study is published, suggesting that each generation appropriates its own *Immensee*.

Starting in 1941, Universum-Film AG, or Ufa attempted to produce movies in color that would establish Germany as an equal of the USA. While the Agfacolor process tends to favor the red-brown spectrum and seems rather dull to someone accustomed to Technicolor's more vibrant and fully saturated blues, one can see that the process underwent refinement. The color of *Immensee*, directed by Veit Harlan, is superior to that of Josef von Baky's *Münchhausen*, finished in the same year. Harlan had already made one Agfacolor film, 1942's *Die goldene Stadt* (The Golden City) when he proposed to Joseph Goebbels a project that was intended to economize on the great expense of an Agfacolor production. *Die goldene Stadt* had cost 1.8 million Reichsmarks, and Harlan now suggested a three-film package that would use the same principal actors and many of the same sets, as he later related in his memoir, *Im Schatten meiner Filme*:

> My suggestions were *Immensee* based on Theodor Storm, *Opfergang* [The Sacrifice] based on Rudolf Binding, and *Pole Poppenspäler*, also based on Theodor Storm. In all of these films, Kristina [Söderbaum, Harlan's wife] would play the lead. She would also play opposite the same male leads. I had chosen Carl Raddatz and Paul Klinger as her partners. The exterior shooting for all three films would be in Schleswig-Holstein. Most of the other players would also be used in all three films. The studio interiors would remain as walls but be redecorated and refurnished after each shooting day, to continue shooting the second or third film there on the following day. "Veit Harlan Production Group" at Ufa had calculated with Production Head Erich Holder and the cinematographers that in this way, three films could be made for the price of two (159).

The production history becomes complicated owing to Goebbels's aversion to what he called "family movie-making," not only in the case of Harlan and his wife, Kristina Söderbaum, but also that of Georg Jacoby and his wife, Marika Rökk, and of Heinz Rühmann, who insisted on co-starring only with his wife, Hertha Feiler. Only after a good deal of argument and negotiation was Söderbaum permitted to play in both

Immensee and *Opfergang*. The third picture, to be based on Storm's novella *Pole Poppenspäler*, was ultimately dropped, but the originally proposed parallel-shooting concept was kept, apparently with some effort, as Harlan recounts:

> These two films, *Immensee* and *Opfergang*, were so fundamentally different from each other that it was not at all creatively simple to shoot them at the same time. Both themes had basically different melodies. Still, we shot *Opfergang* one day and *Immensee* the next. We scheduled shooting around the exteriors, in order to waste as little time as possible moving back and forth. The subtle landscape of Holstein Switzerland, its large lakes, and its marshes were the setting. Following these shots, we traveled to Italy and shot some Immensee exteriors there in the Roman Forum, in front of the Basilica of Maxentius, in front of the Palatine Hill, and in front of St. Peter's Cathedral (165).

In an unusual twist, Goebbels did not meddle with the finished project this time. Harlan seems to have been not only happy with his *Immensee* but also proud of it:

> After I had delivered the film *Immensee*, it was praised by Goebbels with superlatives and labeled a "German folksong." Not one single cut, not one single change was ordered. Of all the films that I had to make during the war, this was the only one which remained exactly as I had planned it and shot it, both in cast and in screenplay (168).

Everything seems so agreeable and pleasant in the context of the making of *Immensee* that one needs to remind oneself of the historical context; the film premiered on 17 December 1943 (Beethoven's birthday), more than ten months after the military disaster of Stalingrad and amidst the nightly bombing of Germany's cities.

How faithful an adaptation of Storm's novella is Harlan's *Immensee*? One of the first postwar critiques of the film was by David Stewart Hull in his 1969 *Film in the Third Reich*. Hull writes that because Goebbels had thought highly of *Die goldene Stadt*, he had allowed Harlan to make *Immensee* without interference. Hull says that Harlan told him he had chosen Storm's "classic novel [*sic*]" because he wanted the film to reflect his love for his wife (216).

Not only is Hull favorably impressed by a film which one can arguably regard as a minor work, but film critic Louis Marcorelles also considers the film in laudatory terms:

> *Immensee* is a film of peace and love. Its love story, filmed in the countryside where Storm himself lived, reflects the director's pagan and brutal lyrical streak. With Kristina Söderbaum in the leading role,

Immensee conveys a strong feeling for nature and a fervent idyllic mood (1955, 68).

It is unclear what Marcorelles means by Harlan's "pagan and brutal lyrical streak" or the oxymoronic "fervent idyllic," but it is clear that the critic is positively impressed.

Hull's critique also offers an oddly skewed synopsis of *Immensee*:

> This fifth color picture follows Storm's book only slightly, and is without propaganda content. It concerns a young girl torn between the love of two men, a music student and the master of a great estate. She prefers the former, but when they are separated by his travels, she marries his rival. The student returns a great conductor and begs his former sweetheart to leave her husband; the landowner, seeing the strength of their love, is prepared to renounce his own happiness. But she remains faithful to her husband, even after his death (216–17).

The emphasis of Hull's capsule plot summary is out of balance, and one can certainly argue about the issue of propaganda content. Hull then concludes with a sweeping self-contradiction, "If Goebbels had ordered a film extolling the purity of love and marriage, he could not have found anything better, and the film is still successful. It has been frequently revived [in West Germany] and its original power remains undiminished" (217).

In the section in their book, *Histoire du cinema nazi*, dealing specifically with film adaptations of literary works, French film historians Francis Courtade and Pierre Cadars refer to *Immensee* and also quote Harlan. They give a plot synopsis that emphasizes the film's symbolism with the caged songbirds, the water lily, the lake, and the rustic bench. They seem rather infatuated with *Immensee* but a bit confused about the foreign location shots:

> From beginning to end, a wonderfully romantic atmosphere pervades *Immensee*, leading us away from the all too difficult reality [of 1943]. Happiness and sorrow replace each other like the movement of waves, underscored by swelling music. Above all, this is a superb color picture (one of the first in the Agfacolor process), in which the landscape is lovingly captured. Not a word about war, National Socialism, or racism. With the exception of a short scene in Rumania [*sic*], the entire film takes place in Germany. All the characters are, in varying degrees, positive and highly moral, in short — exemplary. Each of them remains true to his/her calling: the romantic young woman becomes a model wife, the dedicated husband is ready to sacrifice his happiness for the happiness of his wife, and the brilliant artist elevates his genius above the ordinary. This time Kristina Söderbaum and Carl Raddatz are perfectly cast. Veit Harlan, who . . . in his almost infantile

preference for the grand lyrical, melodramatic style, shows inspiration and grows wings with *Immensee* (149).

A more cynical assessment is to be found in the short evaluation of Immensee in the 1980 compilation *Klassiker des deutschen Tonfilms 1930–1960* by Christa Bandmann and Joe Hembus. Here, Harlan's well-meant romantic intentions are disregarded immediately:

> *Immensee* is a low-grade adaptation of Storm's novella and has, apart from the title, nothing in common with the literary original. The sensitivity and the gentleness that give the material some tension are suffocated in the movie by plodding sentimentality. From the beginning, there is smooching and hugging until the boards of the romantic birch bench bend. Kristina Söderbaum is condemned to play a sad-sack, and you know after a few minutes how this will end — she'll have to reject her great love and arrive at the "painful, yet finest, strong and consoling certainty, that she belongs at her husband's side" — even after death. At this time — it's 1943 — a German woman waits, is true to her husband, and does without (217).

It is true that the film is overly sentimental, and its weepy sentimentality is largely the result of the way in which Harlan chooses to shoot his wife and have her deliver her lines. Moreover, the saccharine tone is made far worse by Wolfgang Zeller's bombastic musical score. Yet, although Harlan took liberties with the story, one cannot argue that the only thing the novella shares with the film is its title.

Harlan took considerable pains to integrate many elements from the novella into his screenplay, some of them even from the original draft of the novella before Storm revised it, such as a scene in which Elisabeth drops in unexpectedly on Reinhard in Hamburg and discovers a woman in his bed. Storm was counseled by friends to drop this scene from the early version of *Immensee,* and did so. By putting it back in, Harlan changes the sexual stakes of the story considerably by introducing desire as a motivation which tends to dilute the chaste quality of Storm's romance.

Most jarring to a reader familiar with the novella is the absence of Elisabeth and Reinhard as children in the film. The initial literary flashback takes the old, white-haired man, who must be at least sixty or seventy, back to the age of ten, with Elisabeth a pre-school girl of five. The novella invests five of its ten segments in their childhood, accompanying them from the ages of ten and five to the ages of seventeen and twelve, then eighteen and thirteen, then twenty and fifteen, respectively. Only in the last third of the novella do we deal with the adult couple, who by then are joined in the triangle with the second man, Erich, the man whom Elisabeth marries after Reinhard has left her.

We can only speculate on why Harlan chose to stay with the single cast and have Elisabeth and Reinhard age, not very convincingly, from young adulthood to early middle age, in Elisabeth's case roughly from eighteen to forty-five. Harlan makes no mention of it in his memoirs. The practice of using child actors to portray characters in flashbacks has become so common in contemporary American cinema that one may be imposing one's own expectations on a German film of 1943. In any event, Harlan made matters vastly easier for himself at the cost of much of the novella's subtlety. The childlike quality of Söderbaum's face and voice may have seemed sufficient. Both Söderbaum and Raddatz were thirty-one when the film was shot. Harlan chose to vary their ages up and down by ten to twelve years. The absence of the children reinforces the film's theme of resignation and tones down Storm's more romantic vision.

Many of Harlan's changes to Storm's original are additions, and some of them work quite well, even as they dilute the miniature quality of the novella. Otto Gebühr, well known for playing Frederick the Great in several popular contemporary films, is moving as the father of Erich. And Reinhard's father, the superb Karl Gülstorff, adds a valuable dimension of reflective maturity and reason. The mothers of the film, in contrast, are shown more negatively. One can argue that Harlan found the basis for the meddling nature of Elisabeth's mother in Storm, but he clearly takes it several steps further.

None of the modest amount of film criticism devoted to *Immensee* has drawn any attention to the shifted time period of the film, which Harlan changes from the indeterminate mid-nineteenth century of the novella — Storm mentions only months and seasons — to contemporary (early 1940s) Germany, notably and jarringly free of any sign of war. The internationally renowned composer Reinhard is shown departing Hamburg for Amsterdam by airplane. In a shot so brief that it must be replayed to make sure, one sees a swastika inadequately painted over on the tail of the Junkers transport plane, patently intended to imply that this is a civilian Lufthansa flight, not a military one. Flying between Hamburg and Amsterdam must have seemed implausibly extravagant for a 274–mile trip, but it served to emphasize Reinhard's celebrity status.

The screenplay adds or changes the last names of the characters. Reinhard — in the novella, only his housekeeper refers to him with an honorific, calling him "Herr Werner" (22) — becomes Reinhard Torsten. In addition, Elisabeth becomes Elisabeth Uhl and Erich is now

Erich Jürgens. Perhaps the change was made for no better reason than that the characters have to mail things to each other with visible mailing labels requiring a last name, a banality which was of no concern to Storm.

Harlan takes advantage of cinematic convention with the use of a photograph to trigger the narrative flashbacks, an entirely appropriate way for a movie to open up memories. The inscription on the photograph of young Elisabeth, "To my dear Reinhard, always yours, Elisabeth" helps establish the romantic relationship, even if she has not remained quite as faithful as she seems to wish to be regarded — it is Elisabeth, after all, who has married, not Reinhard.

A sequence in Italy, missing wholly from the novella, features Reinhard in a delightful relationship with an Italian soprano (played by Germana Paolieri) and shows him in the outside world, actually at work in his profession. He is connected through music to Elisabeth when he considers the soprano's more flamboyant rendition of his song inferior to Elisabeth's simple charm. The contrast between the two women is also ideologically significant, with Elisabeth's sweet, natural German simplicity contrasted unmistakably with the nameless Italian woman's sophisticated, artificial foreignness.

The third character in the triangle, Erich, is a prosperous landowner with an estate, both in the novella and in the film. In the film, a scene is devoted to the grand-opening ceremony of the estate's distillery, an interesting Harlan addition that helps to give some texture to Erich's otherwise long-suffering, flat character. The ceremony also affords the opportunity for some rather bombastic rhetoric, which probably seems more of a parody to a modern viewer than to the moviegoer of 1943.

A sequence involving beekeeping gives Harlan an opportunity to remind viewers of the title's meaning, that *Immen* is another word for the German *Bienen* (bees). The screenplay is, however, heavy-handed in its dialogue when Reinhard speaks of watching "the bees — the bees of Bee Lake Farm [*Immenseehof*]." A brief Darwinist excursus on the battle for the queen bee and the survival of the fittest leave something to be desired by way of lyrical delicacy but do not seem at all out of character for the film Reinhard.

Particularly curious is the subtitle given in the front credits of the film, *ein deutsches Volkslied* (A German Folk Song), accompanied by an oddly awkward and hesitant turning of the credit pages meant to suggest a book. The subtitle seems at first glance to be a possible appellation by Goebbels, but it is not. Here the affinity between the German poetic realism of the late nineteenth century and National Socialism becomes unmistakable in the shared fascination with folkloristic elements, what was widely termed *völkisch* in the Third Reich. The novella *Immensee* was called a folk song in the figurative sense even in Storm's lifetime. Storm was also much concerned with his reputation as a lyric poet — indeed, there are four songs embedded in the text of *Immensee*, all of them central to the story, rather than merely decorative. The novella's Reinhard even refers to the origins of folk songs when he sings some of the songs he has collected as a folklorist in the neighborhood. Elisabeth wonders who wrote the songs, and Erich answers dismissively, "Oh, you can tell just by listening to the things — apprentice tailors and barbers and that kind of airy riff-raff" (29). To this, Reinhard responds with words that reflect German romanticism, "They're not made at all; they grow, they fall out of the sky, they fly across the countryside like spiderwebs, here and there, and are sung in a thousand places at the same time. We find our innermost living and suffering in these songs; it's as if we had all helped make them" (29). Then the three characters hear a shepherd singing just such a folk melody, and Reinhard says, "Do you hear that? That's the way it passes from mouth to mouth," and a bit later, "Those are ancient tones [Urtöne], they sleep on forest floors; God knows who found them" (30). None of this conversation survives in Harlan's film, although Nazism certainly embraced such romantic sentiment.

This tale of shared and revered German virtues will show us an exemplary situation with exemplary figures and an exemplary solution to a primal dilemma, one presumably rooted in the values of the *Volk*. Fifty-five years later, this particular solution of resignation and denial, false choices and missed opportunities, does not look any more characteristic of Harlan's Germany than of Storm's, or, for that matter, of Chekhov's Russia.

Embellishing one scene from Storm's novella, Harlan shows Elisabeth swimming out to the water lilies in the middle of a pond. Kristina Söderbaum had died in earlier NS films by drowning, gaining her the nickname of *Reichswasserleiche* (Reich drowning victim or "floater").[3] Here, she reemerges from the lake alive, however, and viewers are treated to a momentary glimpse of bare Swedish epidermis from behind, no doubt a treat for Söderbaum's many fans. It is, however, difficult to imagine that Harlan was being ironic here; it seems more probable that he was inserting a teasing sequence not unlike the one with Hertha Feiler in *Kleider machen Leute*. Söderbaum was paid 60,000 Reichsmarks for her work in *Immensee*, three times as much as her co-star Carl Raddatz (Drewniak 494).

Both Theodor Storm and Gottfried Keller included in their novellas extremely visual — one is tempted to say "cinematic" — descriptions of landscape, buildings, weather, time of day, facial expressions, gestures, and other details for a screenwriter to work with. One of the central premises of Joachim Paech's *Literatur und Film* is the intimate relation of the earliest motion pictures to the bourgeois narrative tradition of such novelists as Alexandre Dumas, Victor Hugo, and Charles Dickens, in the sense that the pioneer filmmakers simply adapted many of the narrative conventions of the mid- and late-nineteenth-century novel into what one now calls cross-cutting and flashback, for example. The novellas examined in this essay fit cleanly into such a narrative-cinematic tradition with virtually no ideological tailoring necessary. It is not too far-fetched to maintain that in their commitment to the values of traditional narrative filmmaking, the filmmakers of the Third Reich who adapted literary works were part of an unbroken continuum.

Notes

[1] Keller, Gottfried, "Kleider machen Leute," in Klaus Jeziorkowski, ed., *Gottfried Keller: Kleider machen Leute: Text, Materialien, Kommentar* (Munich: Hanser, 1984) 7.

[2] Dieter Krusche, *Reclams Filmführer* (Stuttgart: Reclam, 1973) 638. Käutner (1908–1980) went on to a prominent career after the war, directing such well-received films as *Die letzte Brücke* (The Last Bridge) and *Ludwig II* (both 1954), *Des Teufels General* (The Devil's General, 1955), and *Der Hauptmann von Köpenick* (The Captain from Köpenick, 1956), among numerous others.

[3] Söderbaum's character commits suicide by drowning in *Jugend* (Youth, 1938), *Jud Süß*, and *Die goldene Stadt*. In a fourth film in which water is important, *Die Reise nach Tilsit* (The Journey to Tilsit, 1939), her character prevents catastrophe by discovering that her husband intends to kill her on a boat trip and by reconciling with him.

10

MARY-ELIZABETH O'BRIEN

The Spectacle of War in Die große Liebe

IN THE SPRING OF 1942 the British government implemented a new military strategy of bombing civilian targets, especially working-class neighborhoods, in the hope that it could destroy morale on the German home front. Shortly after midnight on 31 May 1942 the British Royal Air Force launched its first One Thousand Bomber Raid (code named "Millennium") with Cologne its target. Within an hour and a half the RAF dropped nearly half a million incendiaries on the city center. The fireball was visible from over 100 miles away. Upon reaching the devastated city, one British pilot remarked, "It was suddenly silent on board. If what we were seeing was true, then Cologne had to have been destroyed. We looked at the Rhine, but it was no mistake: what we saw down there was reality" (quoted in Paul 111).[1]

Less than two weeks after that bombing raid, on 12 June 1942, Rolf Hansen's home-front film *Die große Liebe* (True Love) premiered at Berlin's largest cinema, the Ufa-Palast am Zoo, and quickly became the most popular film of the year. In the first ten months of its release, *Die große Liebe* earned 8 million Reichsmarks playing to an audience of some 27.2 million spectators (Loiperdinger and Schönekäs 143). The film's touching love story, sensational musical numbers, measured comic relief, and star-studded cast all contributed to its overwhelming popularity. The trade papers, however, praised *Die große Liebe* primarily for its timely subject and realism.[3] What kind of realism did the film offer the masses, especially in the weeks and months following the premiere and massive, persistent bombing raids? What drove audiences in the summer of 1942 to this love story about a revue-singer and a *Luftwaffe* pilot repeatedly separated by the fighting in North Africa, France, and the Soviet Union?

I suggest we take our cue from the Nazi trade papers and examine the way in which this home-front film constructs the reality of war. The vast majority of German feature films made between 1939 and 1945 were set in either a distant, heroic past or a nondescript, seemingly peaceful present. *Die große Liebe*, a striking exception to this pattern, centers on daily life during the Second World War.[4] With its contemporary setting, the film offered audiences a unique opportunity to identify and empathize with characters trying to balance the conflicting wartime demands of love and duty. In this essay I will explore how *Die große Liebe* develops an entertaining and emotionally gripping model for dealing with air raids, rationing, separation, and suppression of desire for the sake of military victory. The film links the conflicts in the homeland and on the battlefield through highly sentimental episodes to illustrate how the nation forms a united front against the enemy. Hansen renders his fictional world with enough authentic details for the audience to see not just familiar characters and situations but also to see themselves in the events unfolding onscreen. Since the main characters are repeatedly depicted as spectators and performers, they hold up a mirror to moviegoers to look at themselves and imagine their own participation in the nation's real-life drama. By drawing structural parallels between musical and military spectacles, the film presents theater as a metaphor for the participatory role war demands of soldier and civilian alike.

Die große Liebe fashions reality in such a way that war functions as a dominant and positive force in the lives of Hanna Holberg (Zarah Leander) and Paul Wendlandt (Viktor Staal). War works as a catalyst for the love story. Paul's battle report brings him to Berlin, while his knowledge of an imminent bombing raid allows him to gain access to Hanna's kitchen, cellar, and eventually her bedroom.[5] As the air raid warden comments about their budding love, "The siren will bring it to the light of day."

For the soldier who knows nothing about blackouts and the singer who is not shaken by them, war changes ordinary experiences into a reality more beautiful than a fairy tale. As they look out over the darkened city in anticipation of a bombing raid, Paul and Hanna discuss how wartime reality, despite its dangers (or maybe because of its dangers) makes the city beautiful. When Hanna mentions that the city looks like a fairy tale, Paul disagrees, saying the city is "even more beautiful. Like reality."

The dangers inherent in war give the everyday a dynamic quality that is both new and exciting. In this highly charged atmosphere of life and death, intense passion and true love can evolve. Despite the characters' disavowal of contemporary life as a fairytale, the narrative continuously associates war with an imaginary kingdom where wishes come true. The film concludes with the song "Ich weiß, es wird einmal ein Wunder geschehen" (I Know, Once Upon a Time a Miracle Will Happen), whose opening lyrics confirm the bond between war and fairy tales. Hanna sings: "I know, once upon a time a miracle will come to pass and then a thousand fairy tales will come true." The song removes "once upon a time," the formulaic introduction of fairy tales, from the remote, make-believe past and situates it in a not too distant Nazi future as suggested by the lyrics "once upon a time it will come to pass." The film links the wish for a miraculous victory to an equally strong wish for a romantic happy ending, so that the former seems to be the only guarantee for the latter.

The battle between love and duty, rather than between Germany and the Allied nations, becomes the principal conflict of the film and, by extension, the times. With war so thoroughly intertwined with the love story, military victory seems predicated on whether or not the pilot and his girl can work out their problems.[6] Because the songs refer ambiguously to developments on the battlefield as well as in the love affair, they reinforce this idea. In the number "Davon geht die Welt nicht unter" (It's Not the End of the World), for example, Hanna sings of overcoming emotional heartaches to a hall filled with injured soldiers. While her song ostensibly deals with the ups and downs lovers suffer because of wartime separation, it could just as easily apply to the vicissitudes of combat. Hanna's lyrics, her gestures, and the soldiers' reactions aptly illustrate this ambiguity. She sings "sometimes things are up and sometimes down," while her hands mimic diving airplanes and the assembled *Wehrmacht* troops link arms to join in the rhythmic movements. Whether a reference to war or to love, the song provides an outlet for frustration and generates an overall optimistic sense of camaraderie.[7]

The film addresses many of the emotional problems created by war, specifically how people waver between hope and desperation, deal with feelings of abandonment, endure loneliness, and successfully adapt to a curtailed domestic life. The main characters, who serve as models, anchor these psychological issues. Nazi film critics and officials maintained that feature films inherently encouraged viewers to identify with sympathetic characters and emulate their behavior. In his 1943 book *Betrachtungen zum Filmschaffen* (Considerations on Film Making), Reich Film Dramaturge Fritz Hippler asserted that if a film gratified viewers' emotional needs, it could also supply influential role models and an orientation in life. Hippler summarized how film could potentially define values and teach behavior:

> Besides the personal connection between the audience and the main character during the course of the movie, film also generates the ambition to be like the star. How he clears his throat and how he spits, how he is dressed, how he behaves, if and what he drinks, what and how he smokes, whether he is a stuffed shirt or a man-about-

town, that all has an effect not only in the film but also in the life of the audience. A powerful and victorious film releases a different public than a tragic or comic film. After an Albers film, an assistant barber is an Albers; nobody had better dare to get mixed up with him (95).

Film scholars in Nazi Germany praised home-front films like *Die große Liebe* because they evoked in viewers "an inner willingness to lose themselves completely and totally in the figures and the events surrounding them." They deemed the effect of these role models as substantial,

> because everyone in the audience, whether soldier or civilian, man or woman, has someone "present" and identifies the fate up on the screen with that of a friend, husband, brother or fiancée. In short, after the first images, every member of the audience sits in the auditorium with a trusting, open heart ("Film und Zeitgeschehen" 8).

Considering the significance attached to the characters, it is no surprise that Hansen chose Zarah Leander and Viktor Staal to play Hanna Holberg and Paul Wendlandt. Best known for her imposing stature, flaming red hair, and legendary contralto, Zarah Leander was by all accounts the diva of Nazi cinema. Directors most often cast the Swedish actress in melodramas where she played seemingly independent, sensual women who suffer unbearable anguish before being redeemed as proper and obedient wives. *Die große Liebe* capitalizes on Zarah Leander's star image to frame the character's education in appropriate wartime behavior within familiar and entertaining melodramatic conventions. As in nearly all her German films, Leander's character is a sensual entertainer who undergoes the painful process of being tamed by a man and disciplined for marriage. What distinguishes her role in this film is that her training directly relates to the contemporary military struggle. Hanna must learn what it takes to be an officer's wife: wait patiently and accept separation without question. She develops from a self-centered prima donna reluctant to sacrifice her own immediate gratification into a selfless wife/comrade committed to victory. While she initially asserts "treat yourself to whatever you like," she eventually comes to accept that separation is part of everyday life, each moment together is precious, and the postponement of pleasure serves a higher goal.

Although Viktor Staal did not possess the same star recognition as Leander, he had already established a solid reputation as a romantic leading man. Starring opposite such popular actresses as Leander in *Zu neuen Ufern* (To New Shores, 1937), Lilian Harvey in *Capriccio* (1938), and Marika Rökk in *Eine Nacht im Mai* (One Night in May,

1938), Staal specialized in roles of handsome and likeable (if somewhat wooden) bachelors who marry exciting, unpredictable women. Typecast as the strong and dependable suitor, Staal brings these qualities to his portrayal of Paul Wendlandt. A dedicated soldier, Paul must discover the value of attachment to a woman and the homeland. Whereas he starts as a daredevil without any emotional ties, he learns that a soldier needs someone special at home waiting just for him. Paul only recognizes how important love is for a man after he assumes the traditionally female role of waiting during war.[8] When Paul tries to visit Hanna unexpectedly, he discovers that she is entertaining the troops in France. Disappointed, he experiences first hand what it is like to wait for a loved one to return from the front. But one aspect of Paul's personality remains constant: he is an officer devoted to the strictest military code of honor. What we hear about Paul in the opening scene characterizes him throughout: "He won't leave his machine in the lurch."

Like all melodramas, *Die große Liebe* needs to place obstacles in the path of the romantic leads to give the characters something to grow around and reach past. One serious obstacle to Paul and Hanna's romance is their different, yet equally valid understandings of *Glück* (luck). Paul, on the one hand, thinks of luck as fortune. During the course of the film, he repeats five times that he has "proverbial good luck." Luck allows him to win Hanna's heart, succeed at games, avoid serious injury, and triumph over the enemy. Hanna, by contrast, talks about luck in terms of happiness. She pictures herself living contentedly with Paul in a cottage, gardening and washing diapers. Ultimately Hanna begins to recognize that personal happiness and the fortunes of war go hand in hand. She eventually develops a realistic attitude and accepts that an ideal married life must wait until after the war. In her final musical performance Hanna acknowledges their common fate: "We both have the same star, and your fate is mine too."

To reinforce the message, *Die große Liebe* mirrors the central plot in two romantic subplots. The first subplot, with Käthe and Albert, mirrors Hanna's search for an ideal relationship with Paul. By rendering the same story with minor characters in the tradition of the *Ständeklausel* (dramatic convention of social rank), the film ridicules unrealistic expectations for personal happiness and takes a humorous look at the ideal man. Käthe fools herself into thinking that the physically powerful acrobat Albert loves her. Only after she finds the ordinary soldier, Maxe, can Käthe have a realistic relationship and perhaps even find true love. Käthe, like Hanna, prefers a man who acts not on stage but in an arena that actually counts — the battlefield. In Käthe's words: "I'd rather have my Max in hand than Albert on the trapeze."

The second subplot deals with Alexander's unsuccessful courtship of Hanna, which helps define the nature of a real man. "Hopeless but cheerful," Alexander serves more as a foil to Paul than as a viable suitor for Hanna. As the sensitive musician, Alexander's inability to be forceful and his tendency to be too nice make him both a comic and a tragic character. Both Alexander and Albert fall short of ideal masculinity. At one extreme stands Albert, seemingly desirable as the strong and silent type, but whose shyness and indecisiveness make him laughable. At the other extreme sits Alexander, an artistic type who is equally inappropriate because he is weak and overly sentimental. Paul thus forms the middle ground, a man who possesses the right mixture of strength, determination, and feeling. A fighter pilot with equal amounts of discipline and sentiment, Paul embodies the virtues Goebbels so often described as "romanticism tempered by steel."

In its presentation of the *Volksgemeinschaft* (national community) gathered together in the cellar during an air raid, the film also works out real-life tensions created by war. Elements of reality enter the scene through stereotypes: the high-strung, screeching old woman; the over-zealously organized family patriarch; the humorless, intellectual complainer; and the hoarder who is generous with other people's property. Each stereotype represents a genuine problem on the home front: fear of bodily harm and death, need for a contingency plan in emergencies, and resentment of hardships, especially rationing. By poking fun at problems in a lighthearted manner, the film shows them to be either unfounded or easily remedied. A cup of real coffee and a good dose of humor seem enough to distract the home front from carpet-bombings and the conflicts of world war.

The images of a community spending an evening together, playing games, knitting, and chatting, portray a sanitized version of life in the midst of Allied aerial strikes. The cellar with its comfortable furniture and friendly atmosphere looks more like a neighborhood social club than a bomb shelter. The film depicts shortages in consumer goods as minor inconveniences, which ultimately teach people to share with the community and forge a cooperative spirit. In contrast to this rather harmless depiction of civilian life, the situation on the German home front in 1942 was serious.[9] According to secret surveillance reports compiled by the *Sicherheitsdienst* (Security Service), food shortages in June 1942 were so severe that many workers complained of "a continuous feeling of hunger." The authorities voiced continued concern over the worsening food situation because "the atmosphere and attitude of the population is still determined by the difficulty in the food sector" (Boberach 263–64, 266, 267).

Despite the discrepancy between the film's depiction of hardships and the state's assessment of them, especially in regard to the severity of the situation, *Die große Liebe* seems to have given audiences a reality compatible with their own. The cellar scene, for example, highlights everyday experiences of adversity, to which many viewers could relate. Moreover, the film offers a remedy by suggesting that humor can be an effective outlet for normal frustrations. When a character loses his sense of humor in the face of minor inconveniences, his attitude is depicted as inappropriate and somehow tied to more deeply rooted personal problems. For example, when Alexander yells at a waiter because he and Hanna cannot get dessert in a restaurant, his anger is plainly an overreaction to the situation. Alexander merely uses the food shortage as an excuse to vent his frustration; the underlying reason for his outburst is the news that Hanna loves another man. Just as the film associates passion with danger to illustrate the inherent connection between love and war, it also associates the frustrations of unrequited love with wartime food shortages to make the same connection.[10]

By constantly presenting contemporary hardships within the framework of the love story, the film obscures any direct correlation between war and bombing raids or food shortages. Wartime dangers and inconveniences, divorced from any geopolitical conflicts, function as catalysts for the love story or as signifiers of romantic intentions. While the film acknowledges wartime problems, it generally frames them as harmless in the short run and even beneficial in the long run. For example, the Allied bombing raid causes no apparent damage, but it allows Hanna to get to know Paul better. Furthermore, although a Soviet pilot shoots down Paul's plane, his minor injury gives him the opportunity to marry Hanna and enjoy a three-week honeymoon.

Die große Liebe provides a good example of how the home-front film highlighted and attempted to forge bonds between civilian and serviceman. These movies stressed the need for all members of the community to unite behind the soldiers, and thus spoke to one of the more haunting myths of the First World War, namely that the German troops were stabbed in the back by the homeland.[11] *Die große Liebe* establishes this crucial link between the armed forces and the folk on the level of performance and spectatorship, uniting individuals through entertainment into a collective act that ultimately supports the war effort. Uniformed soldiers appear alternately as heroes performing a real-life display of martial skills for a captivated audience and as spectators attending an equally stimulating musical variety show. In a similar manner, the film depicts stage performers both as actors entertaining soldiers and as spectators mesmerized by newsreel footage of battle scenes. Since the characters and the scenes share the same properties, the film establishes a nexus whereby war and theater are structurally related. At four moments in particular, the spectacle of the theater merges with the spectacle of war.

The opening sequence blurs the distinction between reality, fiction, and documentary. Set in the skies over North Africa in 1941, familiar elements from contemporary wartime newsreels such as pulsating martial music, flash editing, and aerial shots of Stukas in flight fill the sequence. Into this newsreel-quality footage, the director Hansen intersperses the fictional story of *Luftwaffe* pilot Paul Wendlandt who is unable to engage his landing gear. The use of newsreel conventions heightens the drama of Paul's crash landing, giving the fiction an aura of reality. Because the opening sequence so obviously quotes a familiar newsreel style, it also draws attention to its own construction as a motion picture. This self-reflective narrative creates a decisive link between war and spectacle. While the film renders Paul's crash landing as a real-life military action, it is also a visual sensation witnessed by onscreen viewers. The scene is presented in the same terms as theater, with Paul as an actor on display and his squadron as an onscreen audience who watches the scene intently but from afar. Watching the war thus resembles watching a cinematic or theatrical spectacle.

The second moment comes as Paul's real-life aerial show segues into Hanna's musical extravaganza, where she performs on stage as the object of desire, singing of unbridled passion to servicemen who need to renew themselves emotionally before returning to the front. Not only do structural similarities and visual thrills connect Paul and Hanna's shows, but so does the presence of an onscreen military audience. Paul and his friend Etzdorf, both dressed in *Luftwaffe* uniform, are prominently pictured as members of the audience watching Hanna's show "My Life for Love." A swift tracking shot from the back of the theater to the stage establishes the conventional distance between audience and actor, while numerous close-ups of Hanna and reaction shots of Paul work to redefine the theatrical relationship. The intimate camera work illustrates how emotional involvement can bridge the gap between viewer and actor, soldier and singer, war and entertainment.

The third time we encounter the theater of war, the roles are reversed. Unexpectedly, shots of a dogfight fill the screen, accompanied by the sounds of diving Stukas and dramatic, upbeat music. It appears as if we are watching a newsreel woven directly into the feature film, when an announcer reports that *Luftwaffe* pilots continue to engage the British in a dramatic air battle. Suddenly the camera tracks backward to reveal a movie screen, theater, and audience including Hanna. War is thus rendered as cinema so that Hanna can watch it in the *Wochenschau* (weekly newsreel). The air show unfolding on the screen for Hanna resembles her own performance. Now she is the embedded spectator entranced by the sights and sounds of the Stukas, filled with desire for her fighter pilot conjured up in the newsreel. The military replicates the entertainment Hanna offered the soldiers, so that she can enjoy the captivating pleasures of war.

Finally, Hanna becomes a bridge between war and spectacle when she entertains the troops on the Western front. Like the radio in *Wunschkonzert* (Request Concert, 1940) Hanna overcomes the distance between homeland and front by bringing her musical performance to the soldiers. Whereas she moved Paul emotionally and sexually in her first performance, she now literally moves the servicemen to sway in response to her song, "Davon geht die Welt nicht unter." Both performances send the same message; women are essential to the war effort because they motivate men into action. As long as women fight in concert with men, victory is inevitable. Hansen uses Hanna's participation in a cultural event organized by the *Sonderreferat Truppenbetreuung* (the Propaganda Ministry's special unit for troop entertainment) to help fulfill the state's mission of uniting war and art. As Hans Hinkel, the director of troop entertainment, remarked: "The connection between sword and lyre — as has been validated in troop entertainment for our soldiers — represents the most glorious symbol of German victory over the outdated plutocratic world hostile to us."[12] Maintaining the link between war and theater is portrayed as crucial to military victory and survival. For example, only after Paul and Hanna break up, after they sever the ties between home and war fronts, do the Soviets shoot down Paul's plane. The deadly consequences of autonomy are also apparent when the film cuts to Hanna walking along the Via Appia, where she contemplates the beauty of death and confesses: "Sometimes I too wish I were dead." The symbiosis between Paul and Hanna demands that she understand what it is like to be surrounded by death and experience its fatal attraction, so she can accept the seductive powers of death.

When Paul and Hanna finally meet in the mountain hospital and look together toward the planes flying by, they are united in their role as spectators and in their dedication to the war effort. Again the film structures the scene to have an onscreen military audience. Two servicemen watch Hanna's arrival, nod to each other, and retreat. The camera takes over the servicemen's point of view and allows the film audience to watch the lovers watching the war. The self-reflective narrative provides a point of identification for the film's actual audience, allowing the viewer to participate in the love affair, entertainment, and war (Feuer 329–43).

Self-reflective moments in *Die große Liebe* do not call the film's ontological status or social reality into question. Instead, questions are directed towards the identity of the main characters that masquerade in illusory roles and must find their true selves. At the outset Paul and Hanna confuse the notions of "role" and "self" in respect to both their own identity and the identity of the other. In her first stage appearance, which is also her first appearance onscreen, Hanna plays the role of *femme fatale*. Costumed in a revealing gown and blond wig, she acts the part of an alluring, frivolous woman. Paul mistakes Hanna for her stage role, pursuing her relentlessly half the night. Only after the two share the role of parents in the bomb shelter does Paul see Hanna's hidden potential as a wife and mother.[13] Through the narrative, Hanna travels toward her authentic self, an officer's wife who subordinates her desire (read individuality) to the nation's wartime needs. National Socialism valorized a woman's sublimation of her own interests for the sake of her family and the national family, the *Volksgemeinschaft*. The prevailing view in the Third Reich held that women could only achieve the status of human beings when they accepted the role of motherhood as the genuine self and ceased to exist as an individual:

> If she is a real mother, she loses herself in her familial duties. But wonderfully: exactly therein, she becomes a woman and human being in the deepest sense. The more obvious her surrender, the more so. In losing her life she finds herself, her true dignity, her inherent humanity. . . . She becomes a mother and thus a whole human being by means of self-abnegation, not by self-assertion (Diehl 92).

Reduced to her function as potential mother and deprived of desire and even identity through self-denial, the individual woman vanishes. *Die große Liebe* illustrates this process of self-abnegation in the Via Appia scene, which ruptures the nearly seamless narrative fabric. Hanna walks as if in a trance along the deserted road in a landscape she calls "so endlessly cheerful despite the many gravestones." Her comfort among the graves and her desperate wish to be dead signal her symbolic death, one in which her ego and subjective desires perish. Only after purging herself of all vestiges of individuality does Hanna become reconciled with Paul and worthy of marriage.

Paul also masquerades when he adopts the persona of an adventurous and ardent man about town. Before he meets Hanna, Paul changes out of his military uniform into civilian clothing, thus disguising his real, soldierly self. Paul's protective behavior in the bomb shelter, his concern for the community's well-being, and his ability to distract them from the bombs by organizing a group activity all reveal his potential role as father. Despite these demonstrated masculine qualities, Paul's identity is still unresolved. When Hanna asks him twice who he is, Paul only gives his name and describes himself in mysterious terms as a prophet and a traveler. Weeks later, when she reads his letters from the front, she finally learns his true identity as a *Luftwaffe* pilot. Still, she does not confirm his identity out loud. She merely says to him, "You are," as if to imply that Paul's profession is so integral to his being that he simply "is."

The constant references in *Die große Liebe* to adopting roles, going to the theater and the movies, performing for others and acting as spectators accentuate the pleasures inherent in the communal ritualized act of movie-going. *Die große Liebe* creates an emotionally fulfilling experience of communion with others not only in the fictional narrative but also through the ritual of movie-going itself. Both the fictional and the actual audience can enjoy the collective experience of being transported to a different time and space, a place where magic and make-believe govern the course of events. Günter Berghaus argues that fascist regimes throughout Europe "sought to translate their political creeds into theatrical language that drew heavily on the traditions of ritual and mysticism" to create a belief in the charismatic national community. Berghaus maintains that fascist theater, "like all ritual theatre, had the function of offering a healing power, or *katharsis*, in a moment of crisis and to communicate a binding belief system to the participants" (5). In the crisis of war, *Die große Liebe* offered the home and war fronts a group identity based on a shared emotional release, intimacy, physical closeness, and consumption of entertainment. It also provided a fictional model of viewers united in their consumption of entertainment and participation in war.

But the theater in *Die große Liebe* does not function merely as an escapist illusion or as a means to forge a collective identity. It also becomes a way to control the masses. Since war is defined in terms of participatory theater, civilians and soldiers alike become actors on display constantly exposed to the policing gaze of their fellow actors. Confined in a perfect spectacle or panopticon as both actor and spectator, the individual is under constant surveillance, with the implicit warning to behave. In his celebrated discussion of Bentham's panopticon, Michel Foucault writes, "visibility is a trap" and concludes:

He who is subjected to a field of visibility, and who knows it, assumes responsibility for the constraints of power; he makes them play spontaneously upon himself; he inscribes in himself the power relation in which he simultaneously plays both roles; he becomes the principle of his own subjection.[14]

Die große Liebe presents this system of constant surveillance as a desirable condition. For instance, as an entertainer Hanna is constantly watched on stage. However, when she leaves the theater, she continues to be the object of the omnipresent gaze. The streetcar conductor observes her movements every night and reports on them to a group of men who continuously stare at her. While Hanna seems mildly irritated by this scrutiny, it proves to be beneficial in the end because it allows her love affair with Paul to develop. Only after Paul receives information from the conductor can he follow Hanna into the subway and find a way into her heart.

In a nation permeated by a state-sponsored surveillance apparatus, in a "terrifying social landscape . . . in which ordinary people eagerly helped to police one another," it is fitting that fantasies of an omnipresent gaze would penetrate the cinema.[15] As recent historical studies have demonstrated, the enthusiastic participation of ordinary citizens and not merely the watchful eye of Gestapo officials "kept the machinery of terror going, and constituted a central component of the internal 'constitution' of the Third Reich" (Mallmann and Paul 173).

Die große Liebe contributes to the Nazi cinema of enchantment, creating a place so delightful one wants to share in the illusion at any price. Like all successful entertainment films in the Third Reich, *Die große Liebe* reestablishes the contours of normality. It trains the spectator to fantasize reality in such a way that war becomes a positive force in the end. War brings people together, transforms the ordinary into the spectacular, intensifies feelings, and helps the individual become stronger. Nazi entertainment films work in tandem to allow spectators to insulate themselves from the more upsetting aspects of reality, extricating troubling events and replacing them with palatable alternatives. The mind-set created in the movies is ultimately transferable to everyday life, so that the audience can conceive even the worst circumstances as tenable. Thus, total war becomes thinkable, tolerable, doable, when one keeps in mind that the world won't come to an end and perhaps a miracle will make fairy tales come true.

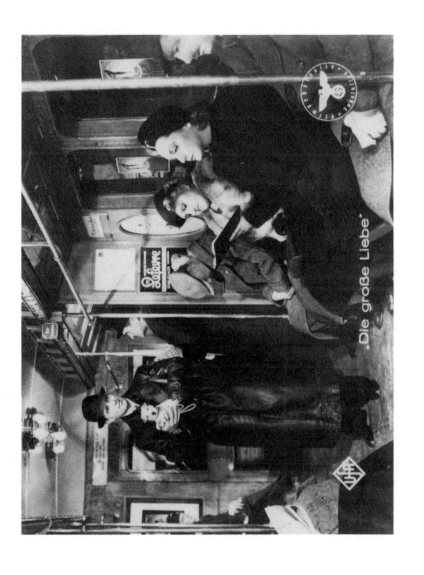

Die große Liebe (1942). First Lieutenant Paul Wendlandt (Viktor Staal), pursuing Hanna Holberg (Zarah Leander), here casts an admiring glance at his future lover. Courtesy Bundesarchiv-Filmarchiv Berlin.

Die große Liebe (1942). Hanna comforts Lieutenant Wendlandt, who is convalescing after his plane has been shot down. Courtesy of Bundesarchiv-Filmarchiv Berlin.

Notes

[1] All translations are mine unless otherwise noted. For a description of Operation Millennium and the Cologne bombing see Wolfgang Paul, *Der Heimatkrieg 1939 bis 1945* (Esslingen am Neckar: Bechtle, 1980) 105–17; Adolf Klein, *Köln im Dritten Reich: Stadtgeschichte der Jahre 1933–1945* (Cologne: Greven, 1983) 252–56; Wilber H. Morrison, *Fortress without a Roof: The Allied Bombing of the Third Reich* (New York: St. Martin's Press, 1982) 24–31; Charles Messenger, *"Bomber" Harris and the Strategic Bombing Offensive, 1939–1945* (New York: St. Martin's Press, 1984) 74–78.

[2] According to Stephen Lowry, the premiere run in Berlin lasted 91 days, while the average run was 28 days, with the range from 6 to 91 days, *Pathos und Politik: Ideologie in Spielfilmen des Nationalsozialismus* (Tübingen: Niemeyer, 1991) 20. Eric Rentschler notes that *Die große Liebe* registered an all-time record of over 400,000 admissions at the Berlin Ufa-Palast am Zoo for the period June 12 to August 29, 1942. *The Ministry of Illusion: Nazi Cinema and Its Afterlife* (Cambridge, MA: Harvard UP, 1996), 260. Klaus Kreimeier lists the film's gross at 9.2 million Reichsmarks and the audience at nearly 28 million based on the period up to November 1944, *Die Ufa-Story: Geschichte eines Filmkonzerns* (Munich: Hanser, 1992) 371.

[3] Typical is this review from Maria Waas, "The film takes its plot from our immediate present, the battle between love and duty grows out of the demands of the day and gives the film convincing true-to-life qualities," Bundesarchiv-Filmarchiv document file 6214, no title, no date. See also *"Die große Liebe: Zarah Leander und Paul Hörbiger in einem neuen Film," Filmwelt* no. 47/48 (26 November 1941): 938–39; "Große Dekoration für Zarah Leander: Bei den Aufnahmen zu dem Ufa-Film *Die große Liebe," Film-Kurier* no. 30 (5 February 1942): 3; Hans Suchen, *"Die große Liebe," Filmwelt* no. 23/24 (24 June 1942): 188.

[4] Fewer than twenty feature films produced in Nazi Germany treated the contemporary Second World War experience. The combat film enjoyed a brief high point in 1941 when five films premiered: *Kampfgeschwader Lützow* (Fighting Squadron Lützow), *Über alles in der Welt* (Above Everything in the World), *Spähtrupp Hallgarten* (Scouting Party Hallgarten), *U-Boote westwärts* (U-Boats Westward), and *Stukas*. Furlough films, in which a soldier finds his true love while on leave, included *Sechs Tage Heimaturlaub* (Six Days Furlough, 1941), *Zwei in einer großen Stadt* (Two in a Big City, 1942), and *Ein schöner Tag* (One Fine Day, 1944). Home-front films like *Wunschkonzert* (Request Concert, 1940) and *Die Degenhardts* (1944), together with related films such as *Auf Wiedersehen, Franziska* (Goodbye, Franziska, 1941) and

Fronttheater (1942), explored the bond between the civilian populace and the front-line soldier in contemporary war-time love stories and family dramas.

[5] At a dinner party Paul hears the announcement: "German National Radio will interrupt its program for a short period," and recognizes that radio silence means a pending Allied strike.

[6] I am grateful to Glenn Cuomo for bringing the following citation to my attention. Joseph Goebbels' diary entry from May 14, 1942 reads: "The new Leander film 'True Love' was shown. It attempts to incorporate a private story into the greater war experience, and it does so rather skillfully. The film can hardly lay claim to artistic merit, but it will certainly be a very effective crowd pleaser." *Goebbels Tagebücher*, Hoover Institute, Reel 3, frames 2750–51, pages 15–16 of typed manuscript.

[7] Micaela Jary relates the genesis of this song in her book, *Ich weiß, es wird einmal ein Wunder gescheh'n: Die große Liebe der Zarah Leander* (Berlin: edition q, 1993) 177–85. She writes that Leander, composer Michael Jary, and lyricist Bruno Balz (who wrote the text directly after his release from Gestapo arrest), considered the song openly subversive. They thought it would be obvious that the song did not refer to the end of the war or separation but to the end of the Nazi regime itself.

[8] In her analysis of the filmic love story, Mary Ann Doane notes, "the genre does seem to require that the male character undergo a process of feminization," *The Desire to Desire: The Woman's Film of the 1940s* (Bloomington: Indiana UP) 116.

[9] As early as late autumn 1939, German consumers were complaining about the inadequate food supplies, coal shortages, and the lack of shoes; see Marlis G. Steinert, *Hitler's War and the Germans: Public Mood and Attitude during the Second World War*, trans. Thomas E. J. de Witt (Athens, Ohio: Ohio UP, 1977) 59, 64–65. By the time *Die große Liebe* began filming in autumn 1941, Security Service reports compiled over the summer warned that the "catastrophic food situation" had triggered widespread resentment and low morale (121). Food shortages and deteriorating public mood only worsened in the winter of 1942, as filming of *Die große Liebe* concluded. The perceived threat posed by British bombing raids escalated in a similar manner. While RAF aerial strikes against the Reich in the summer of 1940 were largely symbolic gestures causing little damage, they nonetheless contributed to low morale on the German home front. The heavy bombing raid on Berlin in August 1940 left many citizens bewildered and discouraged. See Steinert 77; Jay W. Baird, *The Mythical World of Nazi War Propaganda, 1939–1945* (Minneapolis: U of Minnesota P, 1974) 127 ff.

[10] The strong man Albert also uses food to express his love for Hanna. He gives her coffee, a commodity in short supply, which Paul takes control of in a later scene, as if to illustrate the difference between requited and unrequited love.

[11] George Mosse discusses the centrality of the German First World War experience for the rise of National Socialism in his article, "Two World Wars and the Myth of the War Experience," *Journal of Contemporary History* 21 (October 1986): 491–514.

[12] Hans Hinkel, "Der Einsatz unserer Kunst im Krieg," *Der deutsche Film* 5, no. 11/12 (May/June 1941): 217. According to Hinkel, 15,000 cultural events were staged for troops in the West in the winter 1939–1940.

[13] Lowry discusses the centrality of the cellar scene for establishing Hanna and Paul as potential parents (*Pathos und Politik* 164–70).

[14] Michel Foucault, *Discipline and Punish: The Birth of the Prison*, trans. Alan Sheridan (New York: Vintage Books, 1979) 200, 202–3. I am indebted to Bruce Campbell for his careful reading of this essay at an early stage and suggestions on the controlling nature of participatory theater.

[15] David F. Crew, Introduction to Klaus-Michael Mallmann and Gerhard Paul, "Omniscient, Omnipotent, Omnipresent? Gestapo, Society and Resistance," in *Nazism and German Society, 1933–1945*, ed. David F. Crew (New York: Routledge, 1994) 166. For an interesting study of the dream world in Nazi Germany, see Charlotte Beradt, *Das Dritte Reich des Traums* (Frankfurt am Main: Suhrkamp, 1981).

11

ROBERT C. REIMER

Turning Inward:
An Analysis of Helmut Käutner's
Auf Wiedersehen, Franziska; Romanze in Moll;
and Unter den Brücken

L OVE PLAYS AN IMPORTANT ROLE in the Third Reich films of
Helmut Käutner. But then, as film historian Bogusław Drewniak
has written, love plays an important role in most of the feature films of
the Third Reich (239). Whereas many of these films, at least the better
known of them, present love as part of a greater whole, Käutner's films
are about the essence of love itself. While the issues of family, duty, and
sublimation of desire can be found in Käutner's work, his movies are
more about the fulfillment of love than its denial. It is not surprising
therefore that many film historians are reluctant to align his work completely with the film politics of The Third Reich and instead accord him
and his films a special position within National Socialist cinema. Curt
Riess calls Käutner's movies "the most beautiful films of the period"
(1958, 188). Francis Courtade and Pierre Cadars declare Käutner "the
only interesting director of the Third Reich in the realm of the entertainment film" (223). David Stewart Hull places him outside the mainstream when he writes, "The finest director working in the Third Reich
was Helmut Käutner, whose films could hardly be more different from
those of Ritter, Steinhoff, Harlan, and Selpin" (232).[1] Reviewing the
film *Unter den Brücken* (Under the Bridges, 1945; released 1946),
German film critic Wolfgang Ruf places Käutner entirely outside of
Nazi ideology, a position he feels the director earned with his earlier
films *Romanze in Moll* (Romance in a Minor Key, 1943) and *Große
Freiheit # 7* (# 7 Freedom Street, 1944).[2]

Helmut Käutner's Nazi-era films might seem different from other
features made during the Third Reich. Yet, as the following analysis reveals, they never entirely escape the ideological constraints of Joseph
Goebbels's Ministry of Propaganda. Indeed his work seems representative of many of the feature films of the era, which seem free of ideology

and yet not free of the ideological system under which they were created. This essay analyzes three of the seven films Käutner made between 1939 and 1945 — *Auf Wiedersehen, Franziska* (Goodbye, Franziska, 1941), *Romanze in Moll*, and *Unter den Brücken*. I have chosen these three for several reasons. First, they reflect the changing mood in the populace as Germany's war efforts went from victory to defeat to disaster. Second, they are emblematic of the difficulties that postwar viewers have in negotiating the contradictory tendencies of Käutner's films, which suggest being both within and without Nazi ideology. Third, I have chosen the three films because of the nature of their musical scores, which create the stories of these films as much as do the dialogue and visuals. At times the music seems fresh and independent, suggesting to postwar ears non-Nazi qualities, at least different from those heard in the Nazi-era films of other directors. Yet, paradoxically, the music that seemingly places the films outside of the Nazi era also brings them back within Nazi ideology. For if the individual tunes, isolated numbers, and partial melodies suggest nonconformity with other products of the Nazi film industry, when placed back into the context of the respective films, they also suggest compliance with the aims of the Ministry of Propaganda.

Music in Käutner's films supports but also subverts and otherwise adds the meaning to the text that is being created by dialog and visuals. It plays a crucial role in completing the text of *Auf Wiedersehen, Franziska*, the director's fourth film and the only one clearly set in contemporary Germany. The film tells about the love affair and marriage between Franziska, a small town girl, played by Marianne Hoppe, and Michael, a newsreel reporter, played by Hans Söhnker. The newsman travels the globe filming disasters and sports events while his relationship with his wife deteriorates. Käutner sets the film in the years leading up to the Second World War. By focusing the narrative's denouement on the arrival of Michael's draft notice as Germany begins its war against Poland, the director changes an otherwise apolitical satire about male wanderlust into a melodrama about duty and personal sacrifice. Were it not for the topicality of its ending, the film could be seen as a celluloid rendition of the social criticism Käutner preferred in his cabaret skits, which the director described as "ironic criticism of human foibles without an overt political agenda" (Jacobsen 1992, 16). We must ask ourselves however whether the contemporary setting makes the film propaganda or at least gives it a place in the political ideology of the period.

The film's musical score provides the key to understanding its ambiguity. Composed by Michael Jary, with song lyrics by Bruno Balz, the score reflects both official and unofficial musical tastes of the time and includes styles from folk music to jazz, children's nursery rhymes to foxtrots, harmonic musical accompaniment to discordant background music. In its varied tempi and upbeat rhythms, the musical score supports the movie's visuals. Both score and visuals reflect the official optimism of the country as it entered the second year of the war. Newspaper headlines still bannered victories, and speeches referred to mobilization and not yet to "total war" and "pulling through." In this atmosphere, typical of the first years of the war, *Auf Wiedersehen, Franziska* looks outward. It is a love story, set against two backdrops, home and abroad, and it reflects the regime's concern for the sacred and the profane, the domestic and the foreign.

Jary's musical score for the first part of the movie supports the developing love between Franziska and Michael. It accompanies them in a well-choreographed pas de deux as Michael sees Franziska and follows her. The music controls their movement as they start walking, then stop, and then start again. In an early reprise of controlled movement, the two meet again outside a restaurant, walking in choreographed rhythms around each other — a routine that Käutner must have liked as he used it again in *Romanze in Moll* and *Unter den Brücken*. Music directs movement at other times in which Franziska and Michael are together as well. It is synchronized to their walking, provides background for their dancing, and serves as a leitmotif when they part at the train station. A recurring melody in the background, "Man geht so leicht am großen Glück vorbei" (It's Easy to Pass Happiness By) reminds viewers of one of the film's themes, that one finds happiness in one's own back yard.

In contrast, in the scenes that are set outside Germany, the music, hectic and chaotic, underscores the lack of control individuals abroad have over their destiny. The music accompanying the scenes of newsreel footage is exciting. It is also frenzied and noticeably loud. Its entertaining and yet chaotic nature matches the sensational events of the newsreels the cameramen are filming, which include floods, fire, and war that influence the fate of the individuals in the news reports. At the same time the score for these scenes reflects the uncertainty of the lives of the reporters, whose place in the world depends on the next big story.

Music in other sequences that take place outside of Germany likewise fulfills a dual purpose. On the one hand, the jazz numbers lend *Auf Wiedersehen, Franziska* a degree of sophistication not often found in Nazi-era films. Indeed, together with the suggestion of infidelity that is associated with the playing of jazz, American-style music adds a rebellious tone to the film. Historian Michael Kater notes that once the war started in 1939, jazz and swing, which had been a focus of periodic cultural purges, came under a quasi-ban. The Nazis, however, never totally forbade the music with formal laws. Rather, sanctions against jazz and swing were hit and miss. While condemning American musical styles as aberrant and foreign, officials allowed jazz and swing to continue in public performance and on radio. Kater further notes that jazz remained an alternative listening choice for many Germans at home, and especially on the front:

> Goebbels knew well that the soldiers ... loved rhythmically accentuated dance music. ... As much as the minister disliked the pure-jazz extreme, it was difficult for him to draw a line between it and officially acceptable "German" dance music, and so the military fronts ended up indulging in whatever they wanted (118).

Thus, while it is true that the presence of jazz in the movie suggests subversion, it can also be understood as a means to indulge popular taste. In short, the musical score of *Auf Wiedersehen, Franziska* reflects the apparent ambivalence toward jazz and swing of the Ministry of Propaganda. Michael Jary's score for the film alternates between traditional melodies and harmonies and modern discontinuities and discordance.

The polarity in the film's music mirrors the ambivalence within the main characters, who, like the music, are caught between tradition and modernity. Franziska wants to be independent and sophisticated, yet she also wants a traditional domestic life. Michael wants to be a husband and father, yet he wants to continue his career as a globetrotting reporter. Thus, in its characters, story, and music, *Auf Wiedersehen, Franziska* emphasizes the tension that exists between traditional conformance to the norms and expectations of the community and a modern expression of individuality. Reflecting the importance that a sense of belonging and conforming to the *Volksgemeinschaft* (national community) had within Nazi Germany, the film resolves the tension always by privileging tradition. About a third of the way into the film, the story cuts from Germany to Michael and his friend Buck sitting on a veranda in South Africa, listening to a nostalgic melody that comes from a record player next to their lounge chairs. Apropos of nothing except perhaps the mood music, Michael asks his friend where he considers home. Buck has to admit that he has no home, having parents of different nationalities and having been born, grown up, and worked in different parts of the world. Michael, on the other hand, replies with dreamy eyes that his home is Germany, which he says first in English (the men have been conversing briefly in English) and then repeats in German. That he repeats himself in his own language — his home is *Deutschland* — confirms for viewers that even Michael's language makes him a part of something special. Furthermore, his repetition underscores Michael's sense of belonging to something special, the National Socialist community. In contrast, Buck's answer reveals his loneliness, dissatisfaction, and anger. Confirming his frustration at being without a country and therefore without a national identity, he throws his drink at the record, stopping the music.

Michael's epiphany precipitates a change in the story that the film's visual and musical structure reflects. Until this point, the images and music have supported the blossoming love affair between Michael and Franziska, underscoring their trysts with romantic melodies and simple dance tunes. Furthermore, in the initial stages their love has been a personal matter, the affair being carried out either in Michael's house or Franziska's apartment. But as Drewniak notes, love stories in German films of the period are more than personal love affairs. They integrate romance into the family-values rhetoric of the Third Reich. Even simple love stories, according to Drewniak, serve to underscore the joy of marriage and having children (239).

From the time when Michael identifies himself as a German, the central focus of the film aims at getting him to recognize the importance of family life as a means to integrate him into the national community. The visual and aural tracks, which had been objective in their depiction of Michael's lifestyle, begin to reinforce negative and positive stereotypes by juxtaposing foreign and domestic scenes. Michael and Buck leave the veranda, where Michael had begun to feel the special quality of being German. They visit the Seaman's Paradise Club, a bar with an international and erotic atmosphere. The syncopated rhythms of a jazz number play, its frenetic and atonal quality amplified to the point of producing discomfort. On the dance floor, scantily clad women of color gyrate. One of them scats the lyrics to a song, as if language has lost not only its social value, but also its ability to structure human activity. The excess found in a combination of atonal sounds, syncopated rhythms, and frenetic movement emphasizes the chaos and decadence of the bar's foreign environment. Judging from reviews at the time of the film's release, the depiction of an establishment where moral control is lacking draws attention to the superiority of German culture. Hermann Wanderscheck, music reviewer for *Film-Kurier*, refers to the provocative "Negermusik," the Nazi pejorative for jazz, that is heard in the club Michael visits (16 May 1941). A summary of the film, which appeared as part of a pre-release review, likewise focuses on the scene in the Seaman's Paradise Club, contrasting its seedy atmosphere with family-oriented Christmas activities in Germany. The review likens Michael's joyous reaction at the news he is to be a father to that of "a kid on Christmas Eve . . . and suddenly in the middle of this miserable, African dive, he sees home [Heimat]" (*Film-Kurier* 9 January 1941). The pre-release publicity thus suggests a way in which viewers should understand the film, as a conflict between the negative values of foreign elements and the positive values of the German community.

Musicologist Claudia Gorbman has identified two types of film music, each having its own distinct effect on viewers. She refers to one as "intimate 'identification' music." Its purpose is to draw viewers into the film and is generally "not to be heard." The second type she calls "epic 'spectator' music." The spectator notices this music, "which punctuates a pause in narrative movement in order to externalize, make a commentary on it, and bond the spectator not to the feelings of the characters but to his/her fellow spectators" (68). Borrowing this distinction from Gorbman, we can see that in *Auf Wiedersehen, Franziska*, these different types of film music help to structure the tension between non-German and German values. Furthermore the music plays a major role in resolving the conflict in favor of the latter.

The non-diegetic score that plays in the scenes set in Germany draws viewers into the movie, creates identification with Michael and Franziska, and establishes their relationship as occurring within the German community. Although the music remains in the background, it is never incidental. Rather, as mentioned earlier, its pleasant-sounding melodies and motifs choreograph the love affair, punctuate the partings at the train station, and reinforce familial relationships. The diegetic score that plays in the German scenes is comprised of simple foxtrots, waltzes, and a children's song. Regardless of the exact musical form, the tunes are harmonic, melodic, and soft, calculated to unite viewers in a feeling of a healthy Germany. Both diegetic and non-diegetic tracks meanwhile bring viewers into the movie and help them identify not just with the main characters but with the choices about family and country that the characters make. In contrast, the music that plays when Michael is abroad — both non-diegetic and diegetic — calls attention to itself, reminding viewers of the strangeness of the settings. The music accompanying the newsreel inserts may be non-diegetic for the newsreel itself, but for the film it is diegetic (its source being the newsreel); and its cacophonous tones capture the excitement but also the emptiness of the images of disaster represented in the newsreel. Without question the most striking example of music that calls attention to itself comes in the jazz club. Its loudness and fast tempo function to push viewers out of the scene. It causes them to react to and reflect on the excess of the images, rejecting what they see as foreign and unpleasant and accepting that as a comment on Michael's exotic lifestyle.

The music in *Auf Wiedersehen, Franziska* functions similarly to the score in Gustav Ucicky's *Heimkehr* (Homecoming) one of the few blatantly propagandistic films that the Ministry of Propaganda produced and released in 1941. *Heimkehr* sets up a polarity between good German values and bad Polish values as a means to create an aversion among German viewers to that which is foreign and to make viewers thankful for being part of a German national community. In reviewing the film in 1941, Wanderscheck writes how the composer used dissonance in the musical score to announce the arrival of Polish troops and how jazz helped underscore the chauvinist actions of the Poles (10 November 1941).

Although never intended as a propaganda film on the order of *Heimkehr*, *Auf Wiedersehen, Franziska* sets up a similar opposition. The foreign elements of the film's score, which include swing, jazz, and scatting, and the exotic and erotic elements of its visuals, which include scanty sarong skirts and revealing tops, alienate viewers from the foreign. On the other hand, the familiar sounds and sights of family life reinforce the integrative and healing quality of things German. As Michael leaves the Seamen's Paradise Club and reads his letter from home again, the jazz becomes quieter and hints at more traditional melody. In a similar juxtaposition, Michael is tempted by an American career woman in a bar as swing plays in the background. A few scenes later, back in Germany, Michael and Franziska stop arguing when they notice their two children standing on a stair landing, looking out a window and singing for the rain to go away. The scene's seductive sentimentality suggests that the glamour of the outside world cannot match the purity of the family idyll of mother, father, and children.

But before Michael and Franziska's story can reach resolution, the couple has to solve one more problem. Michael has been drafted into a military unit that will produce material for the *Wochenschau*, a newsreel covering events on both the war front and the home front, which was part of the movie bill in theaters at the time. He does not want to leave again, but Franziska, who has had an epiphany of her own, convinces him in a patriotic speech about duty and responsibility that he must leave once more, for the sake of his family and out of duty to his country. After the war the scene's overt propaganda caused the film review board of the Allies to withhold *Auf Wiedersehen, Franziska* from the list of movies cleared to be shown. Käutner, in an attempt to convince the review board that his film was free of Nazi ideology, removed this particular scene, claiming that the Ministry of Propaganda had required the speech:

> I received a request from the Ministry of Propaganda to film an additional scene of about 7–8 minutes in length and work it into the film. The scene shows the reporter's wife telling her husband clearly that now that he was going to war he would finally be doing something worthwhile for Germany (Cornelsen 50).

Käutner argued that he placed the scene into the film in such a way that it could be removed without damaging the film's continuity. Indeed, when he removed the scene, he convinced the film review board of the film's lack of other political content, and the authorities cleared *Auf Wiedersehen, Franziska* for postwar audiences.

Analysis of the film, however, suggests that Käutner may have engaged in wishful revisionism and that the review board was liberal in its clearances. For even without the offending seven minutes, the film text supports an ideologically based reading. Michael goes off to film the images of battle to be sent back to the home front — which would have been similar, one could suppose, to the images in the *Wochenschau* newsreel that preceded *Auf Wiedersehen, Franziska* in theaters of the period.[3] This time, though, at the train station, instead of Michael calling out "auf Wiedersehen, Franziska," Franziska, calls out "auf Wiedersehen, Michael." In the scene, Käutner uses the same musical motif he has been using to characterize scenes of departure in the film but adds several softly played bars from the folk song "Muß i' denn," reminding viewers of the brave women — those in the audience — awaiting the return of their men.[4] Publicity in the *Film-Kurier* describes the scene as follows: "They remain united even though they are separated by geography" (17 April 1941). Moreover, the conclusion, even if not preceded by Franziska's speech about duty and sacrifice, makes clear that Michael's wanderlust, directed now to supplying news for the German home front, serves the general community and not just himself.

Two years later the optimism reflected in *Auf Wiedersehen, Franziska* had given way to shock and pessimism after the German Sixth Army was defeated at Stalingrad. While never trumpeting defeat as they had victory, newspapers nonetheless eluded to the enormity of the setback for Germany by running essays on heroism and poems about fallen comrades. Yet films of the period either ignore totally what was occurring on the front and at home or sublimate defeat into a philosophy of pulling through. Rolf Hansen's *Die große Liebe* (*True Love* 1943), for example, may take place on a home front beset with food shortages and bombing raids; but shelters resemble social clubs rather than bomb cellars, and everyone looks well fed. Moreover, the film counters any lingering pessimism through its lead character, Zarah Leander, Germany's favorite film diva at the time. In two musical numbers that became hits, Leander's character admonishes viewers that the world is not ending and promises them a miracle. Other films simply ignore the contemporary world altogether.

Käutner's *Romanze in Moll* outwardly ignores the situation of Germany at the time of its making, its story being set in nineteenth-century France. Unlike the other escapist films of 1942 and 1943, however, *Romanze in Moll* reflects the external situation in tone and structure. The music and story of the film push forward to the film's tragic outcome, suggesting the pessimism viewers must have felt after the Battle of Stalingrad.[5] The film's somber tone moved Goebbels to decry what he perceived as its defeatism, and he initially banned its domestic release. Apparently he would have preferred a happy ending, one in which the heroine didn't let herself be seduced and certainly one in which she didn't commit suicide (Riess: 1977, 190). In spite of its unhappy ending, the film received good press coverage in Germany and eventually found a loyal following through word-of-mouth publicity (*Film-Kurier* 3 March 1944).

After the war, *Romanze in Moll* found strong acceptance from French critics, but the film had its detractors as well. Mihal Régine Friedman, for example, fairly bristles at the notion that the movie should be considered apolitical and criticizes those who praise the film for obscuring a discourse that is misogynistic in the way it controls the fate of women (1987, 55). Friedman argues that Madeleine's death is neither tragic nor heroic, as critics claim, but the result of suicide, which has been forced on her by an ethos that accepts self-negation of the individual. Indeed, she likens the acceptance of Madeleine's suicide by film critics to the way a death was viewed by Edgar Allan Poe who had said a century earlier that a woman's death was "without question the most poetic topos that exists in the world" (57). Marc Silberman likewise locates a fascist subtext in the film, which leaves the viewer "betrayed and abandoned, [ready to] transfer any sense of responsibility to those who misuse their authority while maintaining the very system of hierarchy and subordination which supports it" (96).

Friedman's and Silberman's readings are exhaustive and consistent. Their arguments are convincing. So too, however, are the glowing reviews of Swedish critics during the war and the reviews and analyses by German and French critics after the war.[6] Yet, Friedman's and Silberman's deconstruction of the film's formal beauty to expose a National Socialist core of *Götterdämmerung* and the efforts of postwar critics to turn Käutner into a maverick among Nazi directors raise additional questions. How, for example, does the film's treatment of marital infidelity fit into the tradition of bourgeois works of cinema, theater, and prose that place the theme of adultery at their center? Is the film's fatalism total or does its structure allow viewers to question the actions of the characters? How does the film's bourgeois morality reflect the official morality of the National Socialists? Finally, is Madeleine's suicide punishment for her adulterous affair or merely a reflection of the film's literary antecedents? Not surprisingly, *Romanze in Moll* calls forth different opinions, for Käutner structures his film around polarities of entrapment and freedom, containment and openness, duty and self-fulfillment, fatalism and free will.

Romanze in Moll fits easily into the film program of National Socialism, suggesting why Goebbels eventually relented and released it domestically in spite of his initial reservations about the film's fatalism. Although the film may seem an exception for its times, *Romanze in Moll* reflects the industry's penchant for recycling or appropriating forms for its own purposes. Thus films such as *Hitlerjunge Quex* (Hitler Youth Quex, 1933) traded on viewers' familiarity with Weimar cinema's forms, comedies such as *Glückskinder* intentionally copied Hollywood stories, and dramas with musical inserts, such as those of Detlev Sierck, successfully imitated a Brecht-Weill strategy of integrating musical numbers into dramatic action. Käutner's *Romanze in Moll* likewise mirrored a preference for recycling a familiar form, namely the bourgeois tragedy. Indeed, the bourgeois tragedy of Germany and Europe's literary canon was the source for a number of Third Reich films. Veit Harlan's *Jud Süß* (Jew Suess, 1940) appropriates elements of Gotthold Ephraim Lessing's *Emilia Galotti*, and *Die goldene Stadt* (The Golden City, 1942) borrows from Lessing's *Miss Sara Sampson* and from Friedrich Hebbel's *Maria Magdalena*. Nazism was prudish in its social values. So it is not surprising that the film industry of the time would favor stories in which death was portrayed as preferable to loss of virtue. Considering the long tradition of bourgeois tragic heroines who have served as inspiration for Käutner's Madeleine it is likewise not surprising that the film eventually passed the censors. She owes little to the heroine of "Les Bijoux" ("The Jewels"), Guy de Maupassant's short story on which the film is based. Maupassant's Madeleine accepts multiple gifts of jewelry, seems more in love with the accoutrements of her affair than the affair itself, and dies of natural causes rather than of suicide. In contrast, like the heroines of bourgeois drama, Käutner's Madeleine enters an untenable relationship in order to escape suffocation in a failing marriage. And like her predecessors, she dies because of the love affair. Madeleine is a cinematic relation of the confused wife of an Ibsen play, the impassioned heroine of a Tolstoy novel, and the adoring lover of a Schnitzler tale. Käutner's use of camera angles, symbolism, choreography, and atmosphere seem reminiscent of Max Ophüls's 1932 classic *Liebelei*, based on Schnitzler's play of the same name. Madeleine's direct model, however, is more likely Effi Briest, the heroine of Theodor Fontane's novel of the same name. Marianne Hoppe, who plays Madeleine, had recently portrayed Fontane's adulterous and remorseful heroine in Gustav Gründgens *Der Schritt vom Wege* (Step from the Path, 1937), a movie based on the novel.

Romanze in Moll thus functions similarly to Käutner's other Nazi-era films, criticizing within the National Socialist world those things that could be criticized, privileging the bourgeois ethos of self-fulfillment, and yet warning against excess. That Käutner was a cabaret artist who became a film director, whose cabaret works were social rather than political commentaries about vice, is apparent in this film and in his other films, both those made during the Nazi period and those made after the war. In a review at the time, Hermann Wanderscheck, one of the *Film-Kurier*'s main reviewers, asks, "who in the audience would want to condemn the behavior of the heroine, who has suddenly regained her life?" (11 November 1943). Who indeed, would want to deny her happiness, considering the narrowness of her petit bourgeois world? Her husband hardly fits the description as a "troubled exemplary spouse" (Bandmann and Hembus 148) given him in some reviews. Rather, camera angles and distance collapse time and space, restricting the husband's movements and revealing him to be a repository of boredom and pettiness. Käutner has given additional form to the outline of the husband of "Les Bijoux." In Maupassant, as befits the nature of his tale, only the wife has vices, spending too much time at the theater and too much money on baubles. Her husband merely indulges her in her diversions. In the film, the man indulges his wife also, but he does so because he views her as possession. "Buy yourself something" — he excitedly tells her as he fans the money he has won at cards and places it next to her bed, as one would for a prostitute, not a wife.

Throughout the opening scenes, the relationship of money and love is re-established time and again, even in the wife's absence. At the hospital, where his wife lies dying, the husband tells the doctor he won't spare any expense to save her. At the pawnbroker's he attempts to sell her things, and afterwards at the cafe, he gives money to a prostitute sitting next to him in a card game, paralleling the gift of money to his wife. In turn his gift to the prostitute parallels the gift of the pearl necklace Madeleine had received from her lover Michael. Käutner underscores the parallelism by having a third party comment on the gift: "One wants to be generous and so one gives presents." Thus even though the film criticizes the husband, it also portrays Madeleine as weak for bartering her affection in exchange for gifts.

Differences in style of presentation, as captured by camera angle and situation, establish two perspectives of love, one confining and the other expansive. The husband is constantly presented as constricted. The camera exaggerates the lack of space in which he must maneuver, controlling him with walls, partially open doors, and mirrors. He seems the architect of his own tragedy, much like Professor Rath of Joseph von Sternberg's *Der blaue Engel*, (*The Blue Angel*, 1929), a film whose tone and style Käutner at times seems to be quoting. As in the great classics of Weimar cinema, the director delights in overt symbolism, compounding tropes of freedom and entrapment, juxtaposing them in a fashion that suggests both life and death. Käutner compares Madeleine to the caged bird that her husband keeps: she flings open the windows to their apartment, reflecting her confinement and the possibility of escape. At the estate to which she and Michael escape for a tryst, the freedom suggested by an expansive sky is tempered as a farmer with a scythe passes in front of the lovers.

In his review of the film's music, Wanderscheck grants the heroine's passing chance at happiness, suggesting a liberal spirit unseen in most German films, and certainly unheard of in official Nazi reviews. Reviews by other critics, however, reveal another text in the film. Robert Volz, for example, focusing on the beauty of Madeleine's death, comments that it was unnecessary for the heroine to yield to her oppressor's blackmail before killing herself (*Völkischer Beobachter* 28 June 1943). Werner Fiedler writes that if Madeleine had not given in, her death by suicide would have seemed "more meaningful, dramatically more necessary, and would have had greater ethical justification" (*Deutsche Allgemeine Zeitung* 26 June 1943). In spite of the liberal and tolerant spirit evident in Wanderscheck's review, Nazi ideology nonetheless defines the heroine's death, and Madeleine becomes victim to an ethos that punishes women for indiscretions. In that respect, both Friedman and Silberman, who argue this point along different lines, perceive in the film the Nazi's cynical attitude toward women. Officially, Nazi-era ideology may have claimed to value nothing higher than love, marriage, family, work, and honor, but in reality, as the reviews indicate, just the reverse is true.

And yet, in spite of the discourse of death that surrounds *Romanze in Moll* in Nazi reviews and the fascist subtext that one can certainly find in it, the film retains a modern spirit. Käutner includes enough intentional irony and satire in the film to counter its darker moments, which may help explain its relatively positive postwar reception in spite of what Friedman recognizes as its received misogyny. From the opening scene and the opening chords of the music track, *Romanze in Moll* is a story still in progress but near its end. The opening shot carries viewers through flowing drapes of a second-story window to focus on the serene face of a sleeping woman, who, the following scene reveals, has attempted suicide and lies in a coma. The soundtrack offers an off-screen variation of the musical romance's thematic melody, which is not introduced into the diegetic world until later in the movie. The film then goes into a flashback, telling the heroine's story from her point of view. Yet the story is clearly told for a short while by a jeweler and for the most part by Michael, the romantic composer who causes the tragedy. The film ends with a shot of the heroine's face. Once again, the shot focuses on her smile, but we see that she is now dead and that a hand (Michael's) lays the pearls, the ones that led to the revelation of the story, on her body. Again we hear the thematic melody on the non-diegetic soundtrack. *Romanze in Moll* is more though than a romantic story behind the enigmatic smile of a *fin-de-siècle* heroine. On the one hand, the elements of this oft told tale — unhappy marriage, adultery, discovery, blackmail, duel — portend the film's tragic outcome. Their presence relates the film to the tradition of bourgeois love tragedies, as mentioned above, and lends the film the fatalistic tone that brought about Goebbels's initial ban. On the other hand, the self-reflexivity that is imbedded within the film's narrative, formal, and cultural codes suggests a more distanced reception to the material. For as the story within the frame begins, Madeleine has not yet died, and the doctor tells her husband that although he must reckon with any possibility, it is his duty to keep hoping for the best. Throughout the film Käutner requires viewers to negotiate between accepting his tale as a finished story, as his use of a conventional frame suggests, and seeing it as a work in progress, as the fugue-like telling of the tale suggests. As I have already mentioned, although the film relates events from Madeleine's perspective, Michael is the true narrator, telling the story to his brother after Madeleine's act of suicide. This is the story that goes along with the musical romance he has composed.

Käutner introduces this musical composition, which plays for over fifty percent of the film, only in incomplete segments. The soundtrack teases with bits of the romance, even introducing the composition on the off-screen track before it is introduced in the story. It is as if the music has to be brought to life by the flashback. The music and the story are a creation of Michael's talent and Madeleine's inspiration. The music needs the story as a source of images just as Michael needs Madeleine to inspire him. The story however also needs the music to give the images structure just as Madeleine needs Michael to help her experience love and also to tell her story. The non-diegetic performance of the music, with its starts and stops and variations of the melody, retard any viewer satisfaction that could be derived from its resolution. The story too stops and starts, first at the pawnbroker's and then at the jeweler's. Not until Michael takes over telling Madeleine's tale and eventually plays the leitmotif "between wakefulness and dreaming" do the film's music and visuals permit at least partial resolution. But even here, the melody plays in the major key and only later in the minor. It is first heard at Michael's mansion and then in Madeleine's small apartment. If music controls the characters' movement in *Auf Wiedersehen, Franziska*, here it controls the love story itself; and since Michael writes the music, he also "writes" Madeleine's story. Musical control of the story reaches its highpoint when the composition is finally performed in concert. The musical performance is the culmination to the flashback that tells of Madeleine and Michael's affair. As Michael conducts his composition, Madeleine listens and daydreams about her life during the affair. The camera focuses in close-up on her face. Superimposed over her image is a collage of scenes that reprise the major stages of the affair, its unraveling, and the assault on her virtue by her husband's boss, who has discovered her affair with Michael.

The series of images in the concert hall is on the one hand hypnotic and cannot be ignored in analyzing the film. Friedman, for example, deconstructs the sequence, which she labels a *mise-en-abyme*, to expose what she sees as the film's fascist subtext, the negation of the individual. Silberman likewise focuses on the sequence, including the leitmotif's music and lyrics in his discussion of the film's brooding romanticism. On the other hand, music does not simply pull us into a film's world. Gorbman's distinction between music of identification and music of spectacle is useful in interpreting the concert hall sequence. Performed now as a completed composition, the musical romance may cause us to feel a sense of finality, to feel that the story is over. Yet it also forces us to review the affair just as Madeleine reviews it. We are helped to do that by the spectacle of the music and also by the husband who asks as he sits down next to his wife, "Have I missed anything?" He has indeed, and to remind viewers what the husband has missed, the collage passes in front of Madeleine's smiling face. Marianne Hoppe has a seemingly ambivalent response to the effect of this sequence on the film's meaning. In an interview conducted on the set of the film in 1942, Hoppe talks about the way in which the collage passing in front of Madeleine's eyes recaps the events that entangle her more and more in her fate. She points out that the presentation leaves room for the imagination of the actress and the viewers. Hoppe concedes that not many women would be able to withstand their destiny, regardless of the outcome. Yet, as if in anticipation of Goebbels's reaction — that the story is too pessimistic — she emphasizes the necessity of women serving as an example for others as they withstand the vicissitudes of fate. They must carry on "in the office, in the factory, at the front, and above all in the family" (*Der Angriff* 13 November 1942). Hoppe's interpretation of the scene of events is of interest because it anticipates the pessimism of later critics, but also suggests an alternative reception by contemporary viewers, one that could lead them to question the heroine's suicide, not accept it.

The ambivalence of the images, suggesting being caught between wakefulness and a dream-state, can be found within the narrative and its multiple references to beginnings, endings, and modes of reception. Just as the melody seems caught, endlessly repeating the short refrain that accompanies the words "between dream and wakefulness," the narrative's doubling and redoubling creates an uneasy mood in the viewer, a feeling that one is caught in a story cycle endlessly repeating. But the repetition also creates distance from the film by calling attention to itself, leaving even a contemporary viewer free to negotiate the film's story without being dragged into its emotional center. For example, a visiting poet at the country estate of Michael's brother disputes an assertion that Madeleine would provide a good model for the heroine of a narrative. The visitor, played by Käutner, maintains that her life offers no possibilities for producing conflict since she is happily married to Michael (she and Michael are pretending to be married). However, if Michael and Madeleine were not man and wife, the case would be different. At this point the romantic couple join in to tell their story as it has actually unfolded, but pretend that it is a fictional one. Their playful creativity reprises an earlier scene from before they were lovers, in which they envisioned a similar scenario on how their relationship might unfold. The scene at the estate in which they tell their story under the guise of fiction is inter-cut with an episode that shows the husband examining the books of an accountant who stole money to keep an expensive wife. This inter-cut scene in turn is reprised back in the apartment when Madeleine tells her husband of the return of their upstairs neighbor to her husband and their reconciliation. After this fourth iteration of Michael and Madeleine's story, viewers prepare for the worst and yet hope for a miracle, as the doctor had admonished the husband when he visited Madeleine in the hospital. Audience members, who have participated in Madeleine's tragedy by following the stops and starts of the music and narrative, are free to question her actions during the montage, recognizing where the story went wrong, because they have witnessed its unfolding. Like Goebbels, reviewers for the *Film-Kurier*, and Marianne Hoppe, viewers can question the necessity of the heroine's defeatism, of her suicide, and ask if the situation was really so hopeless. As Goebbels's initial objections to the film suggest, he suspected that the film's defeatism might influence viewers in a way that would be detrimental to the war effort by turning them inward. In Käutner's earlier film, *Auf Wiedersehen, Franziska*, when Michael, the cameraman, asks Franziska to be his wife, she replies: "Haven't I been your wife for a while already," making a word play of their affair. But the story shows that marriage is more than sex and resolves the affair with a family idyll. In *Romanze in Moll*, when Michael, the composer, asks Madeleine to become his wife, she replies with the same word play: "Haven't I been your wife for a while already?" But the two years be-tween the movies have eliminated the possibility of a happy ending. The only alternatives are suicide or carrying on.

Many postwar critics consider the last film that Käutner made under the Nazis, *Unter den Brücken*, to be the director's best. Wolfgang Ruf calls the film "anachronistic" (*Süddeutsche Zeitung* 12 March 1973). Jan Schütte describes it as an "idyll that steadfastly avoids taking part in the spirit of the times" (171). Reviews from immediately after the war, during the film's initial release, even find elements of protest against the Nazis. A review in the Neue Züricher Zeitung reads: "A film such as this could only have been made with an ensemble in which every member was prepared to protest business as usual or at least had the will to no longer fall into line" (11 November 1947). The critic for the *Neue Filmwoche* used even sharper rhetoric in that publication's Febru-ary 1947 issue, writing:

> The film was made during the last years of the war. But Goebbels's Ministry barred it from reaching the public. The little man in the Ministry of Propaganda indeed had good reasons for sending the film to the vaults. For the film did not fit into the political landscape. . . . [It] contained nothing of what the ministry wanted: [It was] not heroic paraphrasing, not a historical battle composition: rather [it was] a mood, an idyll (17).

Schütte and the other critics are wrong though if they mean to im-ply that the film's avoidance of allusions to the situation in Germany at the time is meant as a political protest against Nazi policies. To be sure,

Unter den Brücken neither directly nor indirectly makes reference to a battle scarred Berlin, but the film hardly protests the war or the regime. Moreover it fits very well into a politics of film that with few, even if major exceptions, avoided explicit Nazi rhetoric and symbolism.[7] As early as 1933, Goebbels had admonished directors that SA troops should not "march through the film or over the stage. They should march through the streets." He equated the use of National Socialist symbols as a "failure of imagination" [wenn einem nichts besseres einfällt] and a sign that "[artistic] ability was lacking" (Albrecht, 1969, 442). Even through the last years of the war, Goebbels's policy of avoidance of overt ideological reminders remained, with the important exception of big budget propaganda extravaganzas like *Kolberg*, *Jud Süß*, or *Ohm Krüger*. Nazi film studios continued throughout the Third Reich to produce musicals, melodramas, comedies, and literary adaptations. That *Unter den Brücken* was not released before the war ended probably had more to do with timing than censorship. *Kolberg* had become an obsession with Goebbels, and other films had to wait their turn to be approved by his ministry. Evidence that the film was not "sent to the vaults" by the "little man in the Ministry of Propaganda" is provided by the favorable pre-approval publicity from the *Film-Kurier*, the official film daily of the Third Reich, which praises the simplicity of the film's story. "This film, whose title reveals that it plays for the most part under the bridges of the rivers, becomes a kind of big city melody, by means of which one can observe the life of the big cities from the water" (23 May 1944).[8]

Of his film, Käutner said after the war: "This film was a peaceful documentation of our own wishes. We lived as though in a dream disconnected from time and by working [on the film] diverted our attention away from all the terrible things" (in Cornelsen 66). The director's avoidance of any allusion to the contemporary situation in Germany troubled some postwar critics who "held it against" Käutner that he "filmed an idyll in the midst of a hail storm of bombs" just outside camera range (in Cornelsen 66). Thus the charm of the movie, its magical setting in a contemporary Germany that didn't exist, became a liability. Indeed, *Unter den Brücken* tells its simple story in such an unadorned and understated fashion that the film is sometimes compared with postwar Italian neorealism. Actually the film's highly choreographed movement, a holdover from Käutner's cabaret days in which he learned that the effect of spontaneity required careful planning, displays little deviation from his other films, which, as already noted owe their style to poetic realism, Weimar symbolism, and the rhythms of cabaret.

As charming as the characters of the film are, the true stars are the music, composed by Bernhard Eichhorn, and the city of Berlin, or a mythical representation thereof. Two melodies dominate the track of *Unter den Brücken*: "Auf der Brücke Tuledu" (On the Tuledu Bridge) and "Muschemusch, es sprach die Sonne" (Muschemusch, So Said the Sun). Hendrick, the man who will eventually win the love of the heroine Anna, and Willi, his business partner, friend, and rival in love, sing the first melody together as the film opens: the scene is set, true to the film's title, below a bridge. Through the lyrics, which tell of watching girls on the bridges above and of love affairs, the melody becomes associated with the friendship between the two men. The song has two distinct tempi. The stanzas are fast, almost agitated, reflecting the brief nature of the affair and the lack of commitment on the part of the men. The refrain is slow, almost melancholy, suggesting the desire of the men for a more permanent attachment. Hendrick performs the second song, "Muschemusch, es sprach die Sonne," which becomes a leitmotif of his and Anna's growing love for each other. The lyrics tell of listening to waves and of watching ships sailing for Zanzibar. The nonsense syllables of *Muschemusch* recall the sound of the waves, but they also give erotic meaning to Hendrick's longing. Instrumental versions of the two songs are also part of the non-diegetic soundtrack of the film. Here, the first song comments on the strength of the friendship, playing as the men vie first for the hand of a waitress and then for Anna's favor. The second song signals the outcome of the rivalry, playing when Anna and Hendrick are together. The one time it plays when Willi is with Anna, Hendrick, in spite of his physical absence, is present as the topic of the conversation.

Berlin, the second true star of the film, grounds *Unter den Brücken* in a physical and geographical reality. Käutner, however, does not present the city as metropolis, filled with the exciting sights and sounds that viewers associate with large cities. It would have been difficult, if not impossible, to refer to contemporary Berlin without reference to the war if Käutner had depicted the street landscape one associates with the city. Rather than include the usual clichés of urban life — nightclubs, alleyways, and bustling streets — he presents the city as the destination and point of departure for the three principle characters, keeping as his focus the waterways that lead to and away from Berlin. When Anna throws money into the Havel River, a gesture that the men believe signals her plans to commit suicide, Berlin also becomes a place to find love. For Anna does not plan to commit suicide. She throws the money into the river to overcome her loneliness and to forget that she earned the money as an artist's model. The men are also lonely and come to view Berlin as a place to commit to love.

Loneliness was clearly also a concern in the real world outside the movie house. Detlev Peukert in his book *Inside the Third Reich* quotes a diary written during the war:

> And the world? The best thing is to shut your eyes to it and to stop hearing and seeing all the dreadful fuss and bother that is getting more and more confusing and difficult to sort out. No one has any idea where it is all going. Most people have completely stopped even asking, and are just sticking to the tiring daily business of shopping and thinking about food. The emptiness inside one is getting more and more noticeable. . . . (79)

Käutner's film captures the writer's sentiment, which must have been prevalent at the time. Hendrick, Willi, and Anna search for love to still the emptiness inside caused by the unsettling conditions of physical and emotional deprivation. The songs may tell of love under bridges or of distant shores, but the trio feels that they will find love where they are, in the city.

Scenes in which the characters visit a museum and an atelier give clear evidence that the setting is contemporary Berlin. Yet, because of the war situation, Käutner has to present the city as outside of temporal reality. The physical locations of restaurant, river, bridges, docks, art museum, atelier, and Berlin apartment exist in a timeless universe that viewers enter by means of the musical score. Gorbman's theories of music in film can again be useful here. She writes that music in film has the power:

> [to remove] barriers to belief; it bonds spectator to spectacle, it envelops spectator and spectacle in a harmonious space. Like hypnosis, it silences the spectator's censor. It is suggestive; if it is working right, it makes us a little less critical and a little more prone to dream. (55)

Eichhorn's score and Käutner's lyrics would have allowed viewers to forget what was outside the theater, in spite of the reminders of the city that the locations provide. But ironically, due to the shelving of the film, they did not have a chance to see the film before the war ended. The film presents Berlin as viewers might have wished it were, unaffected by five or six years of war. The lyrics of the film's melodies ask them to girl-watch and lie on the shore listening to ships sailing for Zanzibar. The melodies are so hypnotic that viewers could willingly suspend disbelief and overlook two seemingly anachronistic moments in the film. When Anna first comes on board, she is unable to sleep because of the strange shipboard noises. She comes on deck and is joined by Hendrick, who calms her fears. He points out that she hears nothing more than the sounds of frogs, the wind, the creaking steering mechanism, and other natural shipboard noises. Telling her that the noises are more like shipboard music, he proceeds to demonstrate this by imitating the various sounds. As some critics have noted, it is one of the more musical moments of the film, even though no music plays on the track, but it is also one of the more hypnotic moments (Cornelsen 69). Hendrick tells Anna that she has to learn how to listen, and that when she does, she will no longer find the sounds strange and frightening. That is a daring scene to put into a film this late in the war when air raids were a regular occurrence, and the intended audience for the film had been living with frightening noises for several years. It remains unanswered how a contemporary audience might have reacted to the scene, although the pre-release reviews accepted this peaceful world as real. The second anachronistic scene comes shortly afterward, as the boat finally reaches Berlin. In an abrupt shift from natural lighting and setting, the film cuts to stock footage of a healthy, vibrant industrial city. This could be prewar Berlin, and to be sure, the time remains somewhat undetermined. Nothing in the story, however, suggests that the narrative takes place at any time other than the present.

Käutner's *Unter den Brücken* may thus seem as if it does not belong to the Nazi-era. Yet the film's imaginary world differs little from that found in the director's other works or in the films of other directors. It was also designed to offer dreams and help its intended audience turn inward and forget reality for a while. The world of Nazi-era German films is after all a world of false normalcy. It is a place where men and women have an idealized existence and play out traditional roles. As such, characters become role models offering images of friendship and love that were meant to help viewers once they left the theater. Yet, by avoiding all reference to the Third Reich, the images also appeal to postwar sensitivities. *Unter den Brücken* is as much part of the postwar spirit of humanity as it is of the Nazi film world. To be sure, the film was meant to help viewers forget the war by offering a place of respite. But turning inward had to be of limited duration if citizens were to continue to carry on their duties outside the theater. Even if the war had been lost by the time the film was made, the pretense of carrying on had to continue. The situation toward the end of the war was thus no different than earlier in the regime when the Nazi government fostered non-ideological entertainment because it distracted citizens from reality. Detlev Peukert points out that:

> . . . *passive* consent — accepting the regime as a given, and being prepared to do one's day-to-day 'duty' — rested on a process which the Nazi regime simultaneously combated and fostered: a retreat from the public sphere into the private (77).

Thus, turning away from outer events had a clear programmatic objective, getting citizens to accept what was happening by focusing their attention inward. But the retreat from reality could not be so drastic or complete that it prevented meeting the personal and social duties necessary for carrying on. And all of Käutner's films, after offering a temporary illusion of normalcy, allow viewers entry back into reality.

Käutner's films help viewers dream because the stories play in a timeless space, an interior world. *Romanze in Moll* is set in nineteenth-century Paris, although the vague nature of the background (the only French being the word *étage* on the landings of an apartment building) suggests that the film could be taking place in Vienna just as easily. In one scene Käutner even foregrounds his delight at frustrating viewers' attempts to learn where they are, having the husband rebuffed by Michael when he asks for the name of the station. *Unter den Brücken* plays in contemporary Germany, but the shots of the Havel River avoid the ruins present in the background when the film was being shot, and stress instead the flow of life that the river represents. Only *Auf Wiedersehen, Franziska* seems to keep viewers in a real present, to keep them active and engaged in events of the day. Coming so early in the war, when there was no need to escape harsh reality, this is to be expected.

But Käutner's films are also grounded in reality, both through the characters and the locales. The decadence of *Romanze in Moll* is familiar, known to viewers from novels, dramas, and films. Thus it is of no consequence whether the setting is the *art nouveau* of Paris or the *Jugendstil* of Vienna. Even if war seems far from the Berlin of *Unter den Brücken*, it also seems near because of the careful way in which Käutner creates its absence. On the one hand, as reviews from postwar critics attest, Käutner's films burst the bonds of Nazi ideology to enter into a more humanistic and liberal film world. The jazz and swing music in *Auf Wiedersehen, Franziska*, the *fin-de-siècle* decadence and pessimism of *Romanze in Moll*, and the lyrical realism of *Unter den Brücken* all create an illusion of films free of Nazi ideology. On the other hand, forces operating within the films pull the works back under the Nazi umbrella, reinforcing prejudice against the foreign other as in *Auf Wiedersehen, Franziska*, indulging a national mood of mourning as in *Romanze in Moll*, and encouraging escapism as in *Unter den Brücken*.

Auf Wiedersehen, Franziska (1941). *A dancer at the Seaman's Paradise Club gyrates and scats to a jazz number. Courtesy Library of Congress and Transit Film GmbH.*

Romanze in Moll *(1943). Helmut Käutner uses
closed and open spaces to reflect Madeleine's (Marianne Hoppe)
feeling of entrapment at home with her husband (Paul Dahlke)
and her sense of freedom with her lover Michael (Ferdinand
Marian) at his brother's estate. Courtesy Library of
Congress and Transit Film GmbH.*

Unter den Brücken *(1945). Willy (Gustav Knuth) smiles at the end of the film, although he ends up with the dog, not the girl. Courtesy Library of Congress and Transit Film GmbH.*

Notes

[1] The four directors Hull cites form an unholy grouping of sorts, having directed such notorious propaganda pieces as: *Stukas* (1941, Ritter), *Hitlerjunge Quex* (Hitler Youth Quex, 1933, Steinhoff), *Jud Süß* (Jew Suess, 1940, Harlan), and *Carl Peters* (1941, Selpin).

[2] Wolfgang Ruf, *Süddeutsche Zeitung* 12 March 1973: 9. Other attempts to distance Käutner from the Nazis can be found in the analyses of Bogusław Drewniak, Georges Sadoul, and Christa Bandmann and Joe Hembus. Drewniak writes that the film *Romanze in Moll* doesn't seem to have been filmed in the middle of wartime at all. In *Der deutsche Film 1938–1945: Ein Gesamtüberblick* (Düsseldorf: Droste, 1987) 259. Georges Sadoul calls *Romanze in Moll* "the best German film that was made during the war." In *Le cinéma pendant la guerre: 1939–1945* (Paris: Éditions Denoël, 1954) 31, quoted in Mihal Régine Friedman, "Die Ausnahme ist die Regel: Zu *Romanze in Moll* (1943) von Helmut Käutner," *Frauen und Film* 43 (December 1987): 48. Finally, Bandmann and Hembus enthuse that *Unter den Brücken* "has nothing to do with the films of the Third Reich era." In *Klassiker des deutschen Tonfilms 1930–1960* (Munich: Goldmann, 1980) 151.

[3] David Welch details how after October 1938 the showing of newsreels had been made mandatory at all commercial film programs. Moreover, according to Welch, the newsreels were often a bigger draw than the feature film. In *Propaganda and the German Cinema 1933–1945* (Oxford: Oxford UP, 1983) 191–99.

[4] Friedrich Silcher's nineteenth-century folk song, "Muß i' denn zum Städtele hinaus," known in English as "Wooden Heart," tells of departure and return from the perspective of the departing man. Käutner used the song again in his film *Große Freiheit # 7*.

[5] That the film reflects Nazi Germany's pessimism after the defeat at Stalingrad is coincidental since the film was begun before the battle took place.

[6] See for example the reviews of Swedish critics quoted in the *Film-Kurier* of 18 July 1944: 1–2, and Theo Fürstenau's introduction in *Filmographie Helmut Käutner*, edited by Rüdiger Koschnitzki (Wiesbaden: Deutsches Institut für Filmkunde, 1978) 7–14. Also see Klaus Wischnewski's essay, "Eine Augenblick der Freiheit oder Helmut Käutners *Romanze in Moll*, "in *Mitten ins Herz*, edited by Helga Hartmann, and Ralf Schenk, 170–73 (Berlin Henschel, 1991). In addition see postwar critic Louis Marcorelles, "Käutner, le dandy," *Cahiers du Cinéma* 73 (July 1957): 27, and the postwar French critics quoted by Friedman in "Die Ausnahme ist die Regel."

[7] Although they were important in the overall program of Nazi film production, films such as Eduard von Borsody's *Wunschkonzert* (Request Concert, 1940), Rolf Hansen's *Die große Liebe* (True Love, 1942), and Werner Klingler's *Die Degenhardts* (1944) were the exception among the almost 1100 feature length films made by the Nazis.

[8] Similar comments can be found in a feature article also appearing in the *Film-Kurier* (20 June 1944: 3).

12

JOHN E. DAVIDSON

Working for the Man, Whoever That May Be:
The Vocation of Wolfgang Liebeneiner

T HE ESSAYS IN THIS VOLUME share a commitment to enlarging the
frame in which we view Nazi cinema. They further our understanding of film's role in National Socialism because they broaden the
field of consideration in important ways. These include but are not
limited to: examining the realignment of nineteenth-century texts and
national traditions under the Nazi regime; tracing the fate of motifs
and genre from Weimar film; exposing the pedagogic mechanisms at
work in both serious and light works; highlighting the identifying processes at the heart of Nazi entertainment; and, complicating the often
facile notion of a non-political aesthetic sphere in order to uncover the
contradictions of the Nazi period. The contributions in this volume
follow on and complement important recent scholarship that has consistently distanced itself from simplistic visions of propaganda as the
heart and soul of Nazi cinema. Many of these scholars stress instead
that the Nazi film industry was not really an exception, that its products show marked similarities not only to pre-1933 and post-1945
German cinema, but also to genre developments in other national
cinemas, particularly in regard to gender discourse.[1]

These shifts in contemporary criticism point to important areas yet
to be studied and serve as vital corrections to widely held but false perceptions about what the term "Nazi" means. It seems to me, however,
that we are prevented from fully benefiting from these advances by the
exceptional status accorded the Nazi period within the disciplinary
boundaries of German Studies. Understandable though this status is, it
exerts a nearly irresistible pressure to return to a somewhat myopic
search for the Nazi element in films despite the acknowledged need for
broadening our scope. Without being able better to analyze the specif-
ics of the Nazi moment within a more general understanding of the
way cultural institutions work, we will find ourselves ironically unable
to counter the step to an ahistorical notion of this cinema, a step which
will become increasingly tempting for students and scholars as historical

distance to the period increases. The question that plagues me, then, is how to continue and further a rigorous examination of Nazi films as historically specific artifacts, while at the same time generating knowledge that will help us better understand the role of dominant cinematic culture more generally. If we continue to read films as individual texts, can we do something more useful with both the obvious German specificities and the equally obvious generic similarities at work in them? I believe we can, but to do so requires that we not simply seek out specific ideological messages emanating from, or discourses circulating through the films. We must also analyze the formal and structural elements that, within the context of particular institutional policies and practices, encourage a seemingly neutral reception. Such a reception rests on identifications that are not specifically National Socialist, even though they stabilize the social base upon which the Nazis built their state.

In the following I provide an example of such an analysis by looking at works by Wolfgang Liebeneiner, a director who made a smooth, nearly seamless transition from the Nazi cultural world to that of post-Second World War West Germany. Liebeneiner was one of the most important but least talked about figures in German film at the end of the war. He appears only once in the text of Gerd Albrecht's invaluable *National-Sozialistische Filmpolitik*, and is listed incorrectly in the index as "Rolf." Liebeneiner's seems a particular and interesting case for a number of reasons. Though having been an actor during Weimar, he only began directing under Nazi rule. He made films in almost every genre prevalent in the Nazi-era: comedies, melodramas, historical dramas, propaganda films, tendentious historical biopics, and Heimat-like films. He even made one film about flying, a theme popular with the Nazis, and had plans made up for a film that takes place at sea as well. Not surprisingly for someone who made neither particularly good nor particularly bad films, Liebeneiner had smashes and flops at the box-office, but also with Hitler and Goebbels. He ascended steadily during a career marked by honors and hard work. In 1936 he was named *Staatsschauspieler* (State Actor) for his work under Gustav Gründgens at the National Theater in Berlin and in 1938 was named to head the artistic faculty at the Babelsberg Film Academy. His *Der Florentiner Hut* (The Italian Straw Hat, 1939) was chosen as the christening film for the new flagship *Robert Ley* — Hitler attended this secret premiere — and three of his other films were awarded National Film prizes. Liebeneiner was one of only three directors to receive the German Film Ring, was given the title "Professor" (along with Veit Harlan) by Goebbels personally in 1942, and was Chief of Productions at Ufa from 1943 until the end of the war. At that time he was hard at work on *Das Leben geht weiter* (Life Goes on), an uncompleted *Durchhaltefilm* (a film encouraging viewers to struggle through the increasingly hard times) in both senses of the term: on the one hand it was to satisfy the Propaganda Ministry that commissioned it as vital to the war effort; on the other hand it was an attempt to keep himself and his crew alive until the Allies took control.

After the war Liebeneiner never enjoyed the same amount of power as he had in the late Nazi years, but he continued to work and prosper. After receiving a license from the British as early as 1945, his first engagement was the theater premiere of Wolfgang Borchert's *Draußen vor der Tür* (The Man Outside, 1947). He soon produced a film version of this work about coming home under the title of *Liebe 47* (Love '47, 1947). Active as a feature film director until 1978, Liebeneiner predictably made both hits and flops in almost all genres, including one of the best-loved films of the Adenauer period, *Die Trapp-Familie* (The Trapp Family, 1956). Liebeneiner also did his own share of remakes, mostly of apolitical films from the Nazi era, but some of his remakes actively de-politicized the originals by removing very specific nationalist and National Socialist content: *Urlaub auf Ehrenwort* (Leave of Honor, 1955), for example, remakes Karl Ritter's 1937 version of this nationalistic story. He branched out into television and was important in setting the tone for West German TV films: among other TV fare he directed *Tom Sawyers und Huckleberry Finns Abenteuer* (Tom Sawyer and Huckleberry Finn's Adventures, 1968), the six-part *Schwejk* series (1972), and the thirteen-part *Spannagl & Sohn* (Spannagl and Son, 1975–1976). He continued to cast his wife, Hilde Krahl, as often as possible, and also continued to act nearly until the time of his death at the age of eighty in 1985.

Whatever else one might say about Liebeneiner, one could hardly accuse him of not working diligently. Like many others, he was an opportunistic careerist both during and after the Third Reich, but rather than using that fact to dismiss him from serious consideration, we might more productively make that a point of entry into his films. In what follows, I maintain that the hard work that is the touchstone of Liebeneiner's career must be taken seriously as a theme in his movies as well. For it provides a point of confluence for the production and reception of culture that is neither specifically fascist nor German, yet remains vital to the cultural politics of the Third Reich and the Federal Republic. A close reading of Liebeneiner's directorial debut, set in the context of contemporary Nazi cultural policy, will yield a notion of "work" that picks up on and further modernizes the sense of *Beruf* (vocation) that Max Weber saw as one of the enabling myths of capitalism. Vocation aligns a careerist's hard and steady approach to his work with a more general sense of work as the grand project that unites us all in generating capital, yet removes the stigma involved with earning money for money's sake, which indeed is the essence of modern capitalism in Weber's view. A more cursory and yet directed review of some of Liebeneiner's most popular feature films shows that this element remains a constant in his movies, positing and affecting a unification of audience, artist, and work through the mechanism of cultural production *and* consumption. In this we will see not only the ways in which Liebeneiner remained tied to the program he began under the National Socialists, but also how their program paralleled and accommodated the programs that came to dominate post-Second World War cultural production in the West.

When addressing the problem of Liebeneiner's move from National Socialist film into post-Second World War cinema, one finds that two critical tendencies surface most frequently. The first is to assume that nothing "Nazi" was really integral to his work: Nazi content was merely tacked on as necessity that kept one working, prolonging a career that this mode of thought often reads as one of resistance.[2] Such an assessment claims that Liebeneiner produced mostly comedies with no manifest political content, ignoring that even Albrecht's notoriously generous categorization lists his apolitical work as outweighing the political by only one film. Paradoxically, the analyses of Liebeneiner's most frequently studied film, *Ich klage an* (I Accuse, 1941) underscore this tendency by claiming that the real issue of the film — the eradication of defective children — is relegated to a side-issue (Brandt 1993; Rost 1987, 1990; Roth 1987). By tying the film's ideological content directly to a specific euthanasia program aimed at handicapped children, critics have overlooked the manner in which that film's very structure is infused with signs pointing to the "eradication of life unworthy of living" right from the start.[3] But however marginal Nazi issues may be in Liebeneiner's Third Reich works, one cannot deny that they often correspond to strategic points in the development of Nazi social and cultural policy. This has been noted often in relation to *Ich klage an*, given its direct relation to the "T-4" and child-murder euthanasia projects, but also seems evident in other films. Liebeneiner's two Bismarck films — *Bismarck* (1940) and *Die Entlassung* (The Dismissal, 1942) — certainly correspond to the shifts in demands on the film industry brought on by the opening of the war and the initial stalling of the march on Stalingrad respectively. Timely productions of a historically displaced celebration of Germany's expansionist military prowess or an equally displaced treatment of devastating setbacks as necessary and temporary seem to be part and parcel of the cultural work of his cinema.

The correspondence to contemporary events also underscores at least one of Liebeneiner's comedies, according to Karsten Witte, who in his treatment of 1941's *Das andere ich* (The Other I) forcefully maps out a second approach to this filmmaker (1981). For Witte, scholars such as Albrecht have judged propaganda only with their ears, leaving the equally important messages that are "latent in the imagery" of films out of consideration. This *Latenz der Bilder* normalizes the symbols of oppression by aligning them with non-political elements, loading compositions so that the viewer processes visual, political data while partaking of light, often insipid, entertainment. Witte also fits Liebeneiner's lighter fare into the larger discussion of "what is fascistic about comedy," not just in the Third Reich but throughout Western cinema, which has to do with properly aligning gender roles by mobilizing women to render themselves emotionally immobile (25). In the context of the increased production demands of the total war economy, *Das andere ich* maintains the ideology of privatization in a nationalized economy in which a woman's sexuality should serve the owner of the means of production even more than production itself (Witte 1981, 32). The heroine's double shifts at work, vital to the concerns of the nation, must give way in the face of the demands of the owner / lover, who undertakes the labor of recasting the world of work as a male sphere.

Witte's brilliant analysis explains how it was so easy for similar films — such as Liebeneiner's 1942 *Großstadtmelodie* (Big City Melody) — to be shown on West German television with only minimal change. For removing background Nazi imagery maintains their status as films that speak a very generalized language of gender and capital. But, sympathetic as I am to Witte's desire to make what is specifically filmic — the visual — his focus in analyzing the ideology of these films, he perhaps overestimates the weight of specific elements of production in its historical context (the factory and its machines, Nazi paraphernalia). In turn he underestimates a more general, less easily pinpointed construction of work that is latent in nearly all of Liebeneiner's films before and after the war. By turning to Liebeneiner's first film, 1937's *Versprich mir nichts* (Don't Promise Me Anything), which can be seen as paradigmatic in regard to his future development, we will find that what is latent in the images is a self-reflexive concern for cultural work that models itself on Nazi policy and yet fosters the development of consumer culture that is often assumed not to have entered German film until the 1950s (Fehrenbach).

The opening of the Degenerate Art Exhibition and of the House of German Art in the summer of 1937 provide the connection to public cultural policy in *Versprich mir nichts*. The attempt to refashion and reclaim art as a Nazi sphere opposed to expressionist modernism had long since been underway, but these two exhibitions marked a new turn in the Nazi assault on high modernism. While many have noted the conflation of cultural and social policy in these events, it is important to remember the specific functions of these two institutions. On the one hand, both maintain the traditional function of the nineteenth-century state museum through the "rhetorical incorporation of the public . . . into the form of power which the museum itself displays," attempting to educate and construct a public by reinforcing a reactionary bourgeois artistic taste (Bennett 29–30; Duncan 448–69). Here the exhibits were two sides of the same coin: the Degenerate Art Exhibition worked on the principle of negative integration of the public into a bloc against what is shown and hence with the power that puts on the display; the House of German Art sought a positive integration through identification, but went one step further, for it functioned like an extremely large gallery in which the artworks were both displayed and marketed, attempting to enlist investing in culture (quite literally) as a means of building support. This additional step is important because unlike the traditional museum, which strove to equate the citizen with a shareholder in the common culture, the Nazi's commonality of the *Volk* had no use for this rhetorical concept of citizenship.[4] In essence, the contradiction of the public museum was that the citizenship was concrete, while shareholding was an illusion; in the House of German Art, the common feeling of belonging was the illusion, while the prospect of purchase opened up shareholding as a concrete possibility. Since the psychological investment that accompanies capital investment made the bonds to culture stronger, the artworks from the House of German Art were also mechanically reproduced and sold in travel markets at reduced rates so that all could participate as shareholders displaying their *völkisch* (nationalistic) affiliations.

Just as Joseph Goebbels was preparing the decree that allowed Adolf Ziegler access to the holdings of all state museums to choose the examples of so-called art for the eponymous exhibit, he was paving the way for stock acquisitions that would change the cinema by making the government the film industry's majority shareholder (Hüneke 121–34).[5] The cultural and financial developments we saw at work in the two massive exhibitions also had repercussions in cinematic policy, as

Goebbels outlined it on the brink of the fuller integration of the state in the private concerns of the industry in March 1937 (Albrecht 1969, 447–63). Goebbels frames his concerns for the industry in a circular conception of culture validated in consumption by a public that itself is validated by participation in the culture through consumption. Art shapes feelings, according to Goebbels, and politics shapes the people. These parallel processes rely on aesthetics, mobilizing pleasure to ensure participation, but the world of mass reproduction has opened up a new and necessary mode of exhibiting participation — consumption. Of course, Goebbels addresses precisely the business of film, but covers this in claims about putting "die Film*kunst*" (film *art*) before "die Film*industrie*" (film *industry*) (453, italics in original). Paraphrasing Göring's assessment of the German theater, Goebbels diagnoses the situation:

> The artistic German film pursues money, which is why money has been as difficult to get a hold of as a beauty who won't let her defenses down. As soon as the artistic film puts aside its monetary desires in order to serve Art, money will begin pursuing it (455).

According to Nazi rhetoric, maintaining an artificial separation between the artist, the art world, and the *Volk* denies the public the chance to participate as consumers.

Along Goebbels somewhat tortured line of reasoning, German artists must cease chasing the desires of the public and return to their true duty: creating true art in which the *Volk* will innately recognize and literally invest itself. The circular sense of "true art" under National Socialism allows this to function. Art is by definition connected to the soul of the *Volk*, and the true artist, like the true leader according to proto-Nazi philosophers such as Moeller van den Bruck and Oswald Spengler, is able to give form and expression to the essence of the *Volk*. In turn the art will be recognized by the people as their true expression and, hence, become popular and make money. But this tortured logic belongs neither solely to Goebbels nor the National Socialists: it inheres in the spirit of capitalism as analyzed by Max Weber. According to his analysis, the spirit of capitalism, that is, that capital accumulation has come to control humans, contradicts a fundamental impulse held over from an earlier ethos, namely that pursuing money for its own sake is immoral. Mediating this contradiction is the notion of work as a calling or vocation, which one can (indeed must) pursue in order to attain an honorable name. As long as one follows one's vocation to the best of one's ability, no stigma is attached to accumulation, provided one avoids ostentatious consumption. This is clearly one impulse at work in the rhetoric of Goebbels's speech: strictly pursuing profit is not only questionable morally but, worse still, pragmatically. And yet, this speech, like the shift in museum policy embodied by the House of German Art, introduces an element in the development of capital that had not flourished in Weimar: fostering consumption is necessary to capitalism to ensure its continued existence. Taking account of this Fordist notion, the Nazis present a model in which conspicuous accumulation remains stigmatized, but consumption becomes a necessary mode of (being recognized as) participating in cultural life.

By taking these contextualizing moments in cultural policy into consideration, we find that Liebeneiner's *Versprich mir nichts* epitomizes Goebbels's message about the look of healthy art and its mode of public integration as if it had taken the Propaganda Minister's speech as a blueprint. To describe the necessary form of true art, Goebbels refers to the "unity of place, time, and characters," which he attributes to the German tradition through Lessing. In the following section I will show how *Versprich mir nichts* takes this aesthetic principle a step further, synthesizing a unity of place, action, and people through the circulation of art within the film. It insists on the importance of getting the art to the public so that the money can flow back to the artist, allowing the *Volk* to find itself reflected in the product developed by and bought as culture. First, art and artist have to move into the public arena. Then the film begins to eradicate the distances between what at one point were distinct interior spaces separated by cultural and economic hierarchies. This creates a unity between the art gallery, the elite Wannsee villa where Felder, the art expert, lives, and the Spartan artist's atelier in Berlin-Mitte, often referred to as the rathole. Much like at the House of German Art, the vital thing here is not simply to celebrate National Socialist art — but to sell it to a public only waiting for the chance to buy it! Thus, the urge to participate through consumption goes hand in hand with the creation of an illusory social unity mediated by art that can be interpreted as the Nazi *Volksgemeinschaft* (national community) but is not directly encoded as such, even within the film itself. Despite the partial obscuring of class distinctions, commercial circulation is vital to this unity, which simultaneously derives from and reaffirms culture. In the final segment of this essay I will suggest that developing the relationship between the work of culture and the facilitation of consumerism in *Versprich mir nichts* may help us to understand both the tenor of Liebeneiner's Nazi-era films and his success in the media-world of postwar West Germany.

Versprich mir nichts is Liebeneiner's only film form the Nazi period to center directly on artistic creation, and it leaves no doubt about the tenor of real art. Heinrich George portrays Felder, Berlin's most knowledgeable and successful gallery owner, who booms that he wants to see "optimism" and thus sets the criteria for judging works of art both in the market and the academy. Though he has more opportunity than usual to show off his charm in this role, George reverts to a more familiar bluster when he instructs his dandyish assistant on the failings of most contemporary art. Liebeneiner shoots Felder's pronouncements against a background of parodies of Expressionist works, the art that the Nazis called "degenerate," and which the assistant has acquired during the gallery owner's absence. Given the obvious parallel to discrediting of Expressionism in the *Entartete Kunst* Exhibition, it comes as no surprise that Felder demands that such "crap" be cleared away. *Versprich mir nichts* eventually culminates its ruminations on art by offering the "Lukas Kranach Prize" to a kitschy fresco in neo-classical style, a direct celebration of the House of German Art. The sense that works of art reflect the character of individual artists springs from the film's circular condemnation of degenerates and a valorization of healthy, optimistic art even though it is accompanied by the somewhat contradictory notion that the real artistic achievement transcends the individual as well.

The twist here is that — naive genius though he may be — the individual artist involved is not alone, and none of the artistic (and ideological) work in this film would be possible without the love story. Martin Pratt, a naive and gifted painter, together with his wife of two years, Monika, have devoted themselves each in their own way to serving art. Monika does this by sitting as Martin's model and handling all the mundane daily affairs; Martin, on the other hand, thinks only of his work. The trope of the starving artist is expanded to a starving artist-couple here, but with the difference that Martin refuses to sell or show any of his paintings until he feels himself ready. Thus the film makes clear that the artist himself rather than an unappreciative public is to blame for his lack of public success. Driven to desperation by hunger and impending homelessness, Monika takes a picture Martin has given her to Felder and presents it as her own (it is signed "M. Pratt"). Felder finds the optimism he has been looking for in this image of the Prussian landscape of the Havel region and, though he has trouble believing that a woman composed this work, puts Monika under contract.

Versprich mir nichts clearly pursues the dual aims of defining proper art and proper gender roles, as do so many light films of the Nazi period. The work and work ethic of the young painter Martin tell us a great deal about the pedagogic process used to steer the viewer properly in these two domains. He is a genius, naive in the extreme, although exceptionally hard working and, to a certain extent, aware of his own failings. He is also a regular guy, although radically immature in several respects, and a healthy man, but hardly an Aryan from a propaganda poster. He maintains the "perpetual adolescence" that Siegfried Kracauer and others have found at the heart of both the proto-fascist films of the Weimar era and Nazi-era films: he remains passionate, obsessive, and even selfish throughout. Monika gives him what he needs to be whole, serving as mother, sister, lover, and, as Martin confesses near the film's end, inspirational supplement. His art — and the film repeatedly stresses that it can only be his — springs from their union, the balance of which is threatened by success and recognition and must be re-established, but without the threat of poverty, to resolve the conflict.

In the opening credit sequence, cinematographer Friedl Behn-Gund begins a nearly full 360° pan in the clouds and traces the skyline of downtown, establishing the setting as the nation's capitol, Berlin. Nothing will remind us of that setting again, however, until a reference late in the film to the fact that Felder lives in a Villa at Wannsee. Though much of the film takes place in public spaces, they are all enclosed — the gallery, the school, a shop.[6] The film shows no further interest in exterior spaces, and indeed seems bent on eradicating them. The opening sequence ends in an artist's atelier, which we enter as the crane moves up to reveal Martin, painting, through the window's glass, while the open window pane frames Monika, posing, draped in fabric hung to look like a low-cut gown.

The opening dialogue stresses that we are watching not simply a painter and his model, but a couple engaged in loving banter. Monika responds with a simple "yes" to Martin's successive questions as to whether she loves him "as a brother," "as a lover," and "as a husband." Feigning confusion, he demands to know exactly how she loves him. "Like all of those together" is her response, which he accepts with a knowing "aha." Vital here is our sense of the couple as a unit bound by her unswerving devotion, by his need of such devotion, and by his work, from which his eyes never stray during the exchange. The sequence concludes as the lovebirds whistle a popular love song back and forth.

The harmony of this little scene will soon be broken by the entrance of the butcher, baker, grocer, and landlord demanding that their bills be paid. Martin has no idea about how bad things are — or anything else for that matter. His response to the suggestion that he sell some of his works, even if they are not quite ready yet, is that his direct connection to his work makes it physically, spiritually, and psychologically impossible for him to sell them. This establishes the immediate link between artist and work as a given, but also as inadequate to the modern situation. The trajectory of the film will bring this initially private and unique relationship to the work of art (as both artwork and ideological endeavor) into the public eye and economic circulation.

Despite this seeming shyness about displaying his work, Martin shows his conceit about it often enough. Though it is not yet ready in his eyes, he bristles at the suggestion that someone had "seen better pictures." In a dreamy reverie, he even claims that he would be the first to praise these paintings if she had painted them (and this gives Monika the idea about selling the works as her own), mentioning the rare combination of "strength and gentleness" in these landscapes to an imaginary audience of "honored philistines." However, Martin never explains the theory of his great art, never talks about the thing that makes his art different — he simply creates it. From the many shots we see of Martin quickly trying to capture a pose or facial expression, we conclude that this art is mimetic, even though we rarely see the paintings or sketches. Indeed, we never see a full frame of the fresco that wins the nation's highest art prize, although we can tell it looks exactly like a sketch made by Martin in about thirty seconds while engaged in a heated debate, an image we do catch an upside-down glimpse of at the close of an earlier scene.

As Karsten Witte has remarked in relation to the Revue Film, this combination of insisting on and yet showing no evidence of talent is often the case in Nazi films. In these films about song and dance talent, "as long as applause is offered by someone in the film audience [onscreen], who turns directly to the movie audience, the actual proof of accomplishment is not necessary" (1981–1982, 247). Similarly in *Versprich mir nichts*, it is left to others to tell us about the greatness of Martin's work. Though the film repeatedly makes fun of little minds that pretend to understand something of the power of art, it addresses its audience much like Martin does his "honored philistines." Herr Felder offers an important mediation here with his mixture of being a regular guy (despite his bluster, he jokes around with his office boy and lets his underling joke with him) and *the* art expert, for this creates an illusory bridge for the movie audience to the world of art that seems largely populated by the rich, effete, and/or academic. Felder's gut assessment of "Monika's work," an assessment born of both his good nature and his expertise, leaves no doubt about Martin's talent. These two sides of his character come into play again after Monika causes a scandal by refusing the Kranach Prize because it should belong to her husband (and thus exposes herself as a fraud). Felder responds first as a critical authority:

> I thought the Lukas Kranach Prize was awarded for an artistic achievement . . . this painting is great, grandiose, yes a completely unique achievement. Ladies and Gentlemen, we should understand one thing. This is not about Martin or Monika Pratt — first and foremost this is about the work of art . . . All other consideration must be silent in the face of the greatness of the work.

And then in the next breath he adds:

> But Ladies and Gentlemen, let us have a sense of humor. Let's have humor enough to look this once at the light side of this surprise. Enjoy the rare good fortune of the birth of a genius.

Felder's arguments convince his audience of experts, just as his authority convinces the film audience that it will indeed be possible finally to recognize Martin without damning Monika. But notice here two things: the valorization of the "work" as that which transcends sensibilities, social conventions, and rules of etiquette; second, despite localizing the source of the work in the individual artistic genius, Felder insists that the genius is born only by entering into the public realm and gaining recognition. Since the Pratts have succumbed to the pressures of misplaced success and quarreled, leading Monika to attend the Fresco-unveiling alone and to disappear afterwards, the private dilemma of the film remains to be resolved; however, the discourse about the work and its creator has been solidified.

The work, as art, is universal — or, better, generic — rather than specifically national. The film makes no pronouncement about the German, Teutonic, or national nature of art. Still, clearly some reason exists to connect this sense of the universal to the German particular, as I pointed out in my discussion of the scene in which *Entartete Kunst* provides the backdrop. Although those negative examples are not explicitly labeled as non-German art, the film is set in the year of its making, 1937, and the socio-political context of that period in Germany enters the moment the first distorted face appears in the background at Felder's.[7] And yet, those negative images are not intrinsic to the film in any convincing sense and do little to add to the latent potential of the images in *Versprich mir nichts*.

It is at this point in the film that we are reminded indirectly of the setting in Berlin: Herr Felder lives in a villa at Wannsee. Soon after, the Berlin offered to us in the opening pan returns, for in the final sequence the Berlin skyline reappears. This time it is seen out of the window through which we entered Martin and Monika's old rathole in

Berlin-Mitte, to which they have both separately returned to seek sol-
ace from their present plight and try to recapture some of their earlier
happiness. As Martin puts candles around the image of Monika he was
painting at the outset, she appears from behind a pillar, as if the work
conjures her up to reinstate the bliss that they once knew. Behind and
above them, the Berlin skyline dominates the window, creating a unity
of place, actors, and action. Much like the opening shot, we have come
full circle, to the point of even repeating the opening dialogue, until
Martin begins promising to change his ways for her. Monika then covers his mouth and implores him to make no promises, giving us the
film's title in its last line. The camera pans from a close shot of their
faces down and left, coming to rest on the painted image of her surrounded by candles on the floor, bringing us literally back to the
"work" which embodies their work in serving art, each in their own
way.

   This final sequence enacts the metonymic slippage toward which the
film has steered all along, positing the unity of place (Berlin, Germany,
the present), figures (the lovers, *das Volk*, the artists), and action (existing as inspiration and artist, giving expression to that love-bird like
existence, working). This unity has been carefully prepared in situating
the spaces just prior to the reunion. After the disaster at the unveiling
ceremony, Martin leaves in search of Monika, visiting all the places that
have played an important role in the film: the fancy new apartment, the
gallery, Felder's Villa, and the rathole. In other words, he leaves the
one truly public space in the film — the school hall dominated by the
fresco that Martin had secretly finished the night before — and will visit
the private spaces that the film has opened up as semi-public ones.[8] The
first stop is the fancy atelier apartment they have lived in since becoming successful. Here we have seen them grow farther apart, Martin turn
into a tyrant with the servant, and Monika struggle to maintain her deception in the face of increasing publicity and attention, even as she
conspicuously consumes their newfound wealth. Liebeneiner shoots the
final scene in this space in a medium shot framing Martin and the servant against the door just inside the entrance. As Martin storms out
through the door, the cut moves to a shot from inside Felder's gallery,
looking out through a glass door in the same screen location, with
Felder's two assistants at a desk lower left. The seconds that it takes for
Martin to enter the image and then to enter the room indicates a separation between the new apartment and the gallery. Martin storms out
after learning that Felder has gone home to his villa in Wannsee, sur-
mising that Monika might be there. Again Liebeneiner cuts on motion
as he exits, but this time cuts immediately to Martin entering the door

at Felder's villa. The distance between the gallery and the villa is erased in this editing. After a discussion in which Felder confesses his envy of Martin's talent, and "his irresistible child-like spirit," and Martin in turn confesses that he could never have painted a single picture without Monika, Felder sends him off to the rathole, certain that that is where she will be. Before departing, Martin turns back to Felder and asks for twenty marks for a taxi, "since it's such a long way." The geographic and social distance between them is evoked only to be eradicated by another cut on the motion of Martin leaving Felder's and appearing in the stairwell to his building, effectively joining the two places across spatial and social separation. The unity of semi-public private spaces in Berlin has been achieved.

The loop of gallery — villa — rathole is unified as the space in which Martin's work comes into being and has effect. By keeping the new apartment out of this loop, Liebeneiner leaves behind the public inversion of gender roles by abandoning the site where Monika was forced to act out her dominance of Martin in the public eye. This simultaneously removes the site where "M. Pratt's" work was transformed into material comfort and gain, where what was hard-gained by the devotion of Martin's vocation became acquired material, concretized in the packages Monika steadily brings home. This reinstates the sense of work-as-vocation in the sense that Weber uses it — as the pursuit of something that is an end in itself — but now freed of the infantile attitude that made Martin dysfunctional at the outset. He was dysfunctional as a husband since he was not providing for his family and as an artist because his material was separated from the public or *Volk*. The mandate of Goebbels's address rings true here: as we have seen over the course of the film, the work of the artist is not just to produce the work, but to produce it for a public, which will pay to see its own reflection. The return to the rathole again conjures up the private bliss of Martin and Monika as belonging to us all, mediated by the authority of Felder and the money of the public tucked away behind the skyline of Berlin.

Versprich mir nichts is thus finally about work in a variety of ways. It refers not just to the industry of the individual, but to toil in pursuit of a calling, the product of such toil, and the semi-public private sphere of circulation where this product meets the people. When Martin rants about his labor in the opening, he dedicates himself completely and yet does not produce real works of art, since he refuses to put them in public circulation. Then in the middle of the film when his work is in public circulation, he remains invisible behind Monika's name and does not pursue his vocation openly. Martin works at night when no one can see him creating the miracle of the fresco that she could not paint: in his drunken revelry after finishing his masterpiece he calls himself Rumpelstiltskin and sings that little man's song in celebration of his anonymity. But the important aspects of the vocation as a modern virtue — one that Weber's analysis indicates is not limited to the Nazi period but belongs to capitalism in general — are that it is public, that one is known to pursue it, that its pursuit is an end in itself, and that the money it generates is secondary. One cannot keep one's name out of it. Clearly this is the message that the ending of Liebeneiner's first film evokes, with the vital addendum that the mode of recognizing the artistic calling is to purchase it, to contribute to the work. *Versprich mir nichts* internalizes the Fordist notion that fostering consumption of goods is integral not only to the general economy but to the cultural economy as well.

I would argue that the concept of work as a vocation that goes beyond mere occupation undergirds nearly all of Liebeneiner's major productions. The sense that work is an artistic work in progress provides — along with the consistently conservative gender politics of his films — the constant thread that may be the key to his easy transition to post-Second-World-War film. One certainly does not have to look hard to find this thread in his more tendentious films of the Nazi period, although in those cases the term "calling" (with its echo of religious zeal) might indeed be more appropriate than the less fanatical "vocation." In *Ziel in den Wolken* (Goal in the Clouds, 1938), a Prussian officer's calling to develop planes for Germany and the German army leads him to resign his commission, suffer disinheritance, risk his true love, and, ultimately, because he receives no money for his undertaking, to stoop to stealing a colleague's materials in order to produce his machine. Still, the audience is never led to question this calling and by film's ending we find the officer's love, honor, family, and, not incidentally, income all restored in a resolution that visually anticipates the famous last shots of Rolf Hansen's *Die große Liebe* (True Love, 1942).

In *Ich klage an*, the physician's vocation is the focus of this discourse about work, with a healthy income being ever present and yet only a byproduct of the calling. The film opens with the doctor being called (the German term, *berufen*, is significant in relation to Weber's terminology) to a professorship in Munich. Having begun penniless and having been subjected to ridicule for the radical nature of his ideas, which included a proto-Nazi belief in the determinacy of blood in inheriting characteristics, Doctor Heydt (Harald Paulsen) views this honor as a well-earned and yet inevitable triumph. However, one of the interesting twists in the film is that it provides two exemplary figures, celebrating both the praxis and the theory of medicine in the calling of a tireless general practitioner and an equally tireless researcher. Though once friendly rivals for a woman's affections, the two men *qua* modes of medicine are united in the film's finale, when the generalist (Mathias Wieman) comes to realize that a doctor's job is not simply to maintain life, but maintain life "worthy of living" at all costs and to put others out of their (and society's) misery. In the final sequence, the researcher, who is accused of killing his wife, turns the accusation on the court — and thus on the state and the people — demanding that they judge his work according to this standard.

Paulsen had already played a very similar role in *Bismarck*, whose drive to serve his king and country provides us a classic example of work as a calling that pays, in part by becoming "the work" of creating the nation. Though compensated handsomely for his efforts, the true reward for Bismarck's life's work comes at the end of the film, in which the crowning moment of his career becomes a painting that provides the film's final image. Depicting Bismarck handing the crown of the newly united Germany to Wilhelm, this painting of the genesis of the German Empire at Versailles in 1871 reappears in *Die Entlassung*, the sequel that shows the trials of the Iron Chancellor (now played by Emil Jannings) after the founding of the Second Empire.[9] In his final monologue, a dejected but not defeated Bismarck stands in front of the art work, claiming that "Germany has been my work" and asking "who will complete it now?" The calling of Bismarck has been the project of Germany-in-progress throughout these films, and his pursuit of this calling alone demands unquestioned respect from the audience — but that pursuit also makes him wealthier at every turn, though accumulation has never been the direct goal. While these more overtly political films tend to stress the ideological aspects of the reward for pursuing the calling, they neither divorce the calling from the career nor erase the aspect of earning completely: those connections remain essential components in Liebeneiner's films. Here might be the reason Liebeneiner never made a so-called genius film, for they tend to require the social and/or economic failure of the genius (Herbert Maisch's *Andreas Schlüter* and Hans Steinhoff's *Rembrandt* [both 1942] offer illustrative examples): his definition of genius seems more closely tied to the pragmatics of finding common ground between the one with a vocation and the people of the time, and that results in a career rather than failure.

This brings us perhaps to the most crucial issue, namely the place where the metonymic conflation of work and vocation within the films becomes the implicit extension of Liebeneiner's own career. Here we must again turn to the apolitical, light works, such as his 1939 comedy of errors, *Der Florentiner Hut*. The film opens with an organ grinder's *Moritat*, which gives a comical condensation of the movie as a work at the outset. This credit sequence begins a broadsheet depiction of the production staff and players and then offers a truncated version of the plot. While looking at a dark screen we hear a bell ringing, which continues as the shot opens up centered on the grinder's organ as he takes his place behind it, flanked by his female assistant and a small crowd (mostly children), which grows as he speaks, and then begins his song:

> You people, hear my *moritat*
> Of how it was recently that
> Many ladies and gentlemen
> Worked on a Terra-film and then
> It was called 'The Italian Straw Hat'
> [Refrain — twice] Doo, doo, doo, doo, It's sad, but oh it's true.

This opening, besides providing an interesting alternative to the normal credit sequence, rehabilitates the popular tradition of the street ballad which had been associated with the worst impulses of communist brainwashing in 1933's *Hitlerjunge Quex* (Hitler Youth Quex). It also presents a vivid pictorial caricature of the players in the now nationalized Nazi film world as part of a very rationalized cultural business. This caricature seems at odds with the image of German cinema that Liebeneiner once described as film-art freed from industrial conditions of production by the Nazi movement.

The three-minute sequence offers a visible image of the work of art that is indicative of the sense of vocation operating in Liebeneiner's films, bringing the artists into the open so that the public can acknowledge their work as the result of a vocation. One image even shows money being thrown out of the window to make this film, giving visual form to the kind of disregard for economics that Goebbels calls for in his program. But we also see the desire of the careerist in the Nazi period to create a freely unified audience that participates in the economy joining artists, works, and the public as one. After about a minute the grinder makes a good-natured, sweeping gesture with his left hand and calls "Everyone, sing along" at the refrain, which the crowd gladly does. The next verse, the last one concerned with the production team, ends with an ironic reference to the director — "ok, there's no one missing/ oh of course, Wolfgang Liebeneiner was directing!/ Doo, doo . . ." The singer then repeats his encouragement for all to join in, but this time looking directly and sternly into the camera and dropping the friendly tone we heard before. Though surely intended as a moment of comic sternness, the mock threat of the *Moritat*, a performance usually concerned with death, unveils the emptiness of the urge to bind an audience in its fictions. Neither sad nor true in itself, *Der Florentiner Hut* begins with a performance of an archaic form of popular culture that creates an image of film work as openly celebrating the system of its production, which is presented as precisely the impulse that the audience should get behind.

The story that follows is quite simple: a wealthy philanderer, Herr Farriner (Heinz Rühmann), decides to reform himself because he has fallen in love and, since he cannot get time alone with his new flame away from her family, wants to marry as soon as possible. Unfortunately, his horse eats the hat of a woman who is cheating on her husband in the woods with a young Lieutenant. They threaten to ruin his marriage that afternoon by pretending Farriner was having the affair with the woman unless he replaces her hat, without which she cannot return to her cuckolded husband. All his attempts to do so fail, yet he is bailed out in the end by the wedding present of his Uncle, which has been sitting under his nose all along. Striking in relation to the film's credit sequence, which concerns itself so directly with the people and processes of film work, is the relative absence of the theme of work in the body of the film. Although he is not of the aristocracy, Farriner is simply rich; we hear about an income of 1,500 Marks per week, but for doing what we do not know. Yet while having riches is not frowned upon here, the message about the immorality of making money an end in itself is imbedded in the film's condescending depiction of the bride's father, who owns a simple flower business and whose first concern is always money. The positive side of work itself is underscored as well, comically encapsulated in the way Farriner's turning over a new leaf is presented as his vocation, to which he has devoted himself completely. The bride is given no character: what the audience infers from the visual and voice-over presentation is that neither her status as a true prize or the relationship as true love are at issue here. This aligns the audience's emotional engagement with the "work" of Farriner's getting married, which involves resisting many advances and solving the dilemma of the hat.

To sum up, Liebeneiner's productions during the Nazi years constantly rest upon a valorization of vocation as an end in itself, infused with a discourse about public participation in culture being rooted not simply in identification but in consumption as well. As we saw in *Versprich mir nichts*, a semi-public private space develops in all of these films that both facilitates and masks the economic moment of this cultural interaction. Such interaction in the films mirrors the investment of the spectators in the audience so as to allow the overt ideological content of the culture at work in the transaction a flexibility that adapts to and transcends the imperatives of the immediate historical situation. Thus, we might say that the brilliance of Witte's insight into *Das andere ich*, in which he links the love story both to the tradition of the *Hosenrolle* (a "woman-in-pants" film) and to the immediate economic need of increasing women's roles in the armaments industry after the shift to the total war economy in the early 1940s, also blinds him to a more general sense of "work" being shaped in that film. Hilde Krahl's character, Magdalena, pursues two different jobs in the same business and cashes in twice: not only does she fail to pursue a vocation (which the film ultimately insists is to serve her man, as Witte rightly points out), but she is in this for the money. The message latent in the *mise en scène* of one image Witte reproduces in his article goes unnoticed. Magdalena sits with money spread out in front of her, holding a shiny coin up to the light and gazing up at it beaming. In the background, centered between the coin and her face, a painted face that seems directly borrowed from the degenerate material discarded from Felder's gallery leers at the camera — the lighting unifying the face's blank eyes, the coin, and Magdalena's eyes and mouth. The taboo of raising money to the level of an idol complements the distrust of one who works solely to attain it. Magdalena is ultimately saved by marrying the boss's son, but what she is saved from is not work in itself, but working for the wrong reason.

Moving now to Liebeneiner's productions in the Federal Republic of Germany, I would like to present two brief examples which, like *Versprich mir nichts* and the opening sequence of *Der Florentiner Hut*, center around the production of art and its relation to the public sphere and public economy. In *Die Stärkere* (The Stronger Woman, 1953), a traffic accident confines Elisabeth, a star opera singer, to a wheelchair, seeming to put an end to her career and endangering her marriage. Her husband Jochen, a successful architect who had once struggled and was forced to rely on his wife's income, is to oversee the conversion of an old castle in another part of Germany into a resort. While away at the site, he becomes involved with a very young and exuberant interior designer representing another firm, who is working on the project. Half sensing that something is going on, half-succumbing to self-pity, Elisabeth begins divorce proceedings in order to free Jochen to join his new love and have children, which, we learn roughly two-thirds through the film, has always been his most fervent wish. However, as Elisabeth begins recording again from the safety of her own room, things begin to shift. Jochen convinces her that he still loves her and only her and, in order to hammer home the point, adopts two children for them to raise. The final resolution of the film, however, requires that Elisabeth return to the public stage, one that is now connected to a broader audience. She keeps her early promise to sing Mozart at the ribbon-cutting ceremonies for the hotel, a performance broadcast live over the radio to incorporate a larger and less elitist audience than the opening concert-hall performance. Liebeneiner intercuts images of the singer's happy family, sitting in the audience and commenting on their mother's beauty, with shots of the younger woman crying at home by the radio. We are left with a close-up of the singer's radiant face, once again at one with herself, her art, and her family.

Die Stärkere stresses the importance of Elisabeth's returning to her vocation of art in public, in much the same configuration that we saw in *Versprich mir nichts*. The onus of earning money has been removed in the present, and in the future. Nevertheless, the film also insists upon money's importance through the sub-plot of her having supported her husband in leaner times. For example, one flashback takes us back to their courtship, which is given no specific temporal markers, but must correspond to the immediate postwar period. Having no money, Jochen must steal their wedding roses from a public park, since it is the man's duty to provide the bouquet. A further reference to the problem of earning is a discussion of a couch Elisabeth's money bought for him early in their marriage. Her earnings allow him to pursue his vocation as an architect — a rebuilder of the old into the new — but the construction of gender identity confounds this situation. After Jochen becomes successful, the film shifts to focus on her return to herself and her art. The upper middle-class status that is projected as their world is, of course, posited as the world in which they will continue to exist, though the monetary aspect of that position has been pushed out of view, leaving them free to follow their respective vocations as extensions of themselves. The inclusion of the radio-microphone in the final sequences again posits the crossover area between public and private spaces in which we all participate in the cultural calling, an area we have seen in so many Liebeneiner films. At the same time, this final performance sanctifies the shift in structures from a traditionalist to a contemporary economic scheme, symbolized in the conversion of the castle to a resort, and the concert hall to a radio performance. While the film's first scene depicts the last concert performance before Elisabeth's accident, the final appearance takes place in a space that breaks down the traditional divisions of public and private, old and new, locating the entertainment industry as that which allows the people, family, individual, and art to coalesce in commerce.[10]

A similar conversion plays an important role in *Die Trapp-Familie*, Liebeneiner's greatest success ever and one of the most popular films of the 1950s. Having transferred his wealth from banks in England to an Austrian bank in 1937, in a move portrayed as motivated by both patriotism and friendship to the bank's director, Baron von Trapp lets himself be convinced that the family castle can be turned into a hotel under the direction of his wife, Maria. At the same time that the family home is opened to an international public, the family singing group makes its first public appearance, against the express wishes of the Baron. The movie audience, having witnessed the family's singing in its pre-commercial phase, knows that it comes from the heart rather than the pursuit of money. The onscreen audience recognizes this, too. The Trapp family's performance of an Austrian hunting song wins them not only first prize, but also an agent's offer to help them tour the U.S. and the Prime Minister's invitation to sing at the next state reception. The Baron, having left before the performance and fearing for the good name of Trapp, categorically refuses to allow his family to become part of the entertainment industry, at least until hearing of the state invitation, at which point their performing becomes a matter of national — or nationalist — importance; Germany's annexation of Austria, however, makes this plan short-lived. Refusing to hoist the Nazi flag, the Trapps barely escape imprisonment and flee to America, where they hope to take Mr. Saemig up on his offer to act as their agent.

From their escape into the Austrian night, we cut to the family interred on Ellis Island, penniless and waiting in vain for their agent to answer their telegram. Saemig's partner feels that the promise to host these singing children was a mistake and accompanies Saemig to the authorities to tell them so. Through the ruse of the good-hearted American bureaucrat overseeing the prison, the agents are forced to see the Trapps, who begin singing in their despair, a moment that fuses the fragmented international populous around them into one people. Their performance, which is presented as authentic Austrian folk-culture, becomes the basis for reclaiming a kind of internationalism under the image of the Statue of Liberty. The shot composition here is very similar to that used in the final scene of *Versprich mir nichts*, with the singers centered low in the frame, with a window as a backdrop above them through which the synecdochic image of the Statue of Liberty appears at top-center of the screen. The song ends with a slight shift in camera perspective that includes the American flags that earlier symmetrically framed the Baron in his moment of near despair along with his family and part of their audience. Petroff, the senior agent, is won over, for he recognizes in the song the sound of money to be made. The next sequence shows the Trapps going out for their sixth encore at their debut performance, framed symmetrically by American flags positioned similarly to those we saw earlier. The public is giving them their hearts, souls, and money, as the Trapps come to express the heart of the new world just as they did the old.[11]

A cut integrated into this sequence shows Saemig and Petroff backstage counting off telegrams containing engagement offers in exactly the manner that they will count the dollars that the Trapps bring in, as Petroff gleefully proclaims that they will be rich. Here again Liebeneiner reinforces the essential separation of the vocation and the money it generates, in this case concretizing this distance by cutting from the joyful, emotive performance on stage, in which the Trapps act out exactly what they are (authentic vessels of folk art untainted by *völkisch* politics), to the performance of the agents' avarice backstage. We have seen the ruthless and amoral side of this strict concern for making money in the first scene of the two agents together, where they are willing to send the Trapps back to the clutches of the Nazis rather than spend money. Of course, the subsequent sequences at Ellis Island, and indeed, the film as a whole, have demonstrated the absolute necessity of making money both for the good it can do and for its ability to keep the art flowing to a public that takes joy in it. Just like the German *Volk*, who, albeit invisibly, support M. Pratt in *Versprich mir nichts*, this American audience participates in "authentic" culture by becoming willing consumers and is renewed by the optimism and flattering self-reflection that are the marks of that culture. Much as Goebbels prescribed in 1937, the Trapps do not chase after the money of this public by trying to pander to it, but simply pursue their vocation of producing folk art, whereupon, or so the film implies, the public throws its money at them. This art is, indeed, nothing but the shaping of emotions, which becomes exceptionally good business as well.[12] The folk song functions as an emblematic unit of art, which is the function it served in so many Nazi films. The shift to Austrian and then American culture provides viewers a degree of comfort by allowing them to separate out the good from the bad Germans. In this way the film helps viewers accommodate the new post-Second-World-War Western situation perfectly.[13]

In many ways, *Die Trapp-Familie* is as odious as anything Liebeneiner produced under the Nazis. The depiction of the agents as Jews, one through his stereotypical *mauscheln* (Yiddish speech pattern), the other through his stereotypical appearance, calls up all the negative associations traditionally used to align Jews with speculative capitalism, even while celebrating the marketing of culture in capitalism. The film exhibits a disdainful attitude toward the internationalism forced upon the Trapps early on, when they have to mingle with the dark-skinned southerners who overrun their family castle and assault the senses with a crescendo of unintelligible babble. The film depicts the mouth of the melting pot of America at Ellis Island — so long seen by nineteenth- and early twentieth-century nationalists as the home of a soulless *Mischkultur* (mixed culture) that would crush what was German in immigrants — as a sinister place of foreignness and poverty. Ellis Island is also the most unremittingly public space in the film: with no back-stage wings to whisper in, no private rooms to retreat to, no door-handles to escape by, it is indeed a prison. The international harmonizing Liebeneiner performs through the art of the Trapps moves us beyond that view of the U.S., pragmatically implying that such ideas have been relegated to the dustbin with other Nazi regalia even while applying precisely the same formulae and valorizing the same careerist ethic about film art he employed during the Nazi period in a new context. A sanitized version of America stands in for the context of the post-Second World-War world here, just as the backdrop of Berlin once stood in for Goebbels's Germany: in both contexts the private vocation of the artist comes in contact with the public to create the semi-public sphere that enables capital to flow through culture. The key to that in-between realm is the same artist-art-people (worker-work-people) continuum Goebbels stressed and Liebeneiner employed during the Nazi period, in which the work becomes the site where viewer investment and public pedagogy meet. If we begin to view other films with an eye to this structure, we will discover that the foregrounding of the work is a moment of individual education and *Volksbildung* (education/formation of the people) in a wide variety of national-historical contexts after the mid-1930s. At work on the work, class and caste differences disappear, and labor is recouped in a system of meaning in which ideological value rests firmly on surplus value. That value is generated by a labor force that does not see itself (represented) as such, but rather sees the invisible imperatives of capital made visible and pleasurable as a return on its own investment.

Versprich mir nichts (1937). To help their financial situation, caused by Martin's refusal to sell his paintings, Monika sneaks past her sleeping husband with a painting she will pass off as her own to the art dealer, Felder. Courtesy Library of Congress and Transit Film GmbH.

Die Trapp-Familie (1956). Baron von Trapp (Hans Holt) and his wife Maria (Ruth Leuwerik) look on as their children emerge out of the subway into Manhattan. Courtesy Library of Congress and Transit Film GmbH.

Notes

[1] Several scholars, following a logic laid out by Fredric Jameson in "Reification and Utopia in Mass Culture," *Social Text* 1.1 (1979): 130–48, convincingly explain the appeal of conservative gender models in these films by showing the manner in which they raise real problems faced by women and then proceed to provide the conditions creating those problems as the answer to them. The impossibility of true wish fulfillment is mediated by the always renewed possibility of wish fulfillment that is provided through the containment of these utopian drives. See Stephen Lowry, *Pathos und Politik: Ideologie in Spielfilmen des Nationalsozialismus* (Tübingen: Niemeyer, 1991), and Ute Bechdolf, *Wunsch-Bilder? Frauen im nationalsozialistischen Unterhaltungsfilm* (Tübingen: Niemeyer, 1992). While not wishing to replace these explanations that rely on psychoanalytic notions of repression and repetition compulsion, I do want to supplement them with an analysis of a more affirmative mode of audience reception that can, but does not have to be understood by the audience as affirming the culture at hand.

[2] See, for example, Curt Riess, *Das gibt's nur einmal: Das Buch des deutschen Films nach 1945* (Hamburg: Henri Nannen Verlag, 1958). In different and much more apologetic ways, this is how Hans Blumenberg treats Liebeneiner's last, incomplete work from the Third Reich in *Das Leben geht weiter: Der letzte Film des Dritten Reichs* (Berlin: Rowohlt, 1993).

[3] From the opening sequences, Hanna (who eventually begs to be released from her tortured life as an invalid) is encoded with an over-stimulated nervousness that was a marker of degeneracy in the late-nineteenth-century medical discourses that provided the underpinnings of Nazi racial and medical science. Her appearance (the first frontal shot is lit to give her a "negroid" look, reinforced by her headscarf), movement, dress, sterility, and the ambiguity of her name (lacking only the final "h" to lengthen the last vowel into one of the two generic names given to Jewish women in the Third Reich), all align her with a modern degeneracy that eventually will take control of her in the form of an incurable degenerative disease, multiple sclerosis. Tracing the trope of nervousness throughout the film shows that Hanna becomes the equivalent of a good Jew, as described by Otto Weininger in *Geschlecht und Charakter* (Vienna: Braumüller, 1903), who recognizes the inescapable nature of the disease of Judaism and bravely asks to be spared this torture.

[4] Of course, as Bennett points out, the museum's theoretical, democratic mission and its practical function of furthering social distinction were and are constantly in tension with one another. One might say then that the commercial aspect of the House of German Art maintained the public function of constructing common cultural tradition even as it fostered class distinction

and generated income for the state, while dispensing with the illusion of the democratic. The conspicuous consumption of cultural goods by the leading figures in the party who visited the House of German Art was in this case exemplary.

[5] It is often overlooked that the film industry remained private until 1937 and (at least technically) remained so after the acquisitions by the Reichsbank. For documentation on the financial arrangements leading up to the acquisitions, see Gerd Albrecht, *National-Sozialistische Filmpolitik* (Stuttgart: Ferdinand Enke Verlag, 1969) 12–35, 524–26.

[6] Monika is seen outside twice briefly: once, returning from the store early in the film, she runs into an old schoolmate who has married well, but the framing encloses them in the shop's windows; and, once on the step going into Felder's Gallery, which she enters quickly. Both are clearly studio shots used to establish Monika's and Martin's standing outside the spaces of social, monetary, and artistic success (the posh dress shop and the major art gallery). While reclaiming the notion of art in Berlin from the vestiges of Weimar decadence is vital to the film, the streets of the city are not the issue here.

[7] As Eric Rentschler points puts in the introduction to *The Ministry of Illusion: Nazi Cinema and its Afterlife* (Cambridge MA: Harvard UP, 1996), the image of one aesthetic extreme is only made sensible by knowledge of the other: in that sense the few shots here of pessimistic art recur under erasure in all of the optimism that dominates the film.

[8] I refer to these as semi-public private spaces because the private homes are clearly marked as places of public work: Martin paints images of the people; Felder selects the images for the nation. The gallery is also kept from being completely public by the private space of Felder's office, in which most of the scenes are shot. There he consumes vast quantities of cake and, under the knowledge of being alone, jokes with the office boy.

[9] Though this may not seem to be the case from the brief description of *Die Entlassung* offered here, the film does indeed align Bismarck with the people through an artwork. In a seeming digression in the film's central section, Kaiser Wilhelm II arrives early for a portrait sitting and interrupts the artist's work on an image of Christ. The model turns out to be an unemployed Social Democrat, who nevertheless remains absolutely true to the Kaiser. In an over-the-top and yet powerful sequence, this subject — still decked out in a robe and crown of thorns — explains to his sovereign the reasons for having joined the party. Wilhelm misinterprets the people's voice here as a call for him to become more personally involved, which leads him to countermand Bismarck's policies and lose ground in the next election. The film often maintains that Bismarck, because he is conscientious in his duties as a landed nobleman, remains close to and understands the people, whereas the Kaiser's court of dilettantes and professional politicians are estranged from the people since they try to rule from behind the scenes but never "dare to come into the public light" (Bismarck). Thus the man pursuing the calling, the people,

and the work of the nation are united in this film as well, which again makes it a kind of tragedy, but one that can be corrected by those who may yet "finish his work."

[10] The parallel here to the function of the radio and music in Borsody's *Wunschkonzert* (Request Concert, 1940) bears out, although the impetus in *Die Stärkere* is toward generating a space for individual fate in which we all share vicariously, rather than overtly uniting individual and national goals. The implied audience (i.e. the audience the film hopes to create for its duration), however, is largely the same.

[11] Johannes von Moltke provides an excellent explication of this delicate symbiosis by reading *Die Trapp-Familie in Amerika* (The Trapp Family in America, 1958), the sequel to *Die Trapp-Familie*, both within and against the traditions of the *Heimatfilm*. "Trapped in America: The Americanization of the Trapp-Familie, or Papas Kino Revisited," *German Studies Review* 19.3 (1996): 455–78.

[12] According to the sequel, this good business does not last long, for the Trapp Family singers face a crisis of unenthusiastic crowds and empty houses, because the bulk of their programs are built around devotional music. Their salvation will again be the folk song, combined with a more contemporary mode of dress and performance. Moltke (calling on Maase, 1993) instructively reads this change of attire in relation to the actual historical influence of the American occupation and film industry, which so profoundly affected fashion and style in Germany in the 1950s. One might also usefully view this move as a further development in the discourse about earning and working I have been following, one in which the producers must also become consumers in order to continue to spin the wheel of culture in economic circulation.

[13] *Die Trapp-Familie* even goes so far as to provide a mechanism for making such distinctions among the Nazis, by maintaining the sense that the Hitler period was a kind of colonization by "the gentlemen from the Wilhelmstrasse" (Baron von Trapp), which in essence interrupts the normal modernization of the Trapps from being those who have servants to those who provide service (in the hotel). After the Annexation the long-time family servant reveals that he has been a Nazi party member illegally for years, and suggests they hoist the new flag, which he has acquired. Moments later a local party official (dressed in typical Alpine garb and sporting the thickest Austrian accent heard in the film) arrives to make the same demand. Baron Trapp refuses both men on nationalist grounds. Rather than see the Baron arrested, however, the servant later deceives his party comrade and enables the Trapps' escape, thus giving an alibi to small-time Nazis and fellow travelers everywhere. The troubles back home receive no more comment in this film.

Works Cited

Agoston, Gerty. "Der 'Bergfilmer' auf USA Tournee. Luis Trenker — unvergessen — besucht Amerika." *New Yorker Staats-Zeitung und Herold.* 17–18 Sept. 1983.

Ahren, Yizhak, Stig Hornshøj-Møller, and Christoph B. Melchers. *"Der ewige Jude": Wie Goebbels hetzte: Untersuchungen zum nationalsozialistischen Propagandafilm.* Aachen: Alano, 1990.

Albrecht, Gerd, ed. *Der Film im Dritten Reich: Eine Dokumentation.* Karlsruhe: Schauburg and Doku, 1979.

Albrecht, Gerd. *Nationalsozialistische Filmpolitik: Eine Soziologische Untersuchung über den Spielfilm des Dritten Reichs.* Stuttgart: Ferdinand Enke Verlag, 1969.

Albrecht-Carrié, René. "Foreign Policy Since the First World War." In *Modern Italy: A Topical History since 1861,* edited by Edward R. Tannenbaum and Emiliana P. Noether, 337–54. New York: New York UP, 1974.

Alexander, Helmut. "'Der ganze Tiroler Stamm in einem Reich.' Option und Umsiedlung im Spiegel der *Innsbrucker Nachrichten.*" In *Die Option: Südtirol zwischen Faschismus und Nationalsozialismus,* edited by Klaus Eisterer and Rolf Steininger, 341–63. Innsbruck: Haymon, 1989.

Arnold, Thomas, Jutta Schöning, and Ulrich Schröter. *"Hitlerjunge Quex."* *Einstellungsprotokoll.* Munich: IHSA Arbeitspapiere im Verlag der filmland presse, 1980.

Baird, Jay W. *The Mythical World of Nazi Propaganda, 1939–1945.* Minneapolis: U of Minnesota P, 1974.

———. *To Die for Germany: Heroes in the Nazi Pantheon.* Bloomington: U of Indiana P, 1990.

Bandmann, Christa, and Joe Hembus. *Klassiker des deutschen Tonfilms 1930–1960.* Munich: Goldmann, 1980.

Barz, Paul. *Der wahre Schimmelreiter: Die Geschichte einer Landschaft und ihres Dichters Theodor Storm.* Hamburg: Ernst Kabel, 1982.

Bateson, Gregory. "An Analysis of the Nazi Film *Hitlerjunge Quex.*" In *The Study of Culture at a Distance,* edited by Margaret Mead and Rhoda Métraux, 302–14. Chicago: U of Chicago P, 1953.

Bauer-Hundsdörfer, Lore. "Jeder Einzelne wird gebraucht." *Frauenwarte* 6.16 (1938): 487–89.

Bechdolf, Ute. *Wunsch-Bilder? Frauen im nationalsozialistischen Unterhaltungsfilm.* Tübingen: Niemeyer, 1992.

Bechtold-Comforty, Beate, Luis Bedeck, and Tanja Marquandt. "Zwanziger Jahre und Nationalsozialismus." In *Der deutsche Heimatfilm: Bildwelten und Weltbilder*, edited by Projektgruppe Deutscher Heimatfilm, 33–67. Tübingen: Ludwig-Uhland-Institut der Universität Tübingen, 1989.

Beja, Morris. *Film and Literature*. New York: Longman, 1979.

Bennett, Tony. "Putting Policy into Cultural Studies." In *Cultural Studies*, edited by C. N. Lawrence Grossberg and Paula Treichler, 23–37. New York: Routledge, 1992.

Beradt, Charlotte. *Das dritte Reich des Traumes*. Frankfurt: Suhrkamp, 1981.

Berghaus, Günter, ed. *Fascism and Theatre: Comparative Studies on the Aesthetics and Politics of Performance in Europe, 1925–1945*. Providence: Berghahn, 1996.

Berg-Pan, Renata. *Leni Riefenstahl*. Boston: Twayne Publishers, 1980.

Bettecken, Wilhelm. "Der Film im Dienst der Propaganda." *FILM-Korrespondenz* 34. 4 (1988): 3–6.

Blumenberg, Hans-Christoph. *Das Leben geht weiter: Der letzte Film des Dritten Reichs*. Berlin: Rowohlt, 1993.

Boberach, Heinz, ed. *Meldungen aus dem Reich: Auswahl aus den geheimen Lageberichten des Sicherheitsdienstes der SS 1939–1944*. Neuwied: Luchterhand, 1965.

Brandt, Hans-Jürgen. "Der Propagandakern — *Ich klage an*." In *Widergänger: Faschismus und Antifaschismus im Film*, edited by J. Schmitt-Sasse, 15–37. Münster: MAKS Publikationen, 1993.

———. *NS-Filmtheorie und dokumentarische Praxis: Hippler, Noldan, Junghans*. Tübingen: Max Niemayer Verlag, 1987.

Brockhaus, Gudrun. "Male Images and Female Desire." *Modernism/Modernity* 3.1 (1996): 71–86.

Brown, Royal S. *Overtones and Undertones: Reading Film Music*. Berkeley: U of California P, 1994.

Bucher, Peter. "Die Bedeutung des Films als historische Quelle: *Der ewige Jude* (1940)." In *Festschrift für Eberhard Kessel zum 75. Geburtstag*, edited by Heinz Duchhardt and Manfred Schlenke, 300–29. Munich: Fink, 1982.

Bucher, Willi, and Klaus Pohl, eds. *Schock und Schöpfung: Jugendästhetik im 20. Jahrhundert*. Darmstadt: Luchterhand, 1986.

Carroll, Noel. "The Moral Ecology of the Melodrama: The Family Plot and 'Magnificent Obsession.'" In *Melodrama*, edited by Daniel Gerould and Jeannie Parisier Plottel, 197–206. New York: New York Literary Forum, 1980.

Clausen, Jeanette, and Sara Friedrichsmeyer. *Women in German Yearbook*. Lincoln: U of Nebraska P, 1995.

Cofino, Alon. "The Nation as a Local Metaphor: Heimat, National Memory and the German Empire, 1871–1918." *History and Memory* 5.1 (1993): 42–86.

Cornelsen, Peter. *Helmut Käutner: Seine Filme — sein Leben.* Munich: Heyne, 1980.

Courtade, Francis, and Pierre Cadars. *Geschichte des Films im Dritten Reich.* Translated by Florian Hopf. Abridged German edition. Munich: Hanser, 1975; Munich: Wilhelm Heyne Verlag, 1975.

Crew, David F. Introduction to "Omniscient, Omnipotent, Omnipresent? Gestapo, Society and Resistance." In *Nazism and German Society, 1933–1945*, edited by David F. Crew, 166. New York: Routledge, 1994.

Crew, David F., ed. *Nazism and German Society.* New York: Routledge, 1994.

Dahrendorf, Ralf. *Gesellschaft und Demokratie in Deutschland.* Munich: Piper, 1965.

Denkler, Horst, and Karl Prümm. *Die deutsche Literatur im Dritten Reich.* Stuttgart: Reclam, 1976.

Diehl, Guida. *Die deutsche Frau und der Nationalsozialismus.* 3d ed. Eisenach: Neuland, 1933.

Doane, Mary Ann. "Film and Masquerade: Theorising the Female Spectator." *Screen* 23.3–4 (1982): 74–87.

——. *The Desire to Desire: The Woman's Film of the 1940's.* Bloomington: Indiana UP, 1987.

Drewniak, Bogusław. *Der deutsche Film 1938–1945: Ein Gesamtüberblick.* Düsseldorf: Droste, 1987.

Duchhardt, Heinz, and Manfred Schlenke, eds. *Festschrift für Eberhard Kessel zum 75. Geburtstag.* Munich: Fink, 1982.

Dudden, Arthur Power. "Dimensions of American Humor." *East-West Film Journal* 2.1 (1987): 3–16.

Duncan, Carol, and Allan Wallach. "The Universal Survey Museum." *Art History* 3.4 (1980): 448–69.

Eichborn, Ulrike. "Ehestandsdarlehen. Dem Mann den Arbeitsplatz, der Frau Heim, Herd und Kinder." In *Frauenleben im NS-Alltag*, edited by Anette Kuhn, 48–64. Pfaffenweiler: Centaurus, 1994.

Eisert-Rost, Elisabeth, Katharina Eschbach, et al. *"Heimat."* In *Der deutsche Heimatfilm: Bildwelten und Weltbilder*, edited by Projektgruppe Deutscher Heimatfilm, 15–32. Tübingen: Ludwig-Uhland-Institut der Universität Tübingen, 1989.

Eisner, Lotte H. *Fritz Lang.* London: Secker and Warburg, 1976.

——. *The Haunted Screen: Expressionism in the German Cinema and the Influence of Max Reinhardt.* Berkeley and Los Angeles: U of California P, 1973.

Eisterer, Klaus, and Rolf Steininger, eds. *Die Option: Südtirol zwischen Faschismus und Nationalsozialismus.* Innsbruck: Haymon, 1989.

Eisterer, Klaus. "'Hinaus oder hinunter!' Die sizilianische Legende: eine taktische Meisterleistung der Deutschen." Eisterer and Steininger 179–207.

Elsaesser, Thomas. "Berlin Alexanderplatz: Franz Biberkopf'/S/Exchanges." *Wide Angle* 12 (1990): 30–43.

Estermann, Alfred. *Die Verfilmung literarischer Werke.* Bonn: Bouvier, 1965.

Everson, William K. Lecture on Luis Trenker. Goethe House New York. 15 Oct. 1983a.

——. "Luis Trenker," *Films in Review* 35.5 (1984): 271–80.

——. "Trenker at 91 Still a Hit: Verbal Salvos Re 'Art' Mark 10th Telluride," *Variety* 14 Sept. 1983b: 6+.

Ewers, Hanns Heinz. *Horst Wessel: Ein deutsches Schicksal.* Stuttgart: J. G. Cotta'sche Buchhandlung Nachfolger, 1933.

Fehrenbach, Heide. *Cinema in Democratizing Germany: Reconstructing National Identity after Hitler.* Chapel Hill: U of North Carolina P, 1995.

Feuer, Jane. "The Self-Reflexive Musical and the Myth of Entertainment." In *Film Genre Reader,* edited by Barry Keith Grant, 329–43. Austin: U of Texas P, 1986.

"Feuer und Fett." *Der Spiegel* 15 (1994): 217–18.

"Film und Zeitgeschehen: Zu dem Terra-Film *Fronttheater.*" *Der deutsche Film* 6.1 (1942–1943): 8.

Foucault, Michel. *Discipline and Punish: The Birth of the Prison.* Translated by Alan Sheridan. New York: Vintage Books, 1979.

Frayling, Christopher. *Spaghetti Westerns: Cowboys and Europeans from Karl May to Sergio Leone.* London: Taurus, 1998.

Freund, Winfried. *Theodor Storm, Der Schimmelreiter: Glanz und Elend des Bürgers.* Paderborn: Ferdinand Schöningh, 1984.

Friedman, Mihal Régine. "Die Ausnahme ist die Regel. Zu *Romanze in Moll* (1943) von Helmut Käutner." *Frauen und Film* 43 (December 1987): 48–58.

——. "Juden-Ratten — Von der rassistischen Metonymie zur tierischen Metapher in Fritz Hipplers Film *Der ewige Jude.*" *Frauen und Film* 47 (September 1989): 24–35.

——. *L'image et son Juif: Le Juif dans le cinéma Nazi.* Paris: Payot, 1983.

Fürstenau, Theo. Introduction. In *Filmographie Helmut Käutner*, edited by Rüdiger Koschnitzki, 7–14. Wiesbaden: Deutsches Institut für Filmkunde, 1978.

Gellately, Robert. *The Gestapo and German Society: Enforcing Racial Policy, 1933–1945*. New York: Oxford UP, 1990.

Gerould, Daniel, and Jeannie Parisier Plottel, eds. *Melodrama*. New York: New York Literary Forum, 1980.

Gleber, Anke. "'Only Man Must Be and Remain a Judge, Soldier and Ruler of State' — Female as Void in Nazi Film." In *Gender and German Cinema: Feminist Interventions*, edited by Sandra Frieden, et al., 105–16. Providence: Berg, 1993.

Goebbels, Joseph. *Goebbels-Reden*. Ed. Helmut Heiber. 2 vols. Düsseldorf: Droste Verlag, 1971.

——. "Goebbels Tagebücher." Hoover Institute. Reel 3, frames 2750–51 (15–16 of typed manuscript).

——. "Rede im Kaiserhof am 28. 3. 1933." Albrecht, *Der Film im Dritten Reich*, 26–31.

——. "Rede in den Tennishallen, Berlin, am 19. 5. 1933." Albrecht, *Nationalsozialistische Filmpolitik*, 442–47.

——. "Rede bei der ersten Jahrestagung der Reichsfilmkammer, 5. März 1937, in der Krolloper, Berlin." Albrecht, *Nationalsozialistische Filmpolitik*, 447–63; Albrecht, *Der Film im Dritten Reich*, 32–63.

——. *Die Tagebücher: sämtliche Fragmente*. Ed. Elke Fröhlich. Pt. 1, Vols. 1–4. Munich: K. G. Saur, 1987.

——. *Vom Kaiserhof zur Reichskanzlei*. Munich: Zentralverlag der N.S.D.A.P Frz. Eher Nachf., 1934.

Gorbman, Claudia. *Unheard Melodies: Narrative Film Music*. London: BFI Publishing; Bloomington, IN: Indiana UP, 1987.

Göttler, Fritz. "Kolberg. Nichts geht mehr." Prinzler, 188–89.

Grant, Barry Keith. *Film Genre Reader*. Austin: U of Texas P, 1986.

"Große Dekoration für Zarah Leander: Bei den Aufnahmen zu dem Ufa-Film *Die große Liebe*." *Film-Kurier* no. 30 (4 February 1942): 3.

"*Die Große Liebe*: Zarah Leander und Paul Hörbiger einem neuen Film." *Filmwelt* no. 47–48 (26 November 1941): 938–39.

Gruber, Alfons. "Faschismus und Option in Südtirol." Eisterer and Steininger 227–38.

Hale, Wanda. "'Heroic Fight' Fine Film of Fatherland." Rev. of *Fire Devil*. *New York Daily News* 4 Jan. 1941. Rpt. Leimgruber: 115.

Halliday, Jon. *Sirk on Sirk*. 2nd edition. London: Faber and Faber Ltd., 1997.

Happel, Hans-Gerd. *Der historische Spielfilm in Nationalsozialismus.* Frankfurt: R. G. Fischer, 1984.

Harlan, Veit. *Im Schatten meiner Filme.* Gütersloh: Mohn, 1966.

Hartmann, Helga, and Ralf Schenk, eds. *Mitten ins Herz.* Berlin: Henschel, 1991.

Hasubek, Peter, ed. *Die Fabel: Theorie und Rezeption einer Gattung.* Berlin: Erich Schmidt Verlag, 1982.

Hauser, Johannes. *Neuaufbau der westdeutschen Filmwirtschaft 1945–1955 und der Einfluß der US-amerikanischen Filmpolitik: Vom reichseigenen Filmmonopolkonzern (UFI) zur privatwirtschaftlichen Konkurrenzwirtschaft.* Reihe Medienwissenschaft 1. Pfaffenweiler: Centaurus, 1989.

Herf, Jeffrey. *Reactionary modernism: Technology, culture and politics in Weimar and the Third Reich.* London: Cambridge UP, 1984.

Hinkel, Hans. "Der Einsatz unserer Kunst im Krieg." *Der deutsche Film* 5.11–12 (1941): 214–17.

Hinton, David B. *The Films of Leni Riefenstahl.* Metuchen, NJ: Scarecrow Press, 1978.

Hippler, Franz. *Betrachtungen zum Filmschaffen.* 5th rev. ed. Berlin: Max Hesses Verlag, 1943.

Hitler, Adolf. *Adolf Hitler: Monologe im Führerhauptquartier 1941–1944. Die Aufzeichnungen Heinrich Heims.* Edited by Werner Jochmann. Munich: Heyne, 1982.

——. *Mein Kampf.* Translated by Ralph Manheim. Boston: Houghton, 1943.

Hofacker, E., and L. Dieckmann. *Studies in the Germanic Languages and Literatures.* St. Louis: Washington UP, 1963.

Hoffmann, Hilmar. *The Triumph of Propaganda: Film and National Socialism, 1933–1945.* Translated by John A. Broadwin and V. R. Berghahn. Providence, RI: Berghahn Books, 1996.

——. *"Und die Fahne führt uns in die Ewigkeit": Propaganda im NS-Film.* Frankfurt: Fischer Taschenbuch Verlag, 1988.

Holander, Reimer Kay. *Theodor Storm, Der Schimmelreiter: Kommentar und Dokumentation.* Frankfurt: Ullstein, 1976.

Horak, Jan-Christopher. "Luis Trenker's *The Kaiser of California*: how the West was won, Nazi style." *Historical Journal of Film, Radio, and Television* 6.2 (1986): 181–88.

Hornshøj-Møller, Stig, and David Culbert. *"Der ewige Jude* (1940): Joseph Goebbels' Unequaled Monument to Anti-Semitism." *Historical Journal of Film, Radio, and Television* 12.1 (1992): 41–67.

Horton, Andrew. *Comedy/Cinema/Theory.* Berkeley: U of California P, 1991.

Horton, Andrew, and Joan Magretta. *Modern European Filmmakers and the Art of Adaptation*. New York: Ungar, 1981.

Hull, David Stewart. *Film in the Third Reich: A Study of the German Cinema 1933–1945*. Berkeley and Los Angeles: U of California P, 1969; reprint, New York: Simon and Schuster, 1973.

Hüneke, Andreas. "On the Trail of Missing Masterpieces: Modern Art from German Galleries." In *"Degenerate Art": The Fate of the Avant-Garde in Nazi Germany*, edited by S. Barron, 121–34. New York: Harry N. Abrams, 1991.

Infield, Glenn B. *Leni Riefenstahl: The Fallen Film Goddess*. New York: Thomas Y. Crowell Company, 1976.

Jacobsen, Wolfgang, and Hans Helmut Prinzler, eds. *Käutner*. Berlin: Spiess, 1992.

Jacobsen, Wolfgang, Anton Kaes, and Hans Helmut Prinzler, eds. *Geschichte des deutschen Films*. Stuttgart: Metzler, 1993.

Jameson, Fredric. "Reification and Utopia in Mass Culture." *Social Text* 1.1 (1979): 130–48.

Jary, Micaela. *Ich weiß, es wird einmal ein Wunder gescheh'n: Die große Liebe der Zarah Leander*. Berlin: edition q, 1993.

Jellonnek, Burkhard. *Homosexuelle unter dem Hakenkreuz*. Paderborn: Ferdinand Schöningh, 1990.

Jenkins, Henry. "'The Laughingstock of the City': Performance Anxiety, Male Dread, and *Unfaithfully Yours*." In *Classical Hollywood Comedy*, edited by Kristine Brunovska Karnick and Henry Jenkins, 238–61. New York: Routledge, 1995.

Jeziorkowski, Klaus. *Gottfried Keller, "Kleider machen Leute": Text, Materialien, Kommentar*. Munich: Carl Hanser, 1984.

Kaes, Anton, Martin Jay, and Edward Dimenberg, eds. *The Weimar Republic Source Book*. Berkeley and Los Angeles: U of California P, 1994.

Kaes, Anton. "History and Film: Public Memory in the Age of Electronic Dissemination." *History and Memory* 2 (1990): 111–29.

Kalbus, Oskar. *Vom Werden deutscher Filmkunst*. Vol. 2. Altona-Bahrenfeld: Cigaretten Bilderdienst, 1935.

Kanzog, Klaus. *"Staatspolitisch besonders wertvoll": Ein Handbuch zu 30 deutschen Spielfilmen der Jahre 1934 bis 1945*. Diskurs Film 6. Munich: Verlag Schaudig and Ledig, 1994.

Karnick, Kristine Brunovska, and Henry Jenkins. "Introduction: Comedy and the Social World." In *Classical Hollywood Comedy*, edited by Kristine Brunovska Karnick and Henry Jenkins, 265–81. New York: Routledge, 1995.

Kater, Michael H. *Different Drummers: Jazz in the Culture of Nazi Germany.* New York: Oxford UP, 1992.

Keller, Gottfried. *Kleider machen Leute.* Stuttgart: Reclam, 1969.

Kendall, Elizabeth. *The Runaway Bride: Hollywood Romantic Comedy of the 1930's.* New York: Knopf, 1990.

Kienast, Hansjürgen W. "Luis Trenker — ein europäischer John Wayne aus Tirol." *Sonntagpost* (Chicago) 18 Sept. 1983.

Kirst, Hans Hellmut. *Heinz Rühmann: Ein biographischer Report.* Munich: Kindler Verlag, 1969.

Klein, Adolf. *Köln im Dritten Reich: Stadtgeschichte der Jahre 1933–1945.* Cologne: Greven, 1983.

Klemperer, Victor. *LTI: Notizbuch eines Philologen.* Leipzig: Reclam, 1990.

Knight, Julia. *Women and the New German Cinema.* London: Verso, 1992.

Koepnick, Lutz P. "Unsettling America: German Westerns and Modernity," *Modernism/Modernity* 2.3 (1995): 1–22.

Koonz, Claudia. *Mothers in the Fatherland: Women, the Family, and Nazi Politics.* New York: St. Martin's Press, 1987.

—— *Mütter im Vaterland.* Freiburg: Kore Verlag, 1991.

Koschnitzki, Rüdiger. *Filmographie Helmut Käutner.* Wiesbaden: Deutsches Institut für Filmkunde, 1978.

Kracauer, Siegfried. *From Caligari to Hitler: A Psychological Study of the German Film.* Princeton, NJ: Princeton UP, 1947.

——. "Volkserhebung." Rev. of *Der Rebell. Frankfurter Zeitung*, 24 Jan. 1933.

Kreimeier, Klaus. *Die Ufa Story: Geschichte eines Filmkonzerns.* Munich: Hanser, 1992.

——. *The Ufa Story: A History of Germany's Greatest Film Company.* Translated by Robert and Rita Kimber. New York: Hill and Wang, 1996.

Krusche, Dieter. *Reclams Filmführer.* Stuttgart: Reclam, 1973.

Krutnik, Frank. "A Spanner in the Works? Genre, Narrative and the Hollywood Comedian." In *Classical Hollywood Comedy,* edited by Kristine Brunovska Karnick and Henry Jenkins, 17–38. New York: Routledge, 1995.

Kuhn, Anette, ed. *Frauenleben im NS-Alltag.* Pfaffenweiler: Centaurus, 1994.

Kurowski, Ulrich. *Deutsche Spielfilme 1933–1945: Materialien II.* 2d ed. Munich: Stadtmuseum München, 1978.

Leander, Zarah. *Es war so wunderbar! Mein Leben.* Hamburg: Hoffmann & Campe, 1983.

——. *So bin ich und so bleibe ich.* Gütersloh: Bertelsmann, 1958.

Leimgruber, Florian, ed. *Luis Trenker, Regisseur und Schriftsteller. Die Personalakte Trenker im Berlin Document Center.* Bolzano: Frasnelli-Keitsch, 1994.

Leiser, Erwin. *Nazi Cinema.* Translated by Gertrud Mander and David Wilson. London: Secker and Warburg, 1974; New York: Collier, 1975.

Loeb, Ernst. "Faust ohne Transzendenz: Theodor Storm's *Schimmelreiter*". In *Studies in the Germanic Languages and Literatures* edited by E. Hofakker and L. Dieckmann, 121–32. St. Louis Washington UP, 1963.

Loiperdinger, Martin. "Goebbels Filmpolitik überwältigt die Schatten der 'Kampfzeit': Zur Bewältigung nationalsozialistischer Vergangenheit im Jahr 1933." Loiperdinger, Märtyrerlegenden, 29–39.

———. *"Hans Westmar." Einstellungsprotokoll.* Munich: IHSA Arbeitspapiere im Verlag der filmland presse, 1980.

———. *"Hans Westmar*: Faschistische und kommunistische Öffentlichkeit kämpfen um den Besitz der Straße." Loiperdinger, *Märtyrerlegenden*, 55–76.

———, ed. *Märtyrerlegenden im NS-Film.* Opladen: Leske und Budrich, 1991.

Loiperdinger, Martin, and Klaus Schönekäs. "*Die große Liebe*: Propaganda im Unterhaltungsfilm." In *Bilder schreiben Geschichte: Der Historiker im Kino*, edited by Rainer Rother, 143–53. Berlin: Wagenbach, 1991.

Lowry, Stephen. *Pathos und Politik: Ideologie in Spielfilmen des Nationalsozialismus.* Tübingen: Niemeyer Verlag, 1991.

Lühti, Max. *Once upon a Time: On the Nature of Fairy Tales.* Bloomington: Indiana UP, 1976.

———. *The European Folktale: Form and Nature.* Bloomington: Indiana UP, 1982.

Maase, Kaspar. "'Halbstarke' and Hegemony: Meanings of American Mass Culture in the Federal Republic of Germany during the 1950s." In *Cultural Transmissions and Receptions: American Mass Culture in Europe*, edited by R. Kroes, R. W. Rydell, and D. F. J. Bosscher, 152–70. Amsterdam: VU UP, 1993.

Mallmann, Klaus-Michael, and Gerhard Paul. "Omniscient, Omnipotent, Omnipresent? Gestapo, Society and Resistance." In *Nazism and German Society, 1933–1945*, edited by David F. Crew, 166–96. New York: Routledge, 1994.

Mannens, Jean-Paul Mathieu. "Sudermanns Verhältnis zu den literarischen Strömungen der Jahrhundertwende." In *Hermann Sudermann: Werk und Wirkung*, edited by Walter T. Rix, 175–88. Würzburg: Königshausen und Neumann, 1980.

Maraun, Frank [Erwin Goetz]. "Symphonie des Ekels. *Der ewige Jude* — ein abendfüllender Dokumentarfilm." *Der Deutsche Film* 4. 8 (February 1940).

Marcorelles, Louis. "Käutner Le Dandy." *Cahiers du Cinéma* 73 (July 1957): 26–29.

——. "The Nazi Cinema (1933–1945)." *Sight and Sound* 25 (Autumn 1955): 65–69.

McCormick, Richard W. "Private Anxieties/Public Projections: 'New Objectivity,' Male Subjectivity, and Weimar Cinema." In *Women in German Yearbook*, vol. 10, edited by Jeanette Clausen and Sara Friedrichsmeyer, 1–18. Lincoln: U of Nebraska P, 1995.

McGilligan, Patrick. *Fritz Lang: The Nature of the Beast.* New York: St. Martin's, 1997.

Mead, Margaret, and Rhoda Métraux, eds. *The Study of Culture at a Distance.* Chicago: U of Chicago P, 1953.

Messenger, Charles. *"Bomber" Harris and the Strategic Bombing Offensive, 1939–1945.* New York: St. Martin's Press, 1984.

Mews, Siegfried, ed. *A Bertolt Brecht Reference Companion.* Westport CT: Greenwood Press, 1997.

Meyer, Michael. *The Politics of Music in the Third Reich.* Frankfurt: Peter Lang, 1991.

Moeller, Felix. *Der Filmminister: Goebbels und der Film im Dritten Reich.* Berlin: Henschel, 1988.

Moltke, Johannes von. "Trapped in America: The Americanization of the Trapp-Familie, or Papas Kino Revisited." *German Studies Review* 19.3 (1996): 455–78.

Morley, David, and Kevin Robbins. "No Place like Heimat. Images of Home(land) in European Culture." *New Formations* 12 (Winter 1990): 1–24.

Morrison, Wilber H. *Fortress without a Roof: The Allied Bombing of the Third Reich.* New York: St. Martin's Press, 1982.

Mosse, George L. *Nationalism and Sexuality: Respectability and Abnormal Sexuality in Modern Europe.* New York: Howard Fertig, 1985.

——, ed. *Nazi Culture: Intellectual, Cultural and Social Life in the Third Reich.* New York: Grosset and Dunlap, 1966.

——. "Two World Wars and the Myth of the War Experience." *Journal of Contemporary History* 21 (October 1986): 491–514.

Müller, Ray (director). *Die Macht der Bilder Leni Riefenstahls.* New York: Kino Video, 1993.

Mulvey, Laura. "Visual Pleasure and Narrative Cinema." *Screen* 16.3 (1975): 6–18.

Mundt, Michaela. *Transformationsanalyse: Methodologische Probleme der Literaturverfilmung*. Tübingen: M. Niemeyer, 1994.

Musilli, John (director and producer). *Leni Riefenstahl*. Written by Stephan Chodorov. Narrated by Peter Brandon. Kent: Creative Arts Archive, 1972.

Nadar, Thomas R. "Brecht and His Musical Collaborators." *A Bertolt Brecht Reference Companion*, edited by Siegfried Mews, 261–77. Westport, CT: Greenwood Press, 1997.

Neis, Edgar. *Die Novelle*. Hollfeld: C. Bange, 1980.

Netzeband, Günter. "D. St. Hull und die Folgen. Korrekturen zur Nazifilm-Geschichtsschreibung." *Film und Fernsehen* (DDR) 7. 1 (January 1979): 33–38.

"Neues von der Terra: *Auf Wiedersehen, Franziska*." *Film-Kurier*, 9 Jan. 1941.

Nolan, Mary. *Visions of Modernity: American Business and the Modernization of Germany*. New York: Oxford UP, 1994.

Nugent, Frank S. Rev. of *Sutter's Gold*. *New York Times*, 27 March 1936: 25.

——. Rev. of *Giovanni di Medici, The Leader*. The New York Times 5 Jan. 1940: 15.

Paech, Joachim. *Literatur und Film*. Stuttgart: Metzler, 1988.

——. *Methodenprobleme der Analyse verfilmter Literatur*. Münster: Nodus Publikationen, 1984.

Panitz, Hans-Jürgen (director). *Luis Trenker*. Pt. 1: *Fast ein Jahrhundert*; Pt. 2: *Alles gut gegangen*; Pt. 3: *Von Kastelruth nach Hollywood*. Omega Film, Bayrischer Rundfunk, and RAI Bolzano, 1986.

Paul, Wolfgang. *Der Heimatkrieg 1939 bis 1945*. Esslingen: Bechtle, 1980.

Petley, Julian. *Capital and Culture: German Cinema 1933–1945*. London: BFI Publishing, 1979.

Peukert, Detlev J. K. *Inside Nazi Germany: Conformity, Opposition, and Racism in Everyday Life*. Translated by Richard Deveson. New Haven: Yale UP, 1987.

Prinz, Michael, and Rainer Zittelmann, eds. *Nationalsozialismus und Modernisierung*. Darmstadt: Wissenschaftliche Buchgesellschaft, 1991.

Prinzler, Hans Helmut. *Chronik des deutschen Films 1895–1994*. Stuttgart: Metzler, 1995.

Prinzler, Hans Helmut. *Das Jahr 1945: Filme aus Fünfzehn Ländern*. Berlin: Stiftung Deutsche Kinemathek, 1990.

"Purim." *Encyclopaedia Judaica*, vol. 13, 1390–1395. New York: Macmillan, 1971.

Rauschning, Hermann. *Gespräche mit Hitler.* New York: Europa Verlag, 1940.

Reichel, Peter. *Der schöne Schein des Dritten Reiches.* Munich: Hanser, 1991.

Reimann, Viktor. *Goebbels.* Garden City, NJ: Doubleday, 1976.

Reinert, Charles, ed. *Wir vom Film: 1300 Kurzbiographien aus aller Welt.* Freiburg: Herder, 1960.

Rentschler, Eric, ed. *German Film and Literature: Adaptations and Transformations.* London: Methuen, 1986.

——. "How American Is It: The U.S. as Image and Imaginary in German Film." *The German Quarterly* 57.4 (Fall 1984): 603–620.

——. "Ministry of Illusion. German Film 1933–1945." *Film Comment* 30.6 (1994): 34–42.

——. *The Ministry of Illusion: Nazi Cinema and Its Afterlife.* Cambridge, MA: Harvard UP, 1996.

——. "Mountains and Modernity: Relocating the *Bergfilm.*" *New German Critique* 51 (Fall 1990): 137–61.

——. "Reopening the Cabinet of Dr. Kracauer: Teaching German Film as Film." *Modern Language Journal* 64 (Autumn 1980): 318–328.

——. "There's No Place Like Home: Luis Trenker's *The Prodigal Son.*" *New German Critique* 60 (Fall 1993): 33–56.

Rev. of *Auf Wiedersehen, Franziska.* Film-Kurier, 9 January 1941: 6.

Rev. of *Condottieri. Variety,* 14 July 1937: 21+.

Rev. of *Emperor of California. Variety,* 12 May 1937: 13.

Rev. of *Emperor of California. Variety,* 19 Aug. 1936: 16.

Rev. of *The Prodigal Son. Variety,* 22 Jan. 1935: 15.

Rev. of *Romanze in Moll. Film-Kurier* 18 July 1944: 1.

Rev. of *Unter den Brücken. Neue Filmwoche,* Feb. 1947: 1.

Rhodes, Anthony. *The Vatican in the Age of the Dictators 1922–1945.* New York: Holt, 1973.

Riefenstahl, Leni. *Leni Riefenstahl, A Memoir.* New York: St. Martin's Press, 1992; reprint, New York: Picador, 1995.

Riess, Curt. *Das gab's nur einmal: Die große Zeit des deutschen Films.* Munich: Molden, 1977.

——. *Das gibt's nur einmal: Das Buch des deutschen Films nach 1945.* Hamburg: Henri Nannen Verlag, 1958.

Rix, Walter T., ed. *Hermann Sudermann: Werk und Wirkung.* Würzburg: Königshausen und Neumann, 1980.

Romani, Cinzia. *Die Filmdivas des Dritten Reiches.* Munich: Bahia Verlag, 1982.

Rost, Karl L. "*Ich klage an* — ein historischer Film?" In *Medizin im Spielfilm des Nationalsozialismus*, edited by Udo Benzenhöfer and Wolfgang U. Eckart, 34–51. Tecklenburg: Burgverlag, 1990.

——. *Sterilisation und Euthanasie im Film des Dritten Reiches: National-sozialistische Propaganda in ihrer Beziehung zu rassenhygienischen Maß-nahmen.* Husum: Mattiesen, 1987.

Roth, Karl H. "*Ich klage an*, Aus der Entsteheungsgeschichte eines Propa-gandafilms." In *Aktion T-4 1939–45: Die Euthanasie-Zentrale in der Tier-gartenstraße 4*, edited by Götz Aly, 93–116. Berlin: Hettrich, 1987.

Rother, Rainer, ed. *Bilder schreiben Geschichte: Der Historiker im Kino.* Berlin: Wagenbach, 1991.

Rowe, Kathleen. *The Unruly Woman: Gender and the Genres of Laughter.* Austin: U of Texas P, 1995.

Ruf, Wolfgang. "Verklärung des ungebundenen Lebens: Helmut Käutners Film *Unter den Brücken*." *Süddeutsche Zeitung*, 12 Mar. 1973: 9.

Rühle, Gerd. *Das Dritte Reich: Dokumentarische Darstellung des Aufbaus der Nation.* Das erste Jahr: 1933. Berlin: Hummer, 1934.

Rühmann, Heinz. *Das war's: Erinnerungen.* Frankfurt: Ullstein, 1983.

Rundell, Richard J. "Keller's 'Kleider machen Leute' as *Novelle* and Film." *Die Unterrichtspraxis* 13 (Fall 1980): 156–65.

Salvemini, Gaetano. *Prelude to World War II.* New York: Doubleday, 1954.

Sanders, Ulrike. *Zarah Leander — Kann den Schlager Sünde sein?* Pahl-Rugenstein Hochschulschriften 251. Cologne: Pahl-Rugenstein, 1988.

Sanders-Brahms, Helma. "Tiefland. Tyrannenmord." Prinzler, 173–76.

Schäfer, Hans Dieter. *Das gespaltene Bewußtsein: Über Deutsche Kultur und Lebenswirklichkeit 1933–1945.* Berlin: Ullstein, 1984.

Schenzinger, Karl Aloys. *Der Hitlerjunge Quex.* Berlin: Zeitgeschichte-Verlag Wilhelm Andermann, 1932.

Schickedanz, Hans-Joachim. *Femme fatale: Ein Mythos wird entblättert.* Dortmund: Harenberg, 1983.

Schlüpmann, Heide. "Faschistische Trugbilder weiblicher Autonomie." *Frau-en und Film* 44–45 (1988): 44–66.

Schmitt-Sasse, J., ed. *Widergänger: Faschismus und Antifaschismus im Film.* Münster: MAKS Publikationen, 1993.

Schoenbaum, David. *Hitler's Social Revolution: Class and Status in Nazi Germany, 1933–1939.* Garden City, NY: Doubleday, 1966.

Schriefer, Uwe. "*S.A.-Mann Brand*": *Einstellungsprotokoll.* Munich: IHSA Arbeitspapiere im Verlag der filmland press, 1980.

———. "*SA-Mann Brand*: Die Präsentation der 'NS-Bewegung' von unten." In *Märtyrerlegenden im NS-Film*, edited by Martin Loiperdinger, 77–108. Opladen: Leske und Budrich, 1991.

Schulte-Sasse, Linda. *Entertaining the Third Reich: Illusions of Wholeness in Nazi Cinema*. Durham, NC: Duke UP, 1996.

———. "Leni Riefenstahl's Feature Films and the Question of a Fascist Aesthetic." *Cultural Critique* 18 (Spring 1991): 123–48.

Schütte, Jan. "*Unter den Brücken*. Die Viererbande." Prinzler, 170–72.

Seiler, Paul. *Zarah Leander: Ich bin eine Stimme*. Berlin: Ullstein, 1997.

Seton-Watson, Christopher. *Italy from Liberalism to Fascism 1870–1925*. London: Methuen, 1967.

Siegert, Michael. "*Der ewige Jude*." In *Propaganda und Gegenpropaganda im Film 1933–1945*, 63–79. Vienna: Österreichisches Filmmuseum, 1972.

Silberman, Marc. "The Illusion of Escapism: Helmut Käutner's Romance in a Minor Key." *German Cinema: Texts in Context*, 81–96. Detroit: Wayne State UP, 1995.

———. "Kleist in the Third Reich: Ucicky's *The Broken Jug* (1937)." Rentschler, *German Film and Literature*, 87–102.

———. "Probing the Limits: Detlef Sierck's *To New Shores*." *German Cinema: Texts in Context*, 51–65. Detroit: Wayne State UP, 1995.

Smith, Harry T. Rev. of *The Emperor of California*. *New York Times*, 8 May 1937: 23.

"Spiel und Wirklichkeit: Filmgespräch um eine Romanze, Liebe und Schauspielkunst." *Der Angriff*, 13 Nov. 1942: 3.

Spurgat, Günter. *Theodor Storm im Film: Die Kino- und Fernsehverfilmungen seiner Werke*. Lübeck: Graphische Werkstätten, 1987.

Stacey, Jackie. *Star Gazing: Hollywood Cinema and Female Spectatorship*. New York: Routledge, 1994.

Stecher, Wilhelm. "Liebe zum detail: Gedanken zu einem neuen Käutner-Film." *Film-Kurier*, 20 June 1944: 3.

Steinert, Marlis G. *Hitler's War and the Germans: Public Mood and Attitude during the Second World War*. Translated by Thomas E. J. de Witt. Athens, OH: Ohio UP, 1977.

Steininger, Rolf. "Die Option — Anmerkungen zu einem schwierigen Thema." Eisterer and Steininger 9–31.

———. *Südtirol im 20. Jahrhundert: Vom Leben und Überleben einer Minderheit*. Innsbruck: Studien Verlag, 1997.

Steurer, Leopold. "Der Optionsverlauf in Südtirol." In *Die Option: Südtirol zwischen Faschismus und Nationalsozialismus*, edited by Klaus Eisterer and Rolf Steininger, 209–25. Innsbruck: Haymon, 1989.

Storm, Theodor. *Immensee*. In *Immensee und andere Novellen*. Stuttgart: Reclam, 1969.

—— *Der Schimmelreiter*. Stuttgart: Reclam, 1962.

Suchen, Hans. "*Die große Liebe*." *Filmwelt* 23–24 (24 June 1942): 188.

Sudermann, Heinrich. *Heimat: Schauspiel in drei Akten*. 1893. Stuttgart: J. H. Cotta'sche Buchhandlung Nachfolger, 1906.

Suval, Stanley. *The Anschluss Question in the Weimar Era: A Study of Nationalism in Germany and Austria, 1918–1932*. Baltimore: Johns Hopkins UP, 1974.

Thalmann, Rita. *Frausein im Dritten Reich*. Frankfurt: Ullstein, 1987.

"Theaterleiter, Publikum und Filmerfolg." *Film-Kurier*, 3 Mar. 1944: 1.

Tornow, Ingo. *Piroschka und Wunderkinder oder von der Vereinbarkeit von Idylle und Satire: Der Regisseur Kurt Hoffmann*. Munich: Filmlandpresse, 1990.

Trenker, Luis. *Alles gut gegangen*. Munich: Bertelsmann, 1979.

Trommler, Frank. "The Rise and Fall of Americanism in Germany." In *America and the Germans: An Assessment of A Three-Hundred-Year History*, edited by Frank Trommler and Joseph McVeigh, 332–42. Vol. 2. Philadelphia: U of Pennsylvania P, 1985.

Ulbrich, Walter. "Die Entstehung des Films *Unter den Brücken*." *Neue Züricher Zeitung*, 11 May 1947.

Viering, Jürgen. "'Für Idyllen war kein Platz in meinem Leben.' Zur Familienthematik in Sudermanns Gesellschaftsdramen." In *Hermann Sudermann: Werk und Wirkung*, edited by Walter T. Rix, 113–34. Würzburg: Königshausen und Neumann, 1980.

Villgrater, Maria. "Die 'Katakombenschule': Symbol des Südtiroler Widerstandes. Eisterer and Steininger, 85–105.

Waas, Maria. Rev. of *Die große Liebe*. In Bundesarchiv-Filmarchiv Document file 6214. no date.

Wanderscheck, Hermann. "Ehen in Dur und Moll: Kleine Untersuchen nach jüngsten Filmen." *Film-Kurier*, 11 Nov. 1943: 3.

——. "Filmmusik als gestaltende Macht." *Film-Kurier*, 16 May 1941: 2.

——. "Panorama neuer Filmmusik." *Film-Kurier*, 10 Nov. 1941: 3

Ward, Mark G. *Theodor Storm, Der Schimmelreiter*. Glasgow: U of Glasgow French and German Publications, 1988.

Weber, Max. *The Protestant Ethic and the Spirit of Capitalism*. 1904, rpt. London: Unwin Paperbacks, 1985.

Wehrling, Thomas. "Berlin is Becoming a Whore." In *The Weimar Republic Source Book*, edited by Anton Kaes, Martin Jay, and Edward Dimenberg, 721. Berkeley and Los Angeles: U of California P, 1994.

Weinreich, Gerd. *Theodor Storm: Der Schimmelreiter*. Grundlagen und Gedanken zum Verständnis erzählender Literatur. Frankfurt: Diesterweg, 1988.

Welch, David. *Propaganda and the German Cinema 1933–1945*. Oxford: Oxford UP, 1983.

Werner, Gösta. "Fritz Lang and Goebbels: Myths and Facts." *Film Quarterly* 43.3 (1990): 24–27.

Williams, John Alexander. "'The Chords of the German Soul Are Tuned to Nature:' The Movement to Preserve the Natural Heimat from the Kaiserreich to the Third Reich." *Central European History* 29.3 (1996): 339–84.

Winkler-Mayerhöfer, Andrea. *Starkult als Propagandamittel: Studien zum Unterhaltungsfilm im Dritten Reich*. Munich: Ölschläger, 1992.

Winkler, Willi. "Ein Schlafwandler bei Goebbels." *Der Spiegel* 48 (1990): 236–43.

Wischnewski, Klaus. "Eine Augenblick der Freiheit oder Helmut Käutner's *Romanze in Moll.*" In *Mitten ins Herz*, edited by Helga Hartmann and Ralf Schenk, 170–73. Berlin: Henschel, 1991.

Witte, Karsten. "Der Apfel und der Stamm. Jugend und Propagandafilm am Beispiel *Hitlerjunge Quex* (1933)." In *Schock und Schöpfung: Jugendästhetik im 20. Jahrhundert*, edited by Willi Bucher and Klaus Pohl, 302–7. Darmstadt: Luchterhand, 1986.

——. "Film im Nationalsozialismus." Jacobsen, Kaes, and Prinzler, 119–70.

——. "Die Filmkomödie im Dritten Reich." In *Die deutsche Literatur im Dritten Reich*, edited by Horst Denkler and Karl Prümm, 347–65. Stuttgart: Reclam, 1976.

——. "How Nazi cinema mobilizes the classics: Schweikart's *Das Fräulein von Barnhelm* (1940)." Rentschler, *German Film and Literature*, 103–16.

——. *Lachende Erben, Toller Tag: Filmkomödie im dritten Reich*. Berlin: Verlag Vorwerk 8, 1995.

——. "Visual Pleasure Inhibited: Aspects of the German Revue Film." *New German Critique* 24–25 (1981–1982): 38–63.

——. "Die Wirkgewalt der Bilder. Zum Beispiel Wolfgang Liebeneiner." *Filme* 8 (March-April 1981): 24–35.

Wittmann, Livia Z. "Zwischen 'femme fatale' und 'femme fragile' — die Neue Frau?" *Jahrbuch für Internationale Germanistik* 17.2 (1985): 74–111.

Wolff, Lutz. *Püppchen, du bist mein Augenstern: Deutsche Schlager aus vier Jahrzehnten*. Munich: Deutscher Taschenbuch Verlag, 1981.

Wulf, Joseph. *Theater und Film im Dritten Reich*. Vienna: Ullstein, 1983.

Wysocki, Gisela von. "Die Berge und die Patriarchen — Leni Riefenstahl." In *Die Fröste der Freiheit: Aufbruchphantasien*, 70–85. Frankfurt: Syndikat Autoren- und Verlagsgesellschaft, 1980.

"Zehn Mark, die von der Brücke fielen: Helmut Käutner dreht für die Ufa *Unter den Brücken* . . ." *Film-Kurier*, 23 May 1944: 3.

Zittelmann, Rainer. "Die totalitäre Seite der Moderne." In *Nationalsozialismus und Modernisierung*, edited by Michael Prinz and Rainer Zittelmann, 1–20. Darmstadt: Wissenschaftliche Buchgesellschaft, 1991.

Index

(Page numbers in boldface type indicate illustrations.)